WEST MIDLANDS
TURF WARS

WEST MIDLANDS TURF WARS
A FOOTBALL HISTORY

STEVE TONGUE

First published by Pitch Publishing, 2021

Pitch Publishing
A2 Yeoman Gate
Yeoman Way
Worthing
Sussex
BN13 3QZ
www.pitchpublishing.co.uk
info@pitchpublishing.co.uk

A CIP catalogue record is available for this book from the British Library.

ISBN 978 1 78531 865 8

Typesetting and origination by Pitch Publishing

Printed and bound in India by Replika Press Pvt. Ltd.

Contents

Praise for the *TURF WARS* series by Steve Tongue

WEST MIDLANDS | LONDON | LANCASHIRE

"A WEALTH OF FASCINATING STORIES."

Backpass magazine

"EVEN FOOTBALL HISTORY BUFFS SHOULD DISCOVER SOMETHING."

When Saturday Comes

"A SUPERB ACCOUNT. TELL SOMEONE TO BUY IT FOR YOU."

Red All Over the Land

"I WAS TAUGHT SOMETHING NEW WITH EVERY PAGE."

It's Red And It's White

"A STANDARD WORK OF HIGH CLASS: OBJECTIVE YET DELIGHTFULLY REVEALING. SHEER ENJOYMENT FROM FIRST TO LAST."

Patrick Barclay, Football Writers' Association

Front cover

Top: Stanley Matthews (Stoke City), Jack Grealish (Aston Villa), Dave Bennett (Coventry City). Bottom: Billy Wright (Wolves), Jeff Astle (West Bromwich Albion), Trevor Francis (Birmingham City).

By the same author

Turf Wars: A History of London Football (Pitch Publishing, 2016)
Lancashire Turf Wars: A Football History (Pitch Publishing, 2018)

Acknowledgements

Whatever the collective noun is for journalists (a hackful?), many thanks to Rob Bishop, Colin Burgess, David Harrison, John Homer, David Instone, Paul Joannou, Jeff Kent, Chris Lepkowski, Phil Shaw and Martin Swain.

Also David Bauckham, Steve Carr, Dr Graham Curry, Will Hoyle and John Lerwill.

To Duncan Olner for the cover and all at Pitch Publishing for their continued support.

Introduction

WHEN GÉRARD Houllier took over as manager of Aston Villa in 2010, he was surprised to be told by the police officer in charge of crowd safety, 'You're welcome here, but I can't support you – I'm a Bluenose.' Houllier, Anglophile veteran of a dozen or more Merseyside derbies while with Liverpool, might have been expected to know all about local rivalries; but he was not the first or last to underestimate the strength of tribal loyalty either in Birmingham or the wider area of 5,000 square miles and almost six million people that make up the West Midlands region, where those partisan feelings are as powerful as anywhere in the country.

Most of the rivalries had begun even before Aston Villa, West Bromwich Albion, Wolverhampton Wanderers and Stoke (our definition of the area takes in Staffordshire) were made founder members of England's Football League, the world's first, in 1888.

The first of more than 130 meetings between Villa and Birmingham City, for instance, took place in 1879, at a time when the latter were known as Small Heath Alliance, a name reflecting their own locality – barely three miles from Aston but proudly different. That opening skirmish in the turf wars was suitably controversial – Villa complained about the state of a 'pot-holed' pitch. By 1894 the Heathens had joined their neighbours in the First Division, which one of the many local newspapers felt could help both. 'Birmingham is large enough to support two clubs and the interests of Aston Villa and Small Heath need not clash in the slightest degree. A healthy rivalry, on the contrary, may be beneficial to both clubs,' said the *Birmingham Daily Post*.

So it remains more than 125 years later. 'Healthy' it has mostly been, although the hooligan excesses of the 1970s and 80s often spilled over into something else. Not that crowd trouble was a 20th-century phenomenon. If snowballs being thrown at West Brom players by Small Heath followers in the mid-1880s now seems quite quaint, it was the sort of behaviour that for a time deterred the mighty Preston North End from travelling as far south as Birmingham.

By 1888 they were having to, after Villa's William McGregor proposed that 'ten or 12 of the most prominent clubs in England combine to arrange home and away fixtures each season' – a groundbreaking concept originating in the second city, run in its early years from a small office in Stoke-on-Trent and soon copied all over the globe.

It is a source of pride for the area to have had at least one of its clubs in football's top tier every year since the Football League began and to have supplied the English champions 11 times.

Whether Villa were genuinely the best club in the world at the start of the 20th century, as has been claimed, was unfortunately never tested, but they challenged for the official title in 1982 having famously become champions of Europe. Birmingham City were the first English club to compete in European football, entering the Inter-Cities Fairs Cup in 1955, after Wolves and Albion had paved the way with glamorous televised friendly matches against foreign opposition in the years immediately beforehand; indeed, the European Cup and hence the Champions League could be said to date from the moment in December 1954 when Wolves manager Stan Cullis proclaimed his team 'champions of the world' after victory over the revered Hungarian side Honvéd.

Disappointingly, there has been no league title since Villa's in 1981, 40 years being the longest break in history without one; and a book about the region's football in 2018 by Professor John Samuels of the Business School at Birmingham University was titled *Where Did It All Go Wrong?* His conclusions were poor leadership, poor governance and a poor image, 'problems that have troubled many aspects of life in the West Midlands region, not just football'.

It is true that all the area's biggest clubs have experienced hard times and financial crises. Villa, Birmingham, Stoke and Albion dropped as far as the Third Division, Wolves and Coventry City played in the Fourth. Yet changes of fortune are common from week to week, let alone season to season, and provide part of the sport's charm. Within a year of *Where Did It All Go Wrong?* appearing, Wolves had finished seventh in the Premier League for a second successive season, qualifying for the Europa League, in which they reached the quarter-final; Albion had boing-boinged their way back into the top tier; and Villa were being spoken of as contenders for a Champions League place.

It was hardly coincidence, of course, that the success of those three clubs had been built on foreign money. In the *Birmingham Post*'s West Midlands Rich List for 2020, no fewer than four of the top six wealthiest men were owners of local football clubs – two at Villa (Egyptian and American), one at Wolves and one at West Brom (both Chinese).

A theme of previous volumes in this series, on London and Lancashire, is that in the long term big clubs tend to stay big and small ones stay small. But the democracy of football also allows those of more slender means to rise above their station, however fleetingly. Burton Albion, Hereford United, Port Vale, Shrewsbury Town and Walsall, all featured here, have spent time in the second tier, as well as enjoying famous FA Cup days.

They have also had to be imaginative in employing the sort of manoeuvres necessary to fight turf wars down the years. A town as small as Burton once had two separate Football League clubs (1894–97) before they joined forces and then had to disband; but once established in a town, football is reluctant to die and Burton Albion, founded as late as 1950, eventually emulated them. Similarly, when Hereford United dropped out and suffered severe financial problems, a new phoenix club immediately emerged. In 1926 Port Vale supporters had to fight off a proposed merger with their great rivals Stoke City; and in the financially problematic 1980s Walsall (themselves the product of a merger between the town's two biggest clubs) might have moved to either Molineux or St Andrew's, before deciding to build a new ground. Later Coventry – victims rather than beneficiaries of foreign owners – also moved to a new stadium but later found themselves groundsharing at Birmingham and out of the region altogether at Northampton.

All have fought the good fight and contributed to the life of their communities, as have the many clubs mentioned in the Non-League chapter here; from Worcester City, who once knocked Liverpool out of the FA Cup, to Kidderminster Harriers, taking 114 years to become Worcestershire's first Football League team and staying for only five.

Famous clubs, players, managers and administrators – and, yes, a few charlatans too. The characters and tall tales from more than 150 years of West Midlands football can be found within these pages.

1

Beginnings 1860–1887

'Association clubs have sprung into existence rapidly all over the town, and this year I can name more than a dozen clubs playing Association rules in Birmingham alone; while wherever a field can be obtained in the Black Country an Association club will be found enjoying the healthy exercise.'

Birmingham Daily Post, March 1876

'There can be no possible objection to the recognised payment of men who cannot afford to play for amusement.'

Sporting Life, September 1884

'The time has now arrived when some radical reform is necessary to save the club [Aston Villa] from utter collapse.'

Athletic News, December 1885

'The Birmingham rough seemed compelled to demonstrate his presence and snowballs were hurled about. It looked as if they were intended for the West Bromwich Albion players.'

Sporting Life, March 1886

'I understand that… Preston North End positively refuse to play again in Birmingham and will not come nearer than Wolverhampton.'

Birmingham Daily Post, March 1886

'No one would have ventured to prophesy that the game could ever attain its present popularity, or that it could involve so much science.'

Pall Mall Gazette, April 1887

JOURNALISM IS only the first draft of history but, rough as it may be, it can sometimes end up as the only record. The problem in regard to the history of football clubs is that most began in such a small way that not even local newspapers were sufficiently interested to write about them. As we will see, this has led to confusion about the origins of several clubs, including Stoke City, West Bromwich Albion and Port Vale. In addition, original club minutes and manuscripts also tend down the years to have been lost or long forgotten.

Up until the formation of the Football Association in 1863 and subsequent agreement on the Laws of the Game, there was dispute too about which sport many enthusiasts were actually playing: rugby with its handling and 'hacking' (at shins) or what became known as the association version.

There was clearly a football club at Cambridge University as early as 1846, recognised by the National Football Museum as the oldest in the world; two years later in rooms at Trinity College, the Cambridge Rules were formulated and then nailed to a tree in a city-centre park where the young gentlemen kicked footballs around. Cambridge brought together men from public schools like Eton, Harrow and Rugby who had taken part in their own versions of ball-chasing, and these in turn became the basis for the Laws of the Game 15 years later when the FA's first secretary Ebenezer Morley said, 'They embrace the true principles of the game, with the greatest simplicity.'

Variations were apparent, however, in different parts of the country such as Sheffield and Nottingham, two provincial centres in which the game took hold earliest. Indeed, when the Birmingham and District Football Association was founded in December 1875 it was Sheffield Rules they adopted before accepting London's version two years later. They were no doubt influenced by a Birmingham representative team having been invited to play Sheffield at Bramall Lane the previous month (losing 6-0) and arranging a return for Christmas week at the Aston Lower Grounds (lost 4-0).

Because the Cambridge University club was part of a larger existing institution, Sheffield FC is the one recognised by FIFA as the world's oldest, dating back to 1857, and followed by neighbours Hallam three years later. In the meantime the Forest club in east London was started by former pupils of Harrow and Forest School in 1859, later becoming Wanderers and winning the first FA Cup of 1872. Cray Wanderers, the oldest surviving club in Greater London, claim 1860 for their formation and so did Oswestry Town, straggling the Anglo-Welsh border until becoming part of Total Network Solutions 143 years later.

With the exception of Wrexham (1864), evidence of earliest present-day professional clubs from the mid-to-late 1860s centres on a notably small geographical area in Nottinghamshire (Nottingham Forest and Notts County), Derbyshire (Chesterfield), Sheffield (Sheffield Wednesday) and Staffordshire. This brings us to **Stoke City**.

* * *

The Potters' claim to have been born in 1863 is contradicted by press reports five years later of Stoke Ramblers, as they were originally known, playing their first game against 'Mr E.W. May's Fifteen' on 17 October 1868, in which 'some excellent play was shown'. It was drawn 1-1, with Henry Almond, captain and one of the founders, appropriately scoring the first goal. The report in *The Field* stated that the club was 'recently started' by former pupils of Charterhouse School (then in central London, now near Guildford); so Stoke – who dropped the name 'Ramblers' within two years and did not add 'City' until 1925 – can be considered the oldest survivors among Premier or Football League clubs in the West Midlands.

The old boys were working for the North Staffordshire Railway Company, and the headmaster of the local St Peter's school, Mr J.W. Thomas, is cited in the club's centenary handbook as the first club secretary and 'virtually the father of Stoke football'.

Like that first match, many games in those days, only five years after the Football Association was founded, were 15-a-side and may still have featured aspects of the rugby code; as late as 1870 a Stoke match against Whitchurch was rumoured to have been played with a rugby ball, which may explain why only one goal was scored (by Whitchurch). Newcastle-under-Lyme and Leek were other early opponents.

According to one local spectator around that time 'when offside was called, everyone pleaded ignorance, so the game was played without the new-fangled offside rule' (the offside law was introduced in 1866).

Home games were played at a variety of small venues until 1875 and then at Sweeting's Field, home of the Victoria cricket team. In 1878 Stoke merged with the cricketers, moving across the road to what became known as the Victoria Ground, originally an athletics venue that kept its oval track and would be home for almost 120 years – one of the longest reigns at any club ground in history.

By that year there were sufficient clubs in and around the heavily industrialised Potteries to form a Staffordshire Football Association. With it came competitive football and the Staffordshire Senior Cup, won in 1878 and 79 by Stoke, who defeated two clubs from Burslem – Talke Rangers and Cobridge – in the finals, and in the first season set a club-record score of 26-0 against Mow Cop. The captain that day was Thomas Slaney, who acted as the club's first secretary-manager from 1874 to 1883 and later became a referee.

By September 1879 the *Staffordshire Sentinel* was previewing 'the most important season they have ever had' with matches against 'many of the most important clubs in the country'. Stoke were among more than 40 clubs who entered the third Birmingham Senior Cup competition that season, drubbing the romantically named Hill Top Athletic 12-0 and Aston Clinton 8-0 before losing to the second city's Saltley College. Heavy defeats by Small Heath Alliance (the future Birmingham City) and Aston Villa in the following two seasons suggested they were still a little way behind the Birmingham pair.

In 1883 shirts of blue and black hoops were swapped for red and white stripes, though only for eight years. The club entered the FA Cup for the first time, losing 2-1 to Manchester FC despite a goal by Edward 'Teddy' Johnson, who a few months later became the club's first international. The forward, 'a splendid dribbler with remarkable speed and a deadly shot', had earned an England cap while playing for Saltley College in 1880, but now brought Stoke recognition, scoring two of the goals with which England won 8-1 away to Ireland in Belfast.

The club's opportunity to meet the mighty Glaswegians Queen's Park, the previous season's beaten finalists, in the FA Cup of 1884/85 was passed up when they decided to scratch from the away tie, presumably fearing the costs involved, if not a heavy defeat. Queen's Park would remain pure amateurs until a historic vote 135 years later, but even in the early 1880s talented Scottish players were migrating south, being found jobs by northern and Midlands clubs who were far from averse to handing them the occasional brown envelope.

The FA, fiercely against any form of professionalism, regularly expelled teams from the FA Cup for breaking the rules, and matters came to a head when Preston North End, thrown out of the 1883/84 competition, openly admitted paying players and found considerable support. 'There can be no possible objection to the recognised payment of men who cannot afford to play for amusement,' said the *Sporting Life* the following September. Lancashire clubs led the way in proposing a breakaway British National Association and by the end of 1884 had support from so many others, spread geographically from Birmingham to Sunderland, that the FA knew the (purely amateur) game was up. They finally gave in during the summer of 1885.

Stoke had been illegally paying players for the previous two years at a rate of up to half a crown (12 and a half pence) per game but when some of them discovered before the first official season of professionalism that one team-mate was to receive double, they went on strike until parity for all was agreed. Thus rewarded, the team set a club record still in existence (though not listed in many record books) by beating Caernarfon Wanderers 10-1 in an FA Cup qualifying round in October 1886, Alf Edge claiming five of the goals. They lost in the next round, 6-4 at Crewe after extra time, but the following season enjoyed their best run while remaining a non-league club, starting with a first major tie against local rivals Burslem Port Vale, which was won 1-0. The Potters went all the way to the quarter-final before losing to eventual winners West Bromwich Albion. It was a useful time to underline their improving credentials with Football League membership about to be decided.

* * *

The initial spread of organised football in the Midlands from the Potteries and East Midlands was south to Birmingham and west to Burton-on-Trent. In 1871 the Burton and District Football Association was formed for numerous clubs mostly based either at churches or in factories.

The original Burton Football Club, like many of the early pioneers, played both rugby union and association football, settling around the middle of the decade for the former game (and is still going strong). More significant for our purposes were a club who would bring the Football League to the town, and another with whom they later merged to keep it there – all many decades before the current Burton Albion were thought of.

Burton Swifts and **Burton Wanderers** were formed in the same year of 1871, the former possibly descended from Burton Outward Star and playing on the west side of the canal at Horninglow. Wanderers, in the north-east, had the better facilities at the Derby Turn ground in Little Burton and won the Burton and District Challenge Cup in 1884 and then 1885 by beating the Swifts. In 1886 Swifts had their revenge but a year later Wanderers beat them again 3-2 after extra time, drawing rave reviews, with one report exclaiming, 'A more intensely exciting and evenly contested game has seldom been played in Burton.'

Both paying at least some of their players by then, they entered the FA Cup initially in 1885, going out in the first round to stronger opposition: Swifts to Wednesbury Old Athletic (5-1) and Wanderers to Small Heath Alliance (9-2).

In April 1888 the *Athletic News* correspondent reported that 'the Burton clubs look like finishing the season well' with Wanderers having made amends for another heavy defeat by Small Heath by winning a thrilling return game 5-4. Clearly the two leading clubs in the area, they would both be Football League teams within a few more years (see next chapter).

* * *

By midway through the 1870s, amid favourable social conditions among a rapidly increasing urban population, football's tentacles had reached England's second city and the Black

Country. The economy was buoyant as the second industrial revolution began; transport networks were spreading out, with Birmingham now served by three major railway companies; press interest was reflected in the publication of *Athletic News* from 1875; and working hours were being reduced. Men seeking leisure activities on their Saturday half-day were happy to go straight from the workplace to a football ground and middle-class benefactors and employers were prepared to help finance their sport.

So it was that in December 1875 the Birmingham District and Counties Football Association was founded at a meeting at Mason's Hotel, Church Street. Calthorpe FC, made up of members of the Birmingham Clerks Association, and Aston Unity were the prime movers at an initial meeting attended by nine other clubs, their names hinting at a wider area than just Birmingham itself. As well as Unity and Calthorpe, plus Aston Villa, Birmingham FC (not the present-day club), St George's and Saltley College, there were five representatives from further west: Wednesbury Old Athletic, Wednesbury Town, Tipton, West Bromwich (Dartmouth, not the Albion) and Stafford Road Works, based in Wolverhampton and who supplied the first president, Charles Crump.

Glaswegian John Campbell-Orr of Calthorpe FC was made secretary, and in March 1876 he wrote proudly to the *Birmingham Daily Post* from Sherlock Street about the spread of the game locally: 'It was not till the year 1873 that the Association game was introduced into Birmingham by the Calthorpe Football Club. Since then Association clubs have sprung into existence rapidly all over the town, and this year I can name more than a dozen clubs playing Association rules in Birmingham alone; while wherever a field can be obtained in the Black Country an Association club will be found enjoying the healthy exercise.'

As mentioned earlier, two representative matches had already been played against the Sheffield FA. The clubs now agreed to compete during 1876/77 in a Birmingham Senior Cup, which thus became the first such county cup competition, just ahead of those in Shropshire and Staffordshire.

Of the original 11 members Birmingham FC did not take part, but half a dozen extra teams did so to make up a neat figure of 16 for a knockout cup, also helping to spread it geographically. In the first game, on Saturday, 14 October 1876, Wednesbury Town narrowly beat Walsall Victoria Swifts 2-1. In fact, in the whole competition, **Wednesbury Old Athletic**'s 13-0 first-round demolition of Harborne was the only big win, hinting at their eventual triumph in the final by beating Stafford Road 3-2 in front of an estimated 2,500 at Bristol Road, Calthorpe's ground. Charles Crump, the association president, scored both goals for the Stafford Road team who took a 2-0 lead but were overcome in the second half. 'The play was very fine throughout,' according to the *Birmingham Daily Gazette,* which reported 'a very large concourse of spectators' at the ground.

Widely known as the Old Uns, Wednesbury Old Athletic, founded as early as October 1874 by scholars of St John's Athletic Club, were formidable competitors in the early years of the Senior Cup and then the Staffordshire Cup too, as well as forging great local rivalries with the town's other major clubs, Wednesbury Strollers (1875), Wednesbury Town and works firm Elwells. Such was the enthusiasm for football in the town that by 1881 the Wednesbury FA boasted 45 teams.

As holders of the Senior Cup, Athletic reached the semi-final the next season only to be knocked out by **Shrewsbury**, a team based around the ancient public school of that name rather than bearing any relation to the present-day Town club that would not be founded until 1886 (see end of this chapter). A crowd estimated at 6,000 turned up to see Shrewsbury win 2-1, after which they successfully saw off the Old Uns' protest that one of their players lived more than the maximum 15 miles away. They went all the way to the final and there beat Wednesbury Strollers 2-1, adding their more local Shropshire Cup in its inaugural season a year later.

By 1879, however, the Shrewsbury club had dissolved. The Old Uns meanwhile were winners of the Birmingham Senior Cup again, beating Tipton 11-0 along the way before repeating the 3-2 victory over Stafford Road of two years previously. They reached two more finals in succession, both lost against an Aston Villa side who were beginning to dominate the competition, winning 2-1 in 1882 and 3-2 in 1883; both finals attracted near-10,000 crowds.

Winners of the Staffordshire Cup of 1880, also against Villa, the Old Uns entered the FA Cup regularly in the 1880s, although only once in 15 games were they taken outside the Midlands. In their first tilt at the trophy in 1881/82 they were drawn away to the already famous Blackburn Rovers, who after demolishing bitter local rivals Bolton Wanderers and Darwen beat the Old Athletic by only 3-1 and went onto the final, losing to Old Etonians. That was the first appearance in the final by a northern club and the beginning of the end for all of the southern amateur teams, who never again won the world's first domestic cup competition.

The Old Uns had knocked out teams of the calibre of St George's, Small Heath Alliance and Villa in a memorable run, but never progressed as far as the fifth round again, losing three times in six seasons to an improving Villa and in the other three to West Bromwich Albion. Their last two ties in the competition proper emphasised how the likes of the Wednesbury clubs were being left behind by professionalism and then league football: in 1886 the result was Villa 13 Old Uns 0; in 1887, WBA 7 Old Uns 1.

Wednesbury Strollers, although formed a year later than their neighbours, entered the FA Cup earlier, albeit without making as much of a mark. Previous finalists Oxford University saw them off 7-0 in their first tie, played amid the dreaming spires in November 1878, and in four seasons their only victory was over Stafford Road three years later. Next up in that campaign unfortunately were Notts County and after a successful protest following their 5-2 defeat, the Strollers went down 11-1 in the replay. In the Birmingham Senior Cup, they followed defeat by Shrewsbury in the 1878 final with a couple of quarter-final appearances before becoming victims of the growing Villa-Walsall duopoly. After a heavy 5-0 defeat by **Wednesbury Town** in 1884/85 their maroon and white hoops were seen no more.

Nor were the Town, who had enjoyed one extended FA Cup run when they beat West Bromwich Albion, Walsall Town and Derby Midland to reach the fourth round in 1883/84, losing to the old boys of Westminster School.

So by 1885 **Wednesbury Old Athletic** were carrying the flag alone for their town. In 1890/91 they joined the Birmingham and District League, then played in the Midland League for two seasons, which proved too much. Their final Senior Cup match was a quarter-final defeat in 1893 by Small Heath, the Football League Second Division champions in March, and four months later they disbanded.

Two 'phoenix' clubs emerged later; one lasted for only half a season with the second initially taking the name Wednesbury Excelsior before reverting in 1897 to Wednesbury Old Athletic. Twice champions of the Walsall and District League and winners three times of the Staffordshire Junior Cup, they showed renewed ambition in the Birmingham Combination, then the Birmingham and District League, but found both competitions a struggle against either future Football League clubs or existing reserve teams of the area's biggest clubs. They eventually gave up the ghost in 1924 after half a dozen successive seasons in the bottom two.

* * *

Other original members of the Birmingham and District Association managed varying degrees of longevity. **Aston Unity**, founded the same year as Aston Villa and playing as their name implied in the same area – as well as identical maroon and blue hoops, before switching to blue and white – were early opponents of the club that would make the district's name famous. For a while they were superior to Villa, knocking them out of the Senior Cup of 1878/79, only to lose to them the following year after hammering St George's 9-1, and in 1882/83 they suffered the humiliation of a 16-0 local derby defeat. Unity continued to play in the FA Cup for another five seasons, losing in the first round each time to stronger opponents, and 1887/88 was the last season they competed.

Calthorpe, dating from 1873, supplied the first secretary of the Birmingham Association and the ground for the first final of the Senior Cup, as well as contributing most money to the new competition (a handsome seven guineas). Founded by two Scots in an early example of heavy Scottish influence on the city's football, they suffered from playing in a public park with no way of charging admission and made no great impression in the Senior Cup. By the early 1880s they were losing ties heavily and scratched the last time they entered in 1886, before drifting into junior football.

Tipton were one of the very oldest local clubs, dating back to 1872, but they appear to have lasted no more than half a dozen seasons, featuring barely if at all even once newspaper coverage increased. Different to most in their plain dark blue shirts as opposed to more popular hoops or stripes, they beat Villa in one of the first official games organised by the newly formed BFA early in 1876 (often wrongly listed as the first Senior Cup Final) and repeated that success in the first Senior Cup tie played by both teams in November that year. But they were not heard from again following an 11-0 defeat by Wednesbury Old Athletic in the quarter-final of January 1879.

Saltley College, founded by students of St Peter's College, a teachers' training college in east Birmingham, may well be the oldest team in the second city if founded as early as 1870. They were another of the founder members prominent in the Senior Cup for a few years. Semi-finalists three times in the first four seasons, albeit often benefiting from a bye, they lost the final 3-1 to Villa on the last of those occasions in April 1880, watched by a healthy 4,000 crowd. Some heavy defeats followed by equally well-established clubs, and the qualifying competition of 1888/89 was their last recorded entry. By then the local works team Saltley Gas were representing the district just as prominently, reaching the final of the first Birmingham Junior Cup when they lost to Aston Victoria in 1888.

As already mentioned, **Birmingham FC**, like West Bromwich and Shrewsbury, bore no relation to the clubs of the present day. The Birmingham team comprised mainly workers from the Aston Lower Grounds leisure complex. They did not enter major cup competitions until 1879/80, losing 6-0 to Oxford University in the FA Cup and 4-1 to Saltley College on their 'home' ground in the Senior Cup. Those reverses lessened their appetite.

St George's, founded in 1875 and playing at Fentham Road, eventually became strong enough to be mentioned as potential members of the original Football League 13 years later. Apart from reaching a semi-final of the Senior Cup in 1882/83 where they lost to Villa, the Dragons found it hard to make progress earlier in the local competitions or the FA Cup, which would not help their argument. In 1884 they managed to win the Staffordshire Senior Cup for the first time but the best evidence of their potential was well timed, coming in the FA Cup of 1886/87. Victories over sides as strong as Small Heath, Derby County and Walsall Town (7-2) took them to the fourth round before a 1-0 defeat by eventual winners West Bromwich Albion. By that time they had gained from amalgamating with the works side Mitchells of Mitchells brewers, changing their name to Birmingham St George's in 1888 and prompting the *Birmingham Post* to declare them one of the four best teams in the West Midlands, along with Villa, West Bromwich Albion and Wolves. Further attempts to join the big boys would only meet with frustration (see next chapter).

Various other clubs bearing the name of the city took part as the Senior Cup peaked at 60 entries in 1883/84. Quality varied with double-figure scores not uncommon, but it had become a genuine Midlands competition, including clubs from Shropshire to Nottingham and north Derbyshire.

Also worthy of mention are **Birmingham Excelsior** (1876–88). Playing in Witton and featuring the Devey brothers, who would become important players for Villa (see below), Excelsior were regular FA Cup competitors in the 1880s, beating Small Heath Alliance for two seasons running but finding Derby Midland too strong when forced further afield. An all-round sports club with a strong interest in athletics, their greater claim to fame was as forerunners of the Birchfield Harriers athletics club in 1877.

Despite the spread of teams, however, the Senior Cup was from 1884 onwards dominated by a small group of clubs still recognised today – and one in particular.

* * *

Many football teams, ancient and modern, were formed from churches, others from cricket clubs: the city of Birmingham's two biggest clubs combined the two. Further north Sheffield FC, officially the world's oldest, came about because cricketers wanted sport more suited to the climate of winter months and so it was with **Aston Villa** and a local church cricket team. In 1874 the pioneers are believed to have met in Heathfield Road about a mile to the west of today's Villa Park after watching a rugby match and decided that association football would be the more enjoyable game. They immediately settled on a name for their new venture that would become world famous.

In an article about Villa on 28 November 1891, the *Illustrated Sporting and Dramatic News* confirmed, 'The club was started from a young men's class in connection with the Aston Villa Wesleyan Chapel in 1874 under the captaincy of W.H. Price, who held that office until 1875.' It listed the captains since then as 'G.B. Ramsay, the present secretary, and from 1881 to 1889 Archie Hunter'. All three had a significant part to play in Villa's early history, which for all its very local origins would be dominated by a Scottish influence reflected most obviously in the team's shirts bearing a large badge of the Lion Rampant during the 1879/80 campaign.

Local man Walter Price set the ball rolling, almost literally, as first captain. It was George B. Ramsay, a 21-year-old Glaswegian clerk, who in 1876 spotted a group of young Villans at practice in Aston Park by Aston Hall and impressed them sufficiently with the deft touches of the more skilful Scottish game to be taken on and soon made next captain. This new tactical approach added in no small measure to the degree of success already achieved by the time, two years later, another significant figure arrived all the way from Scotland – though only by chance. Archie Hunter, a draper, travelled south from Ayr with the intention of joining leading Birmingham club Calthorpe (see above), but being unable to find their ground, he was directed to Aston and went on to succeed Ramsay as one of the club's great leaders; in his case for their first FA Cup Final.

Then there was William McGregor, a heavily bearded teetotaller and church-goer, born in Perthshire, who moved to Birmingham to join his older brother in 1870, keeping a draper's shop in Aston. Initially involved in football with fellow Scots at Calthorpe, he was enticed to Villa by Ramsay in 1877 and soon became a vice-president. Before long he would be a key administrator as committee member, president and chairman before moving the whole of English football on to a new level and earning the statue that stands outside Villa Park today.

Birmingham, like Manchester, was more of a rugby city in the early 1870s before football began to take hold amid the favourable conditions outlined above. Latest research suggests that Villa's first game of some sort was probably played in autumn 1874, though one well-documented match the following March was one of not just two halves but two codes – the first being rugby football, the second 'association', and both 15-a-side. Aston Brook St Mary's, essentially a rugby club, provided the opposition and were beaten 1-0 in the second half of the fixture, once the oval-shaped ball was exchanged for a round one, by a goal from one Jack Hughes, appropriately another of the original founders. The venue was just off Heathfield Road.

The following season they used the Aston Lower Grounds, a popular amusement park at the bottom of Aston Hall transformed from a wilderness that would become the site of present-day Villa Park. Word soon spread and in a first full season crowds of 1,500 or even 2,000 were reckoned to have turned up for games against St George's Excelsior and Wednesbury Old Athletic. Ramsay was then instrumental in finding the new ground that he felt was needed if the Villa were to charge gate money and progress. It was discovered on a stroll through the neighbouring suburb of Perry Barr one Sunday. For an initial £5 a year in rent the roped-off ground in Wellington Road was acquired in 1876 – such a good choice that it sufficed for the next 21 years, during which the club would make spectacular progress. For the first game there in September 1876 Wednesbury Town were the visitors and the receipts were just over five shillings (25p).

It might be said that there were four key steps for any club with serious ambition to be counted among the best in the land: enter the FA Cup, get international recognition for one of the players, turn professional, and join the Football League. Between 1879 and 1888 Villa achieved all four.

For the first Football Association Challenge Cup competition of 1871/72 there were only two teams from outside the Home Counties among 15 entrants: Donington School from Spalding, Lincolnshire, withdrew without playing a game and Queen's Park from Glasgow were probably favourites but played only one match – a goalless draw with Wanderers – being unable to afford another trip to London for a replay.

Villa were confident enough to enter for the first time only five years into their existence and in the competition's ninth season. On 13 December 1879 they travelled to play Stafford

Road, the strong Wolverhampton works team, for a second-round tie and forced a 1-1 draw with a goal by Hunter's brother and wing-half Andy, winning the replay 3-1 (not 3-2 as often reported). Sadly they then scratched, choosing to play a Birmingham Senior Cup match instead of a third-round tie against the toffs of Oxford University, who had beaten Birmingham FC 6-0 and would go on to reach the final for a second time.

There was success, however, in the Senior Cup that season, winning 3-1 against Saltley College in the first of no fewer than six successive finals, and losing only one of them. Walsall Swifts beat them by the only goal but Villa then completed four wins in a row, over Wednesbury Old Athletic twice and the Swifts twice. In the 1882/83 competition there were embarrassingly big wins of 21-0 and 16-0 over Small Heath Swifts and Aston Unity.

As well as emphasising their strength in comparison to the city's longer-established clubs, Villa were showing up well against those from further afield. It was the custom of leading Scottish clubs to venture south over the festive period and on New Year's Day 1881 Villa beat the highly regarded Heart of Midlothian 4-2, before going on later in the season to win the Staffordshire Senior Cup for the first time.

Another important step towards wider recognition was the awarding of caps. The club's first internationals were forwards Howard Vaughton and Arthur 'Digger' Brown, who scored nine goals between them on their England debut against Ireland in February 1882 – the first match between the countries – which England won 13-0.

The FA Cup meanwhile helped spread the fame of both the club and the city's football. Sheffield and Nottingham may have been the provincial pioneers, while Blackburn (Rovers and Olympic) and Preston were among the prominent north-western clubs. But for two years running, in 1881 and 82, Villa beat both Nottingham clubs, County and Forest, in reaching the fourth round each time.

In 1883 County had their revenge by 4-3 in the quarter-final, Villa having equalised at one stage from 3-0 down. The next season brought a 6-1 hammering by Queen's Park up in Scotland and in the following two seasons there were defeats by Midlands rivals West Bromwich Albion and Derby County. Suddenly there was talk of crisis, *Athletic News* reporting in December 1885 that Villa 'has receded in the public estimation to such an extent that the time has now arrived when some radical reform is necessary to save the club from utter collapse'.

McGregor took over as treasurer, finding a parlous state with debts of almost £300 despite Ramsay's efforts in securing well-supported fixtures against Scottish opposition after Preston and then Queen's Park cried off from scheduled friendlies.

But Ramsay's appointment from 150 applications to be secretary-manager was a turning point and in 1886/87 Archie Hunter's team, now fully professional like all their major rivals and wearing claret and blue stripes, would be FA Cup winners. As such they were entitled to call themselves best team in England – if not Britain, since the competition included 131 other teams some of them from Wales, Ireland and Scotland. Wednesbury Old Athletic were drubbed 13-0, with three players scoring a hat-trick, and Derby Midland were beaten 6-1. Wolves took four exhausting mid-winter games to submit, before Villa received the relief of a bye in round four. Horncastle from Lincolnshire were seen off and then Darwen in the quarter-final 3-2, after Villa, leading 3-0 at half-time, had prematurely indulged in champagne. They had run up 35 goals in eight ties and it was 38 in nine after a Glasgow Rangers side full of Scottish internationals were beaten 3-1 in the semi-final at Crewe, with Hunter (two) and Albert Brown scoring, to set up the first Midlands derby final against none other than West Bromwich Albion.

Excitement was intense, drawing a record final crowd of some 15,500 to Kennington Oval, the usual venue until 1893. Albion, fielding eight players from the previous year's replayed final, which they lost 2-0 to Blackburn Rovers, were regarded as favourites but they lost a controversial match by the same score. Denny Hodgetts, Villa's sturdy winger with an impressive moustache, opened the scoring against the run of play, a goal which Albion protested so strongly was offside that play was held up for several minutes. Skipper and centre-forward Hunter confirmed victory just before the finish while lying on the ground after a collision with the goalkeeper.

When the *Birmingham Daily Times* sent a reporter to doorstep the victorious captain the next day, Hunter said that

Albion had become 'very downhearted' after the opening goal, which he denied should have been disallowed: 'A fairer or more deserving goal never was scored. We simply ran away from them subsequent to half-time. I hardly expected that the change of ends would have such a discouraging effect on the Albion. With the exception of Green, they almost all appeared to have lost their heads.'

1887 FA Cup Final: Aston Villa 2 West Bromwich Albion 0
Aston Villa: Warner, Coulton, Simmonds, Burton, Dawson, Yates, Davis, Brown, Hunter, Vaughton, Hodgetts.
West Bromwich Albion: Roberts, H. Green, Aldridge, Horton, Perry, Timmins, Woodhall, T. Green, Bayliss, Pearson, Paddock.

An article in London's *Pall Mall Gazette* made a wider point about the quality of the game and football's progress as a social phenomenon: 'To those who remember the game as it was played 20 or even ten years ago, Saturday's match was a marvel by comparison. No one would have ventured to prophesy that the game could ever attain its present popularity, or that it could involve so much science.'

It was an opportune time for both sides to reach the final, confirming their position among the country's elite, which would stand them in good stead when Villa's William McGregor composed his famous letter of invitation to a league competition exactly 11 months later (see next chapter). And a week after the final, Villa followed up their semi-final success over Rangers by beating the new Scottish Cup winners Hibernian 3-0 to justify the *Birmingham Daily Post*'s description of them as 'champion team of the United Kingdom'.

Villa's defence of the trophy comprised three easy victories and a bye, before they came up against a club who would become national rivals. Seeing off Oldbury Town, Small Heath Alliance 4-0 in the club's first FA Cup meeting and Shankhouse from Northumberland 9-0, the Villans welcomed to Birmingham in January 1888 a Preston North End side whose scoring feats in the competition made their own seem modest. The Lancastrians were run by the formidable Major William Sudell, whose illegal recruiting of mainly Scottish incomers had effectively forced the

FA to accept professionalism. In 1885/86 they played more than 50 games before losing one and the following season beat Queen's Park 6-1 then lost narrowly to Hibernian in a game billed as the unofficial world championship.

In Jimmy Ross and fellow forward John Goodall they had prolific scorers from north of the border who helped the team pile up no fewer than 45 goals in just four FA Cup ties before meeting Villa. It was a run that included the competition's record score of 26-0 against poor Hyde FC (whose goalkeeper later said the total could have been 40), and Villa could not stop it. At least the 3-1 defeat, adjudged to be a fair outcome, was more respectable than most of North End's opponents managed.

The game attracted tremendous interest, and a record crowd of almost 27,000 overwhelmed the Wellington Road ground, crowding the touchlines so much that mounted police and even a few Hussars twice had to clear spectators from the muddy pitch. Some reports on the day suggested that because of these incursions the match had been reduced to a friendly, but Villa's hopes of a rematch were quickly dashed by the FA who added insult to injury by rebuking the club for not maintaining better order.

Beating West Brom in the final of the Birmingham Senior Cup for the first of four successive wins from 1888–91 was a consolation, but by then McGregor, a strong supporter of professionalism, was formulating his visionary plans for a new competition that would transform English football.

* * *

Early **West Bromwich Albion** history has been a subject of some confusion, not to say misinformation. They were not directly descended from the West Bromwich (Dartmouth) club who were founder members of the Birmingham FA, and latest research by reliable local historians suggests that matches like that on 23 November 1878 against a team called Hudson's, from the local soap works factory, were actually played by a separate club, West Bromwich Strollers.

One of the Strollers' founders, Harry Bell, said in a later newspaper interview that they disbanded and several of the players, including future England goalkeeper 'Long' Bob Roberts, formed a new club the following season. The name 'Albion' is believed to have been taken from a small local district with an industrial estate.

In 1879/80 this new club played a full set of matches, beginning on 25 October 1879 with a thumping 7-0 win over West Bromwich White Hart. There were several others well before the December fixture against Black Lake Victoria which is sometimes cited as the first match.

As with both Villa and Small Heath Alliance, many of the pioneering players were cricket enthusiasts, in this case from the George Salter Spring Works factory team. They reputedly had to trek to Wednesbury to acquire a football but George Salter himself, a goalkeeper for the West Bromwich (Dartmouth) team, and a figure of considerable local influence, encouraged the new club and would become chairman and then president.

Changing grounds almost every year in those earliest days illustrated the club's ambition. The initial campaign of 1879/80 had been at Cooper's Hill, the second at Dartmouth Park. After two successful seasons there, another new venue was found in Walsall Street, on the opposite side of the current Expressway, where crucially the club were able to charge admission, albeit for very basic facilities. It opened in September 1881 with a visit from Oldbury but served them for only one season. Confident enough not only to charge at the gate but to enter the Birmingham Senior Cup, in which the original West Bromwich club were also competing, they reached the semi-final, losing 3-2 to Wednesbury Old Athletic.

Next stop was the Four Acres ground off Seagar Street shared with the West Bromwich (Dartmouth) club who began concentrating on cricket. The same Wednesbury team beat them in the quarter-final of the Senior Cup after Albion had thrashed Coseley 26-0 (it was 17-0 at the interval before they generously eased up). They then won a first meeting against Wolves 4-2 and in the Staffordshire Cup they went all the way to the final and beat Stoke 3-2 with George Bell's header. Having beaten Villa in an earlier round before almost 10,500 spectators they were now a force, finishing the 1882/83 season beaten only five times in almost 40 matches.

By November that year it was time to go national and attack the FA Cup, although their inaugural tie brought a 2-0 home defeat by more Wednesbury opposition, this time the Town. Albion would, however, soon reach a remarkable three successive finals to establish them as one of the top teams in the country. Beating the mighty Preston North End on Boxing Day confirmed the progress being made which was enhanced the following season, 1884/85, with an excellent second tilt at the rapidly expanding national cup competition.

Four wins (one against Villa) and one bye took them to a home quarter-final against another of Lancashire's finest, holders Blackburn Rovers, who proved too strong, coming through 2-0 and going on to win the trophy for a second successive year. 'Those who witnessed the match must unanimously agree that though beaten, the Albionites were certainly not disgraced,' reported *Athletic News,* which may have underestimated the crowd in reporting 12,000.

In the summer of 1885, having turned professional like most of their serious rivals, Albion were on the move again, this time a short distance away to Stoney Lane, and a new era of success. For three successive years they were finalists in the Birmingham Senior Cup, winning against Walsall Swifts (1886) but losing to Long Eaton Rovers (1887) and Villa (1888); and regular finalists too in the Staffordshire Cup, adding to the success of 1883 against Stoke with four successive finals from 1886–89, winning three of them against Stoke, again in 1886, Walsall Swifts (1887) and Leek (1889).

More remarkable were the three successive FA Cup finals from 1886–88, a feat not matched after that until Arsenal did it nearly 100 years later. In that time they played 26 ties, losing only twice. It was a settled squad in which seven players played in all three finals: Bob Roberts in goal, the first Albion man to be capped, for England against Scotland in March 1887; full-back Harry Green; half-backs Ezra Horton, Charlie Perry and George Timmins; and forwards George Woodhall and Jem Bayliss. Perry, Woodhall and Bayliss were England players too.

The 1885/86 cup run started with Albion's ten-shillings-a-week (50p) men now playing in blue and white stripes after a bewildering variety of colours and styles. After comfortable wins over local rivals Aston Unity, Wednesbury Old Athletic and Wolves (3-1), they saw off two lots of southern amateur old boys teams, from Charterhouse and Westminster. A first semi-final was played at the familiar Aston Lower Grounds, where Small Heath Alliance were comfortably beaten 4-0 to earn a final against holders Blackburn.

The final at Kennington Oval was a goalless anticlimax for 12,000 spectators. West Brom had the better of it and Rovers, in poor form according to their local reporters, were reluctant to play an extra half hour. An impromptu FA committee meeting voted narrowly for a replay at Derby a week later. It was threatened by a morning snowstorm that abated in time for Rovers to run out 2-0 winners, completing a hat-trick of FA Cup triumphs. 'Play in no way realised expectations,' said the *Daily Post*, and Albion 'never looked like winning.'

Their run to the following year's local derby final against Villa (teams above) was tougher, including four single-goal victories after Burton Wanderers had been beaten 5-0, and a replay after the Sheffield works team Lockwood Bros successfully protested their extra-time defeat.

In the semi-final at Trent Bridge, Preston were beaten 3-1, despite goalkeeper Roberts not arriving until the team were on the pitch warming up; and the same day Villa defeated Rangers in the last FA Cup game the Scottish side ever played. The Midlands then descended on London for the final where, as described above, Albion appeared demoralised by feeling the first goal should have been disallowed and conceded a second before the end. Their secretary offered the rather lame excuse that the players should not have insisted on going for special training at Ascot, but should have stayed at home as they had for previous rounds. 'We have discovered since the match that the air at Ascot was not bracing enough,' he told the *Birmingham Daily Times*.

Albion won the Birmingham and Staffordshire cups as small consolation and no excuses were necessary a year later when the FA Cup finally made its way to West Bromwich. Wolves were again among their victims (2-0) in a run of five successive home ties as centre-forward Jem Bayliss led the goalscorers throughout the campaign. He hit a hat-trick against old but now fading rivals

Wednesbury Old Athletic (7-1), got all four goals against Stoke (4-1) and in the semi-final at Stoke's Victoria Ground against Derby Junction he scored again in a 3-1 win.

The final was the occasion on which over-proud Preston – who had beaten Hyde by the record score of 26-0, then knocked out Villa, and were now clear favourites – requested a photograph with the trophy before the game, while their kit was still clean. 'Had you not better win it first?' enquired regular referee Major Mandarin.

They were unable to do so. Albion's teenage forward Billy Bassett, a future club chairman, was the star, laying on the first goal for Bayliss early on. Fred Dewhurst deservedly equalised in the second half as Albion protested the ball had not crossed the line but in the 77th minute local man Woodhall scored the goal that gave Albion their first national trophy. The *Daily Post* felt Preston had the better of the first half but praised Albion's defenders and also Bassett. Much local pride was evident in the paper's opening line that, following Villa's win the previous year, 'The English Cup is to remain in the Midlands after all.' Twelve months later it would be Wolves' turn in attempting to keep it there.

1888 FA Cup Final: West Bromwich Albion 2 Preston North End 1

West Bromwich Albion: Roberts, Aldridge, Green, Horton, Perry, Timmins, Woodhall, Bassett, Bayliss, Wilson, Pearson.

Preston North End: Mills-Roberts, Howarth, Holmes, N. Ross, Russell, Gordon, J. Ross, Goodall, Dewhurst, Drummond, Graham.

As English champions, Albion were invited to meet their Scottish counterparts in a game variously described as the championship of the United Kingdom, or even the world. Unlike the Wolves when Stan Cullis described his team as world champions some 65 years later (see Chapter 6), Albion could not claim that boastful title: in May, amid a Glaswegian thunderstorm, the Scottish Cup holders Renton beat them 4-1.

* * *

Few major or even minor clubs can have sprung from a pair of families in quite the same way as the one that would come to be known as Birmingham City, but began under the name of **Small Heath Alliance**. An alliance it was, of the Edden and James clans, no fewer than five of whom played in the team's first recorded match, in November 1875. Had Arthur James, later to captain the club for seven years, been available, it would have been six who took on Holte Wanderers, a team who, as their name hints, came from Aston. The result was a 1-1 draw in a 12-a-side game, one David Keys scoring the club's first goal.

The two sets of three brothers had come together, just like Aston Villa, in a church cricket club, in their case from Holy Trinity, Bordesley, which decided to start a football section in September of that year. Pleasingly, the venue for the first match was a piece of wasteland on Arthur Street barely a couple of hundred yards south of St Andrew's.

Ambition was such that for only their second season they found an enclosed ground, just over a mile south in Sparkbrook, only to return closer to their origins in Muntz Street. Sloping, uneven pitch or not, loathed by most visiting teams, the ground would be home for almost 30 years from September 1877 and may well have contributed to an undefeated first season there of 22 matches.

The following year the Heathens – who would not wear blue until 1890, preferring navy shirts most of the time before then – competed in the Birmingham Senior Cup for the first time in 1878/79, its third season, although Muntz Street saw a 1-0 first-round defeat by more experienced visitors Calthorpe. In September the following year there was a first game with Villa, which was won by what was described as 'one nil and a disputed goal to nil'.

The Senior Cup was a competition that, apart from occasional results like the 13-0 win over Coseley in 1886, never brought them much joy until finally winning it as late as 1905. The first trophy was therefore the Walsall Cup of 1882/83, after accepting £5 from Wednesbury Old Athletic, one of numerous opponents who disliked the Muntz Street pitch, to give up ground advantage in an earlier round and winning 4-1 anyway.

Nor did the FA Cup bring much joy early on after the 4-1 debut win over Derby Town in October 1881, including a goal from Arthur James, the brother who missed that opening match six years earlier; Jones was a star captain from 1878–85 and a regular for the Birmingham Association in matches against Sheffield, Glasgow and London. In the next round Wednesbury Old Athletic knocked the Heathens out 6-0. First-round defeats followed in the next three seasons, all by local opposition, before the dramatically improved run of 1885/86 carried the new professionals all the way to the semi-final.

Victories over Burton Wanderers (9-2), Darwen, Derby County, Davenham and Redcar led to the excitement of a local derby tie against West Brom at the Aston Lower Grounds. As mentioned above Albion won 4-0 on a snowy March day which did nothing to enhance the Heathens' reputation on or off the pitch. 'So far the spectators had conducted themselves properly but towards the end the Birmingham rough seemed compelled to demonstrate his presence and snowballs were hurled about,' reported the *Sporting Life*. 'It looked as if they were intended for the West Bromwich Albion players.'

A letter to the *Birmingham Daily Post* also complained about 'rowdies' snowballing Albion players, especially goalkeeper Roberts, and bemoaned the presence of only one policeman for a crowd reported to be upwards of 10,000. Such behaviour, the writer added, was not unknown, claiming, 'I understand that ... Preston North End positively refuse to play again in Birmingham and will not come nearer than Wolverhampton.' Half a crown in appearance money was small consolation for the beaten players.

Further painful derby defeats in the FA Cup followed for three more seasons against Birmingham St George's, Villa (4-0) and Albion again, underlining that Small Heath were not quite at the level of other Midlands clubs pressing claims for Football League membership. One major step, nevertheless, was to become a limited company in July 1888 and announcing a handsome profit 12 months later. 'Alliance' was also dropped from the club's name, and would take on a new meaning when they joined a league of that name in the new decade.

* * *

By the mid-1870s Wolverhampton had a thriving cricket and rugby club bearing the town name, while Stafford Road FC on

Fox's Lane, the railway works team, were regarded as the strongest in the immediate area. It was to their match at home to West Brom on 11 November 1876 – one of the first fixtures played in the new Birmingham Senior Cup competition – that those who had attended a meeting called the night before by a putative Goldthorn Football Club at St Luke's School in Blakenhall for 'any Gentleman interested in the game' were taken to have their interest piqued.

Goldthorn Hill are recorded as having played a Stafford Road reserve team in mid-January 1877. In that year the school leaving age was raised to 14 and St Luke's pupils were clearly encouraged by young headmaster Harry Barcroft, who noted in one of the school logs having let the boys out early one Friday afternoon 'and they had a Football Match'. He was almost certainly the Barcroft listed as playing in goal for that January match when in his early 20s.

Like Villa, Small Heath and others, there were strong links with local cricket clubs and, in the summer of 1879, it appears that one of them – possibly Blakenhall Wanderers – merged with the best of the local football teams to become the **Wolverhampton Wanderers**.

From the Windmill Field in Goldthorn Hill they then moved to Harper's Field in Lower Villiers Street. One of those connected from earliest days told the *Express and Star* years later that the name Wanderers was copied from the London side of that name who had just won five of the first seven FA Cups.

Jack Baynton, a vigorous half-back and one of the founding members from St Luke's, who played in the January 1877 game, was still in the side for that first season under the Wanderers name and was listed as captain (and treasurer) early in 1880/81. In 1889 he would be their goalkeeper in the Football League and an FA Cup Final.

Local interest was no doubt stimulated during that season by Stafford Road's exploits in the FA Cup, winning through three rounds, the last of them away to Villa, before narrowly losing 2-1 at home to the Old Etonians, who went on to a second final in three years.

Ensconced at Dudley Road opposite the Fighting Cock hostelry with only a small shed for cover, Wolves were considered ready for the Birmingham Senior Cup in 1881 but lost 3-2 to Walsall Alma Athletic in a replayed first-round tie. The overall playing record, however, showed only four games lost from 18 including two against Alma, and treasurer Baynton was able to record a profit of £5 6s (£5.30).

The quality of opposition was becoming stronger, with a 1-0 win over Stoke at Christmas and then the first reported meeting with WBA in the Birmingham Cup third round, when 3,000 watched a 4-2 win for the Albion. And by 1883, when the old red and white school colours of St Luke's were adopted (old gold and black would not be seen until 1891), smaller teams were being swatted aside: victories of 9-1, 10-0 and 15-0 in the first three rounds of the Birmingham competition brought another competitive meeting against Albion, who won the quarter-final 2-1 after a 1-1 draw, both games attracting good crowds.

The two clubs were mirroring each other's progress, both entering the FA Cup in autumn 1883. Unlike their rivals, Wolves were victorious in the first round, beating Long Eaton Rangers 4-1 with two goals each from Jack Brodie and John Griffiths before losing 4-2 to Wednesbury Old Athletic despite two more from Brodie. Reaching a first final of the Staffordshire Senior Cup the following season was a further small sign of progress and when professionalism was declared legal in the summer of 1885 Wolves were ready to take on another challenge, joining the major Midlands clubs – a group of which they could now count themselves members – among the paid ranks.

In fact, a table of those leading clubs published at the end of the 1884/85 season based on the number of games lost had Wolves on top with only two defeats in 22 matches. Awarding two points for a win and one for a draw (a system not introduced until midway through the first Football League season) would have given them an average of 1.59 points per game, with Albion and Small Heath on 1.48 and Villa, who lost half a dozen of their 18 games in a weaker season than normal, on 1.22.

Two of those other big rivals, Albion and Villa, both proved a nemesis in the FA Cup, knocking them out in the three successive years before league football began; the fourth-round defeat by Albion in 1885/86 after three wins (including one over a declining Stafford Road) being their best run. The following year's defeat by Villa came in a third replay, a special train carrying Wolves supporters to swell the crowd at Perry Barr to 10,000. Earlier, there had been a record-breaking 14-0 win in the previous round against Crosswell's Brewery from Oldbury with Tommy Hunter (four) one of three players to score a hat-trick; it remains the club's biggest victory in any major competition.

In 1887/88 Wolves took revenge on Albion by 2-1 to win the Staffordshire Cup Final in a second replay. Much better was to come in the FA Cup; and with the club's reputation firmly established, international recognition quickly followed. Right-back Charlie Mason played for England against Ireland, followed within a year by four team-mates (see next chapter). Now the Football League awaited.

* * *

The number of different Walsall clubs already mentioned a good few times confirms the town's importance from earliest days. To recap, one Saturday in October 1876 **Walsall Victoria Swifts** took part in the first match played in the new Birmingham Senior Cup, losing out 2-1 to Wednesbury Town. By the fifth edition of the competition in 1880/81 four other teams all bearing the town's name – Albion, Athletic, Town and White Star – were taking part, though it was already evident that the Swifts were the strongest of them.

They soon became strong challengers in local competitions: semi-finalists in the third and fourth years of the Birmingham Senior Cup, winning the next one in 1881 by surprising Aston Villa in the final, stealing a goal and clinging on. *Sporting Life* commended 'splendid goal keeping of Hobson for the Swifts, saving his charge on several occasions'. Villa had been heavy favourites, a feeling strengthened when the Walsall team were involved in a crash on the way to the game as their 'brake' lost a wheel.

They had beaten **Walsall Town** 3-0 on the way to the final and the pair would regularly meet in the competition and the Staffordshire Cup. In the Birmingham version in 1881/82 holders Swifts beat their rivals again 2-1 in front of some 4,000 at the Chuckery, which may have prompted their unneighbourly opposition when Town applied to join the Walsall and District Association that summer, having implied that they would only field their reserves in the local cup competition. The *Walsall Observer* reported that a motion supported by Swifts was passed, rejecting the application because it conveyed the impression that 'clubs connected with the association are only equal to the second team of the Town club'.

Swifts were Birmingham semi-finalists in 1883 and beaten finalists for the next three years (twice to Villa and once to West Bromwich), knocking out Town again along the way in 1885 and 86. One of their star individuals was full-back Alf Jones, who in 1882 became the first international from any Walsall club, playing for England against Wales and Scotland.

One competition in which Town narrowly surpassed them was the FA Cup, progressing as far as the last 16 in 1883 and only losing 2-1 to Villa.

By 1887/88, however, as thoughts turned to league football, the Birmingham Cup semi-finals gave clear indication of the respective strengths of West Midlands clubs: the four teams were Aston Villa, Albion, Stoke and Wolves. Defeats for the two Walsall teams by Wolves and Mitchell St George's suggested they were not ready for the Football League and the decision was taken to amalgamate as **Walsall Town Swifts**. Donning red and white for the first time, they played away to Villa in the Birmingham Charity Cup semi-final (not the final as sometimes stated) with six former Swifts and five from Town, forcing a draw after extra time in front of a five-figure crowd. Having failed to have the replay scheduled for their Chuckery ground, the new club declined to play it in Birmingham again and withdrew, leaving Villa to play Mitchell St George's in the final.

* * *

Port Vale are another club whose early history is so uncertain that they almost certainly celebrated their silver jubilee and centenary prematurely in 1926 and 1976 respectively. In doing so they were ignoring a letter appealing for funds written by the club chairman Robert Audley in 1907 that talks about 28 years of existence, and a long newspaper article from 1898 (*Golden*

Penny, 12 November) that also suggests 1879 as the founding date. They also appear to be yet another club with cricketing origins, as suggested by the first football captain, Enoch Hood.

According to the *Golden Penny* article, members of Porthill football club playing in Wolstanton held a meeting in Limekiln Lane, Longport, and decided to start a new club nearer their Burslem homes. At a further meeting they settled on the name Port Vale and played at a patch of ground in Longport dignified with the semi-official name The Meadows. A second venue, from 1881, was at Westport meadows, where the club grew and began charging admission.

There was little publicity, however, in the local press at the time apart from a mention of one reserve game in October 1880 and then the club joining the Staffordshire FA in September two years later.

There were at least a dozen teams in and around Burslem, one of the six towns of the Potteries, the others being Fenton, Hanley, Longton, Stoke-upon-Trent and Tunstall. Novelist and football enthusiast Arnold Bennett, born in Hanley, confused matters by writing about the fictitious 'five towns', turning Burslem, which lay in 'a heavy pall of smoke', into Bursley.

By 1879/80, Burslem (formerly and later known as Cobridge), Stoke and Fenton Sutherland were all competing in the Birmingham Senior Cup. After joining the Staffordshire FA, Vale first took part in the association's Senior Cup competition of 1882/83 and in the second round had what was almost certainly their first joust with Stoke, losing a replay 5-1, in which Enoch Hood is listed as captain. They managed to win the North Staffordshire Charity Challenge Cup by beating Leek.

In the 1883/84 season double-figure wins over Newcastle St Giles and Middlewich proved that some opposition was becoming too easy, although results against the more established clubs were mixed: a 1-0 win away to a modest Everton team in November and a draw in the return next month gave a less reliable impression than defeats by Preston (4-1), West Bromwich Albion (6-0), Birmingham St George's (7-1 in the Staffordshire Cup semi-final) and Stoke (3-0, 5-3). The local paper did, however, refer to one of the Stoke fixtures as a meeting of 'our two local champions'.

In 1884 there was also a change of name to Burslem Port Vale and a move to the Moorland Road ground next to Burslem Station, only a third of a mile south of the current Vale Park and now part of Burslem Park. The first game on the sloping pitch there was a handsome win over Everton by either 6-0 or 7-0 (sources differ), followed by heavy defeats against the stronger Blackburn Olympic and Bolton Wanderers. But at more local level Vale won the Burslem Challenge Cup 12-0 against Ironbridge and shared the North Staffordshire Charity Cup with Leek. Early rivalry with Wolves centred on a Staffordshire Cup tie that was ended early because of failing light; Wolves were found to have an ineligible player and Vale lost the away replay which they felt should have been on neutral ground.

In the summer of 1885 the club felt sufficiently confident to turn professional and form a limited company with £2,000 capital. Entry to the FA Cup followed with a good run to a controversial tie against Brentwood. After two draws Vale scratched rather than travel to Brentwood as the Essex amateurs did not charge gate money.

The first two appearances in the Birmingham Senior Cup also brought impressive campaigns, before ending in each case with heavy defeats in the semi-final to West Brom. There was a drawn friendly against FA Cup holders Blackburn Rovers, but Stoke could still not be beaten, despite the presence of a record 10,000 crowd on May Day 1886. They saw Vale's star goalkeeper Billy Rowley break a rib, souring relations between the clubs even more when Stoke wanted him to break his contract with their neighbours and join them. The dispute, which went to court, resulted in a fine for the Potters, whom he nevertheless joined early in 1887, going on to win two caps for England and later becoming Stoke manager.

For 1886/87 there was another new ground, at Waterloo Road, Cobridge, where Preston unkindly won the opening game 7-0, and another FA Cup controversy when drawn against Leek in the third round. The away game was a 'fast and exciting' 2-2 draw, abandoned in extra time because of failing light, after which Vale's secretary wrote to *Athletic News* to complain about its comment that striker Billy Reynolds should have been sent off. After an abandonment and another draw, the fourth attempt at Stoke brought a goal for Leek within ten seconds and an early curtailment with Leek deemed 3-1 winners after Vale players walked off in protest that their third goal was offside.

Stoke beat them twice more before the end of the season and in 1887/88 knocked them out of both the Staffordshire Cup and by 1-0 in the FA Cup after Vale in the latter game 'lost several easy chances by wretched shooting'.

A table of results for the main north, Midlands and Scotland clubs put Vale 37th. Stoke cannot have been pleased with a ranking three places below them.

* * *

The first team from Coventry to enter the Birmingham Senior Cup, as early as the second season of 1877/78, were from the private school **Allesley Park College**, an establishment charging up to 50 guineas a year. Narrowly beaten in the first round, they did not take part again. The college's first matches were in December 1875, both against a side described as 'Coventry Association Football Club', the college winning both of them (*Coventry Herald,* 18 December 1875).

Rugby union was more popular in those parts until the growth of local industry in the 1880s and Coventry City, of whom we will hear much more, did not begin until 1883 as **Singers FC**, a works team of the bicycle factory, with company founder George Singer as president. Given impetus by an employee named William Stanley, they started playing on a pitch to the east of the city centre between the London Road and Gosford Park.

By 1887 they were a club on the way up with an enclosed ground off Stoke Road; too late for consideration as Football League members, though within a couple of years of winning a first trophy, the Birmingham Junior Cup.

* * *

Shrewsbury Town were not founded until 1886, being unique in having their origins in a riot. A team called Castle Blues, one of around 40 in the town, developed such a rivalry with Wellington Town that some of their players were among spectators arrested when the Wellington team were attacked during a match in 1886 against another local side. Castle Blues soon folded in disgrace and in May that year several of their more innocent players joined a new Shrewsbury Town club, who became winners of the Shropshire FA Cup in their first season, beating Wellington Town in the replayed final. Entering the FA Cup the season after, they defeated Macclesfield 3-1 with a hat-trick from captain Harry Pearson before going down heavily to the Welsh Cup holders Chirk 10-2.

Home was the Racecourse Ground at Monkmoor, north-east of the town centre, where they stayed until 1889, the course having staged its last race meeting in October 1887 amid allegations of widespread fixing.

One last club deserving a mention in this chapter are **Shropshire Wanderers** (1872–1880), also based in Shrewsbury, who were involved in the only FA Cup match ever decided by tossing a coin. After two goalless draws with Sheffield FC in their debut in 1873/74, the teams declined to play a third game and Wanderers lost the decisive toss and were eliminated. In the first round the following season they were again drawn against Sheffield, who scratched, whereupon the Wanderers won two ties to reach the semi-final, losing only 1-0 to Old Etonians at Kennington Oval.

The club did not play in the FA Cup after 1877 and disbanded within three years. Their most notable player also achieved an unusual distinction: John Edwards, later known as John Hawley Edwards, won a cap for England against Scotland in 1884, and after moving to the London-based Wanderers and scoring for them in the 1876 FA Cup Final he played for Wales, also against the Scots.

2

The 12 Apostles 1888–1900

'No more debts. Both ends to meet. Plain sailing. These, we suppose, are the ideas of the promoters of the new Football League.'

Cricket and Football Field, April 1888

'The new ground of the Wanderers – Molineux Grounds – is one of the finest in the kingdom, exceedingly suitable for the play and the spectators.'

Express and Star, August 1889

'Birmingham is large enough to support two clubs and the interests of Aston Villa and Small Heath need not clash in the slightest degree. A healthy rivalry, on the contrary, may be beneficial to both clubs.'

Birmingham Daily Post, April 1894

'It would indeed have been a pity had so historic a club been obliged to sever their connection with the senior division. Nevertheless the "Throstles" have had a narrow escape and it was only their plucky play when at home that saved them.'

Derby Daily Telegraph, April 1896

'These test matches have proved an utter farce. A change of some kind is absolutely necessary.'

Manchester Guardian, May 1898

AT THE first annual general meeting of the Football League in May 1889, secretary Harry Lockett (who still worked primarily for Stoke, running the organisation from a small office in the evocatively named Brick Kiln Lane) declared proudly, 'Members cannot but acknowledge the immense amount of good that has been done to the game since its institution. Districts that seemed dead to football have come out again in large crowds, and new homes for Association football are springing up all around.'

The world's first football league, a logical and necessary result of professionalism being legalised three years earlier, was an undoubted success, although it clearly contributed to the growing gap between major and minor clubs. Aston Villa, Stoke, West Bromwich Albion and Wolverhampton Wanderers all became founder members; Small Heath Alliance, Walsall, Burslem Port Vale and the two Burton clubs had to wait and, with the exception of the first named, might be said never to have caught up. At least those five were all admitted to the Football League by the turn of the century, an achievement that eluded the other local club who always felt they should have been among the favoured few, Mitchell St George's.

The Football League has come to be known as the brainchild of draper and Aston Villa committee man William McGregor, but the idea may at the very least have been sown in his mind by Villa fan Joe Tillotson, a future president of the Birmingham FA, who ran a coffee shop a few minutes away in Alma Street, Aston. Supporters, he told his friend, had had their appetite for competition sharpened by big games in the FA Cup and occasionally the Birmingham or Staffordshire cups, but were fed up with meaningless and frequently one-sided friendlies.

It is also probable that either or both men would have been aware of a front-page article in the influential *Athletic News* on 7 June 1887 which suggested that instead of depending on cup games, 'I fancy that the systems of leagues, followed by the Base Ball Clubs of America where eight or more teams unite, and play each other to see which is the best of them, would be much more sensible and remunerative business.' The article listed 12 leading clubs who could be considered for such a competition – of whom ten would eventually be included.

As a keen sports fan who developed a particular interest in baseball, McGregor would almost certainly have known about the National League, founded as early as 1876 with six American teams. The sport would be introduced to England in 1889 and played at Perry Barr that summer. A team playing as Aston Villa took part, as did Derby County, Preston North End and Stoke; Derby took to the game so enthusiastically that the Baseball Ground was already an established venue when the football club moved there from the Derbyshire county cricket ground in 1895.

Having been Villa treasurer, McGregor was well aware that the very nature of knockout competitions made income unpredictable, as did varying levels of interest in friendly matches, often arranged or cancelled at short notice because of cup-tie dates. As was pointed out in his famous letter, sent out in March 1888 after consultation with other Villa committee men and a preliminary tour of the northern clubs he would need to convince, 'Every year it is becoming more and more difficult for football clubs of any standing to meet their friendly engagements and even arrange friendly matches. The consequence is that, at the last moment, through Cup tie interference, clubs are compelled to take on teams who will not attract the public. I beg to tender the following suggestion as a means of getting over this difficulty – that ten or 12 of the most prominent clubs in England combine to arrange home and away fixtures each season.'

How to select those lucky 'ten or 12'? There was arguably an elite quartet of English clubs in Villa, West Brom, Blackburn Rovers and Preston North End, all professionals from day one and winners between them of every FA Cup Final from 1884–92. The original letter also went to Bolton Wanderers, whose influential secretary John Bentley was asked to recommend other potential members. He came up with eight names, of whom Notts County, Stoke, Wolves, Accrington and Burnley were eventually accepted (as well as Derby County and Everton), whereas Mitchell St George's, Halliwell and Old Carthusians were not.

St George's and Bolton's Halliwell fell foul of the decision that only one club should be invited from each town or city, which stemmed from McGregor's belief in the importance of attendance figures; Old Carthusians, the one southern amateur team mentioned, were never likely to accept even if invited.

The official founding date of the Football League was 17 April 1888 following a meeting at a Manchester hotel. In fact, the names of the 12 clubs had effectively been decided a month earlier, at a get-together in London on the eve of the FA Cup Final. A circular issued on 26 March by Harry Lockett echoed McGregor's letter in saying 'a strong feeling was evinced that something should be done to improve the present unsatisfactory state of club fixtures'. It listed the 12 founding fathers, a happy half-dozen each from the north and Midlands. It added that clubs should play a full-strength team in all matches; the league table would be decided on 'an average of wins, draws and losses'; and that the four clubs with the 'lowest average' each season would have to apply for re-election.

The Manchester meeting, also attended by disappointed representatives of Nottingham Forest and The Wednesday, decided on the name (although McGregor had preferred 'Association Football Union') and amended the criteria for league positions to number of wins, with a play-off if teams were level. Oddly, it was not until halfway through the first season that a points system and goal average were decided on.

Press reaction was initially mixed, with widespread sympathy for clubs left out. Leading journalist J.A.H. Catton called it 'a mere money-making scheme'. *Cricket and Football Field* ran a long article on 21 April headed 'The 12 New Apostles' which began, 'No more debts. Both ends to meet. Plain sailing. These, we suppose, are the ideas of the promoters of the new Football League.' The paper provocatively listed 20 other clubs 'who can quite hold their own with a good proportion of the New League', among them Derby Junction, Derby Midland, Leek, Long Eaton Rangers, Mitchell St George's, Burslem Port Vale, Small Heath Alliance and Walsall Town Swifts.

The writer felt, 'There are only three pre-eminent clubs in the country [presumably Villa, Blackburn and Preston] and a selection of the other nine would always be a delicate matter. It has further to be considered whether the object aimed at – the increased interest in ordinary club matches – will be at all achieved by the proposed league.' Secretary Lockett was able to claim with justification a year later that that was the case.

One reason for not using the title of English Football League was McGregor's belief that Scottish clubs, seven of whom had previously taken part in the FA Cup, might one day join. Instead, the Scots followed his lead and formed their own league within two years. He was also open to the possibility of a 'Second League' if the first one succeeded, and he hoped eventually for a 'truly national' competition, mentioning Southampton, Tottenham Hotspur and the original Portsmouth club (though not the as yet little-known Woolwich Arsenal) as future contenders from the south of the country.

Fixtures were arranged by what was described as a ballot, somewhat randomly with Wolves, for instance, starting with four home games followed by four away; and despite the rule about league matches taking priority, Blackburn were allowed to play a pre-arranged friendly against Newton Heath, delaying their league debut for a week (when they drew a local derby 5-5 with Accrington).

The opening Saturday produced two derbies each for the Midlands and the north and, amid good weather, average gates of just over 5,000 were regarded as more than satisfactory. The New Apostles were spreading the word.

8 September 1888: First Football League matches

Stoke 0 West Bromwich Albion 2 (4,500)
Stoke: Rowley, Clare, Underwood, Ramsey, Shutt, Smith, Sayer, McSkimming, Staton, Edge, Tunnicliffe.
WBA: Roberts, J. Horton, H. Green, E. Horton, Perry, Bayliss, Bassett, Woodhall, Hendry, Pearson, Wilson.

Wolverhampton Wanderers 1 Aston Villa 1 (3,000)
Wolves: Baynton, Mason, Baugh, Fletcher, Allen, Lowder, Hunter, Cooper, Anderton, White, Cannon.
Villa: Warner, Cox, Coulton, Yates, H. Devey, Dawson, Brown, Green, Allen, Garvey, Hodgetts.

Also: Bolton Wanderers 3 Derby County 6 (3,000); Everton 2 Accrington 1 (10,000); Preston North End 5 Burnley 2 (5,000); Blackburn Rovers and Notts County did not play until the following week.

* * *

It was appropriate that **Aston Villa**, having proposed the whole concept, should prove the main challengers in that first season to the team who became known as Preston's Invincibles. Villa were the only team to take a point from Deepdale and at home they lost only the last game, to Preston, but away defeats proved costly at Everton, Blackburn (5-1), Burnley (4-0) and Derby (5-2). The Burnley game was a bad day all round, illustrating some of the problems of the time with travel, when Villa had to kick off with eight men after three were caught up in heavy fog. Only two made it in time to take any part.

The opening game at Wolves was dominated early by the home side, who went ahead when the ball 'struck Cox's body and went through the goal'; for some years this was assumed to be the first goal in Football League history but the unfortunate Villa right-back Gershom Cox was saved by some later detective work proving that the match kicked off after several others, so that the honour goes to Bolton's James 'Kenny' Davenport. Green equalised off a post for the Villans shortly before half-time and there was no further scoring in a game the *Stoke Sentinel* called 'a fast one all through, and very even'.

The belatedly agreed points system of two for a win and one each for a draw (West Brom suggested no points for draws but were outvoted) was finalised in the third week of November, by which time most teams had played a dozen games. Preston were already out in front and by the time of their visit to Perry Barr for the penultimate game on 9 February the title was won and their objective was to finish unbeaten in all 22 games. On a snow-covered pitch two second-half goals by Fred Dewhurst, a schoolteacher and their only amateur, ensured they did so, the *Birmingham Daily Times* praising their 'superlatively fine individual and collective work'. The following month they would underline it by winning the FA Cup Final against Wolves to complete a historic first Double (see next section).

The crowd of 12,000 was Villa's best of the season, though overall their figures were a little disappointing: from just 2,000 to see Stoke in Perry Barr's first Football League match (a 5-1 win) they were never close to double figures until the last two matches, 10,000 having turned out to see West Brom beaten 2-0 in the derby before the Preston game.

The league average of all clubs was 4,500. Villa, fifth highest with just over that, were the best of the Midlands contingent while Lancashire, with its slightly longer tradition, had the top four. Everton would remain best supported for the first ten years until Villa, in their second season at Villa Park in 1898/99, averaged just over 23,000. Albert Allen led the Villans' scorers in the first season with 18, including the club's first Football League hat-trick in the 9-1 demolition of Notts County.

The following two seasons of league football were a huge disappointment for the club, something hinted at in the last couple of results of 1888/89: a 5-2 defeat at Derby came a week after a shocking 8-1 capitulation to Blackburn Rovers in the FA Cup third round. Subsequently beating Walsall Town Swifts, Ironbridge (9-1) and then Wolves to retain the Birmingham Senior Cup could not erase that embarrassment.

In 1889/90 Villa were capable early on of beating the champions Preston 5-3, Burnley 6-2 and Derby 7-1, only to concede seven goals at Blackburn and Everton and finish so poorly that they were almost among the bottom four clubs having to apply for re-election; and the following year they did have to do so. Like West Brom, who finished bottom, there was nevertheless no danger of being voted out as the league was being extended by two extra clubs.

Enter Fred Rinder, who became financial secretary, determined to put the club's finances in order. For all McGregor's abilities – he also became FA chairman in 1888 – many felt Villa were not being run well. A programme article from the early 20th century said of Rinder, 'When he started that now historic agitation in 1892, the club was being run by a lot of well-meaning but hopelessly incapable men who held large committee meetings, talked of all sorts of things other than football, made so many mistakes and lived so greatly on the reputation of the Villa and then generally left things in a muddle for the secretary to clear up as best he could ... it was a daring thing to attack the citadel in those days, since certain traditions had grown with the club, but Mr Rinder was an iconoclast, and he not only had his own way in the matter of management, but secured the distinction of leading the reform party.'

The simple expedient of installing turnstiles improved takings, though it may have harmed the pockets of unscrupulous gatemen. For two seasons in a row Villa improved to fourth place, the first of those campaigns including a record 12-2 win over Accrington on 12 March 1892 in which John Devey and the Scot Lewis Campbell scored four apiece. Devey, a handsome captain and one of the best goalscoring forwards of his day, notched 29 league goals in 25 games, the best Villa return until 1926, when the offside law was eased to benefit forwards.

And 1892 also brought the first of three FA Cup Final appearances in six seasons, this one ending in a bitter 3-0 defeat by rivals Albion (see Albion section below), who thus gained revenge for the 1887 defeat. Goalkeeper Jimmy Warner took much of the blame and had his pub windows smashed after what the *Daily Post* called 'without doubt the severest blow Aston Villa have ever received'.

Two years later, however, Villa were Football League champions for the first time. With the speedy Charlie Athersmith an outstanding right-winger, Devey either inside him or at centre-forward and Hodgetts still on the left, there was a powerful attack, but the best defence too with Bill Dunning from Bootle replacing Warner in goal. Devey scored 20 goals, the first of them in a 3-2 victory over Albion on the opening day and a couple more in the 6-3 return game.

Wolves were one of only five teams to lower the Villa colours and only Bolton managed to win at Perry Barr, where Darwen were beaten 9-0. Villa finished six points clear of Sunderland, their greatest rivals in this period, who had won the two previous titles and would take the next one, in 1894/95, but lose an FA Cup semi-final that took Villa back to London for their second final in three years, both against the Albion.

Having finished third in the league, ten places above their neighbours, and beaten the champions-elect in the semi-final at Ewood Park, Villa were favourites, a tag they justified by winning with what remains one of the fastest goal ever scored in a final. At the new venue of Crystal Palace, after two seasons in the north, many of the huge crowd of 42,560 were still trying to gain admittance when Bob Chatt hit a shot that went in off Devey. It came within an estimated 40 seconds.

Wing-half John Reynolds, scorer of Albion's third goal in 1892, was now in the Villa team after an acrimonious transfer, and like his team-mates was not overstretched in holding on to the lead. For the *Sunday Times* correspondent, much impressed by the new ground, 'the quality was far above the average of final ties' and the winners were 'far superior in combination to their rivals'.

1895 FA Cup Final: Aston Villa 1 West Bromwich Albion 0
Aston Villa: Wilkes, Spencer, Walford, Reynolds, Cowan, Russell, Athersmith, Chatt, Devey, Hodgetts, Smith.
West Bromwich Albion: Reader, Williams, Horton, Perry, Higgins, Taggart, Bassett, McLeod, Richards, Hutchinson, Banks.

There was a sensation to come five months later, when the trophy was stolen from a local shop window overnight, never to be recovered. The *Birmingham Daily Times* reported that William Shillcock, 'well-known supporter of sport in the city, and a boot and shoe manufacturer of Newtown Row', had been granted permission to display it: 'He walked into a room behind the shop, and on returning saw the cash drawer on the counter. Then his suspicions were aroused, and on looking round he saw the floor at one side covered with plaster, and on looking above there was a hole through the roof.'

The most convincing of the stories to emerge over many years was that four unemployed men broke in through a grate in the roof and removed the trophy, which was then melted down. Fortunately it was insured, though the FA fined Villa £25 anyway. A new one, almost identical to the original, was commissioned from local firm Vaughton's silversmiths, one of whose directors was Howard Vaughton, a member of Villa's winning team from 1887.

In 1895/96 Villa were champions again, by four points from Derby as Sunderland dropped to fifth. Another Scot, John Campbell from Celtic, announced himself as the new number nine with ten goals in his first eight games, four of them coming in the 7-3 win at home to Small Heath (the Heathens had been promoted the previous season, losing the first second city league derby 2-1 at Perry Barr). Campbell finished with 26 from the same number of games and Devey, moved back to inside-forward, had 16. There was a brief internal disruption when yet another Scot, centre-half James Cowan, a rugged but speedy presence throughout the 1890s, determined to enter the annual new year Edinburgh Powderhall sprint and won it under an assumed name, earning a handsome £380. The club imposed a fine and suspension but had him back in action for three successive January victories.

For the following momentous season there was another key signing in Fred Wheldon, an outside-left with a fierce shot who crossed town from Small Heath after racking up 82 goals in 129 games, while Hodgetts moved the other way. At Villa he beat both Campbell and Devey in top-scoring with 22 in the two main competitions as Villa went for a Double previously achieved only by Preston in the first season of league football.

There were only four league defeats, two of them early by Albion and Everton and two in a brief stumble at the start of 1897 by Burnley and Sunderland. On either side, two long unbeaten sequences included revenge over Albion, a double over Wolves and a winning start at the handsome new ground that would come to be known as Villa Park.

The long-proposed upgrade from Wellington Road had come closer in January 1896 when Villa formed a limited company with Fred Rinder as one of the four directors. A share offer enabled the board to rent seven acres of the Aston Lower Grounds with an option to buy. As Villa fan and stadium expert Simon Inglis has written, 'The park's popularity was waning. Football was the new mass spectator sport.' By the time the new stadium was ready 14 months later Villa were Double winners.

If the league title was never seriously in doubt, reaching another FA Cup Final included one particularly tough test. Drawn away in the quarter-final to Preston, still a solid First Division side, Villa forced a 1-1 draw only to be held in a goalless replay. The third game, in neutral Sheffield, was won 3-2 thanks to two goals from Athersmith.

For the semi-final it was back to Bramall Lane and a more comfortable 3-0 win over First Division newcomers Liverpool, who were thus denied their dream of a Merseyside final with Everton. The Blues were only mid-table, despite ending Villa's two-year unbeaten home run earlier in the season, but the interest created by two big clubs led to another record cup final crowd of almost 66,000 at Crystal Palace.

They saw one of the very best finals to date, the only disappointment being that there were no further goals after a hectic period that produced no fewer than five in a spell of 25 minutes up until half-time.

Campbell scored the first of them, only for Villa to fall behind to Bell and Boyle. Back came the favourites with an equaliser by Wheldon and then a header from left-half Jimmy Crabtree just before the interval. That, unexpectedly, proved to be the goal that won the cup, Everton attacking strongly in the second half but being thwarted by a strong defence and Jimmy Whitehouse's goalkeeping.

Villa, with their eight internationals, 'played distinctly the better football, fought a hard fight and won a well-earned victory,' said the *Sporting Life*. For the *Morning Post*, 'There were excellence, keenness, and pace, and from such a combination there came a splendid exhibition of football.'

1897 FA Cup Final: Aston Villa 3 Everton 2
Aston Villa: Whitehouse, Spencer, Evans, Reynolds, James Cowan, Crabtree, Athersmith, Devey, Campbell, Wheldon, John Cowan.
Everton: Menham, Meechan, Storrier, Boyle, Holt, Stewart, Taylor, Bell, Hartley, Chadwick, Milward.

On the morning of the final, Derby County, seven points behind with one game in hand, were the only team who could prevent Villa retaining the First Division title, but that afternoon they lost 1-0 at Bury, so the celebrations at Crystal Palace were doubled – or Doubled. Not that anyone could have imagined such an achievement would take until 1961 for any team to repeat.

Things could hardly have been better set up for the grand opening of Villa Park (although not yet known by that name) the week after the final, but wet Easter weather kept the crowd down to 15,000 for the visit of Blackburn Rovers on 17 April,

Campbell scoring the first goal at the ground in a 3-0 win. The potential of the stadium and the club was better illustrated two days later when 35,000 turned out to see Wolves beaten 5-0 in Villa's penultimate league game of a campaign they finished off with ten wins and a draw from the last 11 matches.

Reynolds, capped by both Ireland and England, now moved to Celtic with Campbell, whose scoring record for Villa was 43 in two seasons. Failing to replace his goals adequately, they dropped to sixth in 1897/98 yet came again to win two successive championships before the end of a tumultuous decade.

There was a dramatic finish in 1899 when Villa thrashed Notts County 6-1 and Albion 7-1 over Easter to set up the finale five days later at home to Liverpool, who were level on points with them. With the better goal average Villa needed only a draw but took no chances, running up a 5-0 lead by half-time as their visitors blew up spectacularly. A capacity crowd of 41,000 made them the first club ever to average 20,000-plus in a league season.

The trophy was handed over on the day and was retained 12 months later, again by only two points, another strong finish bringing five wins and a draw from the last six matches to pip Sheffield United. This time they were not so dependent on Devey and Wheldon for goals, having promoted local lad Billy Garraty – great-great-grandfather of Jack Grealish – who scored 27 in the league in his first full season.

One of Garraty's earliest appearances the previous season came in bizarre circumstances. At Sheffield Wednesday in November Villa were losing 3-1 when the game was abandoned after 80 minutes because of bad light. Rather than replay it, the Football League ordered them to play only the remaining ten minutes in March, when Garraty was brought in without managing to affect the scoreline, Wednesday adding another goal for a 4-1 win; to make Villa's journey a little more worthwhile the teams then played a friendly of 35 minutes each way, which Wednesday won 2-0.

Five championships and three FA Cup finals in a decade had established Villa as the country's top club. But other big beasts were lurking and ready to pounce.

* * *

As well as being Villa's first Football League opponents, **Wolves** were the side who pressed them hardest for the runners-up spot behind Preston, finishing only a point below their Midlands rivals. Following that by reaching the FA Cup Final, although unable to deny Preston their historic Double, added up to a fine first season of league football, which was followed by three more successively in the top six without ever challenging for the title.

Had they held on to the lead in that opening game with Villa, or avoided defeat in the return in November, which was lost 2-1, second spot would have been theirs. There was a double over West Brom by 2-1 and 3-1, the home game bringing the best attendance of 8,600, but Preston were too good, as they were for everyone else. Wolves lost to them 4-0 at home and 5-2 away, which did not augur well for the FA Cup Final that they reached with a semi-final replay victory over Blackburn Rovers after two games at Crewe (1-1 and 3-1).

Thousands of supporters welcomed them back to the local railway station following that victory and accompanied them seven days later to the Kennington Oval where Preston were naturally heavy favourites. Wolves left-winger Tom Knight hit the bar early on (solid crossbars having replaced tape in 1882) but when Jimmy Ross did the same at the other end Dewhurst poked in the rebound. Ross added a soft second before the interval and Thompson a third before the end. It was an unhappy last game for goalkeeper Jack Baynton, one of the four original founders, although fitting that he and his friend Jack Brodie, another of the originals, should feature on the big day.

Many observers drew a comparison between Preston's pleasing passing style and Wolves' more direct play. At the post-match reception Wolves president Charles Crump could not resist a dig in pointing out that his lads were a proud local team, whereas North End had recruited from all over Britain.

Success in the first season was reflected in as many as five players winning England caps, joined by full-back Dick Baugh and inside-forward Harry Wood a year later. The five were full-back Charles Mason, half-backs Albert Fletcher, Arthur Lowder and Henry Allen and centre-forward Brodie. That first league season was played at the Dudley Road ground, where average crowds of under 4,000 were only ninth best of the 12 clubs. It took almost 50 years until Wolves could call themselves one of the best supported clubs in the country but at least from the summer of 1889 they had a smarter ground, which they still occupy today.

Molineux was until then a leisure park like the Aston Lower Grounds, described by one local paper as Wolverhampton's closest thing to Hyde Park, and the team had occasionally played there in local cup competitions. Named, like the hotel overlooking it, after a prosperous local family, the new stadium had covered accommodation for 4,300 and was 'one of the finest in the kingdom', according to a proud *Express and Star*. For several games in the first season, however, the attendance was barely half that number, the average being lifted only by a huge turnout of almost 20,000 for the Boxing Day visit of Blackburn.

After Villa opened the ground with a friendly match, Notts County were beaten 2-0 in Molineux's first Football League game, while Blackburn and the champions Preston were the only visitors to win a league game there; and with their 2-0 success at Preston in October, Wolves became the first visiting side ever to win a league game at Deepdale. Finishing fourth in that second season, just above Albion, made them the highest placed of the Midlands contingent. One of the smallest crowds of the season saw Burnley beaten 9-1 in December and there was another big win in the FA Cup, when Stoke successfully protested about the Molineux pitch in their 4-0 defeat but lost the replay by double that, Brodie scoring five times to earn a second successive semi-final against Blackburn. This time the Lancastrians were too strong, going through 1-0 with a late goal and then demolishing The Wednesday 6-1 in the final.

A second successive fourth place and then sixth were satisfactory, that latter 1891/92 season featuring a piece of football history in the opening league game when one of the five goals against Accrington was from the first penalty kick in the Football League, converted by inside-forward Billy Heath (until that season, an indirect free kick was the only punishment available). Wolves' slump to 11th twice and then 14th in 1896 was disappointing, but throughout the 1890s, with old gold and black replacing the red and white stripes, they remained a good FA Cup side. It took a good team to knock them out: Blackburn twice, Villa twice and West Brom, then Derby twice; but in 1893 and 96 they were finalists again with differing fortunes.

Thoughts of cup glory were far away one dismal rainy day in October 1892 when Wolves paid their first league visit to Newton Heath – the future Manchester United – and suffered a humiliating 10-1 defeat (still their heaviest, and United's largest). Newton Heath would finish bottom of the table and the Wolves committee offered to resign en masse but were given a stay of execution for a year.

The return game two months later was won 2-0 but league form was fitful and collapsed once the FA Cup Final was reached with wins over Bolton, Middlesbrough, Darwen and familiar semi-final opponents Blackburn, who were beaten 2-1. Among the run of defeats was a 4-2 home loss against a weary Everton, who took sufficient confidence from it to win their FA Cup semi-final second replay against Preston.

Five days after that, Merseyside descended on Fallowfield, a cycling and athletics stadium in Manchester that proved to be a hopelessly inadequate venue for its first and last cup final. Wolves were well represented too and a ground with a capacity of 15,000-20,000 was overrun by more than twice as many, barriers round the pitch being broken down well before the start, so that there was some doubt about whether the game could be played.

Even those who could see anything – among them three Wolverhampton town councillors who climbed a tree – were unsure about the identity of the unlikely match-winner, who turned out to be centre-half and captain Harry Allen. His long lob from far out after 60 minutes caught the Everton goalkeeper dazzled by the sun and dropped over the line.

There were frequent incursions by the crowd, almost 200 policemen on duty being criticised for being 'singularly inactive in the performance of what might be supposed were their duties' (*Sporting Chronicle*), and Everton made a formal protest in vain that the game should have been declared a friendly.

1893 FA Cup Final: Wolverhampton Wanderers 1 Everton 0
Wolverhampton Wanderers: Rose, Baugh, Swift, Malpass, Allen, Kinsey, Topham, Wykes, Butcher, Griffin, Wood.

Everton: Williams, Kelso, Howarth, Boyle, Holt, Stewart, Latta, Gordon, Maxwell, Chadwick, Milward.

Another two modest league campaigns had included the shock of an 8-0 home defeat at Christmas 1893 by the Albion, who then knocked them out of the 1894/95 FA Cup. The worst league performance yet, with only Small Heath and West Brom below them, followed in 1895/96, but was redeemed by the cup run, taking in wins over Notts County, Liverpool and Stoke before a 2-1 semi-final win over Derby at the Perry Barr home of champions Villa.

The Wednesday, who did not adopt the name of their city until 1929, were mid-table opposition and had lost 4-0 at Molineux in the league, but proved too strong in the final. Their England left-winger Fred Spikesley scored twice in the first 18 minutes, David Black equalising in between times.

It was a much-changed Wolves side after finally joining the fashion for Scottish imports like Black, many of the local lads having moved on – or in the case of Harry Allen and David Wykes died shockingly young; Wykes from pneumonia two days after playing against Stoke in October 1895.

There were financial problems too, with debts of £900 reported as attendances remained low in comparison to other First Division clubs and even some in the Second Division. The cup run therefore provided some welcome gates, as did Villa's visits, attracting a crowd of 22,000 that season and one of over 27,000 at Christmas 1896 that would not be bettered until after the First World War. Fewer than half of them came back to see West Brom beaten 6-1 two days later, although it was still the only other five-figure crowd of the season.

Among the spectators from time to time was one of the first celebrity supporters, Edward 'Land of Hope and Glory' Elgar (knighted in 1904), who composed a piece in tribute to right-half Billy Malpass, named after a line from a match report of a Wolves game, 'He Banged The Leather For Goal'.

Elgar and fellow fans witnessed a welcome improvement in league performances to finish third in 1898 and fourth in 1900, but in the FA Cup there was more hope than glory, with defeats by Southern League clubs Millwall and Queens Park Rangers.

The new century would also require a new goalscorer after Harry Wood departed for Southampton, good payers in the Southern League, with 126 goals to his name.

* * *

Until the Football League began, the team who would go into each new season with a target on their back were the FA Cup holders. That was **West Bromwich Albion**'s fate for the historic 1888/89 campaign, in which they began well against some of the First Division's weaker teams but suffered against the stronger ones and finished no higher than sixth, well behind local rivals Villa and Wolves, from whom they took only a single point in four games.

Rivalry with Stoke was also developing, which made for an interesting inaugural league game, only decided in the last six minutes when winger Joe Wilson and then George Woodhall scored Albion's goals. If the Potteries crowd of over 4,000 were disappointed, they had witnessed 'a grand exposition of Association football' according to the *Stoke Sentinel*.

Villa more than Wolves were the team Albion wanted to beat most, and the one their supporters wanted to see most, which meant the two league meetings, a week apart in January, drew the highest crowds of the season at each ground. Having lost at Villa Park, the Throstles managed a 3-3 draw in front of double the 4,000 people who had seen them against Wolves three weeks earlier.

In the FA Cup, another local side, Small Heath, were put in their place and Burnley were beaten 5-1 before a 10-1 romp against Chatham raised hopes of a fourth successive shot at glory. Unfortunately the Preston team beaten in the previous season's final had become an immovable object. They won the semi-final 1-0 at Bramall Lane and Albion's hopes of having the tie replayed after several pitch invasions by the huge crowd were in vain.

The cup continued to provide more excitement than the league in the 1890s for a team never better than mid-table and much worse than that in the third and fourth seasons of the competition. In the inglorious 1890/91 campaign, failing to win from the end of October to the beginning of March meant finishing bottom of the table and having to apply for re-election.

Like Villa, who were fourth from bottom, they received maximum votes, but it was a warning shot – as were the attendances of just 405 for Derby's snowy visit and 800 to see Accrington.

Even then, however, there was an FA Cup semi-final, lost 3-2 to Blackburn, and a year later came another run all the way to the final in defiance of a second successive poor league season. Only struggling Stoke and Darwen ended up below Albion in the table, but in knockout football they raised their game to beat Blackburn and two Alliance clubs, The Wednesday and Nottingham Forest, for whom a Football League scalp would have been a point proved.

Forest took three games to overcome in the semi-final but the prize was worth waiting for: Villa themselves had already qualified and would be the opposition in London on 19 March 1892. Having suffered heavy defeats by their neighbours in the league, 5-1 and 3-0, Albion were the underdogs. 'If ever a team looked like winning the cup it is Aston Villa,' wrote the *Daily Post* correspondent. But form was confounded. In the fourth minute little left-winger Jasper Geddes, who had scored a hat-trick in the semi-final, converted right-winger Billy Bassett's cross. Geddes helped centre-forward Sam Nicholls score the second before half-time and victory was assured with a long-range drive by 'Baldy' Reynolds, after which Joe Reader's goalkeeping kept Villa scoreless.

So by Monday the *Post* was forced to reconsider, admitting, 'It would be an injustice to attempt to lessen the merit of as fine and courageous an exhibition as the Kennington Oval has ever witnessed. No good Birmingham sportsman will attempt to minimise or explain away a victory by three goals to none.'

1892 FA Cup Final: West Bromwich Albion 3 Aston Villa 0
West Bromwich Albion: Reader, Nicholson, McCulloch, Reynolds, Perry, Groves, Bassett, McLeod, Nicholls, Pearson, Geddes.
Aston Villa: Warner, Evans, Cox, H. Devey, Cowan, Baird, Athersmith, J. Devey, Dickson, Hodgetts, Campbell.

With four league games still to play after the final, Albion were able to relax against Darwen and Stoke, ten of the cup winners helping to beat the Lancashire side 12-0 for a victory margin that the club have never again matched. Despite having only those two teams below them, Albion were even spared a re-election ballot on grounds of having won the FA Cup.

Inside-left Tom Pearson hit four goals against Darwen and was top or joint-top scorer for the first five seasons of league football, the lack of a prolific partner for him being one reason the team were not stronger. Unfortunately he had been forced into retirement at the age of 28 before the 1895 FA Cup Final, the third against Villa in just nine seasons. Small Heath and Wolves were beaten along the way but this time Villa, with Reynolds now in their side, won by the only, early goal. It was little consolation that, according to the *Sunday Times*, 'Bassett was the best forward on the field'; or that the 1-0 scoreline was reversed when the sides, both fielding full first XIs, met in the replayed Birmingham Senior Cup Final.

Centre-forward Tom Hutchinson, one of Albion's Scottish recruits, won that game and took over from Pearson as leading scorer in his one full season but soon returned north, and goalscoring was a real problem for the rest of the decade.

Bottom again in 1895/96, they were required along with Small Heath to play off in the test matches introduced three years earlier, the two Midlands clubs taking on the top two Second Division sides, Liverpool and Manchester City. Winning at home against the latter pair enabled Albion to survive but Liverpool replaced Small Heath for the following season. 'It would indeed have been a pity had so historic a club been obliged to sever their connection with the senior division,' commented a sympathetic *Derby Daily Telegraph*. 'Nevertheless the "Throstles" have had a narrow escape and it was only their plucky play when at home that saved them.'

Albion followers expressed their disenchantment rather than relief by staying away from a delayed final midweek league game against Blackburn, only 560 attending. That was in stark contrast to the 17,510 October crowd for the visit of Villa, who as champions four times in five seasons were by now not so much overshadowing as totally eclipsing their old rivals.

As with Wolves, Albion's gates were below average in the top division and in 1896 and 1899 were the worst of any club. The

Stoney Lane ground was of poor standard in comparison to most and, reluctant to spend on a rented property, the directors began looking elsewhere. The next chapter, and many more thereafter, would take place on a piece of land known as the Hawthorns estate.

* * *

Even though the Victoria Ground became an international venue in February 1889, **Stoke** were another club with lower than average crowds, caused to some extent by poor results. Bottom of the Football League in its first two seasons, they were voted out in favour of the much better-supported Sunderland, and although returning after only one year, struggled to establish themselves even in mid-table.

Five defeats from the opening six games of the inaugural league season had those who questioned the Potters' suitability as members nodding in 'told you so' mode. By the end of the 22 matches, only four had been won, two of them 3-0 against Notts County. County finished level on points but with a better goal average, Stoke having managed barely a goal a game at a time when such parsimony was almost unheard of.

The club's longevity and popularity ensured their re-election with more votes than anyone else, but after a second successive failure, the other clubs decided that affluent Sunderland, agreeing to pay the extra travelling expenses involved in going to the north-east, were a more deserving cause; faith justified when they became champions three times in their first five seasons.

Harry Lockett, secretary-manager of Stoke since 1884, resigned to concentrate on running the Football League full-time, but under Joe Bradshaw the club found their level by dropping into the Alliance for 1890/91 and winning the title with only two defeats – both, oddly, while conceding five goals away to Birmingham clubs, Small Heath and St George's. Expansion of the Football League to 14 clubs meant they were then voted in with Darwen, who became the only team to finish below them. It was the season Darwen lost 12-0 at West Brom while conceding a record 112 goals, though Stoke still managed to lose 9-3 to them in finishing second-bottom. Once again the Potters benefited from an extension to the First Division, increasing to 16 clubs at the same time as introducing a Second Division comprising most of the Alliance clubs, including Small Heath, Burton Swifts, Burslem Port Vale and Walsall Town Swifts.

So although testing the patience of their fellow clubs, as well as needing a public appeal to reduce debts of £900, Stoke stayed up and justified their retention with a much more successful 1892/93 season in seventh place, ahead of both West Brom and FA Cup winners Wolves. They even supplied the goalkeeper, Bill Rowley, and both full-backs, Alf Underwood and Tom Clare, for England's 2-0 win away to Ireland; and forward Joe Schofield played against Wales the same day (for three years from 1890–92 England took on both countries on the same day with different teams).

Clare had made his debut against his former club Goldenhill Wanderers, who were captained by his brother. He was a future manager of Port Vale after suffering a broken leg, which for most players of that era was career-ending.

A top-six place for the first time in 1896 was sandwiched between two nervous play-off seasons, the second of which ended in a scandal leading to the whole system being abandoned. The 1894/95 campaign ended in the bottom three, necessitating a one-off test match against Newton Heath that was won 3-0 at the scarcely neutral venue of Port Vale.

Three years later Stoke were one of five teams all level on points at the bottom of the First Division but with the worst goal average. That meant they and Blackburn would have to meet the Second Division's Burnley and Newcastle over ten days at the end of April. The Potters and Burnley both had two wins and one defeat going into their last game against each other, which was sufficient to guarantee them the two First Division places if they drew.

To nobody's surprise, that was the goalless outcome in a game that became in the words of the *Staffordshire Advertiser* 'a complete fiasco ... without much effort on behalf of the players'. Neither side showed any interest in scoring, while the Victoria Ground faithful resorted either to keeping the ball whenever it went out of play, or kicking it on to the roof of the stand.

'These test matches have proved an utter farce,' the *Manchester Guardian* thundered. 'A change of some kind is absolutely necessary.' One came about immediately, the Football League management committee introducing automatic promotion and relegation while expanding the two divisions to 18 teams each, which allowed Blackburn and Newcastle to play in the upper division. There would be no more play-offs for almost 90 years.

Untroubled by relegation worries in the last two seasons of the decade under new manager Horace 'Denny' Austerberry, Stoke achieved little in the FA Cup until one semi-final place in 1899. It took replays to see off The Wednesday and Small Heath with important goals by Willie Maxwell, a native of Arbroath who joined his first English club in 1895 and went on to be top scorer for five successive seasons. Spurs from the Southern League were then beaten 4-1 to set up a semi-final against Derby County at Molineux but despite taking the lead through Maxwell, Stoke lost 3-1 to a hat-trick by Steve Bloomer, one of the greats of the era. They would have to wait until 1971 for the next such adventure.

* * *

Even before a first match had been played in the Football League, many of the clubs not included could see that William McGregor's brainchild was the way forward. Once the lucky 12 were named in the spring of 1888, Crewe Alexandra immediately suggested a second league and hosted a meeting of interested parties. Midlands representatives were Burslem Port Vale, Derby Junction, Leek, Long Eaton Rangers, Notts Rangers, Small Heath (who dropped their 'Alliance' tag that year) and Walsall Town Swifts. Birmingham St George's did not attend but ended up joining them in the Combination, which with no central organisation proved to be not so much a competition as a series of friendlies similar to previous seasons, with the usual range of cup matches to be added on.

Fortunately, a properly organised non-league competition, the Alliance, was introduced for the 1889/90 season and after three years the majority of its clubs – though not the unfortunate St George's – joined the expanded Football League.

The *Birmingham Daily Post*, though regularly covering Football League matches and many other local teams, rarely mentioned the Combination as any sort of tournament. The paper did reveal at the start of October, however, that **Small Heath** had won their first six games of the season. The opener was against St George's (see below), who were clearly the main local rivals at their level; by the end of January the pair had met three times, the last game attracting some 3,000 spectators; 4,000 came to see Walsall Swifts beaten earlier.

With no great interest in the Combination, the FA Cup was looked forward to all the more eagerly and the Heathens enjoyed a good run. In the qualifying rounds, which had been introduced for the first time, they beat Burslem Port Vale, Leek and Burton Wanderers, the latter by 9-0 with Ted and Will Devey, two of the five Birmingham footballing brothers, scoring four goals each. That meant a home tie against holders West Brom in the first round proper, when 3,000 saw Small Heath go 2-0 up at half-time, only to be denied a giant-killing by the odd goal in five.

A poor sequence of FA Cup seasons thereafter included losing to Wolves (1889/90), being disqualified for fielding an unregistered player (1890/91) and going out in the first round proper for five years in a row; but at least by then they had genuine league football.

The first two Alliance seasons were disappointing, resulting in no better than tenth place out of 12 each time. For the last one, in 1891/92, things were looking up and Small Heath finished third, ensuring that they would be among the dozen clubs elected to form the Football League Second Division. Nottingham Forest, Newton Heath and The Wednesday went straight from the Alliance into the First Division while Burslem Port Vale, Northwich Victoria and Sheffield United joined from other regional leagues.

That first Football League season was a triumph as the Heathens swept to the Second Division title, winning 17 of their 22 games and scoring 90 goals – almost 30 more than anyone else. The biggest win was 12-0 against Walsall Town Swifts in mid-December, the first of a run of nine straight wins to finish the campaign a point clear of Sheffield United. Five players reached double figures, led by Fred Wheldon with 25, and goalkeeper Chris Charsley, a future Chief Constable of Coventry, became the club's first England international.

To earn promotion there was still a test match on neutral ground to win against Newton Heath, who had finished bottom of the First Division, but had shown they could score goals by beating Wolves 10-1 and Derby 7-1. After a 1-1 draw at Stoke, the Manchester side walloped their fellow Heathens 5-2 in the replay in Sheffield, ensuring that both teams stayed where they were for the following season.

Twelve months on they were destined to change places after all. In 1893/94 Small Heath finished second behind Liverpool in another strong season, this time scoring 103 goals in 28 games; 22 to Wheldon and 24 to Frank Mobley, who had joined from Singers. Stoke was again the venue for the test match, this time against Darwen, who were beaten 3-1 while Newton Heath lost their game to Liverpool the same day.

Attendances were normally no more than 3,000 – less than a third of Aston Villa's – and the *Birmingham Daily Post* had a warning about future prospects: 'No one can deny that Small Heath have not fully deserved the success. It is to be hoped that they will now receive the support which has been denied them in the past and that their league matches next season will be well patronised. Birmingham is large enough to support two clubs and the interests of Aston Villa and Small Heath need not clash in the slightest degree. A healthy rivalry, on the contrary, may be beneficial to both clubs.'

With St George's having disbanded for lack of support and finance, the paper even made a dramatic claim about the importance of Small Heath's test match victory, 'Defeat would in all probability have meant the disbanding of the club. The committee have been hard-pressed many times during the season just passed, but the hope of fighting their way into the first division, and so retrieving their position, has sustained them in all their difficulties. Now that they have attained the goal of their ambition, it will behove the managers of the club to make real effort in several directions. In the first place, they will have to strengthen their team, for it cannot be expected that 11 or 12 men will stand the strain next season amongst the first division clubs. Then, the accommodation of the spectators will have to be attended to.'

Although only one new player was recruited, regular league fixtures against the country's top teams doubled the average gate, five-figure crowds turning up for the visits of Villa, champions Sunderland and Everton. All three games were drawn and, after heavy defeats away to Sunderland (7-1) and Blackburn (9-1), winning the last game at Sheffield United spared the Heathens from one of the three test match places. In a tight finish, they were 12th of 16 teams, sandwiched in between Wolves and West Brom, with Stoke also beneath them.

The first league meeting with Villa was the away game in September 1894, lost 2-1 after taking a very early lead. 'There are few teams, we venture to think, who will make a more creditable display at Perry Barr than Small Heath did,' said the *Daily Post* correspondent. The result was certainly closer than the FA Cup tie between the clubs seven years earlier (4-0 to Villa) but still a harbinger of things to come: the 1895/96 season brought defeats by 7-3 and 4-1, and the pair would meet 13 times in league and FA Cup games before the Heathens finally beat their neighbours, in September 1905.

Personnel did not change until the second season in the top flight, partly out of desperation as another relegation struggle loomed. Again they finished in between Wolves and West Brom but the West Midlands trio were the bottom three in the division. Under the new system, that meant Albion and Small Heath each playing the Second Division's Liverpool and Manchester City twice in a mini-league. Albion survived with five points but their neighbours did not win any of the first three games, so beating City 8-0 in the last one was in vain.

Relegation cost the services of Wheldon (82 goals in 129 games), who immediately became top scorer for Villa, and Mobley (64 in 103), though Walter Abbott took over with 53 in two seasons to earn a move to Everton. He featured prominently with 13 goals in the Heathens' extraordinary run in the autumn of 1898/99, when successive home wins in the Second Division and FA Cup were gained over Chirk 8-0, Luton 9-0, Druids 10-0, Darwen 8-0 and Port Vale 7-0. Yet a weak finish to the season meant that despite being the second-highest scorers they finished only eighth.

Walsall again provided the nearest thing to be a big local derby, with gates stuck at around 5,000 and money still tight. It would take five seasons in all to return to the big league.

* * *

Neither of the main Burton clubs were spoken of as potential league members even among the 20 left out that *Cricket and Football Field* listed as worthy contenders. Yet within six years the brewery town of Burton-upon-Trent had two separate teams competing in the Second Division. It was a remarkable achievement for a town with a population of fewer than 50,000 people at the time, considering that the only other places with two league teams were Birmingham, Liverpool, Manchester, Nottingham and Sheffield; not even London, where Woolwich Arsenal remained the only representatives until 1905.

The pair may only have spent three seasons together in the Second Division before eventually merging and then dropping out of the league in 1907, but a legacy of football in the area had been established and would continue until the emergence of yet another Football League representative in the 21st century.

The blue-shirted **Burton Swifts**, like Small Heath, had one year of Combination games, then in 1890 bought the Peel Croft ground previously used by the rugby club and had three seasons in the Alliance, finishing fifth in the competition's final year. In knockout football the undoubted highlight was victory over Aston Villa to win the 1892 Staffordshire Cup.

Moving up into the inaugural Football League Second Division, they made a dramatic debut on 3 September 1892 by scoring five goals in the first half against visiting Crewe Alexandra and winning 7-1. They finished sixth and did so again the following high-scoring season, recovering from a 6-1 home defeat by Small Heath to bring off an astonishing 8-5 home win over Walsall in February in 'a game of a most sensational kind', *Sporting Life* reported, adding unsurprisingly that the Brewers' Welsh international goalkeeper Sam Jones, signed from Wrexham, 'was not so safe as usual'.

A long FA Cup run that first season included a 3-2 victory over main local rivals **Burton Wanderers** in front of a record crowd of 5,500 to earn the dubious pleasure of an away game with Preston North End, which ended in a 9-2 defeat. Two years later Wanderers had their revenge by 5-2 before losing at home to Blackburn.

As unbeaten Midland League champions in 1894, Wanderers, who sported blue and white halves, were elected along with their runners-up Leicester Fosse to fill one of the Football League vacancies. They started with a 3-1 win at Rotherham and the first home game was won 1-0 against Newton Heath at the newly improved Derby Turn ground in Little Burton. Some remarkable results included beating Newcastle United 9-0 (still the Geordies' record defeat), Manchester City 8-0 and Walsall 7-0. Wanderers finished seventh of the 16 teams, fully ten points ahead of their neighbouring Swifts. They lost the first Burton derby in the Football League 2-1, which proved their only defeat of the six league meetings between the clubs.

In their second season Wanderers did even better, drawing in the FA Cup at Sheffield United and ending up fourth, only four points behind the champions Liverpool, but the third, 1896/97, was a bad one for the town. Amid the first talk of possible amalgamation, both clubs were forced to apply for re-election with bottom team Lincoln City and the voting for three places went: Lincoln 21, Burton Swifts 15, Luton Town (Southern League) 13, Burslem Port Vale (Midland League) 11, Burton Wanderers 9.

So Luton joined Arsenal as only the second southern club in the league, replacing the unfortunate Wanderers, who returned to the Midland League for four unsuccessful years, at the end of which in the summer of 1901 they finally merged with the Swifts, who had just finished bottom of the Second Division.

As Football League teams, the two clubs' gates had been similar at around 2,500–3,000 but Swifts did not seem to benefit from their neighbours' return to non-league football and after three more seasons in the bottom six, burying the hatchet and joining together was the sensible option.

For the small town dubbed 'Beeropolis', as an ironic reflection of mighty Manchester's Cottonopolis, the Football League years were quite an achievement, and were not yet finished.

* * *

Walsall pre-dated Burton by combining its two strongest teams in 1888 in the hope of making serious progress for the dawn of league football. As **Walsall Town Swifts** they held Aston Villa in their first match, the Birmingham Charity Cup semi-final (not the final, as often reported), and were among the half a dozen teams with the best records in the Combination season of 1888/89.

Life was tougher in the Alliance, with finishing positions of ninth, seventh (including an 11-1 defeat after the long trip to Sunderland Albion) and 11th out of 12. That bottom-but-one placing suggested that the Football League Second Division might be a struggle too and so it proved, starting at home to Darwen and a crowd of 4,000 that was never matched again that season, as one of five successive defeats. An improved run climaxed with the bizarre 6-5 win at Crewe, appropriately on fireworks night, but by the end of the campaign the Swifts were bottom of the 12 teams, Burslem and Burton being two of the few among their other victims.

Local residents were not the first or last to disapprove of league football on their doorstep – even if the average crowd was only 1,300 – and the club received notice to quit the Chuckery. A replacement ground on the West Bromwich Road was not ready for the beginning of the 1893/94 season, the two earliest home games being played in Wednesbury in another poor start, but the new stadium brought an immediate upturn with a 5-1 success over Crewe.

Youthful 'rowdyism' in a home game against Burton was punished by banning anyone under the age of 17 from the next two matches and after the 8-5 defeat in the return game at Burton mentioned above, another bottom place was on the cards; but the defence tightened up, the forwards kept scoring and five successive wins helped finish the season in tenth place. Inside-forward Walter McWhinnie topped the scorers in his first season.

McWhinnie departed early in the third league campaign of 1894/95, however, which ended with the club being voted out. A run of nine successive defeats either side of Christmas included heavy ones at Newcastle (7-2), Leicester (9-1) and Burton (7-0), and a brief revival was interrupted by similarly depressing results at Newton Heath (9-0) and Woolwich Arsenal (6-1). The Manchester result could have been worse: on the original date Walsall lost 14-0 but were able to claim the pitch was in such poor condition that the game should be replayed a month later. Conceding 92 times in 30 matches meant finishing 14th out of 16 and this time the clubs were less forgiving, Walsall having complacently assumed they were safe and neglecting to undertake any serious canvassing. Although above Port Vale and Crewe in the table, they were voted out in favour of Loughborough Town.

The last two home games attracted fewer than 1,000 people and serious financial concerns had to be addressed. Happily the exile lasted only one season, the 1895/96 Midland League campaign ending in third place and re-election to the Second Division with Gainsborough Trinity and Blackpool, replacing Burslem Port Vale.

The return to the Football League after 12 months' absence was with a new name – plain Walsall – new colours of white shorts with blue shorts and another stadium in Hillary Street. It would become known in the 1930s as Fellows Park and was home for 94 years apart from a brief return to West Bromwich Road in 1900 because of difficulty in meeting the rent.

Still obliged to play in the FA Cup qualifying rounds, they responded with a club-record victory in demolishing Dresden United 11-0 and in the league justified their fellow clubs' faith with crowds of almost 4,000, enjoying three comfortable seasons. In the first two a slow start was redeemed by a good finish to end up 12th and 10th, and the 1898/99 campaign was the most successful yet, which made a subsequent disastrous decline all the more of a shock. Sixth place was an excellent achievement, climaxed by a run of only one defeat in 13 games that included the highest league win by 10-0 over doomed Darwen, playing their last Football League season. It compensated for a joint-record defeat away to the Lancashire club on Boxing Day 1896 when, the day after drawing 3-3 at Small Heath and possibly excessive celebrations, the Saddlers had turned up with only eight players and went down 12-0.

Top scorer in the 10-0 win (with four) was a rare character in Jack 'Soldier' Aston, bought out of the Army when under arrest, and regularly falling foul of authority once his career ended after later spells with Woolwich Arsenal and Small Heath among others. 'Soldier Aston again' headlined the *Walsall Advertiser* a little wearily after he was sentenced to two months in prison following another failure to pay maintenance to his wife.

From the heights of sixth place meanwhile, the Saddlers' fall was dramatic. In 1899/1900 they were 12th of 18, the best moments coming with two exciting local derbies in the FA Cup. Small Heath were beaten in the final qualifying round and the mighty West Brom were held 1-1 in front of almost 10,000 at Hillary Street thanks to a goal from Scottish winger Hugh Dailly. But they were clearly destined to live in the shadow of Albion, who won the replay 6-1, and Wolves, who had knocked them out of the cup by an identical score 11 years earlier.

The first season of the new century then brought demotion from the Football League again, an exile that this time would last 20 years. In December, unable to pay the rent they were forced to move back to the old West Bromwich Road ground, where after three unbeaten games in three days at Christmas, form collapsed with one win in 17 matches. That made it essential to win the final one at home to Middlesbrough in order to avoid a re-election ballot, but the town was hardly rallying round by now and only 800 were there to see a goalless draw. Stockport and Burton Swifts still finished below them but were voted back, while the Saddlers would spend the next two decades back in the Midland and Birmingham leagues.

* * *

While neighbouring Stoke struggled from the start in the Football League, **Burslem Port Vale** (the 'Burslem' tag adopted in 1884 was not dropped until 1907) had a season of glorified friendlies in the Combination and then played in the Midland League before joining a majority of Alliance members in the new Football League Second Division, which they briefly dropped out of in 1896 before regaining their place.

In the meantime there was little glory to be found in the FA Cup. From being knocked out 1-0 at Stoke in 1887, they did not survive the qualifying rounds for another ten years, losing several times to the Burton clubs.

In the Combination the Valiants managed to fit in 26 games, far more than anyone else, but lost more than twice as many as they won. The Midland League was more of a success and in 1892 they were the only club from it to be elected to the Second

Division. A tragedy six weeks before the season cast an early shadow, however, when Scottish striker Frank McGinnis died of kidney failure, aged only 22. Signed after scoring five against the Vale for Halliwell in a Combination game in December 1888, he had been leading scorer for three successive seasons.

Without him, an opening-day defeat by 5-1 at Small Heath with only ten men (Billy Beats missed his train to Birmingham) suggested the new level would be testing, which was confirmed with only three wins before Christmas and the humiliation of a 10-0 home defeat by Sheffield United in December that still stands as a record loss for any Football League team on their own ground. Average gates of 1,200 were the lowest in the division, as was the total of 30 goals from 22 games, with only Walsall Town Swifts finishing below them.

An improvement to seventh place the following season, scoring at least four goals in the opening six games, was not maintained, the next campaign being summed up by another 10-0 hammering, this time away to Notts County with only eight men. The regular goalkeeper, gypsy Martin Frail, who lived in a caravan throughout his career, failed to make it through the snow; two others misread the train timetable; and two outfield players taking a turn between the posts conceded five goals apiece, although the *Lincolnshire Echo* reported that 'Baddeley performed splendidly in goal' – which was probably just as well. Again they avoided bottom place, with Crewe below them, and in 1895/96 were above Rotherham and Crewe but were still voted out with that pair as Walsall returned.

Expansion of the Second Division to 18 clubs two years later presented an opportunity to return, which was granted, Vale's case having been helped by a sensational FA Cup giant-killing. First Division champions-elect Sheffield United – possibly expecting another double-figure win – were held 1-1 at Bramall Lane and bested 2-1 after an extra-time goal by Lucien Boullemier, a wing-half and ceramic designer whose French father had moved to the Potteries in the 1870s. The winner came after United had sent their famously heavyweight goalkeeper William 'Fatty' Foulke upfield and he was, in the words of a disgruntled *Sheffield Independent* reporter, 'unable to get back to his place in time'.

The handsome Boullemier was influential again in a first season back in the league, 1898/99, which began with six successive wins and included a record Cobridge attendance of 12,000 for the drawn game at home to champions Manchester City. Vale finished ninth and established themselves for several seasons in mid-table.

* * *

In May 1888 the *Birmingham Daily Post* declared **Birmingham St George's** to be one of the four best teams in the West Midlands, along with Aston Villa, West Bromwich Albion – who had for the past two seasons beaten them by a single goal in the FA Cup – and Wolves. The difference, of course, was that two months earlier the other three had been chosen as founder members of the Football League, McGregor's insistence on only one representative from any town or city ruling them out of contention.

It was a blow from which they never quite recovered. The following Easter, after a 4-1 win up at Darlington, another local paper would praise them as 'displaying more consistent form than any in the Midlands during the past month or two ... possessed of more ability than most people give them credit for'. Some were prepared to, and at the end of that season in the Combination they gained most votes of the clubs trying to win admission to the First Division, but were still two short of replacing Notts County.

Instead they joined the Alliance and could have finished fifth had they won a match they refused to fulfil against Sunderland Albion after being ordered to replay it. In its second season they were fourth but the last one in 1891/92, which included an 11-1 defeat by Crewe, was a bad one that ended in bottom place. St George's were the only one of the 12 clubs not to be elected to the new Second Division and soon disbanded, their financial problems illustrated when Harry Davies, who had moved to The Wednesday, was successfully sued by his old club for five guineas despite arguing that St George's no longer existed. 'What are you going to do with the money?' his counsel asked, but was told that the club was £60 in debt and had creditors to pay.

* * *

Warwick County, who played at Edgbaston Cricket Ground, collapsed at around the same time, with one minor record to their name. By beating Stoke City in an FA Cup qualifying round in October 1888 they became the first non-league side to knock a Football League team out of the competition. Defeat by Birmingham Excelsior in the first round proper followed and within three years the club had disappeared.

* * *

Singers, who did not become **Coventry City** until the end of the 1897/98 season, remained essentially a works team until well into that decade, even after turning professional. Lagging a good way behind the Midlands' major clubs, they first played competitively in 1887, by which time Aston Villa and West Brom had both been FA Cup finalists.

The cycle factory team began in the Birmingham Junior Cup but quickly made a mark as semi-finalists in 1887/88, wearing navy and white stripes, and then winners three years later in an unusual all-black kit. The season after that they achieved a notable treble of successes in the Birmingham Junior, Walsall and Wednesbury Cups. There was a real star in Frank Mobley, born in Handsworth, a slight but dangerous centre-forward who knocked in 26 goals in 16 cup ties in 1891/92 before being snaffled away by Small Heath and helping them into the First Division. He would return for one final season early in the next century.

By 1894 Singers were ready for league competition, starting in the Birmingham and District League with an exciting 4-4 draw at home to Kidderminster Harriers, who had been one of the league's 12 founder members in 1889 (see Non-League chapter). It turned out to be one of the better results that season. Only seven games out of 30 were won and amid results like 8-0 defeats by the reserve teams of West Brom and Wolves (Villa's second string were a little more lenient, though not much), they finished 13th of 16.

It took another two seasons in the doldrums before reaching seventh place for two years running in a league dominated by those reserve teams. A first FA Cup venture in 1893 brought defeat by Football League club Burton Swifts, and after losing to the same opponents three years later in the third qualifying round there would not be another win in the competition until 1902. There was similarly little success in the Birmingham Senior Cup from 1892.

Civic pride may have been enhanced with the name change, but in Coventry's local papers 'football' still tended to mean rugby. A crowd of 3,000 for the opening game at the new Highfield Road ground in September 1899 was three times the average and presaged a disastrous campaign at the bottom of the table. The most spectacular match was a 7-6 defeat away to Bristol Rovers' reserves and the Football League seemed a long way away.

* * *

Shrewsbury Town also moved up to the Birmingham and District League in the mid-1890s, in their case by way of the Shropshire equivalent, which they joined in 1890, immediately finishing as runners-up to Ironbridge and seeing Welsh winger Charlie Bowdler honoured as their first international. Just before that they had begun competing in both the FA Cup and the Birmingham Senior Cup, albeit learning hard lessons. In the first FA Cup season of 1887/88 an away tie at Chirk brought a 10-2 defeat and the following year a crowd of 2,000 at the Racecourse Ground watched the mighty Wolverhampton Wanderers also run up double figures, this time without reply.

There was a considerable success, however, when allowed over the border to play in the Welsh Cup, a competition instigated in 1877 and mostly dominated by Wrexham and the Ruabon club Druids. In 1891 the Town drubbed Mold 5-0 in the semi-final and then Wrexham 5-2 in the final at Oswestry after trailing 2-0 at half-time. 'There was the largest attendance ever seen at a football match in Shropshire,' reported the *Sporting Life*. 'The game was fast and exciting throughout.' The crowd was said to be 4,000-strong.

They would have reached the final again a year later after a 4-0 win against Westminster Rovers (another Wrexham club) but the result was erased over a protest about the state of the pitch, and Rovers won the rematch. And in October 1894 the Town ran in no fewer than 21 goals without reply in the same competition against the unfortunate Mold Alyn Stars.

Three years in the FA Amateur Cup also led to a semi-final place in the last of them, 1895/96, after which they turned professional, but still found the Birmingham League a struggle. The Town finished one place above Singers for two years running but were never in the top ten for the five seasons before the century's end.

3

Down, Down
1901–1919

'Players wanted for all positions. Apply stating wages required, age, height and weight to Frank Heaven, Secretary, The Hawthorns, West Bromwich.'

Athletic News, April 1901

'It is generally considered that a new and far more prosperous time is about to begin for Association football in Burton.'

Athletic News, August 1901

'At last, a final worthy of the name and of the occasion. The Villa won in undeniable style.'

Birmingham Gazette, April 1905

'The weakness of the Wanderers is distressing to those who have a warm corner in their hearts for a club which has never been out of the first class and which has accomplished much on a limited income and with, as a rule, English players. The present plight of the Wolverhampton warriors is pitiable.'

Athletic News, April 1906

'The Potteries public do not deserve a football club if this is the way they show their support.'

Stoke chairman, June 1908

'We view with indignation and alarm the persistence of Association Football Clubs in doing their best for the enemy.'

The Times, November 1914

BY THE turn of the century, football matches were becoming more recognisable to modern eyes. Goal nets and penalty kicks had been introduced and neutral linesmen now replaced the touchline umpires previously nominated by the clubs. Tactics and styles of play were evolving and early experiments with artificial lighting were taking place.

Scotland and Ireland had adopted William McGregor's brainchild and had their own national leagues; Austria were about to play Hungary in the first international match outside Britain and seven other European nations would shortly form a new organisation called FIFA.

The Football League was flourishing with 36 teams, and attendances continued to increase – Aston Villa having become the first to average 20,000 in a season – but the clubs' owners were always wary of costs. In summer 1901, despite opposition from the original players' union (the AFU), the Football Association's annual general meeting introduced a maximum wage of £4 a week and outlawed bonuses. The restrictions did not, however, apply to ambitious Southern League clubs like Southampton and Tottenham Hotspur, who were able to recruit a number of disenchanted older pros to further their FA Cup exploits. And after the sensation of a £1,000 transfer fee, when Alf Common moved from Sunderland to Middlesbrough in 1905, a limit of £350 was introduced – it lasted for just three months.

* * *

By 1900 nine West Midlands clubs had played in the Football League, five of them in the First Division, and the FA Cup had been won by **Aston Villa** (three times), West Bromwich Albion (twice) and Wolves. Small Heath were about to return to the First Division – and adopt the name of their city – but it was Villa who continued to lead the challenge to northern domination.

Champions three times in four years to end the 19th century and boasting the biggest crowds for six successive seasons from 1898/99, they justifiably considered themselves the country's top club. Yet apart from further FA Cup wins in 1905 and 1913, only once more in 15 years before the First World War were they able to break the monopoly of northern title winners: Newcastle United (three), Liverpool, Sunderland, The Wednesday, Manchester United, Blackburn Rovers (all two) and Everton.

The new century began with one of those poor defences of the title that champions are wont to suffer; in Villa's case dropping into the bottom four after winning only one game of the 13 after Christmas. The FA Cup was not so much a distraction as a welcome relief in finding some form to reach the semi-final, beating Small Heath after two games that produced only one goal, scored by Billy Garraty in extra time of the home replay. Sheffield United, runners-up to Villa the previous season, were initially held 2-2 but won the replay at the Baseball Ground 3-0.

Joe Bache, a future England international, was an important signing from Stourbridge, forming a dangerous inside-forward trio with Garraty and Glaswegian Jasper McLuckie. The trio's goals were behind a late Double attempt in 1902/03, before losing the cup semi-final 3-0 to mid-table Bury and finishing a point behind champions The Wednesday after a strong finish.

The following season the cup brought controversy when a huge crowd at Tottenham spilled on to the pitch with Villa ahead through Bache's goal. They declined to leave, causing the game to be abandoned and moved to Villa Park – where Spurs won 1-0.

Controversy too in the league a year later, when Manchester City arrived desperate to win the final game: Villa skipper Alex Leake said the great Billy Meredith offered a bribe but the home team's 3-2 win denied them any chance of success. It eventually cost City far more heavily: Meredith, banned for the following season, turned whistleblower about illegal payments and 17 of their players were also suspended.

By that time Villa had played, and won, another FA Cup Final. Harry Hampton from Wellington Town, another good non-league find, replaced the departed McLuckie at centre-forward, scoring in every round of a comfortable run to the semi-final. He was on target again in the 2-1 replay win over Everton and scored both goals in the final at Crystal Palace against Newcastle. The Geordies had beaten Villa twice in the league as they pushed for a Double, but were below par on a brilliantly sunny day and had to be content with securing the championship.

It was only the second time that over 100,000 had watched the final. 'A stirring spectacle at the Crystal Palace,' headlined

The Referee, in which 'Newcastle United fail to show their form'. The *Birmingham Gazette* (having dropped the word 'Daily' a year earlier) commissioned a special contribution from the great all-round sportsman C.B. Fry, who wrote, 'At last, a final worthy of the name and of the occasion. The Villa won in undeniable style. They beat a team which, inferior as it was on the play, took a lot of beating.'

1905 FA Cup Final: Aston Villa 2 Newcastle United 0
Aston Villa: George, Spencer, Miles, Pearson, Leake, Windmill, Brawn, Garraty, Hampton, Bache, Hall.
Newcastle United: Lawrence, McCombie, Carr, Gardner, Aitken, McWilliam, Rutherford, Howie, Appleyard, Veitch, Gosnell.

Villa's captain, England right-back Howard Spencer, was their only survivor from the previous final of 1897; his playing career finally ended in 1908 after almost 300 games for the club and the following year he joined the board, serving until 1936.

Spencer was in the side that made history in their next FA Cup game, in January 1906, a record 11-0 win against little King's Lynn of the Norfolk and Suffolk League; in the league, seventh place meant they finished for the first time below newly named Birmingham, who did the double over them. In September that year the first *Villa News and Record* match programme appeared for the opening game against Blackburn. Programmes from that season now sell for around £150 each.

Material in them over the next four seasons was generally of an upbeat nature as George Ramsay's team finished fifth, then second in 1907/08 to a Manchester United side winning their first title, followed by seventh place and a sixth championship title in 1909/10.

A total of 84 goals equalled the best by any First Division team (Villa themselves 16 years earlier). Bache reached 20 for the second time in three seasons and Hampton was back on song with 26 after missing long spells of the previous three campaigns. The margin was a comfortable one, runners-up Liverpool only reducing it to five points by winning the last match of the season, between the two teams at Anfield. A 7-1 win over fifth-placed United in February was a highlight, but it was just as well not to know that would be the last championship triumph for 71 years. On the back of it the club purchased Villa Park outright for a total of £9,750.

A record run of nine successive wins in autumn 1910 should have been the basis for retaining the title but United pipped them by a point when Villa lost their final game, which was again at Liverpool.

Hampton had plenty more goals left in him and with the benefit of them – another 122 in five seasons – his team were runners-up twice more and FA Cup winners once. In 1912/13 they ended up four points behind Sunderland but, as with Newcastle eight years earlier, denied north-eastern giants the Double by winning the final. Derby, Crystal Palace and Bradford were all knocked out by the same emphatic 5-0 scoreline, then Oldham in the semi-final submitted to a goal by Clem Stephenson, the little inside-forward signed from Durham City in 1910.

The final was a full-blooded affair. Hampton and Sunderland's balding centre-half Charlie Thomson got stuck into each other but escaped without punishment until after the game, when they were suspended for a month at the start of the following season – as was the referee for not having imposed sufficient order. Sunderland hit the bar or post three times, two of them while Villa goalkeeper Sam Hardy was off injured with centre-half Jimmy Harrop deputising. But Tom Barber headed the only goal from a possibly miskicked corner by Charlie Wallace, who had also sliced a 15th-minute penalty well wide.

It was their fourth win out of four at the happy hunting ground of Crystal Palace, this one in front of a record crowd of 121,919, and press opinion declared it as well merited as the previous triumph over Newcastle. 'The Midlanders showed just that extra cleverness and the unison in attack that justified the win,' said *The Sportsman*, while admitting, 'It was not of the standard that had been fondly anticipated from the two crack clubs of the kingdom. The occasion and over-anxiety caused the players to lose their heads in the heat of the moment.'

1913 FA Cup Final: Aston Villa 1 Sunderland 0
Aston Villa: Hardy, Lyons, Weston, Barber, Harrop, Leach, Wallace, Halse, Hampton, Stephenson, Bache.

Sunderland: Butler, Gladwin, Ness, Cuggy, Thomson, Low, Mordue, Buchan, Richardson, Holley, Martin.

It was the first final between the top two First Division teams and four days later Villa needed to beat the same opponents to have any chance of the title. But Sunderland scored first and held out for a draw, then won their last two games to finish in front. Each team had pushed the goalscoring bar higher with 86, Harold Halse, signed from Manchester United, and Hampton both registering five in one match; in the latter's case it was the 10-0 win over The Wednesday.

Under the shadow of war, the 1914/15 season was an anti-climax, with gates down everywhere, requests from Lord Kitchener in the programme to join up and Villa falling to 14th with West Brom above them. But in a table of First Division points from 1888 to 1915 the Villans came out on top; and had been highest-placed West Midlands team in 21 of those 27 seasons. (See Appendix I).

* * *

A bold step forward for **West Bromwich Albion** in moving from Stoney Lane to The Hawthorns in the summer of 1900 was followed by a potentially disastrous one at the end of the opening season there, with relegation for the first time from the top division of English football. After returning at the first attempt the Throstles went down again two years later and this time took seven seasons to clamber back up, before consolidating and reaching an FA Cup Final.

The new ground, a mile south-east of the town centre, and boasting the old wooden 'Noah's Ark' stand from Stoney Lane (which burnt down on Bonfire Night 1904), needed lots of work before the first game on 3 September 1900 for the midweek visit of Derby County. Charles 'Chippy' Simmons scored the home team's first Hawthorns goal in a 1-1 draw in front of just over 20,000 and five days later a huge crowd of over 35,000 turned up for the Aston Villa game; winning neither before losing 5-0 at Liverpool, then 6-1 to both Bury and Nottingham Forest gave an indication of how the season was going to go.

No team lost more games or scored fewer goals, and apart from the derby at home to Wolves, who followed Villa in taking both points, crowds fell away so badly that for the final game against Sheffield United barely 1,000 people bothered to attend. Yet Albion still managed to reach another FA Cup semi-final, only to lose 4-0 to Tottenham, who then became the first Southern League winners of the trophy.

At the end of the season the club placed an advert in *Athletic News*: 'Players wanted for all positions. Apply stating wages required, age, height and weight to Frank Heaven, Secretary, The Hawthorns, West Bromwich.'

Several were acquired, including a new captain in wing-half Dan Nurse from Wolves, and only three men who endured the pitifully attended last First Division game started at home to Glossop in the new division. A 1-0 defeat watched by 5,000 hardly augured well but the newcomers quickly blended; 'Chippy' Simmons rediscovered his goalscoring touch to total 26 and with only three further defeats Albion bounced straight back as champions, with a record 55 points.

Two contrasting seasons back among the elite brought unpredictability above all else. Under new secretary-manager Fred Everiss, beginning a family dynasty in 1902, Albion went to the top of the table and were dreaming of a first title, before falling apart with only one victory in the final dozen games and ending up seventh. As often happens, a bad finish to one season carried over into the next: a goal-shy team managed only three wins by Christmas and finished bottom for the second time in four years. 'There was general sympathy for the club when they were reduced three seasons ago but very little excuse can be found for them this time,' said the *Birmingham Daily Gazette* in its roundup of the season.

Locals took another relegation badly and when it became clear that there would be no quick fix this time, three games were watched by under 3,000 people. Four better seasons brought a place in the top six and in 1907 a return to best FA Cup fighting traditions. Stoke were overcome in a second replay at neutral Villa Park and home wins over Norwich, Derby and Notts County followed, all bringing in much-needed finance from gates of more than 25,000 and leading to a semi-final against holders Everton at Bolton. Having protested in vain about the choice of venue, Albion pushed the First Division side all the way but went down 2-1 after an unfortunate mistake by the long-serving England full-back Jesse Pennington, who would go on to set the club appearance record with 495 games until Tony 'Bomber' Brown overtook him many years later.

Two years afterwards came an ultimately heartbreaking attempt at promotion. Top with one match to play, Albion lost 2-1 at Derby, whereupon Bolton and Tottenham overtook them. Tottenham's advantage on goal average was so narrow that one extra Albion goal in any of the 38 games would have been sufficient to take them up. The *Gazette* lamented one such goal at Blackpool, not given because 'the ball rebounded out of the net so quickly as to deceive the referee'.

One consolation was the resumption of lucrative derbies with relegated Birmingham, who in two successive seasons broke The Hawthorns' attendance record; first in the FA Cup tie of January 1908 (drawn 1-1) and then in the league the following Boxing Day, when 38,049 packed in for a 1-1 draw.

In 1910/11, Albion finally made it back to the First Division with a revamped team including stalwarts like Pennington, goalkeeper Hubert Pearson, and future England caps Joe Smith and Bobby McNeal. Reliable goalscorer Fred Buck ensured the championship was sealed on the final day with a winning penalty at home to Huddersfield.

Further ground improvements for the new season increased the capacity, which was tested when an early-season game brought the return of Villa. A new record crowd of over 46,000 watched the 2-2 draw in a performance confirming that after wins at Villa Park and over Manchester United and Liverpool, Albion should be comfortable at the new level.

They finished a respectable ninth and ought to have won the 1912 FA Cup. Tottenham, Leeds City, Sunderland, Fulham and Blackburn were all beaten to leave Albion hot favourites in the final against Barnsley, a mid-table Second Division side. The defence, with Pennington and Smith in front of goalkeeper Pearson (who scored two goals from penalties that season), was as solid as any but if there was one fault it was the lack of a top goalscorer. That was proved in both the semi-final, which yielded one goal in two games, and the final itself, which did the same. A goalless draw at Crystal Palace was described as 'dull and featureless' and in the replay at Bramall Lane – another venue Albion protested about as being too favourable to their opponents – Barnsley scored the only goal two minutes from the end of extra time. 'Play was never high class but it was better than at the Palace,' sniffed the *Daily Mirror.*

Three remaining seasons produced little more of note than one fifth place, and another record crowd against Villa (48,057), whom they copied by purchasing the freehold to their ground. A longed-for First Division title seemed some way off. If only they had known.

* * *

Fourth place in 1900 was a high watermark that **Wolverhampton Wanderers** would not reach again for almost 40 years, low tide taking them to rejoin Albion in the Second Division by 1906. One FA Cup success against the odds two years later was the only highlight in a run of undistinguished campaigns in that competition. By the time of relegation they were the worst supported team in the First Division, down to 6,500, while Villa, for instance, were attracting three times as many.

Football Who's Who in 1903/04 was still speaking of the club with high praise, extolling their reliance on local men from Staffordshire and Shropshire: 'They look after purely locals better than any club in England.' The article added an obvious reason: 'They cannot afford to pay the high wages most clubs do.' Debts of £1,400 at the start of the new century necessitated another public appeal, as in 1895, which raised two thirds of the money owed.

One of the local men, Tom Baddeley, was an England goalkeeper, the first of his five caps coming on home ground at Molineux in the 1903 victory over Ireland. As expected, it proved difficult to find a goalscorer to replace Harry Wood, who had taken Southampton's Southern League money. Billy Wooldridge did his best and managed 16 in a rare encouraging 1903/04 season with an eighth-place finish, plus only a second win in a dozen games against Villa, which proved illusory. Within two years supporters were bowing to the inevitable, as spelt out by the *Northern Daily Telegraph* in April: 'There can now be no doubt that the Wolverhampton Wanderers – one of the original dozen clubs – is doomed to the Second Division.'

In 1904/05 Wolves conceded a record 73 goals, and 12 months later, worst fears were realised. By Christmas they were clearly in serious relegation trouble with only four wins, plus defeats of 8-0 at Newcastle and 6-0 at Villa in successive November away games – all those goals going past Baddeley, who retained his place until the bitter end, by which time 99 had been conceded. As is sometimes the way, there was a sudden flourish at the finish when all was lost: home wins of 6-1 over Notts County and 7-0 against Derby. Those clubs were in the bottom six but Wolves were lowest of them all and ended up a full eight points short of survival.

A 5-0 FA Cup defeat when Baddeley was missing at Bradford City, a team from the middle of the Second Division, summed the season up and 'Hopeless Wanderers' was the headline in the *Birmingham Daily Gazette* more than a month before the finish. Under the headline 'The Starving Wolves', *Athletic News* wrote, 'The weakness of the Wanderers is distressing to those who have a warm corner in their hearts for a club which has never been out of the first class and which has accomplished much on a limited income and with, as a rule, English players. The present plight of the Wolverhampton warriors is pitiable.'

The Second Division brought a host of new visiting teams to Molineux, plus old foes in West Brom, who attracted a crowd of 25,000 – literally ten times as many as for the less-attractive Burton United a month later. Poor away form undermined a promotion challenge and so in the second season down below, 1907/08, the FA Cup exploits became something of a sensation.

When the competition proper began in January the only league highlights had been two well-attended games against the Albion, both lost by a single goal. In a first-round visit to Bradford City, Wolves avoided a repeat of the humiliation two years earlier and won the replay 1-0 with a goal by leading scorer George Hedley, once an England cap in his Sheffield United days. Two more crowds of over 25,000 turned out to see First Division Bury and then Southern League Swindon beaten, and an even bigger attendance was at the quarter-final game in which Stoke went down 1-0 on their own ground to a goal by Walter Radford, whose double had beaten Bury.

So to a semi-final against another Southern League side, Southampton, who were overcome 2-0 at Stamford Bridge, which meant that Wolves were in the final after only one victory over a First Division team. They had wound up their Second Division campaign in a modest ninth position and it was hardly surprising that reigning First Division champions Newcastle, 6-0 semi-final winners against Fulham, were strong favourites. United had scored 18 goals on their way to the final but, after being repulsed early on, were shocked when a long drive by Wolves' amateur wing-half Kenneth Hunt, a student at Oxford University, eluded their goalkeeper. Hedley added a second, Howie pulled one back, but right-winger Billy Harrison ran half the length of the pitch to score a third. Thus the Wanderers became only the second team from the lower division to win the FA Cup, while Newcastle lost their third final in four years.

'Among many memorable Cup finals at the Crystal Palace that of yesterday, which saw the third and again unexpected downfall of the classical Newcastle United team, will surely rank as one of the most remarkable,' said the main article in *The Referee*. 'And a more popular victory than that achieved by the hardy wear-and-tear Wolverhampton Wanderers, whose amber and black colours were flaunted on every side, is almost without parallel.'

1908 FA Cup Final: Wolverhampton Wanderers 3 Newcastle United 1

Wolverhampton Wanderers: Lunn, Jones, Collins, Hunt, Wooldridge, Bishop, Harrison, Shelton, Hedley, Radford, Pedley.

Newcastle United: Lawrence, McCracken, Pudan, Gardner, Veitch, McWilliam, Rutherford, Howie, Appleyard, Speedie, Wilson.

The town celebrated wildly; the players less so when Wolves committee man T.H. Sidney successfully opposed a resolution at the FA's AGM that the £4 maximum wage should be abolished. Backing their policy of loyal local lads – eight of whom were in the FA Cup-winning side – and with average gates up to a new record of over 9,000, the club had made a profit of almost £4,000 which they did not intend wasting on mere footballers.

A return to the First Division, however, did not materialise. In 1908/09 every Second Division team wanted a shot at the FA Cup holders, who started by losing 3-0 in the newly elected Tottenham Hotspur's first Football League game, and later returned to near the scene of their cup triumph to play Crystal Palace in the first round but went out 4-2 after extra time, and ended up seventh in the table. In the years before league football ceased they could do no better than seventh, eighth, ninth, fifth, tenth, ninth and fourth. Wooldridge moved on after 11 years' service and although forwards Radford, Billy Blunt and Welshman Frank Curtis proved capable of 20 league goals in a season at various times, there was a lack of consistency all round.

Albion winning promotion in 1910 meant the most attractive local derby disappeared, Birmingham's visit never drawing as many people. With the team mostly in mid-table, Molineux's best attendance over these years was the 25,000 who saw Manchester City beaten in the FA Cup in February 1911. In the last pre-war season, average gates were back down to 7,500, dropping on one occasion to just 3,000.

* * *

Like the Albion, **Small Heath** shuffled between the two divisions of the Football League for a while before settling, like Wolves, in the lower one. Unlike the other pair they achieved nothing in the FA Cup, and so the historically important milestones of this period were adopting the name of Birmingham in 1905 (not yet adding City), then finally beating Villa in a league game and moving to St Andrew's the following year. Royal blue shirts were also established definitively after occasional 19th-century experiments, a large white V appearing later and lasting until the mid-1920s.

Building on the promise of third place in 1899/00, the Heathens won promotion the following year, passing Albion on the way up. Within 12 months, however, the pair had swapped places again.

The potential for larger crowds was shown in March 1901 when, even though admission charges were doubled for the day, 18,000 turned out to see a goalless draw in the FA Cup with Villa, who would regularly break the attendance record for First Division derbies against them. Runners-up, a point behind Second Division champions Grimsby, the Heathens had the tightest defence in either division that season and a powerful centre-forward in the heavily moustachioed Scot Bob McRoberts, who scored five in the 10-1 defeat of Blackpool. The defenders in front of goalkeeper Arthur Robinson were not overwhelmed in the higher league but suffered in one of the closest relegation tussles in history. The Heathens actually scored more than they conceded, yet still went down as the lowest of no fewer than 15 teams who were separated by a mere seven points. With crowds having shot up from the Second Division average of 5,500, almost four times as many came to see the decisive final match, in which a win over Notts County would have meant safety. The home side could only manage a goalless draw, which meant that Stoke survived one point above them. 'A hard-fought and exciting match,' said the *London Daily News*, which was of no consolation in Small Heath.

What would have encouraged them was having won 11 matches, and back in the Second Division, immediate promotion was achieved once more, this time along with Manchester City. Irish inside-forward Arthur Leonard scored more than McRoberts – including four in the record-equalling 12-0 win over Doncaster Rovers.

Two solid mid-table seasons followed, gates being swollen by renewed derbies with Villa, and in 1905/06 the newly named **Birmingham** finished seventh and above their neighbours for the first time, beating them twice. A crowd of 30,000 was at the old Muntz Street ground in September to see Villa overcome for the first time in 14 First Division and FA Cup meetings between them, by 2-0. 'The Villa met their superiors in endurance, pluck and skill,' said the *Birmingham Daily Gazette* report. 'They were beaten by football of an exceptionally fine order.'

Later that season a new site was secured in Bordesley. During ten months of hard labour, a huge Spion Kop (the open side named after the hill in the Boer War battle of 1900) and an equally impressive main stand were built, and the stadium opened on a snowy Boxing Day 1906 for a goalless draw against

Middlesbrough, with 32,000 present – over three times more than for the last game at Muntz Street a few days earlier. By March the new venue was held in high-enough esteem to stage the FA Cup semi-final between The Wednesday and Woolwich Arsenal.

Crowds of 45,000 and 50,000 came to see visits from Villa but only the FA Cup would bring gatherings of that size again until after the war, as the first full season there – like Albion's at The Hawthorns – ended in another relegation. It came as a shock, having finished ninth the previous season, but scoring only 40 goals was a recipe for finishing bottom. Only later did it emerge that Romany travellers ejected from the site had placed a curse on it – which managers like Ron Saunders and Barry Fry were still trying to lift almost a century later.

McRoberts, who had left to join Chelsea's first Football League campaign in 1905, returned as Birmingham's first full-time manager five years later after an even more inglorious season saw them finish bottom of the Second Division with a couple of attendances dropping as low as 1,000. Fortunately the club's history ensured they had enough friends to help them top the re-election poll; Grimsby Town, despite finishing one place above them in the table, were replaced by newcomers Huddersfield Town.

McRoberts brought about a gradual improvement over three seasons, culminating in third place in 1912/13, four points behind runners-up Burnley. The last two seasons before the war were most notable for a home game in January 1915 against Glossop, who were destined to finish bottom in their final Football League season. They went away beaten 11-1 with five goals by inside-forward James Windridge and four from centre-forward Andrew Smith.

* * *

The first decade of the new century was a sorry one for football in Staffordshire. The six towns' pottery industry and Burton's brewing were still flourishing but in the space of 12 months the county lost Stoke, Burslem and Burton as Football League venues; all of the clubs concerned regularly having attracted some of the smallest crowds in their respective divisions. Stoke and Port Vale would regain Football League status in 1919, a Burton team much later.

Stoke suffered financial problems around 1900 and three times in the first four years of the century finished in the First Division's bottom three, avoiding relegation by margins of two points, one point and one point. It was hardly a surprise to make the drop as bottom team in 1906/07.

After joining the fashion for employing Scottish players in the 1890s, the club hoped to help finances by concentrating like Wolves on developing local talent and bringing in amateurs such as the Welsh amateur international goalkeeper Dickie Roose, a bon viveur and ladies' man who has been described as 'football's first playboy'. Full-back Sam Meredith, brother of the more famous Billy, was also recruited and played regularly in the 1901/02 season when the team finished a single point above relegated pair Small Heath and Manchester City. Without a 2-2 draw at City on the final day they would have gone down.

Beating Villa early on and then knocking them out of the FA Cup in a replay at Villa Park with an extra-time goal were among the highlights; a 7-0 defeat at Liverpool in January with half the team suffering food poisoning from a bad fish meal was the lowlight. After less than ten minutes goalkeeper Roose fled the pitch in search of a toilet and failed to return.

For two seasons the Potters were comfortable enough in mid-table, and in the second of them in 1905/06, they led the table after five games, eventually finishing tenth of the 20 clubs. Average gates were more than 8,500 for the first time and on Boxing Day 20,000 came to see eventual champions Liverpool beaten 2-1.

It was soon evident that the following season, which started with four successive defeats, two of them by Villa, would be much tougher and that another relegation struggle was likely. This one was finally lost, the team finishing five points from safety in bottom place as home crowds dropped to 3,000. Going out of the FA Cup to Second Division West Brom in a second replay suggested that the lower tier would not be easy either, although the repercussions were unimaginable.

Another poor start undermined any promotion challenge, and tenth place was as good as could be expected. Off the field, however, things had deteriorated badly. Winning three FA Cup rounds before losing at Wolves brought only a brief financial respite, leading scorer Tom Holford was sold to Manchester City and the last two home games were watched by 1,800 and 1,500 respectively.

'The Potteries public do not deserve a football club if this is the way they show their support,' said the club chairman, W.A. Cowlishaw. They did not have a club for a worrying couple of weeks after he and his fellow directors resigned from the Football League in mid-June 1908 and put it into liquidation, Horace 'Denny' Austerberry, secretary-manager since 1897, telling the League, 'League football has been decadent in the Potteries for a considerable time and the first outward and visible sign of that decay was the disappearance of Burslem Port Vale 12 months ago.'

Respected former Football League referee Alfred Barker got together a consortium to run what was effectively a new club and served as manager until 1914. He told the local *Sentinel*, 'The maintenance of first-class football in the district is worth much more than the biggest day's work I have ever done.'

What the paper called 'the greatest crisis in the club's history' was over, but the Football League would not automatically allow them back into the Second Division as they had officially resigned before changing their mind. The main re-election ballot had already taken place at the AGM in May with Bradford Park Avenue voted in to replace Lincoln City, and so a special meeting was arranged for a new vote at the end of June, in which Stoke finished well behind both Tottenham and Lincoln, the London club then winning the one vacancy on a 5-3 vote by the management committee.

Rumours (denied by Stoke) persisted that Spurs had offered them money to resign in the first place. Had the new owners been able to agree a deal before actual liquidation, the Potters would not have been involved in any voting. But the upshot was that the club were out of the Football League, which now had just four West Midlands representatives for the remaining seven seasons before ceasing operations in 1915: Villa, Birmingham, West Brom and Wolves.

Stoke went into the Birmingham and District League for the 1908/09 season, finishing eighth as the local public confounded the previous chairman's pessimism with crowds of 6,000 to 7,000 and more than double that for the FA Cup visit of eventual winners Newcastle United, who were held 1-1.

From then on they concentrated on the stronger Southern League, earning promotion to its First Division in 1910/11. A crowd of 17,000 turned up for one game there against Queens Park Rangers in December, but when some of them invaded the pitch, causing an abandonment, the FA ordered the Victoria Ground to be closed for three weeks. Despite dropping back to the second tier in 1913, Stoke won that championship under Barker's successor Peter Hodge in the 1914/15 season with 24 goals from Arthur Watkin, who also scored five in that season's 11-0 FA Cup win over Stourbridge. So after all the setbacks, the Potters were welcomed back into the Football League as replacements for ailing Glossop; though they would have to wait four years to take their place.

* * *

The 'first visible sign of decay' of Potteries football that Stoke officials identified was the reluctant resignation from the Second Division in 1907 of their neighbours **Burslem Port Vale**, a year before Stoke were forced to take the same drastic step themselves. Comfortable in mid-table around the turn of the century, Vale began sliding downwards from about 1903 with four seasons in the bottom six. More significantly, they were regularly lower than that in the table of attendances.

Ninth place in 1900/01 and 1902/03 proved to be high marks, and goalkeeper Arthur Box scoring the only goal of the game from a penalty to beat Manchester United in 1906 was one of the talking points. In 1906/07, with former England international forward Billy Beats returning after 11 years with Wolves and Bristol Rovers and still knocking in the goals, Clapton Orient, Chesterfield Town, Lincoln City and Burton United all finished below them, but the directors, having declared a loss of £200, were approaching their wits' end. An appeal in the *Sentinel* for new investment came to nothing, although the club's warning was clear enough: 'unless capital is forthcoming, there must be an end to an organisation of 28 years standing'. So it was.

'No sportsman could expect them to give of their valuable time and of their money any longer,' ran a sympathetic report in the *Sentinel*. 'The club still exists but how much longer that will be the case we cannot say.'

Fixtures for the new season had already been announced – ironically with Vale due to play relegated Stoke in their first match – when the club resigned in mid-June, regular applicants Oldham Athletic taking their place. A 3-0 home win over Blackpool on 27 April 1907, with 3,000 present, therefore turned out to be Vale's last in the Football League for a dozen seasons. It was the same year that Burton lost its league team too – for rather longer.

Most of the players joined other clubs, including Oldham and Stoke, and the distinctive name might have been lost to football forever, but they were taken over by the ambitious locals Cobridge Church, who called themselves Port Vale and were accepted into the North Staffordshire Federation of nine teams, where they were described as 'a young junior Port Vale organisation'. They began with a 6-0 win over a weakened Newchapel United, finishing in mid-table, and stepping up to the stronger North Staffordshire and District League. The second campaign there should have culminated in a championship win – but finished instead with one of the most bitter episodes in the Potteries turf war.

Going into the final match of the 1909/10 season, which was a derby at the Victoria Ground, Vale needed a draw to take the title and Stoke reserves needed a win. To the disgust of the home supporters, Vale, who had recently lost to their neighbours in the Hanley Cup Final and did not want a repeat, boosted their team with four new amateur players including future Arsenal manager Herbert Chapman and Stoke's former goalkeeper, the flamboyant Dick Roose. According to one local paper, the home crowd 'kept up a continuous hooting right through the match' and with the visitors 2-0 up in the latter stages, there was a pitch invasion; Roose was surrounded and Stoke forward Vic Horrocks was knocked down amid the confusion.

The referee felt he had no option but to abandon the game. As recriminations continued in the following days ('Disgusted' of Newcastle-under-Lyme was among those who wrote to the *Sentinel* in bitter complaint), Vale refused to replay, Stoke had their ground closed for a fortnight and the Staffordshire FA decided not to award the title to either of them. Official champions or not, Vale could claim they had more points than anyone else, and had scored 89 goals, 22 of them by centre-forward Joe Brough, who was then snapped up by First Division runners-up Liverpool.

Fourth the following season, Vale moved to the stronger Central League, which contained the reserve teams of most of the big northern clubs. They acquitted themselves well there and were in the top four for every one of the next five seasons, finding a regular scorer in Chris Young from Spurs. He rattled in seven of the goals in the club's all-time record win when they beat Burton Rangers 14-1 in the Birmingham Senior Cup in September 1914. By that time they were at a new ground, having vacated Cobridge for the Old Rec in the centre of Hanley.

* * *

Burton United suffered equally poor gates and even more lowly league positions than the Vale before dropping out of the Football League at the same time in 1907, one year before Stoke. Unlike the six towns pair they did not return.

As recounted in the previous chapter, **Burton Swifts** and **Burton Wanderers** struggled on gamely, but once the former finished bottom of the Second Division in 1900/01 having lost 22 of their 34 games, the long-delayed decision was taken to amalgamate. A 2-0 defeat at Stockport on 27 April was therefore the Swifts' last game and on 15 May the Station Hotel was the venue for the historic announcement. It enabled them to gain joint-top votes two days later in the re-election poll with Bristol City, who took the place of Walsall. A further meeting in July at the Masonic Hall decided the new club should be **Burton United** rather than County.

So the Burton turf wars were over and a peace treaty was agreed. 'It is generally considered that a new and far more prosperous time is about to begin for Association football in Burton,' read a front-page article in *Athletic News*, 'for with the amalgamation of the Swifts and the Wanderers will disappear an amount of rancorous rivalry, which of recent years has been detrimental to the game in that town. Moreover, in certain quarters support was withheld on the ground that the two clubs could not possibly exist separately in a borough of only 50,000 inhabitants. Now all is changed.' The optimism was understandable but proved misplaced within a few years.

Playing at Peel Croft, the Swifts' ground, in a variety of colours starting with the light blue and white of Wanderers and the dark blue shorts of Swifts, later taking in maroon, green and brown, the new club reached a praiseworthy tenth place initially, ahead of such names as Barnsley, Blackpool, Leicester and Newton Heath. The new committee were prepared to invest in players and beating Woolwich Arsenal in London was one of the better results; but the promising crowd of around 4,000 for a first home game against Blackpool was never bettered, and an average of 2,800 at the season's end was only 300 better than Swifts had been drawing.

From then on each season produced a slightly worse league position. In 1902/03 they were 13th, with gates up a little and some extra welcome finance earned from giving up ground advantage for an FA Cup tie against newly named Manchester United – drawing the first game 1-1 before losing the replay. Another good run in the same competition the following year carried them through five qualifying rounds before a 3-0 defeat away to Second Division rivals Burslem Port Vale and another slight drop to 14th place.

From 1904/05 the downward trajectory increased with ultimately predictable results. Watched by crowds of 16,000 for two years running away to Manchester United, losing heavily 5-0 and 6-0 showed what they were up against. Initially voted out after finishing in the bottom two but reprieved because both divisions were expanded to 20 clubs, they finished 19th the next season and then rock bottom.

There was a rare happy day at home to Wolves in early March with a 4-1 win. West Brom were beaten too in what proved to be the club's last Football League game on 27 April 1907 but remaining unbeaten in the last four matches still left them five points behind the rest and, more importantly, persuaded only seven clubs to vote for them; the rest preferred to elect latest

London applicants Fulham, who had promised to pay extra travelling costs for Midlands and northern clubs. New hope when, as noted above, Burslem Port Vale subsequently resigned was quickly quashed, the Football League management committee voting unanimously to bring in long-time applicants Oldham Athletic. (As Oldham and Fulham finished their first season third and fourth in the table with crowds well into five figures, the Brewers could hardly complain).

Finances had remained difficult, crowds hovering around 3,500 and summer wages often not being paid. A serious fire in the grandstand towards the end of the season would also mean expensive rebuilding. But Burton and its 50,000 inhabitants had been blessed with 15 years of Second Division football.

For 1907/08 United were accepted into the Birmingham League, where they started by beating Kidderminster 6-1. After a mid-table finish they managed two more seasons, finishing bottom in the second of them while conceding 121 goals and being denied re-election. The last match on 23 April 1910, like the first, was against Kidderminster, won 3-0 in front of a tiny crowd. 'Good luck to them for a game struggle under adverse circumstances that would have killed many a club,' wrote the *Staffordshire Sentinel*. That luck, like the club's financial situation, was not about to change.

Despite being provisionally accepted into the Southern League Second Division, United were in no state to fulfil their opening fixture and an announcement that they would be ready for the following campaign proved over-optimistic. Instead they merged with Burton All Saints in the Trent Valley League, surviving the First World War but not the Second (see Burton Albion, Chapter 10).

* * *

After eight previous seasons in the Football League – albeit with seven finishing positions in the bottom half of the table – this was a grim period for **Walsall** as a non-league club, struggling financially much of the time but managing at least to stay afloat until the advent of two new Third Divisions after the war offered them a passage back to the Football League. Voted out in 1901, they joined the Midland League, which was dominated by the reserve teams of East Midlands and Yorkshire clubs and provided not a single local derby. There was an ominous start in losing five of the first six games before finding some form in time for a good FA Cup run that brought crowds of over 9,000 to see Second Division Burnley beaten 1-0 and First Division Bury victorious 5-0.

Switching to the Birmingham League after two seasons made sense with less travelling and better attendances against the reserve teams of Villa, Small Heath, West Brom, Wolves and Stoke (even if it often meant some heavy defeats), plus the first teams of Crewe, Shrewsbury and Coventry. A 10-3 loss to Stoke's second string in January 1907 was the worst result, but the Saddlers were capable of putting seven goals past teams like Halesowen or Stourbridge and on one occasion even Villa's reserves, who once drew a crowd of over 8,000.

There was a welcome return to Hillary Street/Fellows Park in September 1903 after a three-year exile for the new competition, although only 1,500 came to the first game and there was no gate higher than 3,000 that season. The best final position was third in 1910/11 and 1914/15, when Arthur Campey scored five hat-tricks. Lowly league status meant always having to fight through the qualifying rounds of the FA Cup, so it was an achievement to reach the first round proper and enjoy a day out at Villa Park (6-0 defeat or not) in 1912; and to come through six qualifying rounds in 1914/15 including a win over Stoke before losing 2-1 to Shrewsbury.

* * *

Coventry City, as they had been known since 1898, were also to be found in the Birmingham League, mainly in the mid-to lower reaches of it until achieving fourth place with 97 goals plus the FA Cup first round proper in 1907/08 to earn a place in the Southern League.

The immediate years beforehand were largely a struggle in the new Highfield Road ground, the worst result being a 14-1 loss to Aston Villa's reserves in December 1900. Also losing 10-0, 8-0, 7-1 and 6-2 that season to the reserve teams of Small Heath,

Wolves, West Brom and Stoke respectively underlined their inferiority to the area's biggest clubs.

Yet by the second half of the decade, City were on a par with those second strings, improvement coinciding with new blood on the board and the pitch. The excellent 1907/08 campaign was notable for the fact that of the above quintet's reserves, only Birmingham were able to win at Highfield Road, where the defeat of Villa was watched by a 4,000 crowd; and on the last day of the season West Brom were humiliated 11-2. The inside-forward trio of Albert Lewis, Willie Smith and 'Tubby' Warren scored 74 of the 97 league goals and another 20 in the club's best FA Cup run yet.

City came through six qualifying rounds to meet Crystal Palace, losing 4-2 at home in front of almost 10,000 spectators. Palace were then the first opposition when the club moved up to join them in the Southern League for a 1-1 draw on 1 September 1908. With few new players signed, it was a tough season in which they started slowly and finished bottom but one, but still managed 15 wins in 40 games.

One of City's stars the following season with ten goals from inside-left was Elias 'Patsy' Hendren, who stayed only two years and later became one of England's best-known cricketers, scoring seven Test match centuries.

Remaining in the league's First Division also meant more chances in the FA Cup proper, meeting some glamorous northern opposition like Preston, The Wednesday (both of whom they beat away from home), Everton (in the 1910 quarter-final), Burnley and Manchester United; visits from United in successive seasons brought gates of 17,251 and in January 1913 a record 20,042.

Relegation in 1914, however, was a bad blow. The Southern League Second Division was a grim place for English clubs, comprising ten Welsh teams plus Stoke, Stalybridge, Brentford – and Coventry. High expenses and low gates meant City might have wished the authorities had bowed to much of public opinion and ceased playing once war began. As it was, they were immensely grateful to David Cooke, a board member since 1909 who undertook to pay off most of the increasing debts.

* * *

Shrewsbury Town continued to struggle in the Birmingham League, finally breaking into the top ten at the eighth attempt in 1902/03 when finishing a commendable sixth. A bad season in 1906/07, conceding 106 goals in the 34 games, was quickly improved with fifth and sixth-place finishes, and the club featured briefly in the FA Cup again, albeit suffering clear defeats by more established clubs like Portsmouth and Nottingham Forest.

Leading scorer Billy Scarratt proved the most versatile of men, appearing in all positions including goalkeeper, in which role he conceded only one goal in three of the FA Cup games.

In 1910 came an important step with the move from the Copthorne Barracks ground to a picturesque site on the banks of the River Severn at Gay Meadow, a name believed to derive in more innocent times from sporting and leisure pursuits there. A crowd estimated at 3,000 watched the opening game on 10 September against Wolves' reserves, lost 2-1. 'Saturday's gate was fairly satisfactory but the club needs all possible support in consequence of the heavy expenditure their new venture has entailed,' wrote the *Shrewsbury Chronicle.*

Three years later came Town's best season yet, scoring a record 76 goals and finishing as runners-up only a point behind Worcester City.

* * *

The decision to go ahead with the 1914/15 football season once the United Kingdom entered the war early in August was widely criticised. War on Germany was officially declared on 4 August 1914 but two days later a Football League meeting decided to carry on with the scheduled fixtures. A month later the FA backed them but asked clubs to make grounds available for drill practice, to hold recruiting rallies at half-time, and it appealed to players and fans to join the armed forces. The Rugby Football League also pressed ahead with its new season, but cricket's County Championship stopped a week earlier than the scheduled finish of 9 September, cancelling the five remaining matches; high-level hockey and rugby union also stopped.

There was, therefore, a clear divide between the mainly amateur sports and the professional ones, with most newspapers taking the side of the former. 'This is no time for football,' the (London) *Evening News* thundered early on. *Athletic News* was one of few publications to stand up for the national sport's stance, proclaiming, 'The whole agitation is nothing less than an attempt ... to stop the recreation on one day in the week of the masses. What do they care for the poor man's sport? The poor are giving their lives for this country in thousands.'

So, on went football, the league's two divisions finally wrapping up a few days after the 'Khaki Cup Final' of 24 April 1915, in which most of the crowd were soldiers in uniform. 'Play with one another for England now,' Lord Derby urged the players of Chelsea and Sheffield United after presenting their medals.

Two years earlier, 120,000 had watched Villa win the FA Cup against Sunderland. Now, fewer than 50,000 saw the Sheffield side's victory, which reflected the overall fall in attendances. Every one of the 40 Football League clubs suffered a decrease on the previous season, by an average of more than 40 per cent. Villa dropped from 25,000 to under 14,000; Albion from 20,000 to 11,000; Birmingham from 17,500 to 12,000; and Wolves from 10,500 to 7,500. Manchester City were the only team to average more than 20,000 (just), which 15 clubs had done the previous year.

War arrived just as Fred Rinder was unveiling great plans for Villa Park, which he intended to have a capacity of 120,000 to 130,000 spectators, easily the highest in the land. Instead, all that was done was to extend the Witton Lane stand and remove the cycle track, creating a better experience for the smaller crowds who came throughout that disappointing season as the team dropped to 14th – the lowest position for 14 years.

For the 1915/16 season four regional leagues were organised on a geographical basis, but there was little enthusiasm for competitive football in the West Midlands. The so-called Midlands section, won by Nottingham Forest, was effectively for East Midlands and Yorkshire clubs, while Stoke played in the Lancashire League, finishing midway; for a later and smaller subsidiary tournament they moved into the Midlands section and were again in mid-table.

In the following wartime seasons much the same arrangements applied, although Birmingham now entered the Midlands competition, initially finishing third of the 16 teams and pulling in surprisingly good five-figure crowds, which peaked at 18,000 for the visit of Leeds in February 1917. Stoke again competed in the Lancashire section and were also third of 16.

For the next two years Birmingham again did well, ending up third and second in the main competition, and winning the subsidiary competition of six matches in the final season. Leeds were again popular visitors, drawing 26,000 in November 1917. Stoke won the Lancashire section that season and then lost a championship play-off against the Midlands winners Leeds City 2-1 on aggregate.

Coventry and Port Vale also competed in 1918/19 but Villa, Albion and Wolves largely remained aloof, doing little more than play occasional charity matches against each other while some of their players guested for other clubs. Guesting was commonplace, so much so that in that final season Birmingham's Frank Osborne played four consecutive games at St Andrew's in the opposition's colours.

As the Birmingham League did not operate, Walsall also showed little interest in playing apart from a couple of years in the more parochial Walsall and District League.

Much more seriously, many former professionals did not come back from the war. It was estimated that about 2,000 players had eventually joined the armed forces, many of them in the Footballers' Battalion, the 17th Middlesex regiment, in which future Wolves manager Frank Buckley was second in command; they suffered heavy casualties.

Villa lost two men in action, the young half-back Arthur Dobson and Tommy Barber, who had scored the goal that won the FA Cup in 1913. West Brom's gifted amateur international centre-forward Harold Bache died in action at Ypres in 1916, the same year that Dick Roose, the flamboyant former Stoke goalkeeper mentioned earlier in this chapter, who also played for Everton, Sunderland, Huddersfield, Villa and Arsenal, was killed at the Somme. Jack Shelton, an FA Cup winner with Wolves in 1908 before joining Port Vale, died while serving with the North Staffordshire Regiment.

Once these sort of losses to football became known and by the time the Armistice was declared on 11 November 1918, public and press opinion had been modified. Whereas, for instance, a letter to *The Times* had stated in November 1914, 'We view with indignation and alarm the persistence of Association Football Clubs in doing their best for the enemy,' an article in the same paper as the first post-war Football League season got under way in September 1919 praised football for doing 'more than anything else to revive tired limbs and weary minds' among the troops.

4

Up for the Cup 1920–1939

'It is a long time since we have had a team which has shown such consistently brilliant form as the men from West Bromwich. They have been the outstanding team of the year of reconstruction, and provide a fine object lesson of the value of fostering local talent.'

Birmingham Gazette, April 1920

'The Commission is satisfied that an arrangement was made that the match played at Bury in 1920 should be won by the Coventry club.'

Daily Herald, May 1923

'The rally of Birmingham stands out as one of the most remarkable in football history.'

Athletic News, October 1925

'Bitter feelings have been aroused in the Potteries by the proposal to amalgamate Stoke City and Port Vale.'

Athletic News, April 1926

'Great defence holds up Arsenal: How Walsall earned fame'

Birmingham Gazette, January 1933

'Major Buckley has been accused of all manner of sinister tricks with his players in order to achieve success, and there have been suggestions that the Football Association should do something about it.'

Sports Argus, April1939

BEGINNING THE post-war years with an FA Cup triumph, **Aston Villa** were almost never out of the top half of the table and often much higher until a sudden decline and the humiliation of relegation for the first time in 1936 – almost symbolically alongside Blackburn Rovers, once their fellow giants.

Even the glory of that FA Cup success had to be shared with West Bromwich Albion, who stormed to the first Football League championship in their history a fortnight earlier. But it was also a season in which two famous names arrived at Villa Park.

The first of them was badly needed. Under the new system of playing the same opponents in successive games, which lasted for several years, Villa had won only one of their first ten matches before recruiting centre-half Frank Barson, a tough Yorkshireman signed from Barnsley, whose unyielding nature not only led to a number of suspensions but meant he only stayed in the Midlands for three seasons.

From the day of his debut at the end of October 1919 the team rose from the depths of the table by winning nine of the next ten, the only defeat being by 4-2 at home to Albion, a week after winning 2-1 away to them; more than 101,000 watched the two games, illustrating how attendances were shooting up again, just as they would immediately after the Second World War. Villa finished with a home average of over 33,000 despite climbing no higher than ninth place.

The other important – and longer-lasting – debutant was centre-forward Billy Walker, a Wednesbury man held back until he was 22 years old but a permanent fixture for the next 13 years, in which time he ran up a club record of 244 goals.

The first two of them arrived in his opening game, a 1920 FA Cup tie at home to Queens Park Rangers that began a run all the way to the final. Walker and leading scorer Clem Stephenson (29 that season) were on target to knock out Manchester United in the next round, Stephenson got the only goal at home to Sunderland and an own goal eliminated unlucky Spurs at Villa Park. In the semi-final Walker put two past high-flyers Chelsea in a 3-1 win, which spared the FA a huge embarrassment: the final was already scheduled for Stamford Bridge, but instead of a home game for the Pensioners, it became Midlands against Yorkshire in the form of Huddersfield Town, Second Division promotion winners after being on the verge of amalgamating with the new Leeds United club.

Town, having knocked out Liverpool and Newcastle, proved obdurate opponents and with Stephenson and Walker for once subdued the final went to extra time. One hundred minutes had been played when inside-right Billy Kirton got the decisive touch to a corner off a defender's face for the only goal, the King's son Prince Henry handing over the trophy to Villa captain Andy Ducat, the Surrey cricketer and double international.

'We can never look back on this, a great final, without vividly recalling the credit due to Huddersfield for having played a fine, sporting game,' Ducat told the newspapers. 'Our Cup! But what a struggle to get it' was the *Birmingham Gazette* headline, while reflecting the general view that 'a shade of superiority all round entitled them to the verdict'.

1920 FA Cup Final: Aston Villa 1 Huddersfield Town 0
Aston Villa: Hardy, Smart, Weston, Ducat, Barson, Moss, Wallace, Kirton, Walker, Stephenson, Dorrell.
Huddersfield Town: Mutch, Wood, Bullock, Slade, Wilson, Watson, Richardson, Mann, Taylor, Swann, Islip.

With this sixth FA Cup success, Villa overtook Blackburn, causing the FA president John McKenna to call them 'the gramophone club – always setting new records'. The needle, however, was about to get stuck.

Neither McKenna nor anyone else could have known it would be 1957 before another major trophy.

Walker, good for 20 goals a season, continued to be prolific, which was just as well, for Stephenson joined Huddersfield who then won three successive league titles. Pre-war star Harry Hampton left to help Birmingham win promotion from the Second Division, and at the end of the 1921/22 season stubborn defensive kingpin Barson refused to move house from Yorkshire and after being suspended by the club he was sold to Manchester United.

League positions were still respectable for a while as top Midlands club in tenth, fifth, sixth and sixth places, and in 1924 there was another FA Cup Final.

The early rounds were routine until an exciting quarter-final win away to Albion, new leading scorer Len Capewell from Wellington Town making his mark again.

In the semi-final lowly Burnley were beaten 3-0 but five days before the final came an unreliable rehearsal when Newcastle visited Villa Park for a First Division game, rested ten players – which cost them a hefty £750 FA fine – and were beaten 6-1. A more solid reason to make Villa favourites was that despite having lost 4-1 at St James' Park on New Year's Day they sat above the Geordies in the league.

Wembley's second FA Cup Final was made all-ticket to avoid the chaos of the first one a year earlier and almost 92,000 saw Villa dominate the first half on a wet pitch but fall away. They were struggling by the last five minutes, when Newcastle scored twice in 90 seconds. The *Gazette* was critical this time, 'One was driven to the conclusion that Villa lost the game owing to the adoption of wrong tactics,' in particular their short-passing game.

Dropping as low as 15th in 1924/25, and going out of the FA Cup in a replay at home to Albion, Villa recovered to a familiar sixth place the following season. It was the one all forwards loved, when the new offside law was introduced requiring only one defender as well as the goalkeeper to be behind the attacker instead of two. A dramatic indication of the effect came at Villa Park on the opening day: Burnley were demolished 10-0 with five by Capewell, who finished the season with 32 of Villa's 86 in the league. Nationwide, goalscoring overall increased by almost 50 per cent.

It was at that point that George Ramsay, one of the club's founding fathers, celebrated 50 years' service and retired as secretary-manager, having overseen six First Division titles and six FA Cup wins.

In 1928/29 as the goal glut continued, Villa scored 98 in finishing third, 25 of them coming from the new sensation Tom 'Pongo' Waring. As the goalscoring successor to Dixie Dean at Tranmere Rovers, Waring was expected to move on to Liverpool, but Rovers did not fancy losing more supporters to another Merseyside club as they had with Dean's transfer to Everton. That favoured Villa, who in February 1928 were able to acquire him for £4,700, though he quickly came to curse a defence that in his second game lost 7-5 at Newcastle after he scored twice.

For several seasons they would regularly concede close to 80 goals, including the extraordinary 1930/31 campaign. Villa scored no fewer than 128 in 42 league games but let in 78, which was 19 more than champions Arsenal, who consequently beat them to the title by seven points. Waring was unstoppable, starting with all four goals in the 4-3 win away to Manchester United and finishing with a club-record 49 in 39 league games, plus a 50th in the FA Cup defeat at home to Arsenal. Left-winger and future manager Eric Houghton backed him up with 30 and went on to reach double figures every season through the whole decade.

Games against the Gunners were epic occasions around that time. Three FA Cup meetings attracted crowds of more than 70,000 at Villa Park, while the First Division matches tended to be full of goals. In 1932/33, for instance, Villa won 5-3 at home but were beaten 5-0 at Highbury in April, a result that meant they lost out again in the title run-in to Herbert Chapman's team.

Runners-up twice in three seasons, the club continued to be proud FA Cup fighters only to have their hopes dashed in three semi-finals. In 1929 they beat Arsenal 1-0 with a Waring goal but lost in the last four to a penalty by lowly Portsmouth.

Five years later, with Waring having been injured in January, Welsh international Dai Astley took over, scoring in five successive rounds including four in the 7-2 fourth-round win over Sunderland. But his strike in the semi against Manchester City was a mere consolation in the catastrophic 6-1 defeat on a heavy Huddersfield pitch.

The other run to the last four was in 1937/38. City were beaten 3-2 in the quarter-final, watched by another new record crowd of 75,540, but at the familiar neutral venue of Bramall Lane, Preston won 2-1 with a goal Villa felt was offside.

By that time the Villans were on their way to winning the Second Division championship, as two seasons earlier the almost unthinkable had happened. Warning signs were apparent in a sharp decline from being First Division runners-up in 1933. While Arsenal went on to a hat-trick of titles, establishing themselves as the dominant force in English football, Villa slipped to 13th for two successive years.

Waring missed most of the second half of each season and in the calamitous 1935/36 campaign he played only the first ten games before requesting a transfer and leaving for Barnsley with a record of 167 goals in 226 games. He remains one of the Villa greats, as well as being a character of whom Billy Walker, who retired in 1933 with 244 goals to begin his long managerial career, wrote, 'Nobody on the staff could do anything with him, although I think I can claim, as the captain in his days, to be the only person able to handle him.'

Even in the relegation season Villa scored 81 goals (20 more than runners-up Derby) thanks to Astley (21) and Houghton (15), but the defence had a dreadful time, conceding a record 110. Three times before Christmas they let in seven at home, against Middlesbrough, West Brom and, most famously, Arsenal. That was the day, 14 December 1935, of 'Drake's Seven'. England centre-forward Ted Drake had eight attempts on the Villa goal, hitting the woodwork with one and the back of the net with all the others.

'Villa's armada sunk – by Drake. Seven "broadsides" and only one Gunner' headlined the *Daily Herald*, whose correspondent George Forrest wrote, 'The like of the sheer smashing certainty of his shooting I have never seen.'

A spending spree of £35,500 on seven players in three months from November brought a slight improvement including away wins against the top two, Sunderland and Derby, but the awful first part of the season was too much of a handicap. Blackburn accompanied them down in bottom place despite deservedly winning the last game 4-2 at Villa Park.

Once again the club's predicament was highlighted in a *Gazette* editorial, this time underneath a more serious one about Germany's increasing political demands. 'To get back to the First Division is going to be a hard job and it may not be accomplished in one season,' the paper correctly predicted. 'Money alone cannot do the trick, any more than money alone could avert the disaster which culminated last Saturday. Whoever or whatever was responsible, it has been all too clear that the lack of teamwork caused the trouble.'

Manager James McMullan was succeeded by Lancastrian Jimmy Hogan, a prophet without much honour in his own country, whose new training methods and emphasis on ball play eventually paid off. Down in the Second Division, Coventry provided the only local derbies, drawing a crowd of 63,686 for the first one (drawn 0-0) and 40,000 for the Highfield Road return (a 1-0 home win). Inconsistent Villa finished one place below them in ninth place but the following season won the title from Manchester United. Frank Broome led the scorers with 28, and in a welcome change the defence conceded a mere 35, the sort of total unheard of at that time in the top two divisions. Crowds reached a new record average of just under 42,000, helped by 68,029 for the 1-1 draw with Coventry; for two years running Second Division Villa had the country's second-highest attendances.

The players were rewarded with a tour to Germany where – unlike the England team that summer – they refused to give the Nazi salute. Hitler's shadow was already hanging over Europe and there would be only one more full season of Football League games, in which Villa consolidated in 12th place in the First Division and recorded the highest average crowd anywhere. Back where they belonged, the club's prestige remained as high as their level of support.

* * *

For **West Bromwich Albion** the inter-war years began in the best possible manner with a first Football League championship, but also included relegation twice to the Second Division, where in 1931 they set a record by winning the FA Cup and promotion in the same season.

The historic 1919/20 campaign began with nine wins in 11 games and continued in much the same vein, allowing for an occasional touch of inconsistency. After beating Notts County and their renowned goalkeeper Albert Iremonger 8-0 in October with five goals from inside-left Fred Morris, losing the return game 2-0 the following week was hardly expected; then an unwelcome home defeat by Villa was righted with a 4-2 win at Villa Park five days later – as mentioned in the section above, both games drew huge derby crowds.

Half a dozen straight wins going into the new year had the Throstles a point clear at the top of the table and two wins out of three at Easter put them within touching distance of that first title. Beating Arsenal in front of almost 40,000 set it up and confirmation came in the next game, a 3-1 win at home to Bradford while two of the club's very best players, Morris and left-back Jesse Pennington, were helping England beat Scotland 5-4 in Sheffield.

They were back for victory over Chelsea in the final game when the trophy was handed over. 'Fred Morris, a Tipton lad and one of the cleverest inside-forwards Albion ever had, set up a new League record by scoring 37 goals,' said the club's golden jubilee booklet of 1950. A fortnight later the Charity Shield, played for in those days against the Southern League champions, was added to the trophy cabinet with a 2-0 win over Tottenham at White Hart Lane.

'It is a long time since we have had a team which has shown such consistently brilliant form as the men from West Bromwich,' wrote 'Look-Out' in the *Gazette*. 'They have been the outstanding team of the year of reconstruction, and provide a fine object lesson of the value of fostering local talent, rather than attempting to build up a ready-made 11 at big transfer fees.'

Three of the next four seasons brought disappointing finishes in the lower half of the table, although some vast crowds were recorded for big games. In 1921 Birmingham were promoted back to the top division after 13 years and their Boxing Day visit to The Hawthorns the following season drew almost 50,000 to see Welsh international Stan Davies score the only goal for the home side. Fourteen months later, during a more successful league campaign (seventh place, a point below Villa), an FA Cup win over championship challengers Sunderland was watched by 56,474, and when Villa arrived in the same competition for a second successive season in February 1925 with Albion themselves in contention for the league title the gate was another new record of 64,612. They saw a 1-1 draw before the Throstles went to Villa Park four days later and won the replay 2-1.

Perhaps the fans had had enough of each other at that point; for the third meeting in a week, only 22,123 were at the important First Division game at The Hawthorns in which victory was Albion's tenth in 12 games, boosting hopes of a second title in five years. They held Chapman's Huddersfield, the leaders and reigning champions, in the next game but dropped too many points over the remaining two months and finished runners-up, two points behind but having won more matches than any other team. Centre-forward George James had his one outstanding season with 25 goals.

A year later came yet another tie at home to Villa, who won it 2-1 in front of over 52,000. And in 1926/27 both Villa and Birmingham were able to look down in glee as their neighbours dropped down to the Second Division after 16 years.

It was the second season of the new offside law favouring attackers but, despite neither scoring the least nor conceding the most goals Albion finished rock bottom, four points from safety. Beating Villa 6-2 in March failed to inspire the late run they needed, the seeds of failure having been sown in a terrible autumn run of 13 defeats in 16 games.

The catalyst for success down below was Jimmy Cookson, a Mancunian centre-forward signed from Chesterfield amid stiff opposition, who averaged close to a goal every game throughout a dozen years of his senior career. In his sixth match for Albion, at home to Blackpool in September 1927, he recorded a double hat-trick in a 6-3 victory and finished the season as the Second Division's top scorer with 38.

In four seasons the team were never lower than eighth and in 1930/31 they emulated the Wolves team of 1908 by winning the FA Cup as a Second Division side – in Albion's case in a local derby final and while achieving promotion too. Finishing the previous season with seven straight wins and a club-record 109 goals (33 more from Cookson) offered reason for optimism, which was sustained even after he was injured in November. Fortunately a new hero immediately stepped up to the plate: 21-year-old 21-year-old W.G. 'Billy' Richardson, a bus inspector signed from Hartlepools.

He would take the headlines at Wembley in the culmination of an FA Cup run that began with three matches against Charlton Athletic, the third being decided at Villa Park. Tottenham were knocked out in the fourth round, Portsmouth in the fifth and the quarter-final brought a much-anticipated derby with Wolves, also having a good season in the Second Division. A 1-1 draw at The Hawthorns was watched by over 52,000 and only 5,000 fewer saw the midweek replay, in which Richardson's goal earned a 2-1 win and a semi-final against Everton, the Second Division leaders and eventual champions. At Old Trafford, right-winger and captain Tommy Glidden scored the only goal on the same day as Birmingham beat Sunderland to set up a West Midlands derby final.

Albion had beaten only one First Division team, Portsmouth, on the way but Birmingham were struggling near the bottom of that league so a close contest was expected. So it proved on a cold, wet day. Blues will always claim they were robbed early on when Bob Gregg put the ball past Harold Pearson but was ruled offside. Richardson gave Albion the lead after 25 minutes, and after Joe Bradford equalised, Blues lost concentration and straight from the kick-off Richardson added his second from close range.

'It had been a great game, and the Albion's victory was well-deserved,' observed the *Staffordshire Sentinel.* 'West Bromwich played the game that paid, the long swinging open game with lightning raids which at times had the opposing defence paralysed. The Albion were a great team – one of the best seen at Wembley.' Skipper Glidden told reporters, 'I thought our success was due to the quickness with which we turned defence into attack.'

1931 FA Cup Final: West Bromwich Albion 2 Birmingham 1
West Bromwich Albion: Pearson, Shaw, Trentham, Magee, B. Richardson, Edwards, Glidden, Carter, 'W.G.' Richardson, Sandford, Wood.
Birmingham: Hibbs, Liddell, Barkas, Cringan, Morrall, Leslie, Briggs, Crosbie, Bradford, Gregg, Curtis.

A week later another Hawthorns crowd of 52,000-plus saw not only the FA Cup paraded but a hard-fought 3-2 win over Charlton, Richardson's winning header sealing promotion with Everton.

Four good seasons back in the First Division followed, culminating in another FA Cup Final. Richardson was still going strong, becoming one of the club's greatest goalscorers with successive league totals in the top division of 27, 30, 26 and 25 earning him his solitary England cap. In November 1931 he hit four in five minutes at West Ham; in September 1933 banged in a six-minute hat-trick against Derby; and in the 1935 FA Cup run scored eight, including a hat-trick in the 7-1 demolition of Sheffield United.

The other Steel City club now stood in the way. Five days before the final, Wednesday drew 1-1 at The Hawthorns, confirming their position a few places higher in the table than Albion, and at Wembley they were too good, winning an entertaining game 4-2. Twice Albion fought back to equalise, through left-wing pair Wally Boyes and Ted Sandford, but Wednesday's winger Ellis Rimmer scored twice in the last five minutes.

In a high-scoring era there were two notable seven-goal away wins. Richardson claimed another hat-trick in the 7-2 success at Manchester City in January 1934 (with the great Frank Swift in goal) and, even more enjoyably, hit four in a remarkable 7-0 win at Villa Park in October 1935 – the record victory margin between the clubs. That came during his best seasonal return, the club-record 39 in 41 games. He also scored, to less effect, in Albion's heaviest defeat, a 10-3 loss at Stoke in February 1937 when goalkeeper Billy Light was handicapped by a heavily bandaged ankle.

Fred Everiss, secretary-manager since 1902, was still in charge but in 1938 found himself presiding over another relegation campaign. In the bottom seven for the two previous seasons, the Throstles could not be saved this time even by Richardson, who was let down once again by the team's defending. His 15 goals came from a total of 74, which was more than the runners-up Wolves, but conceding 91 was by far the worst in the country. A 2-1 defeat at Molineux was one of three losses in the last three games, all away from home, and although only three points separated the bottom nine clubs, West Brom were lowest placed of all. They went down with a Manchester City team who in typically bizarre City fashion were the defending champions and highest goalscorers, having beaten Albion 7-1 three weeks earlier.

* * *

A lowly Second Division side, **Wolves** had to endure a season in the Third Division North during the 1920s before finishing the inter-war years as one of the country's leading clubs again under the controversial 'Major' Frank Buckley.

Unlike Arsenal, who finished two points below them in the final pre-war season, they were unable to talk their way into the First Division and endured a grim first campaign, ending in the bottom four despite eight of the pre-war team being able to resume under long-serving manager Jack Addenbrooke.

After the crowd invaded the pitch and threatened the referee during a home defeat by Bury in October, the ground was closed and two home games had to be played at The Hawthorns. Neither was won, and then in one of those Christmas matches when strange results can occur, Wolves, who had once inflicted Hull's record defeat by 8-0, lost there 10-3.

On Easter Monday there was a record crowd of over 30,000 to see a defeat by Tottenham, the champions-elect, whose next game against Wolves was a famous one for both clubs, in the 1921 FA Cup Final. As in 1908 it was a shock that a moderate Second Division side should progress so far, this time overcoming two renowned clubs from the higher division. A good rivalry had been established by now with Stoke and when the teams were drawn together in the first round of the competition, some 35,000 turned up at Molineux to see Wolves come through 3-2. Even more were present for the second round replay against Derby, who were struggling in the First Division and went away beaten by the only goal, from Welsh international Dick Richards. A single goal by Arthur Potts was good enough to win at Fulham and the public sat up when Everton, top six in the First Division, were beaten at Goodison in front of 55,000 by the same 1-0 scoreline, this goal from leading scorer George Edmonds.

From Goodison it was across Stanley Park to Anfield for the semi-final, the luck of the draw handing Wolves a tie with the other remaining Second Division side, promotion-chasing Cardiff City. A goalless draw resulted but in the replay at Old Trafford, Edmonds scored again in a 3-1 triumph.

The day of the final brought constant rain for a Stamford Bridge crowd of 72,805 but a sodden, muddy pitch did not prove the leveller that the underdogs would have hoped for. They held on until eight minutes into the second half, when Jimmy Dimmock, one of Tottenham's four England internationals, was allowed to score what proved to be the only goal. Reports on the day blamed right-back Maurice Woodward but he later claimed that it was captain Val Gregory who handed possession back to the Spurs man.

The Midlands press complained that as several hundred supporters waited at Wolverhampton station to console their team, players returned either in 'dribs and drabs' or not at all, which was 'a great mistake of policy'.

Fifteenth that season, Wolves dropped two places the following year, and in 1922/23 suffered the shame of relegation to the third tier. The club had been affected by a tragedy early in the season when manager Jack Addenbrooke, off sick since the summer, passed away aged 57. He had been in charge for 37 years, more than twice as long as any future manager. George Jobey replaced him but oversaw a disastrous campaign summed up in a 7-1 Christmas Day defeat by Coventry. The defence, which had conceded only 49 goals the previous season, was now hit for 77.

Molineux's first 40,000 crowd saw the 2-0 FA Cup defeat by Liverpool but barely one tenth of them turned up for the final two home games once the team's fate was sealed.

In the Third Division North, support began to return to see some new places and new faces. For the opening game at Chesterfield, goalkeeper Noel George was the only survivor from the FA Cup Final just two years earlier. A fine replacement for Edmonds, Tom Phillipson from Swindon Town made his debut in the Christmas Day defeat of Durham City during an unbeaten run stretching from early November until 7 April. He averaged a goal every two games, as did inside-left Harry Lees from Ebbw Vale as Wolves just kept their noses in front of Rochdale to claim the only promotion place by a point. Another big crowd saw an FA Cup replay defeat by West Brom.

Jobey stepped down and Albert Hoskins took over during a successful period of rehabilitation in the Second Division. Reacquaintance with Stoke and Coventry brought four wins, and Wolves finished sixth, then fourth, Phillipson grabbing 16 and 36, and then 31 in 32 games during 1926/27; from November to February that season he scored in 13 successive league games, including five on Christmas Day at home to Bradford City. He was also on target in the narrow FA Cup defeat by Arsenal in January 1926, many of the 42,000 crowd watching from the new Waterloo Road stand.

The summer of 1927 brought the arrival of one of the great figures in Wolves history, Frank Buckley. A former Birmingham and Derby centre-half who became a major in the First World War and was badly injured at the Somme, he managed Norwich City afterwards and then Blackpool before moving to Molineux, where an emphasis on discipline was quickly outlined to his new playing staff. Later he would invite controversy by the use of testosterone injections and over-watering the pitch to handicap ball-playing visiting teams and help Wolves' direct style.

The first two seasons were unspectacular and not until the third in 1929/30 did Wanderers rise to even the top half. Phillipson (later a Wolverhampton town councillor and mayor) was allowed to move to First Division Sheffield United for a welcome £4,000 in the spring of 1928 and it would be another three years before his team-mates made the same step up. Fortunately the board saw what an inventive manager they had.

They owed much to the goals of Billy Hartill, one of the few local lads in a team now with a strong Yorkshire influence after Buckley's regular sorties into the transfer market. In 1929/30 Hartill hit 33 goals, including all five in the home win over Notts County. The defence was less reliable, conceding six at Oldham shortly afterwards and seven to West Brom in the Christmas derby.

In 1930/31, finishing fourth with another 24 from Hartill was marred somewhat by Albion winning promotion after beating Wolves twice and again in an FA Cup quarter-final replay.

But the following season it would at last be Wolverhampton's turn. From a 4-0 thumping of Spurs on the opening day they ran in a record 115 goals, 30 of them to Hartill. Heady victories in December alone included 6-0 v Bury, then 7-1 away to Port Vale and 7-0 against Manchester United on Boxing Day. Leeds and Stoke were the main promotion rivals but by beating Vale 2-0 in April Wolves assured themselves of going up as champions.

Back in the top division in 1932 for the first time in 26 years, Buckley's boys endured a season of two halves and just escaped going straight down again; the first half left them bottom after a run of ten defeats in 11 games and hammerings like Arsenal's 7-1 success at Molineux – three years before the Londoners achieved the same result at Villa Park with Drake's seven goals. At Christmas the two games with eventual runners-up Villa were both won by the away side and were each watched by over 50,000.

Hartill was still scoring, getting four in the 6-4 February win over Huddersfield and ending up with 33 as his team won five of their last eight, including the crucial final game at home to new FA Cup winners Everton to secure 20th place, two points clear of relegated Bolton and Blackpool. Average gates of 27,000 were the fifth best in the country.

For three more seasons, all in the bottom eight, progress was slow, making the restoration of Wolves as one of the country's top clubs all the more welcome. There was a notable debut on 18 November 1933 when shy young Welshman Bryn Jones played in a 2-1 win at Everton, and was immediately commended in the press as 'a promising recruit'. He had ten goals by the end of the season and kept a good supply going to Hartill; both men scored in the exciting 4-3 Boxing Day win over Villa, a day after losing 6-2 there. Hartill totalled only 13 that season but 27 the next, which included all five on the September day when the Villans were beaten 5-2.

Hartill went to Everton in the summer of 1935 with 15 hat-tricks in a record 170 goals in 234 games, a total that would not be beaten until the days of John Richards. Apart from an 8-1 win over bottom club Blackburn, he was missed, and Buckley set about revamping the squad, bringing in most notably a converted centre-half called Stanley Cullis.

Brought up in Ellesmere Port, where his father had moved with many other workers from the Wolverhampton Corrugated Iron Company, Cullis was picked out as a born leader early on, captaining the reserves at 17 and given three first-team games a year later – one of which was an unfortunate 5-2 defeat by Albion. From March 1936 he would keep the number five shirt until the war and beyond.

The home crowd were initially not impressed by the comings and – especially – the goings. At the Chelsea game in November that year some of what was now regarded as a small crowd of under 17,000 came on to the pitch to make their displeasure known. The team were third from bottom yet the next home match was won 6-1 against Charlton; Gordon Clayton, moved to centre-forward, started banging in goals and by the season's end Wolves were in the top five. In the FA Cup Middlesbrough and Grimsby were also hit for six and the run only ended after three quarter-final meetings with Sunderland, watched by a total of 168,000 spectators.

For all that improvement it was stunning to finish runners-up to champions Arsenal and Everton in the next two years, not least because, in between the two, Arsenal took Bryn Jones away for a world-record transfer fee. In 1937/38, with Jones still at Molineux and scoring a personal record 15 goals, Wolves lost the title by only a point when they could have been champions for the first time in history. A win at Roker Park on the final day would have done it but Sunderland squeezed home by the only goal and Arsenal crushed Bolton 5-0 to become champions.

There was a new goalscorer in Merseysider Dennis Westcott, signed from New Brighton, who knocked in 19 and then the following season 32, backed up by 26 from Dickie Dorsett, the replacement for Jones. The Welshman had gone to Arsenal for what many decried as the ludicrously high fee of £14,000 as Spurs pushed up the bidding. Yet he never settled and as his new team finished no higher than fifth in the final pre-war season it was Wolves who were second again and FA Cup runners-up too.

Everton, with Tommy Lawton starring, rose from 14th the previous season to take the title by four points despite being furious at a 7-0 Molineux defeat in the February mud; Dorsett scored four after Buckley had the pitch flooded even more than usual. A crowd of 51,000 saw Villa beaten at Easter but the draw with them next day was one of three in the last five games that cost Wolves on either side of the FA Cup Final.

The title was slipping away by the time of the final but it seemed to hold every chance of sweet consolation against lowly Portsmouth, who they had beaten 3-0 in the league. On the way to Wembley there were four home wins (another new record crowd of 61,315 saw Liverpool beaten in round five), then a thumping semi-final success by 5-0 against Grimsby, Westcott scoring four of his 43 that season with a 16-year-old Jimmy Mullen on the wing.

In the final, however, everything went wrong as Pompey scored three goals in the last 15 minutes of the first half, the first of them by Bert Barlow, who Buckley had sold to them earlier in the season. Dorsett got one back but Wolves conceded again before the end to be left with a frustrating double as runners-up in the country's two principal competitions. 'So much had been expected of them: they achieved so little,' wrote the *Sunday Times* reporter at the final.

Any greater success would have been even more controversial, for one of the back stories to the final was that Wolves, like Portsmouth, treated their players with injections of monkey glands – effectively testosterone – believed to improve their strength and stamina. 'Major Buckley has been accused of all manner of sinister tricks with his players in order to achieve success, and there have been suggestions that the Football Association should do something about it,' the *Sports Argus* wrote.

Intrigued by the work of a Russian scientist, Buckley tried the treatment himself and was so impressed that he asked his players to submit to it. A couple refused, which did not go down well, but others appeared to find it beneficial. The FA did indeed hold an inquiry and questions were asked in Parliament by a Leicester MP after his local club lost 10-1 at Molineux in April 1938 – still Wolves' record league win.

Buckley had history with the FA, who in 1937 banned his club from a summer tour to Europe because of their poor disciplinary record. But the governing body found no harm in his injections and one of football's earliest drugs scandals was averted.

The Major had taken the wolf pack a long way, justifying the board's faith in him through a difficult period, and had a new contract running until 1948. But his plans, like those of everyone else in football, now had to be put on hold. It was particularly unfortunate, Cullis believed, because, 'If the war had not come in 1939, this Wolves team would have developed into one of the finest in the history of the game.'

* * *

In the fourth series of the Midlands gang saga *Peaky Blinders,* taking place in the mid-1920s, one of Tommy Shelby's men in Small Heath who is suspicious of outside infiltrators asks a potential new factory worker a question to prove he is a Brummie: 'What's the names of the Villa and Blues goalkeepers?' The response, correctly given (well done, scriptwriters), is 'Tommy Jackson and Dan Tremelling.'

Locals would certainly have known the answer. Tremelling barely missed a game for **Birmingham** from 1919–28, ending up with almost 400 appearances before giving way to the even more revered Harry Hibbs. Local rival Jackson was between the posts at the opposite end in many of the derbies between the two teams during the 1920s, in which results were as even as could be: 18 matches, of which each side won six with the others drawn.

Yet while Villa spent almost all that period in the top half of the table, as well as reaching two FA Cup finals, Blues first had to get out of the Second Division, and once back in the top tier faced a struggle to stay there; one they finally lost just as the Second World War was looming.

There was certainly no shortage of firepower to get the team out of the Second Division, which was achieved in two enjoyable, high-scoring seasons immediately on the resumption of peacetime football, bringing the crowds back to St Andrew's; an average of 23,000 in 1919/20 and over 31,500 for the following championship campaign.

Jack Whitehouse had been one of the most successful players anywhere during the First World War, scoring almost 50 goals for the club in their Midlands section Football League matches. After he helped the team to doubles over Coventry, Wolves and Stoke before Christmas 1919, the squad was boosted by the acquisition of two other prolific forwards.

Villa's record league scorer Harry Hampton had found himself squeezed out of their team despite almost 250 goals in 15 years, and after crossing town aged 34 in February 1920 he made an immediate impact, as did the younger Joe Lane from Blackpool. In their second and third games together, St Andrew's saw Nottingham Forest routed 8-0 and Lincoln drubbed 7-0 with the newcomers claiming ten of those goals.

A strong finish pushed Blues up to third place and the following year they justified the tag of promotion favourites. At Christmas 60,000 turned up to see West Ham beaten with two Hampton goals and he was on target again for the crucial last two games, in which a double over Port Vale meant pipping newly elected Cardiff City to the title on goal average. Scoring 79 goals was 20 more than the Welsh club, and four players all reached double figures: Hampton, Lane, Whitehouse and influential new inside-forward Johnny Crosbie from Ayr.

The whole team understandably found life tougher back in the top division while renewing hostilities with West Brom (two defeats over Christmas) and Villa (a win and a draw in March). Lane and Hampton both moved on after relegation was avoided by five points, but fortunately a bright new star was emerging to go on and become the heaviest scorer in Birmingham's history.

Joe Bradford, born in Coalville, joined the club from junior football aged 19 and from early 1922 stepped up as the most reliable goalscorer for the next dozen years, finishing with 267 of them in 445 games. That was just as well, for he often lacked support. In 1923/24 for instance, when he hit 24 and won the first of a dozen England caps, the best anyone else could manage was four. Not surprisingly it was Bradford who inspired the famous comeback draw at Villa Park two seasons later; with 12 minutes to play Blues were 3-0 down, but in the space of four minutes Bradford scored twice and panicked the home goalkeeper Cyril Spiers into an own goal. 'The finish was certainly the most sensational that had ever occurred between the local rivals,' said the *Sports Argus* that night. 'The rally of Birmingham stands out as one of the most remarkable in football history,' offered *Athletic News*.

Finishing eighth the previous season was a rare sojourn into the top half and the FA Cup was no source of excitement either in the 20s. In 1921/22 Blues even forgot to enter in time, which the secretary tried to pass off as 'just one of those things'. Right at the start of the next decade, however, came a decent cup run at last, culminating in the Wembley meeting with Albion.

Leslie Knighton, formerly manager of Arsenal, was now in charge and Bradford was still leading the attack in every sense, scoring eight goals in the first four rounds as Liverpool at Anfield, Port Vale, Watford and Chelsea at Stamford Bridge were beaten. Harry Hibbs was in goal, promoted from being Tremelling's understudy the previous season, and in the semi-final at Elland Road he kept the favourites Sunderland out under great pressure while Welsh left-winger Ernie Curtis, an FA Cup winner with Cardiff, scored once in each half for the Blues.

So a derby with Second Division Albion it was to be for Birmingham's first final, once they had put together enough points to avoid relegation in another tough league season that included a 9-1 defeat by Sheffield Wednesday (the busy Hibbs saving a penalty to prevent double figures). 'All things considered, I imagine that Birmingham will get the Cup,' wrote 'Corinthian' of the *Daily Herald,* while the *Gazette*'s front page featured a message from each of the captains, in which Blues full-back Ned Barkas suggested, 'I hope our rivals will pardon me for saying that our little touch of class will tell.'

Both were wrong. Albion's young side still had two vital promotion games left but refused to be distracted and benefited, as mentioned above, from an early goal by Blues inside-forward Bob Gregg being chalked off as offside. Bradford's equaliser to Richardson's goal lifted them for only as long as it took Albion to kick off and race downfield again for Richardson to score again.

Bradford had two more good seasons but was on the wane by 1935, when the team was in the bottom four in successive campaigns. In the first one they only survived by virtue of an extraordinary 7-3 win at Leicester in the penultimate game. He departed for one final season with Bristol City in the Third Division South before retiring, watching on as Blues rallied to mid-table for a couple of years in which Villa's 1936 relegation meant they were briefly top dogs in the second city.

In the congested finish of 1937/38, winning the final two games saved them from partnering Albion in relegation, but the next season they left the revival too late – winning three of the last four matches but not the other one, in which Chelsea's draw at St Andrew's turned out to save the Londoners at Birmingham's expense. It mattered not that Blues had beaten the champions Everton, as well as holding them in the FA Cup in front of the ground's record crowd, traditionally given as 66,844 but stated at the time as 67,341.

Villa, back in the top division and winning the derby 5-1 at Villa Park, had the last laugh again.

* * *

Elected back to the Football League just as it was suspended in 1915, **Stoke** (not 'City' until 1925) changed divisions five times in the eventful inter-war years before seeing off a proposed amalgamation with Port Vale and settling down after the emergence of their greatest player.

Stanley Matthews made his debut in March 1932 and within four years had helped them to fourth place in the top division, a position they have never yet bettered and only once equalled – when 'The Wizard of the Dribble' was still starring in 1947. As a small boy in his Hanley home, Stan favoured his local team Port Vale but claimed he could sometimes hear the roar from the Victoria Ground he was to grace in two spells of such distinction.

He was four years old in August 1919 when the Potters played their first Football League game for 11 years, 12,000 turning out to see Barnsley beaten 2-0. They finished in mid-table, just ahead of Vale after winning 3-0 away in the first league meeting between the pair. 'While the Vale had the better of the midfield exchanges throughout, Stoke merited their success because they took their chances,' the *Sentinel* reported.

The following two seasons, however, were typical in their unpredictability. In 1920/21 the Potters were in the bottom three and 12 months later they won promotion. Tommy Brittleton, a veteran pre-war England international from The Wednesday, added experience if nothing else – his last appearance was aged 45 – and the Broad brothers, Tommy and Jimmy, both forwards, proved worth the expenditure laid out by a wealthy director; Jimmy top-scored with 25 league goals as Barnsley were narrowly edged out of second place on goal average. There was a win and a draw against Vale, the home game being watched by 27,000, as well as the bonus of a 4-2 FA Cup success away to them. Almost 44,000 packed the Victoria Ground two rounds later to see a goalless draw with Villa, who won the replay 4-0.

Returning to the First Division, where Villa and West Brom were top-eight teams, proved too much. Eight games passed without a first win and a revival early in 1923 was ended painfully by a 6-0 defeat at Villa Park. Although Jimmy Broad had done well again, the whole team then ran out of goals and a total of only six in the last dozen games meant they ended up four points shy of safety.

Manager Arthur Shallcross was replaced just before the end of the campaign by player-manager Jock Rutherford from Arsenal, who shocked everyone by resigning after two games of the new season (the second of them a 5-0 defeat at Leicester), apparently in a dispute over team selection and transfers. He soon rejoined Arsenal, playing on for four more years with them and Clapton Orient.

Recovering from this setback to finish sixth in the Second Division, the Potters then went through three more eventful seasons. Avoiding relegation by a single point in 1925, they failed to work the same trick the following year and instead went down by a point. It was hardly the most appropriate way to celebrate Stoke-on-Trent having become a city, allowing the club to add that prestigious word to its name. Just as bad, if not worse, was losing four derbies in a row to Vale (who were in the top half of the table both seasons) which led to a sensational development.

Club officials were shocked to learn from press reports that majority shareholder John Slater had gone behind their backs and suggested a merger to the old enemy, whose directors apparently approved it. Vale were prepared to accept playing at the larger and better-equipped Victoria Ground but their supporters were not. 'Bitter feelings have been aroused in the Potteries by the proposal to amalgamate Stoke City and Port Vale,' reported *Athletic News* on 26 April 1926. It took another month to kill off the plan. Slater sold his shareholding and those Vale directors in favour of amalgamating all resigned.

Stoke cheered themselves up by immediately taking the Third Division North title. Charlie Wilson contributed 25 of the 92 goals, including five in the 7-0 home win over Ashington, and the following season set a club record of 38. Six of them came in a run to the FA Cup quarter-final. As the Potters re-established themselves in the Second Division with successive top-six finishes, he became the first player to reach 100 for the club.

A couple of seasons in mid-table followed, but help was at hand. Manager Tom Mather was determined that the young Stanley Matthews, a schoolboy international winger at 13 (though he had mainly played as a centre-half), would join up from the day of his 15th birthday: 1 February 1930. On that morning he walked into the Victoria Ground, where his first contribution to earning a £1 weekly wage was to clean out both dressing rooms.

Within seven months he had made a reserve-team debut and, as his 17th birthday approached, he told Stoke to their great relief that he would sign professional for them despite the interest of Villa, Birmingham, West Brom, Wolves and several others. They rewarded him with the maximum wage of £5 a week during the season, dropping to £3 in summer, plus two appearances before the end of that campaign. On 19 March 1932 he played in a 1-0 win at Bury and a week later had a home debut with a 2-0 win against Barnsley. The four points enabled the Potters to finish third in the Second Division, only two points off promotion.

From then until the Second World War was the most successful period in the club's history to date, and it can hardly be counted a coincidence that these were the years of the first Matthews era. Used sparingly until Christmas 1932, he took advantage of injuries to two senior players to gain a regular place in the new year, and ended up with 15 appearances and a championship medal as Stoke held off Tottenham's late run to take the Second Division title by a point.

Vale were beaten 1-0 in October in front of the biggest home crowd of the season of almost 30,000, and the return game in March contained a historic moment: Stanley Matthews's first goal in senior football.

In the following six seasons he was effectively first choice as the Potters established themselves back in the First Division. They finished 12th, tenth, fourth, tenth, 17th and seventh, the fourth place in 1935/36 being the best in their history; if they had won the penultimate home game against Sheffield Wednesday instead of losing they would have been runners-up.

For 30 successive league games the Potters fielded the same goalkeeper, full-backs and half-backs behind Matthews, who managed a rare hat-trick in the 5-0 away win at Birmingham. Never a prolific goalscorer, he still reached double figures for three successive years, but was forging his reputation as a maker of chances, benefiting from hours as a boy spent dribbling round chairs in the backyard and later perfecting a new style: running at his full-back, feinting one way and swerving the other in a burst of acceleration and cloud of dust. The principal beneficiary was Freddie Steele, a year younger and another Hanley boy, who in 1936/37 scored a club-record 33 league goals and added eight in his six internationals

Typically, the England selectors, having given Stan a stop-start international career that began against Wales in September 1934, paired him with Steele for only one of those games, at Hampden Park, when left-winger Joe Johnson gave the club three members of the forward line.

Stoke's drop to 17th in 1937/38 from fourth two years earlier was a surprise, though nothing like the shock when their supporters learnt what was happening behind the scenes. Bob McGrory, a tough Scot promoted from player-coach to replace manager Mather, was held to be suspicious of individualists in a team game. He spent the summer of 1937 haggling with Stan about a bonus payment before reluctantly agreeing to pay it.

Scoring his only England hat-trick after being moved to centre-forward in a 5-4 win against Czechoslovakia in December cemented Matthews's reputation as a national hero, but increasing rumours of resentment in the Stoke dressing room as the team began to struggle prompted a sensation two months later when he handed in a transfer request. 'Without Stanley Matthews, Stoke City would not be Stoke City,' ran an editorial in the *Sentinel*. 'Stanley Matthews must not be allowed to go.'

Three thousand supporters attended a special meeting at the King's Hall, with many more locked out, and only after a deputation had two meetings with the player himself and one with the directors did Matthews agree to stay. By winning the final game at home to Liverpool the Potters stayed up; had they not done so he would almost certainly have pressed for a move again, as he did in any case early the next season. It was an uneasy truce as the club finished the final full season seventh, while Matthews was about to spend much of his war in Blackpool.

* * *

For **Port Vale** this was a heady period, beginning with an unexpectedly sudden return to the Football League and first meetings with Stoke and then shocking their supporters by initially agreeing to an amalgamation with their rivals, before suffering the same brief drop to the Third Division North.

For the first post-war season the Football League expanded with room for four new clubs, but voting to decide who they would be left Vale missing out by a single vote and forced them to resume against the reserve teams of their betters in the Central League. Not for long. In October, Second Division Leeds City were expelled after being found guilty of making illegal payments in a blot on the fledgling managerial career of the great Herbert Chapman.

Vale jumped at the chance to step up and take over the Yorkshire club's very acceptable record of ten points from eight games. Their first match, on 18 October, was a long trip to South Shields, one of the clubs voted in ahead of them. It brought a 2-0 defeat but the next two, although also lost, felt more like a return to the big time: home and away games with Tottenham Hotspur (that season's champions) played in front of crowds of 16,000 and 30,000 respectively.

The *Sentinel* called the South Shields meeting 'a creditable debut' in a 'keen encounter' and after the White Hart Lane game the headline read, 'Hanley men make another creditable show'.

Some hasty recruitment was necessary to strengthen the team, the best acquisition being striker Bobby Blood for a modest £50 from Leek. He defied serious injuries sustained in the war to score 24 league goals and ensure a respectable final position of 13th – well above both Wolves and newcomers Coventry City. As well as the Spurs game, there was huge interest and big crowds at two other matches at the Old Recreation Ground. In January, Manchester United arrived for a 1-0 FA Cup win, drawing 14,549, and two months later came the long-awaited league games against Stoke. A reported 22,697 saw the Potters win comfortably, but at the Victoria Ground a week later the team now nicknamed the Valiants forced a goalless draw.

It was a blow when Blood left for West Bromwich Albion in February 1921, claiming that the hefty £4,000 fee had helped to save the club, but there was an even better replacement. Local lad Wilf Kirkham hit a record 26 league goals in 1924/25 and beat that two years later with the all-time record of 38. The team stayed well away from the two new Third Divisions until the end of the decade, manager Joe Schofield, the former Stoke winger, getting them as high as eighth in the Second Division for three successive years from 1925–27.

In the first two of those seasons, Vale looked down from a great height on their neighbours, beating them four times out of four as the Potters finished in the bottom three and then went down. But officials at the Old Rec believed the club could climb no further on gates of around 10,500 and as detailed in the previous section accepted an offer in April 1926 from Stoke's main shareholder of a merger and move to the Victoria Ground.

Fortunately those Stoke officials who knew nothing about it were as outraged as Vale supporters, whose vigorous campaign led to a climbdown the following month, with the Valiants directors forced to resign. Suitably inspired, the team went out to enjoy Kirkham's record-breaking season in which average crowds were higher than at the Victoria Ground.

In 1928/29, however, the tables were turned as the Potters made a successful return to the Second Division in sixth place while Vale's defence let them down in conceding 86 goals, leading to relegation with Clapton Orient. Like Stoke, whom Kirkham joined, they returned immediately as champions, scoring 103 goals in a triumphant campaign of only five defeats. Sam Jennings from Nottingham Forest was top scorer with 24 but sadly the man who signed him did not live to reap the reward. Manager Schofield fell ill early in the season and died at the end of September, aged 58. It was the club's second such tragedy in the 20s: in November 1923 the previous season's top scorer, Tom Butler, suffered septic poisoning after breaking his arm in a match at Orient and died in a London hospital.

Kirkham returned from Stoke after two seasons and a broken leg, helping beat the Potters 3-0 in his first game back before the Valiants went on to avoid relegation on the last day. The Matthews years were beginning, however, and Vale, in danger of being permanently overshadowed, even considered a change of name; Stoke United and Hanley Port Vale were among those suggested. Nothing came of it and as Stoke City finished third in 1932 and then top, the Valiants struggled at the wrong end. Kirkham retired with 164 goals for them, becoming a headmaster, and in 1936 they went down again, conceding 106 times.

The season still included the club's greatest giant-killing act, slaying that year's runaway Football League champions. Sunderland let them off the hook in a 2-2 draw at Roker Park when Arthur Caldwell equalised late on and in the replay on a frozen Old Rec pitch Vale scored twice in the first 20 minutes to bring off a remarkable triumph. 'The victory was fully merited, for Vale were superior in all phases of the game,' crowed the *Sentinel*. 'Port Vale won the admiration and respect of the whole football world.'

Defender Harry Griffiths, singled out for praise that day, and club-mate Jack Roberts were both exceptional baseball players, who won international honours at the sport.

Three modest seasons followed before the war, two of them in the Third Division North and then one in the southern section; Vale, like Walsall and Coventry, being a club whose geographical position meant occasionally being switched between the two. But Stoke and Stanley Matthews now ruled the Potteries.

* * *

Coventry City's 100 years in the Football League, celebrated while in exile at St Andrew's in August 2019, might have ended 99 years earlier had the truth about their first season been made known at the time. But the knowledge that they had fixed two crucial games remained no more than rumour until the Football League finally found them guilty three years later, handing out life bans to individuals and only a £100 fine to the two clubs involved.

Celebrations at being elected when the top two divisions were expanded to 22 clubs for the 1919/20 season soon gave way to reality. From the opening day's 5-0 home defeat by Tottenham, City did not gain a point until the tenth game or win until the 20th, against Stoke on Christmas Day. Despite bringing in Harry Pollitt as manager in November, going into the final two matches they were ahead of Grimsby but a point behind Lincoln, with a game in hand and a better goal average. So to avoid applying for re-election three points were needed from two matches in the same week, both against Bury, who were in the top six but had nothing to play for except a little talent money.

At this stage City panicked. Skipper George Chaplin, recounting the whole story many years later (*Coventry Herald,* 22 and 29 January 1938), revealed that he agreed with the club's owner and benefactor David Cooke to visit Bury 'with £200 in my pocket', returning confident that the necessary points would be secured. The away match was drawn 2-2 and three days later a record crowd of more than 23,000 turned out at Highfield Road for the return. At half-time Bury led by a goal to nil and one of their players told a shaken Chaplin that City were playing so badly it was impossible not to be in front. What a jubilant home crowd then saw was outside-left Alec Mercer, a former Bury player, score twice to win the game and keep City out of the bottom two places.

In retrospect it seems unlikely that they would have been voted out, which happened to Lincoln and Grimsby. For one thing, that pair had the worst crowds anywhere of under 7,000 whereas the city of Coventry had proved it would support the local club in good numbers: the Highfield Road average was almost 17,000. Secondly, they had topped the list of applicants only 12 months earlier; thirdly, it was customary to give clubs a second chance even if their first season at the higher level was unsuccessful.

At worst, City would almost certainly have been given a place in the new Third Division formed of Southern League clubs, as Grimsby then were (despite hardly being in the south of England). Lincoln, forced to wait another year until the Third Division North began in 1921, had more of a grievance, which would increase immeasurably when a Football League commission was finally formed in the spring of 1923 to investigate a tip-off.

Its verdict, announced on 29 May, stunned football. Confusingly, it referred only to the away game, but the *Daily Herald* reported, 'The Commission is satisfied that an arrangement was made that the match played at Bury in 1920 should be won by the Coventry club.'

Cooke, Chaplin and City director Jack Marshall were banned for life, along with seven Bury players and officials; two years later manager Pollitt, who had been sacked after those last two matches, was added to the list.

As a scandal it ranked with the infamous Manchester United-Liverpool fix of 1915, when seven players were suspended *sine die*, and for many years the shadow hung over Coventry, who were in relegation danger for the next four seasons and finally succumbed in the fifth. In both 1921 and 1922 they survived by one place, and in the next two by two points, so finishing bottom in 1924/25 had an air of inevitability about it. A new strip of red and green halves, the local authority colours, was quickly deemed to be unlucky and after two seasons blue and white stripes returned.

Not surprisingly, crowds slowly dropped away and in the Third Division North were below a 10,000 average for the first time. The last match at home to Hartlepools United drew barely 1,600. Walsall was the nearest thing to a local derby and although both teams switched to the southern section, City's form was no better. In 1927/28, five years after the Football League's punishment, they were only a point above bottom club Torquay, the fear being that having to apply for re-election would give the other clubs an excuse to turf them out.

Fortunes, league positions and attendances slowly began to improve around 1930, the year that Sunderland's FA Cup visit set a new ground record of 31,673. The following year Harry Storer, a no-nonsense Burnley midfielder and cricketer for Derbyshire, was appointed manager and made an inspired double signing that transformed the club. Clarrie Bourton arrived from Blackburn and Jock Lauderdale from Blackpool for only £1,000 in total to play together in attack. In their first season of 1931/32 they scored 69 league goals between them – a club-record 49 to centre-forward Bourton, which was the highest in the whole country – yet the Bantams finished only 12th, having scored 108 but conceded 97.

Tightening up the defence while still reaching three figures in three of the next four seasons had them at last in contention for promotion back to the Second Division, finally achieved in 1935/36. In this extraordinarily fruitful period, which included their record league win, 9-0 over Bristol City, Bourton had returns in the league and FA Cup of 50, 43, 25, 29 and 24. The two decisive home matches in winning the title, against closest rivals Luton and then Torquay, drew combined crowds of over 73,000.

'The revival received an impetus from the day that Mr Harry Storer joined the club,' reported the *Coventry Evening Telegraph*, the manager addressing thousands of supporters who invaded the pitch to tell them, 'I feel sure we will not be a disgrace to the Second Division.'

That was an understatement. In the first season they were eighth, above Villa, the two derbies being watched by huge crowds, and promotion to the top division should have been won in 1937/38. Losing only one game before Christmas, City were always in among the bunch chasing eventual champions Villa but despite having the second-best defence they needed one more big season from Bourton, who instead left for Plymouth, having scored 180 times in 241 games. Without him no one scored more than 13 and winning only one of the final five games left them a single point behind runners-up Manchester United.

The same weakness was evident in another fourth-place finish the next season, 62 goals being the lowest of almost any team in the top half; relegated West Brom brought in the biggest gate, just as they had at 44,492 for an FA Cup tie two years earlier. It was all a big step up from 1919, but a wonderful opportunity had been missed that would take nearly 30 years to grasp.

* * *

The Second Division, let alone the First, may have been a mere dream for **Walsall** but the inter-war years are nevertheless remembered for the most famous result in the club's history.

Before Christmas 1932, enjoying a better season at last after nine successive finishes in the bottom half of the table, they took advantage of home ties in the FA Cup to overcome fellow Third Division North clubs Mansfield Town and Hartlepools. The third-round draw then produced the tie everyone wanted – at home to the country's best and most glamorous team, Herbert Chapman's Arsenal.

Runners-up in the First Division and FA Cup the previous year, the Gunners were top of the table and heading for the first in a hat-trick of titles. Narrow defeats away to Sheffield

Wednesday and Sunderland in the weeks before the game proved they were not invincible; on the other hand they had earlier crushed Leicester and Wolves (at Molineux) 8-2 and 7-1 on successive Saturdays, and seen off Sheffield United 9-2. Forwards Joe Hulme, David Jack, John Lambert and Cliff Bastin all scored hat-tricks in those games, with Alex James supplying the ammunition.

'They are looking forward quite confidently to a comfortable passage into the next round,' said the *Birmingham Gazette* on the eve of the tie, while astutely adding, 'And this frame of mind, where Cup ties are concerned, is always dangerous.'

Arsenal were missing five senior players through injury and flu, which made more of a difference than might have been expected. Being so successful, they essentially had a regular first 11 – all of whom played at least 25 league games that season – plus a crop of reserves. Chapman, who missed the Sunderland defeat to watch Walsall play poorly at home to Barnsley, made a rare miscalculation in naming four replacements who had only one previous appearance between them; the three making their debut would be sold without ever playing in the first team again.

Of course, they should still have been strong enough, with five internationals in the side and Jack, James and Bastin among the forwards. But Walsall, playing in changed colours of blue and white, were inspired, as well as being helped by a muddy pitch and a physical approach. They had a gifted goalscorer in Gilbert Alsop, who after an hour's play headed in a cross by Freddie Lee. Only a few minutes later, one of Arsenal's debutants, Tommy Black, brought down Alsop with a wild tackle and Bill Sheppard scored from the penalty spot to have the home crowd of 11,150 believing. Half an hour afterwards most of them were invading the pitch to carry their heroes off.

The *Gazette*, which would have been entitled to quote its preview about a dangerous frame of mind, carried the headline 'Great defence holds up Arsenal: How Walsall earned fame' and wrote, 'Their grit and mettle made a big impression upon their more talented opponents and carried the less fancied team to a deserved victory.' The *Walsall Times* correspondent took a more personal approach, 'Is it true? Is it not a dream that I shall awake and smile at? No!'

FA Cup third round, 14 January 1933: Walsall 2 Arsenal 0
Walsall: Cunningham, Bennett, Bird, Reed, Leslie, Salt, Coward, Ball, Alsop, Sheppard, Lee.
Arsenal: Moss, Male, Black, Hill, Roberts, Sidey, Warnes, Jack, Walsh, James, Bastin.

Five days later the Saddlers beat Mansfield 8-1 in a league game before going out of the FA Cup 2-0 at First Division Manchester City, watched by 52,000. Manager Bill Slade, appointed a year earlier, had brought several Coventry players, including Lee and Sheppard, into the side which went on to finish fifth in the Third Division North and fourth the year after. It was also a period (1929–34) in which three Saddlers earned international honours: Mick O'Brien and Robert Griffith for Ireland and goalkeeper Roy John for Wales.

Alsop, the son of a Gloucestershire coal miner, was another former Coventry forward, undistinguished at Highfield Road but a new man after joining Walsall in September 1931. In both 1933/34 and 1934/35 he scored 40 league goals, the all-time club record, before moving on to West Brom. Unsuccessful there but prolific at Ipswich, he returned to Walsall in 1938, by which time they were bottom but one for two years running in the Third Division South. In that last season before the war they did manage to raise their game once more in the FA Cup, Alsop scoring all four goals in victory against Notts County in a run that took Walsall into the last 16 for the first time in 50 years. It was one of his 18 hat-tricks for the club and he would later be honoured by having a stand named after him at the Bescot Stadium when they moved from what in 1930 had been renamed Fellows Park after the long-serving club chairman.

The 1920s had been something of a struggle, too, after returning to the Football League as founder members of the Third Division North. George 'Paddy' Reid, later capped by Northern Ireland, hit the first goal and was top scorer as the Saddlers finished eighth, then third behind champions Nelson and Bradford Park Avenue. In 1925/26 they struggled with the new offside rule, conceding 107 goals but being re-elected comfortably, 21 votes ahead of the unsuccessful Carlisle United. Switching to the Third Division South for four years from 1927 proved beneficial in terms of travel, though money remained tight. Drawn at home to Aston Villa in the FA Cup fourth round in 1930, the directors gave up ground advantage and were rewarded with a most welcome £1,879 share of the massive gate of 74,626, including an estimated 15,000 of their own followers, who saw a brave 3-1 defeat. Goalkeeper Fred Biddlestone impressed the Villa so much that they immediately signed him and made him their first choice for the rest of the season. As for conceding ground advantage, it was just as well Walsall did not make the same decision when Arsenal came out of the hat three years later.

* * *

Shrewsbury Town made such progress during the inter-war years that they felt able to make the first of several applications to bring the Football League to Shropshire. Adding a new £5,000 grandstand at Gay Meadow in the autumn of 1922 proved timely, as that season they became Birmingham League champions for the first time. The margin was three points from Bilston United, who they beat 2-1 away from home to clinch the title. 'There would be fully 6,000 spectators present,' reported the *Birmingham Gazette*, 'a special train being run from the Shropshire capital, while all the charabancs had also been requisitioned.'

Runners-up the following season, Town were rarely down in the doldrums again. In 1933/34 Joe Taylor scored 68 in all competitions. His prolific replacement was Jack Roscamp, who had netted twice for Blackburn in the 1928 FA Cup Final; and for four successive seasons until the Second World War Town recorded over 100 league goals, many of them by the Lancastrian forward Bill Hewitson. In 1935/36 he totalled 72 goals before following Taylor into the Football League, and the next season Ernie Breeze, a converted full-back, registered a double hat-trick in the 11-1 romp against Bangor. Town scored 133 goals but were still only runners-up to Bristol Rovers Reserves. Moving up to the Midland League in 1937/38, they became champions at the first attempt and won the Welsh Senior Cup for the first time since 1891. Coming from 2-0 down at home to Swansea in the final to draw in front of a 14,500 crowd, they took the replay 2-1.

Once the war was over, greater things beckoned.

5

War
1939–1945

'The Football League programme has been interrupted by war and the date of its resumption is at present beyond imagination.'

Birmingham Daily Post, September 1939

'It was obvious there will be no football there for a long time, Hitler having done a spot of ploughing up of the playing space with a series of bombs, before knocking a large-sized hole in the new stand.'

Midland Daily Telegraph, November 1940

'A trainload of Sunderland supporters on the way to the match was machine-gunned by a German raider but nobody was hurt.'

Sunday Mirror, May 1942

'Not since the peace-time days had such a crowd been seen at Villa Park as there was this afternoon… More than half an hour before the kick-off the gates had to be closed.'

Birmingham Mail, May 1944

'It was right and proper that our sport should go on… supplying a much wanted need.'

Staffordshire Sentinel, May 1945

REMEMBERING, PERHAPS, how much criticism football had attracted by carrying on regardless at the start of the First World War, the governing body could hardly have been quicker in calling a halt when the next one began – yet it would shortly have second, more positive thoughts.

When Prime Minister Neville Chamberlain went on the radio on the morning of Sunday, 3 September 1939 to declare that Britain and France were now at war with Germany, the Football League season was suspended with most teams having played just three matches. Crowds of all kinds were immediately banned and as the *Birmingham Daily Post* put it, 'The Football League programme has been interrupted by war and the date of its resumption is at present beyond imagination.' The city's evening paper, the *Despatch,* added that night, 'All contracts are automatically cancelled. Whatever clubs do for players is voluntary.'

Football fans had seemed to know what was coming, for even during August many were not in the mood for sport. From the first day of the league programme to the second, total crowds of 600,000 (already low) had dropped to below 400,000. Then the 11 First Division games on the first Saturday of September attracted just 137,500 and Birmingham's 20,000 at home to Burnley in the Second Division was joint best anywhere in the country.

From the three sets of matches, Blackpool were the only 100 per cent team in the top division. Aston Villa had one of the better attendances, of 36,000 for an opening win over Middlesbrough, but only 8,000 saw the defeat at Derby that dropped them to 14th place. Stoke, with many players already on military duty, were ninth with one win, one draw and one defeat, having suffered a long journey home from Middlesbrough and not arriving back until the early hours.

Wolves, with Stan Cullis, Dennis Westcott and 16-year-old winger Jimmy Mullen playing all three games, were 16th after two draws and a defeat, holding Arsenal 2-2 at Molineux in front of 41,000 but losing 2-1 at Blackpool.

In the Second Division, Birmingham, relegated the previous season, were second to Luton Town on goal average, having won at home to Burnley and Leicester, and drawn at Tottenham. Coventry were fifth, drawing 3-3 with Albion, who sat in 12th place after losing an exciting game 4-3 at home to Spurs despite a hat-trick by Eric Jones.

Walsall were in the middle of the Third Division South with a win, a draw and a defeat but Port Vale were bottom with a single point, having played only two games and not winning either.

Remarkably soon, however, there came a change of heart. With German forces busy in Poland and offering no immediate threat to Britain, the government quickly decided that there could be benefits for national morale if something closer to normal life continued. Friendly matches were played from mid-September, and at the start of October the Football League announced detailed plans for eight geographical groups, which would start later that month.

In the First World War, Villa, West Bromwich and Wolves missed most or all of the competitive football and now Villa again showed no enthusiasm. They declined to compete for the first three years, and with Birmingham and Coventry later suffering from bomb damage and Port Vale sitting out four successive seasons, it was not until 1944/45 that all the West Midlands teams took part.

There were restrictions from the start on travel and attendances: initially crowds were limited to about 8,000 and a 50-mile travel limit was imposed, which at various times would affect far-flung clubs like Carlisle, Hartlepools, Norwich and Bournemouth.

As conscription had been introduced for all males aged 20 to 23, slowly increasing by age, many were sent either to training camps around the country or posted abroad, and clubs rarely knew very far in advance which players would get a weekend pass, be on leave, or arrive on time. Match programmes would include names like 'A.N. Other' and guest players became frequent, which was of huge benefit to clubs like Aldershot (home to the British Army, where many sportsmen joined the physical training course) and Blackpool (an RAF training centre with many nearby camps). Teams would occasionally start a man short and appeals over the public address system for 'any footballers in the crowd' were not unknown. Players were paid only 30 shillings (£1.50) per match with no bonuses, which the players' union protested in vain was inadequate.

The FA, under-secretary and future FIFA president Stanley Rous, made every effort to keep the government onside. Charities, especially the Red Cross, were generously supported by profits from representative matches and then internationals; receipts from entertainment tax proved useful once crowds picked up; and grounds were offered for training and other use. The Trinity Road stand at Villa Park was converted into an air-raid shelter but Birmingham were upset at not being allowed to play at St Andrew's by order of the Chief Constable, who feared the effect of air raids on nearby munitions factories. The order was not rescinded until March 1940, meaning their first 18 matches in the new Midlands Regional League had to be played either away, or in two cases on neutral ground at Leamington.

Their opponents in the eight-team competition were Coventry, Walsall, West Bromwich, Wolves, Leicester, Northampton and Luton; Stoke and Port Vale having been put in the West League, which included Merseyside and Manchester clubs.

* * *

In that first season of **1939/40,** Wolves, Football League runners-up for the two pre-war years, topped the table by a point from Albion, with Coventry third and Blues doing well to finish fourth. Walsall, beaten 8-1 after St Andrew's was reopened, propped up the rest, but results could be as unpredictable as team line-ups; the Saddlers, bottom or not, almost ruined Wolves' title chances by winning 5-1 in Molineux's penultimate match.

Frequent unavailability of senior players meant opportunities for younger ones, something in which Wolves manager Frank Buckley had always believed in any case. Like Albion, they used few if any guests that season. When his team played at Birmingham in March the average age was under 20 and included Billy Wright, who had been given a debut aged 15 for a friendly away to Notts County at the end of September, scoring twice in a 4-1 win; he played at outside-left and made all his early appearances in the forward line as the club tried to decide on his best position.

Stoke, who announced they would field as many local players as possible, had Stanley Matthews playing 15 times and won the

West League with the four big guns of Merseyside and Manchester right behind them. Vale, competing in their only season until 1944, were eighth of the 12 teams. Their goalkeeper was normally Arthur Jepson, who also played cricket for Nottinghamshire, taking more than 1,000 wickets before eventually becoming a Test match umpire.

Meanwhile, a benefit match for Blues goalkeeper Harry Hibbs in April brought a rare outing for Villa, some of whose players took advantage of opportunities elsewhere. Frank Broome and George Edwards turned out a number of times for Blues and enjoyed joining Westcott of Wolves and Albion's Ted Duggan in playing for ambitious Chelmsford City; as non-league clubs were not bound by the 30 shillings maximum appearance fee, City would sometimes pay as much as £4.

A widespread desire for knockout football was met towards the end of the season with a Football League War Cup, played over two legs in the first two rounds. West Brom and Birmingham went furthest but both lost in the quarter-finals, while Coventry put out Wolves 7-2 on aggregate then lost narrowly to Albion. In the final at Wembley in early June, West Ham beat Blackburn in front of a 42,000 crowd trying to forget about that week's retreat from Dunkirk.

International football resumed early, England sending two teams to play Wales in November 1939, of which the first in Cardiff was a London-based XI and the second at Wrexham was picked from northern and Midlands sides. Stan Cullis made the first of many wartime international appearances with Matthews and Villa's Jackie Martin also in the team. The same trio played later that season in what was almost always the best-attended wartime fixture; Scotland against England regularly drew over 75,000 to Hampden Park.

As Dunkirk had illustrated, the so-called phoney war of the first few months was now well and truly over. Winston Churchill had replaced Chamberlain as Prime Minister and the Luftwaffe was bombing England, which meant factories like the Austin and Rover works at Longbridge and Solihull making military vehicles and engines were obvious targets, as well as the major towns and cities.

* * *

For **1940/41** the eight regional leagues were scrapped in favour of a strange system under which teams were placed in either the vast northern or southern section, playing wildly differing numbers of games, and positions were bizarrely decided not on points average but goal average.

All West Midlands clubs were considered to be in the south, the highest placed being Coventry, whose season was brutally ended after only ten games. Through the night of 14 November and into the following morning, the worst bombing of the Coventry blitz caused more than 200 fires, devastated the cathedral, and destroyed more than 4,000 homes. Highfield Road was badly damaged, the *Midland Daily Telegraph* correspondent reporting in surprisingly light-hearted vein, 'It was obvious there will be no football there for a long time, Hitler having done a spot of ploughing up of the playing space with a series of bombs, before knocking a large-sized hole in the new stand.' Having had barely 300 spectators for the previous home game, City stopped playing until August 1942.

St Andrew's was also damaged, not only by bombs but a serious fire accidentally caused by the local fire service, which incinerated all Birmingham's playing kit. Afterwards they had to play at Leamington and Villa Park. The Blues, giving experience to young goalkeeper Gil Merrick, managed only 16 games and like Stoke, who played 36, were in the lower half of the 34 teams. In October 1941, before the worst damage, they were awarded the England-Wales international by a sympathetic FA and with the crowd limited to 25,000 several thousand applications had to be sent back.

Walsall played 32 games and were one of only two teams to score a century of goals, putting them in 12th place, just above Albion, who they beat 10-3 in the final game. In beating Notts County 11-4, the Saddlers benefited from the scoring feats of Manchester United forward Jack Rowley. Back in his native West Midlands, he scored four times in a game on no fewer than four occasions, giving him 23 from 14 appearances – more than he made for his own club. In the cup, however, Walsall were outscored 10-7 on aggregate by Nottingham Forest as the local sides made an early exit. Preston won the final, beating Arsenal after two games attended by a total of 105,000. West Brom, in contrast, had three 'crowds' of under 1,000 at The Hawthorns, even though Billy Richardson played more regularly than the previous season and scored 29 league and cup goals.

Even though players received such small sums, Wolves had lost nearly £18,000 the previous season and decided to drop out of all competitions, during which time teenagers Wright and Mullen gained further experience playing for Leicester, who lost to Arsenal in the semi-final.

* * *

The Wanderers returned, however, for **1941/42** and their young team won the League North Cup. They knocked out Albion in the semi-final – almost 65,000 turning out overall for the two legs – and then beat Sunderland by 2-2, 4-1 in the final, the home leg being watched by 43,000. The *Sunday Mirror* reported grimly on the hazards of wartime travel to games, 'A trainload of Sunderland supporters on the way to the match was machine-gunned by a German raider but nobody was hurt.'

Billy Wright fractured his ankle against Albion and therefore missed the final and also a one-off match against the London Cup winners Brentford, played at Stamford Bridge, in aid of King George's Fund for Sailors. It ended 1-1.

Albion had beaten Wolves 8-2 and 5-3 in the league during a spell of scoring 43 goals in six games in the autumn, when winger Billy Elliott was on target in 11 successive matches. They also had a fine double over Everton in the cup quarter-final by 3-1 and 5-1 at Goodison before Wolves took their revenge, the Baggies' star forward Richardson drawing a rare pair of blanks in a season when 24 games brought him 31 goals.

It was a good time for goalscorers. Villa, slumming it for two seasons below their station in the Birmingham and District League against various RAF teams, particularly enjoyed playing the forces sides of Lichfield and Hednesford, who they beat 19-2 and 14-1 respectively early in 1942.

Even without Matthews, now guesting regularly for Blackpool, Stoke did better than the previous season in a strong

North League. Tommy Sale's goals were an important factor. Having returned from Blackburn Rovers in 1938, he totalled 55 in 1941/42, including a double hat-trick against Walsall, who nevertheless were well placed and ahead of Wolves in the South League.

The second city suffered badly from bombing raids during the summer of 1942 and Villa defender Ernie Callaghan, a constable in Birmingham City Police, was awarded the British Empire Medal for 'conspicuous bravery' during the Blitz.

* * *

By **1942/43** a complicated pattern had been set of league games until Christmas, then a second championship, plus a series of ten qualifying games for the cup, all followed by two-legged knockout football. This time the West Midlands clubs were all in the northern section, playing almost 50 games before the top 32 entered the League North Cup.

Villa, bored with the Birmingham and District League and having won 26 of 31 games in 1941/42, sought stronger opposition, returning in League North. They caused a minor controversy by raising admission prices to one shilling and sixpence (nearly 8p) and a major one when powerful Scottish full-back George Cummings was banned for life. Sent off in the Christmas Day win at Leicester for 'dangerous charging', he became a victim of draconian punishment by the FA, which was reached 'having regard to a warning in May 1940 and his conduct since'.

Mercifully the ban was lifted for the following season, but he missed all the cup games of early 1943 in which Villa reached the semi-final before going out to Blackpool. The inclusion of one Stanley Matthews helped attract 50,000 to Villa Park for the second leg, when a 2-1 win for the home side was not sufficient to take them through. There was then a short triangular championship with Birmingham and West Brom, Villa beating the former but losing 6-2 at home to the latter when Richardson scored five for the visitors to finish with 17 from his final half-dozen games, including two victories over Blues.

Birmingham suffered from lack of a goalscorer but had Merrick as their established number one, hardly missing a game until the end of the war. With Highfield Road available again, Coventry also returned and drew almost 15,000 for their second game back at home to Villa, a 2-1 win. They did well to finish in the top ten of each of the two championships, winning 28 of 48 games in all thanks to plenty of goals from centre-forward Tom Crawley and Welsh international George Lowrie.

Walsall had to do without Jack Rowley, who played once for his home-town club Wolves with a spectacular outcome. Guesting in November for the club that had released him as an 18-year-old without playing a first-team game, he scored all eight goals in an 8-1 win over Derby. Wolves had to rely on Westcott for goals most of the time, though Wright reached double figures. Major Buckley also created a record by giving a debut to an outside-right called Cameron Buchanan at the age of 14 and 57 days in a 2-0 win over Albion.

* * *

In **1943/44** Villa went one better than the previous season by taking revenge on Blackpool to win the League North Cup. Although well placed in both of the league sections, with nine defeats in 39 games, they only scraped through the cup qualifying section by one point, then perked up for the knockout games. They saw off Stoke, Coventry, Bath (who had been drafted in to boost the number of western clubs) and West Brom, and Sheffield United were then ousted 5-4 on aggregate in a semi-final that drew 40,000 to Villa Park and even more to Bramall Lane.

Excitement redoubled for the final against Matthews's Blackpool despite a 2-1 defeat in the away leg. A week later the *Birmingham Mail* reported, 'Not since the peace-time days had such a crowd been seen at Villa Park as there was this afternoon for Aston Villa's decisive game with Blackpool in the final of the League (North) Cup. More than half an hour before the kick-off the gates had to be closed.'

Nearly 55,000 were inside and they saw two goals by Frank Broome in a 4-2 win. Villa gave the trophy to the Red Cross to auction – and the winner sportingly returned it to them. They then met London Cup winners Charlton at Stamford Bridge in a 1-1 draw watched by over 38,000. In October they had suffered a rare shock against Walsall, who from 4-0 down at half-time revived to draw 4-4. Frequently punching above their weight, the Saddlers had Bert Williams in goal and little Johnny Hancocks on the wing, both of whom would soon be off to Molineux.

Birmingham also returned to competitive football, and were back at St Andrew's although the ground still lacked dressing rooms. They made a successful tactical switch in moving full-back Cyril Trigg into attack, where he scored 56 goals over two seasons. Stoke, meanwhile, missed Matthews, who in 1943/44 played only three games for them and 23 for Blackpool. Fortunately Sale was still scoring well, with 30 goals, supported by Freddie Steele's 20.

Coventry centre-forward Tom Crawley was another prolific striker, with five in the 8-0 Christmas Day drubbing of Albion, who again relied throughout the season on Richardson and Elliott.

The sensation of the campaign, however, was the resignation of Frank Buckley. Signing a ten-year contract with Wolves in 1938, he had said that 'no other club could ever interest me'. In December 1943 the *Nottingham Evening Post* revealed that ambitious Notts County had had discussions with him but had been told he was 'not interested'. On 8 February, however, newspapers carried the story that he had obtained his release and was about to join the Meadow Lane club for the huge salary of up to £4,500. The Wolves directors referred to his 'earnest request for release' and the *Express and Star* cited 'private and personal reasons' in his letter to the board. 'I can assure you we shall part on the friendliest terms,' he insisted.

Whether or not it was relevant, the team were having a bad season. In the first league section until Christmas they won only five out of 18 games and were in the bottom ten of the 50 clubs. The second half under Ted Vizard from QPR, a Welsh international and veteran of the 1923 FA Cup Final, was worse with three wins out of 20 – ironically the same record as Notts under Buckley. The move never really worked out for the Major and he left after two years for Hull City.

In April, the biggest crowd anywhere for many years, 133,000 at Hampden Park, saw England beat Scotland for the third time that season, with two players each from Wolves and

Stoke involved: Cullis's club-mate Frank Taylor appearing at left-back, with Frank Soo at wing-half behind Matthews. The elegant Soo was born in Buxton of English-Chinese parentage and won nine wartime caps in all before falling out with Stoke manager McGrory, just as Matthews had done. Earlier in the season England routed the Scots 8-0 at Maine Road, which Cullis, at centre-half as usual, described as the finest football he had ever seen.

* * *

By **1944/45** the country was growing more optimistic after the Normandy landings in May and then the liberation of Paris in August, even though it would be another nine months until VE Day. But crowds picked up again and for the first time all the West Midlands clubs took part in competitive football as no fewer than 54 teams entered the North League.

Birmingham's directors looked forward to a new era by announcing at the annual meeting of October 1944 that the club would henceforth be known as Birmingham City – a little belatedly, some might say, as Queen Victoria had granted city status as long ago as 1889. The same meeting revealed plans for a handsome new cantilevered stand, the first of its kind, though it would not be built until the early 1950s.

There was still time for St Andrew's to be badly hit by fire in 1945 as the Germans made their last desperate assaults with Doodlebugs and flying bombs. But Blues supporters were cheered up at the end of the season by the appointment of Harry Storer, who had done a good job as manager of Coventry. He signed off at Highfield Road with a 3-1 win over Villa, which made some sort of amends for the 9-2 defeat at Villa Park the previous week. And he would be back there in 1948.

Walsall were also under new management when Harry Hibbs, the old St Andrew's hero, left the Blues after having made 388 appearances between the posts.

As cup holders, Villa lasted only one round, losing to Wolves, who then beat Birmingham but lost 4-3 on aggregate in the northern semi-final to the eventual winners, Nat Lofthouse's Bolton.

Albion were only moderate with 18 wins in 50 games, Richardson appearing just four times before moving on for a successful year with Shrewsbury Town. His final goal, at Northampton, gave him a century in wartime matches to go with 202 in the Football League and 26 in the FA Cup.

Stoke saw a bit more of Matthews with 15 games but were well beaten twice by Manchester United in the cup, and Port Vale, returning at last, won only 13 of their 49 games and finished bottom of the 54 clubs in the second half of the season.

Vale had survived a financial crisis by agreeing to sell their Old Rec ground to the local council for £13,000 and leasing it back. As the *Staffordshire Sentinel* described it, 'The Hanley club faced a crisis. Force of circumstances compelled the club to sell its ground to Stoke-on-Trent Corporation. And it was only after long negotiation and contention that the City Council agreed to allow the club the continued use of the ground at a rental, for a period of three years. That respite is to be utilised in an attempt to bring to fruition a scheme for a new ground.'

The move would take another five years. Meanwhile they did give some games to a young Ronnie Allen, as well as a distinguished guest in Irish international (and future World Cup manager) Peter Doherty.

In April another capacity crowd saw England hammer Scotland 6-1 at Hampden with three Stoke players in the team, Soo and Matthews being joined by Neil Franklin, who had succeeded Cullis at centre-half. There had been caps too at various times for Westcott and Mullen of Wolves; Villa's Broome; Albion's Len Goulden and Elliott; plus Bert Williams while still in goal at Walsall; and Coventry centre-half George Mason, the club's first England international.

The end was in sight and on 8 May VE Day was celebrated as Germany surrendered, though war went on in the Far East until the atomic bombs were dropped on Japan in early August. Of course, peace came too late for some. Wolves wing-half Eric Robinson was one of five soldiers drowned on an ill-conceived military exercise in Yorkshire. Centre-half Joe Rooney, who had made a First Division debut just before the war when Cullis was injured, was killed in an air raid in Belfast in 1941. Blues outside-left Tom Farrage died at Arnhem and Jim Olney, a centre-half who had moved from Birmingham to Swindon just before the war, was another casualty.

Football had endured a testing six years and was not quite ready to resume normal service. But the *Sentinel* concluded in its roundup of wartime sport, 'It was right and proper that our sport should go on ... supplying a much wanted need.'

6

'Champions of the World' 1946–1960

'33 trampled to death in Cup-tie disaster'
The People, March 1946

'Stoke should grab the League title today'
Daily Mirror, June 1947

'A city of Coventry's size deserves the highest grade of football. Local supporters have had great demands made on their loyalty since the end of the war.'
Coventry Evening Telegraph, April 1952

'For so long it seemed that fate had decreed West Bromwich were not to win any football honour, after being in the running for the elusive double.'
Sunday Graphic, May 1954

'Hail, Wolves "Champions of the world" now'
Daily Mail, December 1954

'Villa cannot expect excessive sympathy … because they had their chance to escape relegation but failed to take it.'
Birmingham Post, April 1959

BY THE time the 1945/46 season began at the end of August, Japan had unconditionally surrendered, the formal signing for which took place on 2 September, six years and a day after Britain declared war on Germany. One of many ways the nation expressed relief was the huge appetite for entertainment and sporting events, crowds flocking back to football to start a steep upward graph that would peak in 1948/49. It was that very enthusiasm, however, that led to **Stoke City** becoming involved in the worst tragedy seen on an English ground at that time.

Clubs had voted for one more season of regionalised football and although experiencing a moderate campaign in League North, the Potters had Stanley Matthews back in the fold, guaranteed to put thousands on the gate anywhere. So it proved at Burnden Park for the second leg of the FA Cup quarter-final against Bolton Wanderers, the previous year's War Cup winners, who had already won the first match 2-0 at the Victoria Ground.

A crowd estimated at anything up to 85,000 turned up for the game on 9 March 1946 and when a frightened youngster attempted to leave shortly before kick-off, his father unlocked an exit gate, allowing hundreds more to swarm in. The turnstiles were belatedly closed but a surge at one end, already dangerously full, caused at least two barriers to break, and the result was graphically summed up on the following day's front page of *The People*: '33 trampled to death in Cup-tie disaster'.

Stoke's Freddie Steele told how the referee, having taken the players off the pitch after a few minutes of play, went to the dressing room and said he had been asked by the Chief Constable of Bolton to continue with the game, fearing there would be 'a riot' if it was abandoned. The referee knew that spectators had died but did not tell the players, who soon realised; Matthews recalled his shock at seeing body bags at the side of the pitch. Not surprisingly the rest of the game was played out in sombre mood and ended goalless.

Former MP Moelwyn Hughes recommended in his subsequent Home Office report a check on safety standards at larger grounds, and mechanised turnstiles to track admissions, but harshly concluded that the disaster was 'inflicted by a crowd upon itself'.

There was a widespread feeling that something similar could have happened at any of the major grounds – almost all of which had three sides of terracing – where large crowds were being recorded again. On the previous Saturday the first leg of Aston Villa's tie with Derby drew Villa Park's all-time attendance record of 76,588; Derby won 4-3, then held out for a draw in the second match, and their semi-final replay against Birmingham attracted another huge audience of 80,480 to Maine Road, Manchester, four days after 65,000 saw the first match at Hillsborough. Earlier in the season there had been vast numbers too for Moscow Dynamo's historic tour of Britain, when the Midlands was unfortunate to miss out on the four matches, with two played in London plus one each in Cardiff and Glasgow.

In the league, attendances were boosted by a glut of local derbies. At a Football League EGM on 7 May 1945 – the day Germany surrendered – Birmingham's chairman Bill Camkin was among those who spoke against resuming on a national basis. Had that happened, the Blues would have been stuck in the Second Division. Like Villa, Coventry, West Brom and Wolves they were doubtless happy to be placed instead in the South League of 22 clubs; avoiding trips to the north-east, although still needing to reach Southampton and Plymouth.

The smaller clubs successfully protested that returning to the Third Division North and South would still mean too much travel – citing Norwich, for instance, going to Torquay and Cardiff – and so those divisions were further split in two geographically, playing a different competition before and after Christmas and then their own knockout cup.

The League South campaign developed into an excellent one for the West Midlands as Birmingham, Villa, Albion and Wolves all finished in the top six along with the FA Cup finalists Charlton Athletic and Derby. Indeed, Blues and Villa were champions and runners-up respectively, separated only on goal average. The decisive games turned out to be their meetings on successive Saturdays early in the new year, watched by a total of nearly 104,000. Blues, now under Harry Storer, drew their away game 2-2 and won the return 3-1. At the start of May, playing a final game three days after their rivals, they won 3-0 at Luton to seal the title. As the next day's *Birmingham Gazette* pointed out,

'Curious anomaly about this consolation prize for Birmingham, one time favourites for the double honour of League and Cup winners, is that when football reverts next season to its peace-time status, they will figure in the Second Division of the Football League. Blues won the championship by merit alone.'

Villa and Albion both scored more than 100 goals, with George Edwards claiming 39 for Villa and Albion's Ike Clarke and Billy Elliott claiming 19 each to fill the void left by Billy Richardson. Coventry were respectably placed in mid-table but in the FA Cup went out to Villa after two well-attended games.

Lower down the ladder, Port Vale were an excellent third in the first half of the Third Division South behind Queens Park Rangers and Norwich. Walsall went one better by finishing runners-up to QPR in the second section, which qualified them for the last four of the knockout cup. There they beat Bristol Rovers and in the final at Stamford Bridge lost only 1-0 to Bournemouth.

For just about all the local clubs the portents were therefore good for the resumption of normal service.

* * *

It turned out to be **Wolverhampton Wanderers** who led the Midlands challenge once the Football League resumed in its pre-war form – literally from the first day, when they hammered the team of the 1930s, Arsenal, 6-1 and should have gone on to win the First Division title. But, pipped twice for that crown, they had to wait for it until 1954, a year when their most bitter rivals West Bromwich Albion might have done the Double instead.

Half a dozen players from the 1939 FA Cup Final team were still available, augmented now by talent like youngsters Billy Wright and Jimmy Mullen, goalkeeper Bert Williams and winger Johnny Hancocks from Walsall and inside-forward Jesse Pye, a record £12,000 signing from Notts County who thrilled a Molineux crowd of 50,000 with a hat-trick on debut in that opening game with Arsenal.

Pye provided great support for Dennis Westcott, who was still good for goals – a club-record 38 – with four of them coming in a stunning 5-1 win away to leaders Liverpool in December with which Wolves replaced them at the top. Fifteen wins in 17 games put them well clear at Christmas and after a freezing winter in which snow fell somewhere in Britain for 55 successive days, the return game between that pair at Molineux on the last day of May should have given Wolves the title.

Going into it, they led the table with 56 points, ahead of Manchester United on goal average, while Liverpool and Stoke City had 55 with a game each to play. But Wolves, with Westcott out injured, froze on the day in front of another 50,000-plus crowd. They went two goals down before the interval – the second because Cullis refused to commit a 'professional' foul on scorer Albert Stubbins – and retrieved only one of them midway through the second half.

Liverpool then had to endure a fortnight's wait until Stoke finally played the last match of an extended season on 14 June, needing a win away to seventh-placed Sheffield United to take their first championship; they lost 2-1 and so the title went to Merseyside, Wolves having dropped behind United to third place with Stoke fourth.

Before playing in the Liverpool game, skipper and centre-half Stan Cullis had announced his imminent retirement, aged only 30, having become worried by suffering concussion after so much heading of heavy leather balls; after one game at Middlesbrough, where the ball became very wet, he collapsed and was in hospital for a week. He became assistant manager to Ted Vizard, who after taking the team to fifth place the following season – top scorers for the second year running – resigned over unspecified policy differences, which Vizard said had existed for some time.

Cullis, a natural leader who had captained the club aged 20 and his country at 22, was the obvious successor and any doubters who felt him too inexperienced were to be confounded by a record of three league titles, two FA Cups and what should have been at least one Double over the next dozen years. He inherited Major Frank Buckley's widespread scouting network and many of his mentor's attributes, putting equal faith in young talent and direct play, and demanding 'unswerving loyalty and 100 per cent effort'.

In his first season Wolves were again among the highest scorers, even with Westcott having left for Blackburn, as they embarked on an FA Cup run all the way to Wembley. Victories over Chesterfield, Sheffield United and Liverpool brought a quarter-final derby with West Brom, in which Mullen scored the only goal. Drawing 1-1 with the holders Manchester United in the semi-final at Hillsborough with Sammy Smyth's goal, Wolves won the Goodison Park replay 1-0 with another from the former Linfield amateur. Luckily, the final was against not their conquerors of 1939, the champions-elect Portsmouth, but Second Division relegation strugglers Leicester City, who were comfortably overcome 3-1 with Pye scoring twice and Smyth adding an individual effort described in the *Daily Mail* as 'perhaps the finest goal ever seen at Wembley'. The *Birmingham Gazette* reporter felt, 'It is no exaggeration to say that had they got five, it would have been in keeping with their display.'

1949 FA Cup Final: Wolverhampton Wanderers 3
Leicester City 1
Wolves: Williams, Pritchard, Springthorpe, Crook, Shorthouse, Wright, Hancocks, Smyth, Pye, Dunn, Mullen.
Leicester: Bradley, Jelly, Scott, W. Harrison, Plummer, King, Griffiths, Lee, J. Harrison, Chisholm, Adam.

Disappointment at going out of the FA Cup the following season in a fifth-round replay to Stan Matthews's Blackpool was quickly forgotten as another championship challenge resumed. Winning 4-1 away to Villa at Christmas with almost 70,000 packed in had started a successful run and Wolves were level on points with Portsmouth going into the final day. But although they drubbed Birmingham 6-1, Villa could not do them a favour and lost 5-1 to Pompey, who retained their title on goal average. As usual, Wanderers had scored more goals than most contenders, but also conceded more. It was exciting stuff, much appreciated by a record average crowd of over 45,000.

Two seasons spent well down the table, albeit with a 1951 FA Cup semi-final appearance (lost in a replay to Newcastle), prompted Cullis to regenerate the side. By 1952/53 they were challenging again, ending up only three points behind the champions Arsenal and would not finish outside the top six until 1961/62. Footballer of the Year and England captain Wright now had one of the future England internationals Ron Flowers and Bill Slater as his wing-half partner, with Bill Shorthouse at centre-half and a prolific inside-forward trio of young Peter Broadbent, Bilston's Roy Swinbourne and Dennis Wilshaw, who had returned after an impressive spell at Walsall in 1949, scoring a hat-trick against Newcastle in his first game back.

That trio contributed 61 goals between them in the championship season of 1953/54, backed up by a remarkable 25 from winger Hancocks. Yet for much of the season Wolves, chasing their first title, trailed Albion, who were after their second 34 years on. Mullen's goal to defeat the neighbours 1-0 at Molineux in November, watched by more than 56,000, cut the gap to a single point and Wolves went into the new year ahead. In retrospect, the shock of a home defeat in the FA Cup third round by Second Division Birmingham probably helped them, as Albion became increasingly distracted by their own cup run.

The key game was on 3 April at The Hawthorns, where Wolves, two points behind and having played a game more, snatched a crucial 1-0 win with Swinbourne scoring. Albion, preparing for the FA Cup Final, then won only one of their remaining five games so Cullis's men were virtually assured of the title even before they defeated Tottenham 2-0 at Molineux on the final day.

Having taken the maximum four points off Albion, they won the title by exactly that margin. The team, unchanged for the last five games and with Wright filling in at left-back, was: Williams; Stuart, Wright, Slater, Shorthouse, Flowers, Hancocks, Broadbent, Swinbourne, Wilshaw, Mullen.

Two adjustments Cullis made to the pre-war style were to push inside-left Wilshaw further forward as a second striker, and to make greater use of his outstanding wingers Hancocks and Mullen, who ended up with 280 goals between them before bowing out. His stated philosophy, which would be emulated 30 years later by teams like Watford and Wimbledon, was to 'send the ball into the other side's penalty area with a minimum of delay'.

Cullis also noted with satisfaction how the club's junior team were runners-up to Manchester United's Busby Babes in the first two FA Youth Cups of 1953 and 1954. At least half a dozen of them would make it to the first team. He had learnt from Buckley the value of signing players straight from school and like his mentor was therefore able to make huge profits in the transfer market; in his case almost £200,000 in ten years.

The town motto, 'Out of darkness cometh light', was particularly appropriate for the early 1950s, when Molineux's first floodlights enabled Wolves' exploits to be brought to a much wider audience. The lights were inaugurated in a series of midweek friendlies against mainly foreign opposition, starting with a South African XI in September 1953. The following season's floodlit games even led directly to the long-predicted pan-European competition for clubs. Israeli champions Maccabi, First Vienna and Moscow Spartak were followed in December 1954 by Honvéd, a team full of the Hungarian stars like Ferenc Puskás, who had humiliated England 6-3 and 7-1 in the previous 12 months.

Copying an old tactic used by Major Buckley, Cullis ordered three astonished apprentices, including a young Ron Atkinson, to flood an already heavy pitch before the game. The reason became apparent as Wolves, outplayed and 2-0 down in quarter of an hour, eventually powered their way through the mud to win 3-2. Headlines like 'Hail, Wolves "Champions of the world" now' (based on a quote by Cullis) caught the imagination of influential French sports newspaper *L'Equipe*, whose editor used it to drum up support for a European Champion Clubs' Cup which began the following season.

Wolves would have their chance in competitive European football before the end of the decade, when limitations of British style would be exposed. In the meantime there was more success. They could have retained their league title in 1954/55 but faded badly over the last 11 games to allow Chelsea a first championship with the joint lowest number of points (52) since the top division was extended to 22 clubs.

The Busby Babes then came into their own for two dominant years, before the horrors of the Munich air disaster allowed Wolves to become the country's top team again for what should have been a championship hat-trick and the Double. Swinbourne, his career cut short by injury, had been replaced by Jimmy Murray, with Norman Deeley and Bobby Mason promoted to the forward line; for almost two years England regularly fielded an entire Wolverhampton half-back line of Eddie Clamp, Wright (now a centre-half) and either Slater or Flowers.

In 1957/58 they took the title with 103 goals (Murray 29, Deeley 23) and retained it just as easily while scoring 110 (Murray 21, Broadbent 20). After the second triumph, captain Wright, told that he was likely to be replaced before long, decided to retire with 105 caps and almost 550 club games to his name. He managed the England youth and under-23 teams before a less successful spell in charge of Arsenal, returning later to the Midlands as a television executive.

In the first season without him Wolves were agonisingly close to the first Double of the 20th century. Scoring as freely as ever, they became the first team to reach 100 goals for three seasons running (adding a fourth a year later). After winning 6-4 away to Manchester City and 9-0 at home to Fulham, they hammered close challengers Burnley 6-1 at the end of March but then slipped up at home to the other contenders, Spurs. The title hat-trick could still have been theirs, but unfashionable Burnley, needing to win their final game away to City, did so 2-1. The consolation was to win a poor, one-sided FA Cup Final five days later. Having knocked out Villa 1-0 in the semi-final, Wolves beat ten-man Blackburn 3-0 with little Deeley scoring twice.

1960 FA Cup Final: Wolverhampton Wanderers 3 Blackburn Rovers 0
Wolves: Finlayson, Showell, Harris, Clamp, Slater, Flowers, Deeley, Stobart, Murray, Broadbent, Horne.
Blackburn: Leyland, Bray, Whelan, Clayton, Woods, McGrath, Bimpson, Dobing, Dougan, Douglas, McLeod.

Winning those two First Division titles meant an entry into the European Cup Wolves had helped spawn, though it did not go well. Schalke from West Germany beat them 2-2, 2-1 in the first season and after seeing off Vorwaerts of East Germany and Red Star Belgrade the following year, Wolves were given a lesson by Barcelona, who won 4-0 in Spain and 5-2 in another Molineux mudbath. Although Cullis blamed failure in Europe on his refusal to change the team's natural attacking game, one Spanish newspaper commented caustically, 'Wolves, like all

English teams, continue to play football that is 20 years behind the times.'

It seems unlikely that their supporters would willingly have swapped those 20 years for anything else.

* * *

Mid-table in the Second Division when war came, **West Bromwich Albion** had two solid seasons in seventh place on the resumption, then fought their way back into the top division for a fierce spell of rivalry with Wolves in particular.

Only by winning the 1954 FA Cup did they have the better of it but they remained formidable competitors towards the decade's end.

Already possessing two good goalscorers in Ike Clarke and winger Billy Elliott, Albion found another in centre-forward Davy Walsh who, like many of his contemporaries, played for both Northern Ireland and the Republic. He totalled 50 league goals in those first two post-war seasons and topped the list again with 23 in the promotion season of 1948/49 after Clarke had left.

That season was notable for another departure, Fred Everiss retiring after an extraordinary 46 years as secretary-manager. Jack Smith, a coach at Wolves whose playing career ended when a bus ran over his foot during a wartime blackout, was hired as team manager and achieved instant success.

With Birmingham promoted the previous year, Coventry provided the only local Second Division opposition and two crucial games against them in April attracted a combined 82,000 to see each team win 1-0. Just as importantly, Albion held their main rivals Southampton at The Dell and ensured finishing above them by winning 3-0 away to Leicester, who were facing an unlikely double as FA Cup finalists and relegation candidates.

Back in the top division, crowds reached an average of almost 39,000. Nearly 61,000 watched the 1-1 draw with Wolves at The Hawthorns, when the home team's goal was scored by new young winger Ronnie Allen, signed from Port Vale for a record £20,000. For three seasons Albion sat in the lower half of the table without suffering relegation concerns, and from 1953 their sights were set higher following the arrival as manager of the debonair Londoner Vic Buckingham.

A disciple of Arthur Rowe and Tottenham's 'push and run' style, he served an apprenticeship at Bradford Park Avenue and in his first full season at The Hawthorns led the charge towards a league title that only petered out in the last two months, once an FA Cup Final place had been secured. Earlier results included a remarkable 7-3 win at Newcastle and a hat-trick in successive home games for Allen, now moved to centre-forward.

As mentioned in the section above, losing at home to Wolves at the start of April (one of four successive derby defeats) was a serious blow and became one of five losses in the last seven games, leaving Albion four points adrift at the finish. Inside-left Johnny Nicholls scored 28 league goals, one more than Allen, who had a crucial role to play in the FA Cup.

The run to Wembley began with revenge over Chelsea for knocking them out the previous year, thanks to Ron Greenwood's own goal. Allen scored a hat-trick in the fifth-round win at home to Newcastle and found himself having an emotional reunion with his former club Port Vale in the semi-final at a packed Villa Park. Vale had a superb stonewall defence that conceded just 21 goals all season in the Third Division North and at half-time they led 1-0. But goalkeeper Ray King made a rare misjudgement in allowing Jimmy Dudley's cross to curl past him and in the last quarter of an hour Allen converted a disputed penalty in a bittersweet moment.

That proved an invaluable test of nerve for the final against Preston, who despite sitting in mid-table were made favourites, on the basis that they had ended the league campaign in fine form while Albion were throwing away the title. Additionally, most neutrals wanted Tom Finney to emulate Stanley Matthews the year before and earn an FA Cup winner's medal.

But Albion doubled up on him with Ray Barlow dropping deep to help left-back and captain Len Millard, and the Footballer of the Year was unable to influence the final the way Matthews had in 1953.

Preston nevertheless came from behind to lead when Allen's opener was overhauled by goals from Angus Morrison with a header and then Charlie Wayman, who even Finney admitted looked offside. In the 63rd minute Tommy Docherty fouled Barlow, and Allen squeezed home the penalty; just a couple of minutes before the end, winger Frank Griffin, who had been doubtful with an ankle injury, cut inside to win the cup.

'For so long it seemed that fate had decreed West Bromwich were not to win any football honour, after being in the running for the elusive double,' said the *Sunday Graphic*. The *Birmingham Gazette* praised Barlow 'at his dazzling and devastating best' and concluded, 'There was not the slightest doubt that Albion thoroughly deserved their success.'

1954 FA Cup Final: West Bromwich Albion 3 Preston North End 2
West Bromwich Albion: Sanders, Kennedy, Millard, Dudley, Dugdale, Barlow, Griffin, Ryan, Allen, Nicholls, Lee.
Preston North End: Thompson, Cunningham, Walton, Docherty, Marston, Forbes, Finney, Foster, Wayman, Baxter, Morrison.

In September came a thrilling 4-4 draw in the Charity Shield game away to champions Wolves, in which Allen scored a hat-trick, but another charity venture two months later almost had disastrous consequences. Following a specially arranged exhibition game away to Hereford United, which Albion somehow lost 10-5, manager Buckingham was involved in a serious car crash on the way home and was unconscious in hospital for a week.

From finishing 17th they slowly climbed back up the table over the next three seasons and in 1957 should have been involved in a glamorous FA Cup Final against Manchester United. Knocking out the powerful Blackpool and Arsenal on the way, Buckingham's team reached the semi-final in the company of both Villa and Blues. With the West Midlands feverishly excited, Birmingham went out to Matt Busby's Babes but at neutral Molineux, Albion, with two Brian Whitehouse goals, were two minutes from Wembley when Villa's Peter McParland equalised for the second time. The *Birmingham Post* (which had now taken over the *Gazette*) reported that Villa could not play as badly again, but in the replay at St Andrew's they did and still won 1-0. Allen was injured during the game, new England cap Derek Kevan missed three chances and, in the desperate finale,

Joe Kennedy headed against the bar.

In September that year floodlights were installed at The Hawthorns, and the club followed Wolves in inviting over some exotic foreign opposition. The most memorable game was against the Russian army team CDSA, a return match from the one played in Moscow that summer. Broadcast live on BBC television, it attracted over 55,000 to see Albion win 6-5 in driving rain. Their goalscorers were significant: Allen; a hat-trick from 'The Tank' Kevan, who had followed Buckingham from Bradford; and future England team-mates and management partners Bobby Robson and Don Howe. The latter trio, also on the scoresheet in a 9-2 win over Manchester City, all played for England at the 1958 World Cup finals, along with half-backs Clamp, Wright and Slater of Wolves; the two clubs provided over half the first-choice team. Wanderers were at their peak, but Albion also enjoyed three excellent seasons in finishing fourth, fifth and fourth again before and after Buckingham left for undisclosed 'personal reasons', later moving to Holland and taking Ajax to the Dutch title.

Meanwhile the ground the Baggies and their supporters most enjoyed visiting was St Andrew's, where in three successive seasons from 1957–60 they drubbed the Blues 5-3, 6-0 and 7-1.

* * *

Knocked off their perch as the Midlands' leading club in the mid-1930s, **Aston Villa** took an awfully long time to climb back on to it. In the post-war years they were generally to be found about a dozen points behind the champions, until a period of four eventful seasons towards the end of the 50s: finishing only five short of the winners Chelsea in 1955, then surviving a relegation scare, winning the FA Cup and only two years after Wembley sinking briefly back into the Second Division.

Pre-war stalwarts like Frank Broome and Eric Houghton would not last long – although tough-guy left-back George Cummings did three more full seasons – and Scottish wing-half Alex Massie now took over as manager. League football resumed with two home defeats in three days to Middlesbrough and Everton, but a final placing of eighth was improved to sixth the following year after Trevor Ford was bought from Swansea to lead the attack and the scorers. George Edwards's rate dropped off but he did have a role to play that second season in one of the most famous of all Villa Park FA Cup ties.

In the third round on 10 January 1948, Edwards scored within 13 seconds against Matt Busby's Manchester United, who responded with magnificent football to lead 5-1 by half-time. Villa 'won' the second half, recovering to 5-4 before United's Stan Pearson added the tenth goal of an unforgettable game. 'The score perhaps hides the terrific fight Villa put up in the second half,' said the *Gazette*, tipping United to go on to Wembley, where they duly won one of the best post-war finals 4-2 against Blackpool.

George Martin became manager for three uneventful seasons, although his Irish namesake Con Martin, an experienced Gaelic footballer, had an unusual 1951/52 campaign: he played the opening game in defence as normal, then took over from injured goalkeeper Joe Rutherford and started 27 matches between the posts as Villa finished sixth.

Two seasons in mid-table led to the return in September 1953 of Eric Houghton, who had been playing for and then managing Notts County. Danny Blanchflower had now brought his cultured wing-half play from Barnsley and future FA Cup Final captain Johnny Dixon was the prime goalscorer from inside-left, Ford having been moved on to Sunderland for a British record £30,000.

Another important figure, Northern Irish winger Peter McParland, made his debut in September 1952 at the age of 18, and was a regular for the improved 1954/55 campaign in sixth place, which also featured five attempts at settling an FA Cup fourth-round tie against Doncaster Rovers – ultimately lost to the Second Division side.

Blanchflower, however, moved on to Tottenham in search of greater things, summing up some years later the way he felt at the time: 'Things were happening over at Wolverhampton; Birmingham City were fighting their way out of the Second Division; and there was plenty of promise at nearby West Bromwich. But nothing seemed to disturb the sleepy serenity of Villa Park.'

The grand old ground was anything but serene during 1955/56, when relegation was avoided only by winning the last three games. In a dreadful start only one of the first 14 was a victory and Villa were still bottom with ten matches to play. West Brom, of all people, arrived at Villa Park on the final day with no intention of helping their neighbours but also with nothing to play for, and were duly despatched 3-0, leaving Villa safe on goal average alone.

The following season proved far more successful: tenth place in the First Division, Jackie Sewell proving his worth as a goalscoring inside-forward and a first decent FA Cup run since the 1953 quarter-final had been lost at home to Everton. It required replays against Luton Town and Burnley to join Birmingham and West Brom in the last four, where, as described above, McParland's two goals thwarted Albion at Molineux. In the replay Billy Myerscough, signed cheaply from Walsall, scored the only goal.

Like Albion against Finney's Preston in 1954, Villa had few neutrals on their side at Wembley, where the opposition was provided by Manchester United's highly popular young team. Already champions for the second successive season, and European Cup semi-finalists, they were hot favourites for the Double – the first since Villa's in 1897.

The *Birmingham Post*'s football correspondent was one of the few to oppose them, loyally suggesting, 'Where Villa score (and these are the qualities which should see them through) are in their exceptional fitness and remarkable team spirit. Given reasonable fortune, I expect to see them frustrate United's hopes.'

Fortune and huge controversy were factors on the day, McParland being the key figure. Goalkeepers holding the ball were considered to be fair game for a shoulder charge and, as photographs show, the winger was at least a yard away when he launched into one on United's Ray Wood after only six minutes. The referee gave a free kick but said afterwards the challenge was 'not a malicious foul, just a bit too robust'. The result was a fractured cheekbone for Wood, whose team played for most of the game with ten men.

Jackie Blanchflower could do nothing to prevent his Northern Ireland team-mate scoring twice in the second half, Tommy Taylor's late header coming too late to prevent Villa achieving a record seventh FA Cup win.

1957 FA Cup Final: Aston Villa 2 Manchester United 1
Aston Villa: Sims, Lynn, Aldis, Crowther, Dugdale, Saward, Smith, Sewell, Myerscough, Dixon, McParland.
Manchester United: Wood, Foulkes, Byrne, Colman, Blanchflower, Edwards, Berry, Whelan, Taylor, Charlton, Pegg.

United had revenge of a sort the following October by winning 4-0 in the Charity Shield and 4-1 in the league. But by the time they visited Villa Park in March 1958 the Busby Babes had been decimated at Munich, wing-half Stan Crowther had switched sides and Villa had an important new signing in Gerry Hitchens, who scored in their 3-2 win.

In joining from relegated Cardiff City the blond centre-forward assumed he was bettering himself, but after scoring 26 goals in his first season and a half he found his new team dropping down to join the Welsh club in the Second Division. Losses by 7-2 and 5-2 to West Ham and Portsmouth respectively early in 1958/59 suggested all was far from well and Eric Houghton was sacked. After an improvement in the spring under new man Joe Mercer and an unlucky FA Cup semi-final defeat by Nottingham Forest, the run-in was disastrous: the last nine games brought five defeats and four draws. Worst of all it was Albion, hoping to finish third with a win, who administered the *coup de grâce* with a 1-1 draw in front of a 48,000 Hawthorns crowd on a wet Wednesday night. But had Ronnie Allen not scored in the last couple of minutes to equalise Hitchens's goal, Villa would have stayed up on goal average instead of Manchester City.

'Villa cannot expect excessive sympathy, not so much because their position has been gradually weakening over the years, but because they had their chance to escape relegation but failed to take it,' wrote the *Post*'s correspondent. He was pessimistic, however, in suggesting that lack of strength in the reserve team meant they 'obviously have not the players to get back to the First Division in a hurry'.

It took only 12 months, during which Charlton Athletic, losing their goalkeeper to injury, were beaten 11-1 with five goals by Hitchens, who finished with 23, only one ahead of McParland; Bobby Thomson, the new signing from Wolves, weighed in with 20. As well as the championship title, there was even a second successive FA Cup semi-final defeat, this time lost 1-0 to Thomson's former club.

Villa were back where they belonged, but by the end of the next decade, new depths would be plunged.

* * *

Thanks to the old enemy Aston Villa, **Birmingham City** had the distinction of becoming the first English club to compete in European competition.

In the 1950s, FA secretary Stanley Rous was keen on using football to improve international relations across the continent and wanted British teams involved. The Inter-Cities Fairs Cup, as its cumbersome name indicated, was designed for representative teams from across Europe, with matches ideally taking place at the same time as trade fairs in the respective cities. Neither idea proved particularly practical, although it was a London XI drawn from six different clubs that got the ball rolling by winning 5-0 away to a Basel XI in June 1955. England's second city was also invited to enter, but as Villa apparently showed no interest in a joint team, Blues went into battle on their own, setting off for Milan and Zagreb in May 1956 shortly after finishing sixth in the First Division and losing the FA Cup Final to Manchester City.

Seven of the Wembley team and four reserves took the field against Inter Milan, holding the Italians to a goalless draw and going on to beat Dinamo Zagreb with the only goal, scored by Eddie Brown. A livewire forward popular wherever he went, Brown had played for Preston, Southampton and Coventry, clubs where his habits included saluting any policeman who returned the ball or shaking hands with a corner flag. He scored again in the December return against Dinamo, a 3-0 win with more than 40,000 present, and Blues then won the three-team group by beating Inter 2-1.

In the semi-final in October 1957 they won an exciting game 4-3 against Barcelona, then lost the return 1-0 with three minutes to play and were beaten 2-1 in a play-off in neutral Basel. 'Barcelona too fast and accurate' was the *Post* headline but defeat proved no disgrace as Barcelona went on to demolish the London XI 8-2 on aggregate in the final.

In the next tournament, also stretching over two years, Blues did even better by reaching the final after seeing off Cologne, Dinamo again and Union Saint Gilloise of Belgium. Unfortunately, Barcelona, who had beaten Wolves 9-2 on aggregate in the European Cup a couple of months earlier, stood in the way once more and, after a goalless draw that brought 40,000 to St Andrew's, the Spaniards won the second leg in May 1960 4-1 with what the *Post* called 'a superb display'. But the overall experience was enjoyable enough for the club to enter for the next two seasons as well (see Chapter 7).

Domestically, it looked for a while as if City would join Sheffield Wednesday as a club notorious for yo-yoing between the top two divisions. In the end they were promoted twice and relegated once between 1948 and 1955, as well as reaching one FA Cup Final and two other semi-finals during the 1950s to add to the European experience.

On the back of a fine 1945/46 season, winners of the South League and FA Cup semi-finalists, Blues were clearly going to be strong contenders for promotion from the Second Division and after finishing third in 1946/47 they were champions the following year, with the highly unusual record of more points (59) than goals (55). It was the defence that got them there, conceding a mere 24 times, with 21 clean sheets. That formula proved unsuccessful at the higher level, however, and after scoring only 36 and 31 in successive seasons they went back down again.

Harry Storer had made way as manager for Bob Brocklebank, a gentlemanly Londoner known as 'The Toff', who had played for Villa before the war. The desperate measure of moving Cyril Trigg from full-back to centre-forward again did the trick for the 1950/51 season, in which he was top scorer as Blues finished fourth and were close to Wembley, losing only 2-1 to Blackpool in a replayed semi-final at Goodison Park. 'The most telling factor was the masterly brilliance of Stanley Matthews,' reported the *Birmingham Gazette*.

The following season should have brought promotion again but somehow losing the penultimate game 5-0 against lowly Notts County meant finishing third, missing out to Cardiff on goal average.

Arthur Turner, a former Blues captain, took over as manager in November 1954 to inspire a Second Division title win in stark contrast to the defensive triumph of 1948. In his second and third home games City beat Port Vale 7-2 and Liverpool 9-1, and five players ended the season with double figures, led by Peter Murphy's 20. It was still the tightest of finishes, Turner's men needing to win their final game at Doncaster to make sure of going up; they did so by 5-1 to take the championship on goal average from Luton and Rotherham, with Leeds just one point behind. It was the only time the top three have finished level on points.

Now the club settled in for one of their longer stays in the top division, which would last for ten years. In the first of them they finished sixth, with Noel Kinsey, Brown and Murphy a prolific inside-forward trio whose goals also carried Blues to the FA Cup Final – without playing a home game. Picking off Torquay 7-1 and Leyton Orient 4-0, they were too good for sterner opposition in Albion at The Hawthorns and Arsenal at Highbury. Sunderland were next to go, by an unexpectedly comfortable 3-0 in the Hillsborough semi-final, which led to a typical long wait for the final against Manchester City, who finished one point above them in fourth place.

During that seven-week period the teams met in the league at Maine Road for a 1-1 draw. Blues cannily made six changes for the game but the Manchester side left out Don Revie, who although on the transfer list was central to their tactical plan in the final. Taking a leaf from the Hungarian team that had twice demolished England, they used him as a withdrawn centre-forward, with inside-forwards Joe Hayes and Jackie Dyson in the main striking positions.

With eight of the team beaten by Newcastle in the previous year's final, they received the benefit of an early goal by Hayes, equalised by Kinsey within quarter of an hour. In the second half Dyson and Bobby Johnstone gave City a cushion, and they held on despite German goalkeeper and former POW Bert Trautmann being groggy from a blow to the head while saving at Murphy's feet. When he belatedly visited hospital four days later, he was found to have a broken neck.

It was 'a match packed with entertaining football', the former Manchester City goalkeeper-turned-journalist Frank Swift wrote, although the *Daily Mirror*'s Peter Wilson felt 'the winners were so superior for five-sixths of the game'.

The tradition of losing finalists returning to win the following season did not materialise in 1957. Blues lost 2-0 to Manchester United in the semi-final, thereby missing out on a local derby at Wembley against Villa. They were comfortable in mid-table until the final season of the decade, finishing only two points clear of relegation after a 7-1 home defeat by Albion, but also suffered a tragedy with the death of full-back Jeff Hall.

First-choice right-back for Blues since breaking into the side in autumn 1954, Hall played in every England game for two full seasons from 1955–57, until losing his place to Midlands rival Don Howe of Albion. After a 1-1 draw at Portsmouth in March 1959 he complained of feeling exhausted from what he believed to be flu, but it turned out to be polio; within 15 days he was dead. His legacy was that the death of a fit young footballer caused proper awareness of the dangers of polio and a hugely increased take-up for vaccination.

* * *

Just over a year on from the Burnden Park disaster of March 1946, **Stoke City** should have been crowned English champions for the first time. Would they have done it had Stanley Matthews buried the hatchet with manager Bob McGrory instead of leaving before the end of the season, having played only 23 league games? It seems quite possible.

Unfortunately, the effect of the war years had not been to bring the two men any closer. Instead it cemented Matthews's feelings for Blackpool, where he was now living, having bought a guest house with his wife.

In a slow start to the 1946/47 season the mainly local Potters team took only one point from four games before stringing half a dozen wins together in succession. But Stan missed seven of those matches with injuries. After taking part in a practice match ahead of the eagerly awaited next game at Arsenal in October, he declared himself fit and was not pleased when McGrory – possibly seeing the chance to make a point – said he would not be in the team at Highbury. Matthews said he would certainly not be turning out for the reserves as suggested, and once the press got hold of the story, the rift deepened.

With the team going well in the second half of the season matters were then smoothed over until the next little crisis just after Easter. On a run of only one defeat (away to Wolves) in a dozen games, Stoke should have been pulling together for the run-in to a season extended into June because of the bad weather. Instead, headlines like 'Matthews Mystery Crops Up Again' were increasingly common, that one appearing in the *Daily Herald* on the morning of a home game with Brentford on 19 April after its reporter was unable to obtain confirmation that the great man would be playing.

Stan discovered that he had not been listed in the programme and was only included in a 3-1 win because of an injury to Albert Mitchell. 'Fed up and unhappy', he persuaded the board to sell him to Blackpool at the end of the season. Although the news immediately leaked out, what seems extraordinary is that Stoke, having agreed a fee of £11,000, allowed the move to happen when they still had three games left. Blackpool had finished their programme and were out of contention (they finished fifth) but after the matches on 3 May the four teams above them could still win the title: Wolves had 53 points, Stoke 52, Manchester United 51 and Liverpool with an extra game in hand had 50.

The transfer was agreed on 10 May in a Glasgow hotel after Matthews played there for Great Britain against a Rest of Europe team. In a long statement to the *Sentinel* published that evening, he mentioned his business interests in the seaside hotel as a reason for leaving but also admitted, 'There have been disturbing influences behind the scenes which have increased this season.' He concluded, 'I only hope that Stoke succeed in their efforts to win the championship this season.'

But instead of helping them by appearing in the team's next two crucial games at home to Sunderland (0-0) and away to Villa (1-0), he then went off on tour with England to Switzerland and Portugal.

Wolves' home defeat by Liverpool, mentioned earlier in this chapter, meant Stoke could still take the title with a victory away to sixth-placed Sheffield United, who had knocked them out of the FA Cup, in a match finally played on Saturday, 14 June, more than a fortnight after the Villa game. 'Stoke should grab the league title today' headlined the *Daily Mirror*.

In an exciting start each team scored in the first five minutes, John Pickering for United and Alex Ormston for Stoke. Walter Rickett restored the home side's lead soon after half-time and for all their late pressure on a rain-sodden pitch, the Potters 'could not complain' at a 2-1 defeat, the *Sentinel* reported. By Monday the tone had softened: 'They played well enough to win any ordinary match, but Saturday's game was no ordinary match, just as it had not been an ordinary season.'

Having finished fourth for the second time in 11 years to equal their club record, the Potters could not expect they would never do so again in almost 75 years. As for the absurd notion that Stanley Matthews would return to play for them more than a decade later, see the next chapter.

He was back at the Victoria Ground in Blackpool's colours at Christmas and received a fine reception from the biggest crowd of the season at almost 48,000 with thousands more locked out. It was a poor, injury-stricken campaign, however, for Stoke, who ended up grateful to finish six points above relegation. Freddie Steele was one of the injury victims, breaking a leg in September, before moving on to Mansfield Town. In 1950 the Potters were in the bottom four, in 1952 the bottom three and a year after that with former Wolves full-back Frank Taylor taking over from McGrory came relegation – three days before Matthews finally won the FA Cup with Blackpool.

In a fearsomely tight finish the bottom ten clubs were separated by a mere seven points, but Stoke were one behind Manchester City, Chelsea and Sheffield Wednesday, with only Derby beneath them.

By that time they had lost a key player whose departure for foreign climes in the summer of 1950 caused a national sensation. Neil Franklin, having played at centre-half in every one of England's 27 full internationals since the war, went to play for Independiente of Bogota and huge financial rewards in the outlawed Colombian league, taking Matthews's replacement at outside-right, George Mountford, with him. Franklin lasted six games, admitted his mistake and returned but never played for England or Stoke again, joining Hull City. Mountford stayed for a full season and also served a brief suspension before returning to the Stoke team until a 1953 move to Queens Park Rangers.

In the FA Cup the Potters had knocked out Blackpool – Matthews and all – with a Mountford goal in 1949 and two years later came through two close and passionate derbies in the third round with Port Vale, who forced a 2-2 draw at the Victoria Ground before submitting to the only goal two days later, by Frank Bowyer – top scorer for the third year running.

While Stoke were finishing only halfway up the Second Division in 1953/54, Vale were taking the Third Division North by storm, which meant a resumption of league derbies the following season for the first time in 21 years. A 47,000 crowd watched a goalless draw at the Victoria Ground in September and the Potters won the return in April 1-0. That win was not quite enough to secure promotion, just fifth place, two points behind the leading pair. League aspirations had not been helped by no fewer than five meetings with Bury in the FA Cup third round.

The following year Vale even finished one place above them, and the rest of the decade was a vain struggle in the quest for a return to the top division. Brighter moments included, literally, the introduction of floodlights for Vale's visit in October 1956; winger Tim Coleman scoring seven of the eight goals at home to Lincoln later that season; and beating holders Aston Villa in an FA Cup second replay the following one.

At the end of the 1959/60 campaign Stoke were 17th, which cost Taylor his job. His assistant Tony Waddington took over but it would take the return of the prodigal son 18 months later to set up a 1960s revival.

* * *

After six modest post-war seasons in the middle of the Third Division South, **Port Vale**'s fortunes suddenly took off when they were moved to the northern section in 1952 against the directors' wishes.

Under the former Liverpool forward and Lancashire fast bowler Gordon Hodgson, and with star forward Ronnie Allen sold to West Brom, they were playing by then in a ground originally supposed to be 'The Wembley of the North'. But the more grandiose plans for the new stadium in Burslem were slowly dropped as costs expanded. The proposed capacity of 70,000 at Vale Park (for a club whose average crowd in the first post-war season was about 10,500) was reduced to a more realistic 40,000 and three-quarters of that number came to the opening game against Newport on 24 August 1950.

Persistent drainage problems were an issue and denied the club what would certainly have been their best gate of the season after drawing an exciting FA Cup third-round tie 2-2 away to Stoke. The replay also had to be played at the Victoria Ground, where in front of another 40,000-plus crowd, Bowyer's last-minute goal took the Potters through. 'Port Vale, rugged, full of fight and great hearted triers, took most of the honours,' said the *Birmingham Gazette*.

The league game against Bristol Rovers over Christmas also had to be moved to Stoke's ground, and so many other home games were postponed that Vale were forced to play five of them in the space of 11 days, the match against Exeter attracting only 2,630. A typical finish in 12th place was followed by a summer tragedy when manager Hodgson died of cancer, aged 47.

After an unhappy interim period under Ivor Powell in the new season, former Stoke City hero Freddie Steele returned to the Potteries from Mansfield Town as player-manager. He lifted a floundering team from bottom of the table to 13th and after stopping playing began to construct the 'Steele defence' or 'Iron Curtain' that would bring the club to national prominence.

In 1952/53 they had the second-best defensive record in the country and missed out on the Third Division North championship to Oldham Athletic by only one point. Allowing Oldham a late equaliser at Vale Park on Easter Saturday turned out to be the key moment.

The extraordinary season that followed, however, became the greatest in the club's history as the defence tightened up even further, taking Vale to the championship by 11 clear points and an FA Cup semi-final. To put the achievement of goalkeeper Ray King and his defenders into perspective, the champions of the other three divisions – Wolves, Leicester and Ipswich – conceded

56, 60 and 51 goals respectively; Vale let in 21, while playing four games more than the top two leagues.

If Vale Park was not, after all, the Wembley of the North, it deserved the old cliché of 'fortress'. By the end of February, Hartlepools were the only one of 14 visiting teams to score a goal there. The final tally was five conceded at home, one of several new Football League records, including the 21 overall and no fewer than 30 clean sheets. There were only three league defeats in 46 games, all of them on long trips to the north-east – at Gateshead, Hartlepools and Workington.

Restricting the opposition so effectively meant that Vale rarely needed to score many. Their total of 74 (22 of them to Basil Hayward) was perfectly respectable but eight teams in the division scored more. Not surprisingly the league title was effectively wrapped up with five games to spare. A Good Friday crowd of almost 27,000 came hoping to see a repeat of the previous home game – a 7-0 win over Stockport – but in the event a goalless draw against Southport was sufficient, as theoretical challengers Barnsley lost 6-0 the same day.

By then a glorious FA Cup run was also over. It began modestly but took off in the fourth round with a 2-0 win away to Cardiff City, who were halfway up the First Division. The reward was a home game against holders Blackpool, bringing Stanley Matthews back to take on the club he once supported and would later manage. 'Blackpool Never Looked Like Beating The Vale' was *The People*'s headline next day, recording, 'Little was seen of Stan Matthews. In fact he was outshone by his opposite number, 21-year-old Colin Askey.'

Inside-right Albert Leake, emerging as a key goalscorer in the competition, got both for a deserved win in front of a 42,000 crowd. He was the man to settle the quarter-final as well with the only goal away to Leyton Orient of the Third Division South.

Now for West Bromwich Albion, chasing a First Division and FA Cup Double, at Villa Park in the last four. It was Leake again who gave Vale a shock lead and dreams of Wembley just before half-time. The equaliser was credited to Jimmy Dudley's curling cross, though it came off the head of skipper Tommy Cheadle, who King said was too deaf to hear his shout and leave it. Vale supporters are aggrieved to this day by the penalty awarded in the 70th minute when Cheadle's foul on George Lee appeared to be outside the penalty area. Ronnie Allen, of all people, converted the spot-kick in what he called 'the most difficult moment of my career'.

'Petrified Albion pulled out of their semi-final trance just in time to beat perky, punch-packing Port Vale,' said the alliterative *Daily Herald*, while Steele sportingly agreed that 'perhaps promotion is more important'.

Once it was achieved, the manager found that a lack of attacking power made life difficult at a higher level. Scoring 48 was the second lowest in the division and the Iron Curtain was suddenly found to be of less resistant material, being breached 71 times. Despite an average home crowd of over 20,000 it meant finishing in the bottom six, although the following season brought rare bragging rights locally: in October Stoke were beaten for the first time since 1932 and Vale's 12th place was one above them.

After that it all went wrong during a miserable 1956/57 campaign, when the once impregnable defence conceded 101 goals. Steele resigned in January, shortly before a 7-1 home defeat by Nottingham Forest, and the Valiants were doomed to relegation long before a 2-2 draw at home to Stoke in the final game.

Back in the Third Division South, finishing in the bottom half of the table meant being placed in the new Fourth Division for its inaugural 1958/59 season, where a rejuvenated Vale, having won a friendly against West Brom to inaugurate their new floodlights, proceeded to win the title. After a slow start, they knocked in a club-record 110 goals (Stan Steele 22) in the amber and black stripes that lasted half a dozen seasons. 'Port Vale relied on youth,' recorded the FA's yearbook. 'The average age of their regular team was in the early twenties.'

Up in the now-national Third Division, 80 goals guaranteed a mid-table spot in a season most notable for Vale Park's record attendance; 49,768 watched the 2-1 FA Cup fifth-round defeat by Aston Villa.

* * *

From fourth place in the Second Division just before the war and classic battles with Aston Villa in front of huge crowds, to the Third Division South by 1952 and then the new Division Four represented a sad decline for **Coventry City**. The result – or to some extent the cause – was a rapid turnover of managers.

The first of them departed in tragic circumstances. Dick Bayliss, long-serving assistant to Harry Storer, took over when the latter departed for Birmingham City in 1945, but early in 1947 he fell ill after a scouting trip and died in April, aged 47. As if in tribute, the team revived, lanky Welsh forward George Lowrie scoring 17 goals in the last dozen games to lift them to eighth place.

New manager Billy Frith, a pre-war City player who had briefly managed Port Vale, was unable to keep Lowrie from Newcastle United's clutches after a second season in which his goals – 18 in 22 games – ensured a mid-table berth, and after a bad start to the 1948/49 campaign Frith made way for Storer's return from St Andrew's. He claimed to regret ever having left 'my club' but as is often the case the second spell did not live up to the first.

One encouraging period had City top of the table at the end of 1950, watched by regular crowds of 30,000-plus, but too many defeats in the second half of the season ended any promotion hopes. It was a badly missed opportunity and the following season an early 7-1 defeat at Swansea indicated the way the wind was blowing. Storer used 34 players in a vain attempt to stave off relegation, which was confirmed by defeats at home to champions Sheffield Wednesday and away to Leeds.

The Wednesday game was watched by 36,331, underlining once again the club's potential. An editorial in the *Coventry Evening Telegraph* insisted, 'A city of Coventry's size deserves the highest grade of football. Local supporters have had great demands made on their loyalty since the end of the war.'

That loyalty was soon tested in the Third Division South and average gates dropped by 9,000. A younger team featured Reg Matthews in goal and Eddie Brown as centre-forward and leading goalscorer, but failing to win any of the last eight games and then a moderate start to the 1953/54 season led to Storer resigning. 'I have not failed,' he said, blaming a lack of investment in new players and warning, 'While this attitude continues, Coventry City will never be anything but a small club achieving far less than its potential.'

The club's ambition could hardly be faulted when in the summer of 1955 they recruited not one but two manager-coaches with a Europe-wide reputation. Liverpudlian Jesse Carver and Yorkshireman George Raynor had been working for leading Italian clubs and in Raynor's case, the Swedish national team that finished third in the 1950 World Cup. Unfortunately the reality of football in England's third tier was something very different. Carver felt he had made a mistake almost immediately and left four months into the new season, and when Raynor was demoted to coach at the end of it after finishing eighth in the table, he returned to take charge of the Sweden team – and led them to a World Cup Final two years later.

A legacy remained, however. 'They introduced new training and playing methods which at first intrigued and then completely won over their players,' wrote Midlands journalist Peter Morris. 'And they injected into the club a vast enthusiasm for ball-work and practice which had been unknown before.'

The 1957/58 campaign was a critical one for all lower-division clubs, who at the end of it would be placed in either the new Third or Fourth Divisions. After a bad start, Billy Frith returned to replace the unsuccessful Harry Warren and fortunes briefly improved. Following a 6-1 victory over Exeter in November, the match programme's resident poet wrote, 'We trust that they will do it more, and not talk of Division Four.' Alas, going from Boxing Day until mid-March without another league win proved too great a handicap and City, 19th, were destined for the lowest level of the Football League.

From unpromising beginnings in places like Oldham and Gateshead, it proved the making of them. Inside-right Ray Straw from Derby formed a prolific partnership with first Jim Rogers and then George Stewart, Accrington Stanley's record goalscorer, and from autumn onwards City were not only up among the four promotion places but fancied themselves as champions – all the more so after 28,000 saw them beat main rivals Port Vale in March.

A slump of five goalless games allowed Vale to overhaul them but City rallied to secure promotion with two games to spare and finish as runners-up. Straw had 27 goals, Rogers and Stewart 28 between them in their half season each.

A second successive promotion seemed possible for a while as Frith's team set off at a gallop in the Third Division. They were still in contention after beating rivals Norwich at Highfield Road in April, watched by almost 28,000, but won only one of the remaining six games to end up a disappointing fifth, seven points short.

The other let-down during the post-war period was the inability to make any impression in the FA Cup, winning only nine ties out of 24. But an infamous cup defeat would soon cost Frith his job and pave the way for greater days ahead.

* * *

Although it had a glorious finish, this was hardly a vintage period for **Walsall**, who in one particularly embarrassing spell in the doldrums were forced to apply for re-election no fewer than four years in succession. Even the legendary Major Frank Buckley could bring about no improvement at that dismal time and his spell in charge was his last in management.

The era began well enough under the old Birmingham goalkeeper Harry Hibbs with fifth and third position in the Third Division South. There was a notable achievement at the start of the latter season when centre-forward Dave Massart, released by Birmingham, scored a hat-trick in each of the first three home games. Before the end of the campaign, however, with 23 goals in 27 games, he had joined Second Division Bury for £2,000.

Like most clubs, the Saddlers benefited from the post-war boom in attendances and that season had a record average of over 15,000. But they were always vulnerable to losing their best players and so it was later that year with Doug Lishman sold to Arsenal and Dennis Wilshaw recalled by Wolves. Losing those three key forwards led to a predictable drop in goals, crowds (below 11,000) and league position, down to a more familiar berth in the lower half of the table.

From bottom place in 1951/52, the following season was even worse with a mere seven wins and 118 goals conceded despite the arrival in April of Major Buckley, who offered his services when his contract at Leeds expired. He was expected to bring about an improvement the next season, yet, although gates increased by 50 per cent to 9,000, the team finished bottom once again as he tried out 42 different players. Among them, playing 22 times, was Jack Flavell, who understandably decided to concentrate on cricket as a Worcestershire paceman, later winning four England caps.

Finally in 1954/55 they crept above fellow-strugglers Colchester United, but although Buckley's contract ran until March 1956 the directors were understood to want a change. After he had signed several new players during the summer including another Worcestershire football-cricketer, George Dews, the Saddlers lost their first three games of the new season and the Major left. Walsall's chairman, Neville Longmore, said, 'We have disagreed on a matter of policy.'

John Love, who had been named the first assistant manager in the club's history, took over and for once four teams finished below them, in Watford, Millwall, Crystal Palace and Swindon.

The worst was over and the very worst outcome – being voted out of the Football League – was never likely, even on the fourth successive occasion. That year they still received 17 votes more than Peterborough United, regularly the most popular non-league club, who would have to wait another five years before deposing Gateshead.

Buckley had made an important acquisition in centre-half Albert McPherson from non-league Stalybridge, who would go on to play more than 350 games for the club. He was captain under new manager Bill Moore, who moved to Fellows Park in December 1957, having been Eric Houghton's assistant with the FA Cup-winning Aston Villa team.

The other particularly important player Moore inherited was centre-forward Tony Richards, once rejected by Birmingham, who became leading goalscorer six times. He hit 28 in the much-improved first season of the Fourth Division to help the Saddlers finish sixth, and then 24 out of a record 102 as they won the title in 1959/60 with four other forwards reaching double figures.

Southport were hammered 8-0, a 4-2 win at Oldham ensured promotion with seven games still to play and the championship was secured by five points from Notts County. 'After many seasons of disappointment and frequent applications for re-election to the League, the success of Walsall is all the more encouraging and refreshing,' wrote the *FA Yearbook*. Richards also had a valuable goalscoring lieutenant in left-winger Colin Taylor, enjoying the first of his three spells, who would eventually join him as the highest scorer in the club's history.

League attendances were back up to 11,000, non-league Peterborough's visit in the FA Cup set a new ground record of 20,646 – and there was more success to come.

* * *

Once the Football League stabilised in 1923 with four divisions of 22 teams each, there was no further expansion for almost 30 years. This became frustrating for an ambitious club like **Shrewsbury Town**, who began applying for election in 1935 (see Chapter 4) and in successive seasons received an increasing number of votes from six to 15 but were still always at least 20 short of what was required.

When they received a mere five votes in 1949, after having been Midland League champions twice since the war, the Third Division seemed even further away. But a year later, with attendances standing at over 40 million in the post-war boom, the Football League management committee proposed expanding the lower divisions by two extra teams each. At last the Town's moment had come. On 2 June at the annual general meeting in London they received easily the most votes for one of the northern section places and became Shropshire's first Football League club. A £100 fine from the Midland League for not submitting their resignation in time was a small price to pay, and in any case leading jockey Gordon Richards, a Shropshire lad, sent the club that amount as part of a fundraising exercise.

Scunthorpe pipped Wigan and Workington for the other place in the northern section, and like Gillingham and Colchester United in the Third Division South, the newcomers were paired together for the opening day of the season. Thus on Saturday, 19 August 1950 all four made their bow, the northern pair sharing a goalless draw at Scunthorpe. 'No goals, but Shrewsbury Town are pleased' the *Birmingham Gazette* headlined, adding, 'Both sides will perhaps find the going hard in their new sphere for a while. But if Saturday's form can be taken as any criterion there will not be a great deal to worry about.'

Only two days later a record Gay Meadow crowd of 16,000 turned up for something close to a local derby with Wrexham and saw a home win. Town conceded early on, but Scottish inside-forward Bobby Brown put them level by charging the goalkeeper over the line in classic 1950s fashion and centre-forward Arnold Jackson with 'a great left-foot drive' won the game. 'Hats and programmes went into the air as Jackson scored the winner,' reported the *Gazette*.

The old Derby and England winger Sammy Crooks had been appointed manager earlier that year, and he told his first press conference, 'Like most non-league clubs we have not much money to spend on players. My job will be to develop young talent.' Football League status did not change that, and it was a tough first season, which finished with four teams below them, after scoring a modest 43 goals. There was no extra income from the FA Cup either as Town declined to enter after being told they would have to play in the qualifying rounds; the following year they lost to the amateurs of Leytonstone but in December 1952 finally beat two Football League teams (QPR and Chesterfield), 65 years after first entering.

Being in the Third Division North meant long trips to places like Carlisle, Gateshead, Hartlepools and Barrow with little in the way of local derbies; Walsall were in the southern section as, bizarrely, were Port Vale, 40 miles north-east of Shrewsbury. So the directors were happy to be moved to the Third Division South from then on, becoming rivals to the Saddlers not just geographically but around the bottom of the table. During Walsall's dreadful spell of four successive years applying for re-election, Town were only one place above them in 1953 and also in the bottom four the following year.

Home attendances, beginning at an average 9,000, remained consistent at 7,000 to 8,000 and the team slowly progressed from 1954–57, before making an inspired signing in June 1958. Arthur Rowley, born in Wolverhampton, made little impression as a West Bromwich Albion winger just after the war and struggled in the First Division with Fulham despite being moved to inside-forward. A move back to the Midlands with Leicester City was the making of him and when they surprisingly released him only 12 months after breaking the club record with 44 league goals in a season, Shrewsbury were delighted to offer the player-manager's job.

He was a great success from the start, scoring 38 in his first season as Town increased their overall tally from 49 to 101. Going into a dramatic final ten days of the campaign Rowley's men were a point behind Exeter City for the final promotion spot from the new Fourth Division. When they led Watford 5-2 at Vicarage Road with 12 minutes left the floodlights failed and a replay was ordered; in the meantime they beat Exeter 3-0 with a Rowley hat-trick and therefore needed a draw from the rematch at Watford. Rowley, 'still one of the sharpest shots in the game' said the *Daily Herald*, scored again in a convincing 4-1 win and Town were promoted for the first time.

In the higher division they invested in floodlights, first used in November 1959, again performed outstandingly by scoring 97 goals, and finished third behind two strong teams in Southampton and Norwich City. Rowley scored 32 and although his team had peaked he was far from finished.

7
'Slump City' 1961–1970

'The Wolverhampton board of directors informed their manager Stanley Cullis that they wished to be released from their contract arrangements with him.'
Birmingham Post, September 1964

'Has there ever been a player like Sir Stanley Matthews CBE?'
Daily Mirror, April 1965

'Jimmy Hill's soccer career has gone on like a series of rocket attacks.'
Coventry Evening Telegraph, August 1967

'Midland soccer, the depression area of the game for the past eight years, has at last come back to life with the success of West Bromwich Albion in winning, if not gloriously, the FA Cup.'
Soccer Star, June 1968

'Villa must face up to the fact that they are a Third Division club. It will do them no good to look over their shoulders and become nostalgic about the past.'
Birmingham Post, April 1970

WHILE LONDON was supposedly 'swinging' in the 1960s, the second city modernised. The £8m Bull Ring shopping centre formally opened in May 1964 and construction of the M6 and 'Spaghetti Junction' – a name given by the local evening paper to the labyrinthine Gravelly Hill interchange – was well under way. But the region's football was far from progressive. Prince Philip opened the Bull Ring with Aston Villa and Birmingham City looking like wounded animals in the First Division's bottom four; 12 months later Blues and Wolves suffered relegation, with West Brom and Villa not far above them. Birmingham football was 'Slump City' according to the *Post* and the 1964/65 season was 'one of the dreariest in the history of West Midland soccer'.

Yet, difficult era as it was for most clubs, two men of stature – and now statues – set their respective cities rocking: Stanley Matthews at Stoke and Jimmy Hill at Coventry.

* * *

Stoke City had made regular attempts down the years to bring Matthews back, and their new young manager Tony Waddington saw the best opportunity yet early in the 1961/62 season. Stan, now 46, upset Blackpool by returning late for pre-season after making lucrative guest appearances in Canada, then suffered a recurrence of old knee trouble. When he was dropped after a 3-0 defeat at Arsenal in October, Stoke moved in and even as a lowly Second Division club were happy to double his Blackpool wages and pay a £3,000 transfer fee that would be recouped in his very first match.

Waddington shrewdly decided to wait for a home game and on 28 October an astonishing 35,974 turned up, paying total receipts of more than £6,500 to see Huddersfield Town beaten 3-0 – the previous home crowd had been 8,409. 'Eager fans cause miles-long jams' was the *Sentinel*'s headline. 'Matthews was cheered each time he made astute passes,' said the *Sports Argus*. Lifting the side by his mere presence, Matthews also eluded England's new left-back Ray Wilson to set up one of the goals and move the Potters away from the relegation trouble into which they had fallen.

Eighteenth the previous season, they were even lower when Stan returned but by the end of the campaign had risen to eighth. Just as important, if not more so, gates virtually doubled as thousands who had left after the old First Division days came back as regulars. Top-flight Leicester were knocked out of the FA Cup in front of more than 38,000 and almost 50,000 paid record receipts to see a 1-0 defeat by Blackburn in the fourth round.

Optimism understandably abounded for the next season and proved justified when a serious promotion challenge was launched with an unbeaten run of 18 games from late August. Waddington was forging a reputation for bringing the best out of players considered by others to be on the slide. Jackie Mudie, aged 32, and 29-year-old Dennis Viollet, the former Busby Babe, led the goalscorers; Eddie Stuart and Eddie Clamp, league championship winners with Wolves, were hardmen whose job was to exact retribution on anyone guilty of kicking the maestro.

Then in March, as football emerged from the great winter freeze, gifted inside-forward Jimmy McIlroy, another title winner, arrived after being controversially shown the door at Burnley. He scored the only goal as Stoke won a crucial promotion game at Chelsea in front of 66,199 spectators and then beat them to the championship itself with a 2-0 win over Luton, Matthews running on to a McIlroy pass to round the goalkeeper for the clinching second. It was a triumph to grace the club's centenary celebrations – almost certainly taking place five years too early – which included a friendly at home to the great Real Madrid, drawn 2-2.

After the Luton game, Matthews, who had rather sentimentally been voted Footballer of the Year again, reminded reporters that it was exactly 30 years since he last won the Second Division title with Stoke, and added, 'I have made up my mind when I will retire. It will be when I feel the rest of the team are carrying me. I don't think it has happened yet.'

So after watching his son win Junior Wimbledon that summer, back into the First Division he went for a protracted farewell of ten more league games and one FA Cup tie, spread over two seasons. In the first of them Stoke finished in the bottom six, albeit ten points clear of relegation, but reached the League Cup Final, losing 4-3 on aggregate to Leicester. In 1964/65 they ascended to mid-table with the newly knighted Sir Stanley playing just once, at home to Fulham on 6 February, aged 50 years and five days. It was his 355th official game for the Potters over a 33-year span.

In April almost 35,000 paid tribute at a glamorous testimonial match against an International XI, on the morning of which the *Daily Mirror* asked, 'Has there ever been a player like Sir Stanley Matthews CBE?'

Sadly the final chapter of his story, up the road as general manager and then team manager of his old favourites Port Vale, did not end well (see Vale section below). But he had revived Stoke from their moribund early-1960s state.

Finishing 11th, tenth and 12th without him in front of regular crowds of around 25,000 confirmed they were an established force again in the top division. Waddington continued to attract such seasoned performers as inside-forwards Peter Dobing, Roy Vernon, George Eastham and World Cup-winning goalkeeper Gordon Banks, as well as having unearthed a fine goalscorer in John Ritchie at Kettering Town.

From 1967–69, with Ritchie sold to Sheffield Wednesday – 'my biggest mistake', Waddington once said – they dipped a little, finishing only three points above relegation each time in tight finishes, but were soon back in mid-table with better to come.

* * *

In doubling his wages when rejoining Stoke, albeit to a modest £50 a week, Stanley Matthews was one of countless footballers who owed a debt to Jimmy Hill. Chairman of the Professional Footballers' Association since 1957, Hill had been as prominent as his bearded chin in bringing about an end early in 1961 to the £20 maximum wage (reduced to £17 in the summer months).

At three regional meetings in December 1960, the players voted overwhelmingly to strike the following month, although Hill found senior Aston Villa players at the Midlands meeting 'apathetic'. The Football League, led by the intransigent Yorkshireman Alan Hardaker, threatened to fill the teams with amateurs and then tried to move all fixtures on the proposed strike afternoon of Saturday, 21 January to the previous day, which alarmed clubs without floodlights. On the Wednesday of that week, an agreement was reached and strike action averted.

That summer, forced to retire as a Fulham player by a bad knee injury, Hill was still involved in preventing the Football League from keeping the retain-and-transfer system, under which clubs could hold on to a player at the end of his contract and simply not pay him if he turned down a new one. About to join a leading sports agency, Hill found his career taking a new direction instead.

Coventry City had endured an undistinguished 1960/61 season in the lower half of the Third Division, scoring 80 goals but conceding 83 in the Football League's highest-scoring post-war campaign. After a bad run in autumn 1961 with crowds down to 8,000, time was running out for their manager Billy Frith. Chairman Derrick Robins, who had met Hill through the Lord's Taverners charity and been impressed, invited him along incognito to watch the FA Cup tie at home to non-league King's Lynn, and a shocking 2-1 defeat made it all too easy to bring about a change of manager.

The club's statement openly admitted Hill had been approached the previous week about taking over. 'This is the start of something really big,' Frith's successor said. 'The potential for a top-class team in Coventry is tremendous.'

The new man won his first game 1-0 against Northampton Town on 2 December, then three of the next four as well, and steered City away from danger to finish 14th. He quickly made a mark too in areas widely neglected at the time like public relations and community involvement – lifting a long-standing ban on Coventry players talking to the press and inviting hundreds of local youngsters to a party after the Boxing Day home game.

In the summer of 1962 Robins made £30,000 of his own money available for new players. The manager knew he needed a goalscoring centre-forward and bought one in Terry Bly, who had hit 52 in Peterborough United's first Football League season (when they totalled an astonishing 134) and added 30 the year after. Three other new recruits followed to use up the full £30,000 including right-back and future manager John Sillett from Chelsea. Later on, inside-forward Ernie Machin arrived without significant damage to club finances: the fee paid to non-league Nelson was £50.

In further pursuit of a new image for a new era, Hill changed City's colours from white shirts to a smart new sky-blue strip and even helped director John Camkin write a club song to go with it, 'Let's all sing together, play up Sky Blues!' Any factory hands in Coventry car plants unfamiliar with the tune of the 'Eton Boating Song' soon grew very used to it, and increasing enthusiasm as the 1962/63 season unfolded lifted crowds to 25,000 at snowy Christmas and then higher still when football finally resumed. In the FA Cup fifth round 40,487 saw City beat Sunderland at Highfield Road with a goal by centre-half and captain George Curtis, and five days later 44,000 were packed in to see Manchester United triumph 3-1 before going on to win the trophy.

Bly scored his 30th goal of the season that March day, but Hill, ever his own man, made the hugely controversial decision to replace him before the transfer deadline with another Peterborough striker, George Hudson. Although Hudson began with a hat-trick on debut, he added only three more goals in the remaining 14 games, of which just four were won. From a position one point behind the promotion places with two games in hand, City ended up fourth, worn out by playing their last 16 matches in seven weeks. 'It ends disappointingly but new standards have been set,' Hill wrote in the *Evening Telegraph*, 'and the football world recognises Coventry City to be one of its progressive clubs.' In the longer term the manager could claim justification too for his transfer dealings: Bly, sold to Notts County, lost his touch and Hudson became the hero of the 1963/64 title-winning team.

Hill's latest proposal was that fireworks should be let off every time his Sky Blues found the net, which even under less stringent 1960s health and safety rules was deemed to be too dangerous to spectators. It would also have been an expensive plan in a season of 98 goals scored: there was an 8-1 win over Shrewsbury Town, and Hudson got a hat-trick in a 6-3 romp away to QPR. Going into the final day City were second, but leaders Crystal Palace surprisingly lost at home to Oldham and after Jimmy Tarbuck calmed down the players with some gags in the dressing room, Hudson's 28th goal in 36 games beat Colchester. A crowd of 36,901 acclaimed the Sky Blues as champions.

Another flying start had them top of the Second Division by winning the first five games of the following season. After one of them, a 5-3 success at home to Ipswich in front of almost 38,000, an enraptured *Daily Herald* reporter wrote, 'This might have been a European Cup match. Not since Wolves in their sparkling days and Spurs in their European extravaganzas have I sampled such throbbing soccer intensity.' Alas, the season petered out in tenth place and contained defeat at Villa Park in the FA Cup as well as a highly embarrassing 8-1 League Cup loss at home to Leicester. Hudson was top scorer again but in 1965/66 many felt a great chance of further promotion was undermined when he was sold to Northampton with a dozen games left. Hill promoted a young Bobby Gould and six of those games were won, but crucially three were lost and City missed out to Southampton for a place in the top division by one point.

The next season, however, Gould was given his head and the number nine shirt, inside-forward Ian Gibson eventually settled after his record £55,000 transfer from Middlesbrough, and a magnificent run of 25 games unbeaten from 19 November until the end of the season brought first promotion and then the Second Division title. Beating closest rivals Wolves 3-1 in a Midlands epic in front of a record 51,455 on 29 April effectively ensured the championship. 'The way Coventry City supporters celebrated on Saturday night, one would have thought their team had won the European Cup,' read the front page of the *Evening Telegraph* two days later.

Yet amid those celebrations, a sensation was brewing. Hill, sensing that, after rising from the Third Division so quickly, establishing City at the highest level would be a long-term project, asked for a ten-year contract. The board offered only five and neither side would compromise. News of the split – 'the best kept secret in British soccer' – did not leak out until he told his players barely 48 hours before the opening First Division game away to Burnley. Even then the real reason was kept quiet, Hill telling the *Telegraph* only about the strain of being a football manager and claiming that five and a half years in the job was long enough (when he had been demanding another ten).

The paper speculated reasonably enough that he would be moving into journalism or television after staying on until a successor was appointed. 'Jimmy Hill's soccer career has gone on like a series of rocket attacks,' said an editorial the next day. In a later autobiography the man himself wrote a little disingenuously, 'I left Coventry City FC not because I wanted to leave but because I wanted to stay.'

Unsurprisingly in those circumstances and with no new signings, the season did not begin well; there were just two wins in 11 games before Hill departed following a 4-0 defeat at Sheffield Wednesday in early October. Brian Clough and Malcolm Allison were both offered the job before it was accepted by the loquacious Irish captain of Manchester United, Noel Cantwell, who had been tipped as long-term successor to Sir Matt Busby. From bottom place at the turn of the year he kept City in with a shout of avoiding relegation and – boosted by a £100-per-match bonus and the promise of a holiday in Barbados – the players achieved it by a point with goalless draws in the last two games away to West Ham and Southampton. Former Albion and Stoke wing-half Maurice Setters and centre-forward Neil Martin had proved important signings.

The following season was a carbon copy, again finishing one point clear after a nervous wait for FA Cup finalists Leicester to play all their games in hand, from which they failed to take sufficient points.

That made a rise to sixth place in 1969/70 as unexpected as it was welcome. Away form was outstanding and a 1-0 win at Molineux in April ensured a top-six place and European football. In the inevitable turnover of players, George Curtis moved on to Villa after 538 games and a badly broken leg, but Ernie Hunt and Willie Carr were established in midfield while John O'Rourke added some valuable goals to Martin's tally. Promisingly, for the second time in three years – and with future conspiracy theorist David Icke in goal – City reached the FA Youth Cup Final. From Bury and Brentford to Bayern Munich (see next chapter) it had been quite a decade. And Jimmy Hill would be back.

* * *

In direct contrast to Coventry's exciting ascent, **Aston Villa** began to decline. They not only dropped to a level below the Sky Blues but ended the decade in the Third Division for the first time in a glorious history.

Before that came a respectable return to the top division in ninth and seventh, plus an immediate if drawn-out impact as winners of the inaugural Football League Cup. Partly because Joe Mercer's team needed two games to beat Preston, three to see off Plymouth and then three semi-finals against the favourites Burnley (1-1, 2-2, 2-1), the final against Second Division Rotherham United did not take place until the start of the following 1961/62 season.

It meant that Gerry Hitchens, whose 11th goal in the competition (out of 42 that season) eventually knocked out Burnley, had moved to Inter Milan before the final, for which new centre-forward Derek Dougan was not eligible. In their joint absence Villa gave a debut to 17-year-old Ralph Brown, who never played for them again after the shock 2-0 defeat in the first leg at Millmoor. 'Hitchens sorely missed' was the *Birmingham Post* headline, and after 68 minutes of the return game the home side were still two goals in arrears. But they took the tie to extra time and with eight minutes remaining and another unwanted replay looming, Peter McParland, the 1957 Wembley hero/villain, who had been moved to centre-forward, scored the decisive goal.

For a much-criticised competition, the healthy attendance of 30,765 in heavy rain was as welcome to the Football League as the *Daily Mirror*'s excitable description of 'the game of a lifetime'. The rival *Daily Herald* in contrast referred to 'the Cup final nobody else really cared about'.

By the time of the third final in May 1963, the second city cared greatly, for it was to be played between Villa and Birmingham. Early in the season Mercer's team would have been clear favourites but after beating the Blues 4-0 in March they lost 11 First Division games in a row. A 3-1 defeat in the first leg of the final at St Andrew's proved too much to recover and four days later in what the *Post* called 'a dreary spectacle' a goalless draw gave their neighbours the trophy. 'Villa kept plodding along in the same uninspiring style,' said the report.

There was no McParland to save them this time; he had gone to Wolves. Perhaps they should have fielded the maverick Dougan, who was so annoyed at being dropped for the last four games that a month later he moved down two divisions to join Peterborough.

Tony Hateley from Notts County, so strong in the air, was an outstanding successor, but his goals alone could not prevent decline. In three seasons he scored 81 times with no greater reward than a losing League Cup semi-final against Chelsea as Villa finished 19th (causing Mercer to resign), then 16th twice running. His most memorable performance was away to Tottenham in March 1966, scoring four times as Villa came from 5-1 down to draw. But when Chelsea signed him in October 1966 for £100,000 he left a team that sank to relegation with one win in the last 13 games and one crowd below 14,000, prompting another managerial change: Tommy Cummings for Dick Taylor.

Relegation meant joining the Blues with a welcome boost from huge derby gates but the former Burnley centre-half and Mansfield manager could not arrest the slide and left in November 1968 to herald the dramatic arrival of Tommy Docherty.

Having fallen out with Chelsea after five largely successful years, bizarrely joined Rotherham (knocking Wolves and Villa out of the FA Cup), and resigned from Queens Park Rangers after less than a month, the charismatic Scot was introduced to Doug Ellis, a Blues director who was about to change allegiance and become chairman of Villa; a club he discovered were 'close to bankruptcy' with debts of almost £200,000.

The desired uplift came with five straight wins and three crowds of over 40,000 before the end of the season; 52,772 watching Blues beaten in the final home game to ensure 18th place. 'Tommy Docherty has revitalised Aston Villa, so much so that the club and its players will be looking forward to next season with great optimism,' wrote the *Birmingham Mail.*

The manager was for once less sure, knowing that Brian Tiler from Rotherham and Bruce Rioch from Luton were the only significant signings he was allowed in revamping the squad. After starting 1968/69 with no wins and four goals from nine games, he was reduced to such wacky ideas as making 15-year-old Scot Jimmy Brown the club's youngest-ever player, then giving him the captaincy before leaving him out again.

Nothing worked and when a 5-3 home defeat by Portsmouth in January left Villa stuck at the bottom of the Second Division, Docherty became the first manager sacked by 'Deadly' Doug Ellis. The chairman – of whom Docherty later said 'he always had the best interests of Aston Villa at heart' – was predictably unmoved by a petition from 8,000 fans urging the manager's reinstatement.

His successor, former Villa and Wales captain Vic Crowe, would be more successful, but winning the last two games of the season still left them two points behind Charlton, confirming relegation to the third tier of English football along with their fellow founding Football League members Preston. The essential reason was not hard to discern: in successive seasons the goals totals of 37 and 36 were the worst in their history and the leading scorer had just six.

'Villa must face up to the fact that they are a Third Division club,' wrote Ian Willars in the *Birmingham Post*. 'It will do them no good to look over their shoulders and become nostalgic about the past.' It was difficult not to.

* * *

Like Villa, **Birmingham City** tasted some welcome cup success at the start of the 1960s – including in their case continued European experience – but the Blues preceded their neighbours into the Second Division and were not far off sharing a descent to the Third.

The Fairs Cup adventures at the end of the 1950s described in Chapter 6 went on for two more contrasting seasons. In 1960/61 an exciting run to a second successive final enlivened another eight months of struggle in the First Division. Újpesti Dózsa of Hungary (3-2, 2-1), Copenhagen (4-4, 5-0) and Inter Milan (2-1, 2-1) were all beaten before a two-legged final against AS Roma, held over to the following autumn. At the end of September 1961 the Italians forced a 2-2 draw at St Andrew's and then won the return 2-0 in October. One month on it was time for the next competition but Blues' involvement was much shorter: against the lesser-known Barcelona club, Espanyol, they suffered a 5-2 defeat in Spain and could only win the return 1-0 in front of a modest crowd of under 17,000.

There was no great interest either in the inaugural League Cup, little more than 15,000 turning up for the first home game to see a goalless draw against Second Division Plymouth, who won the replay 3-1. For the semi-final two years later at home to another lower-division team, Bury, the crowd was barely 11,000 but a 4-3 aggregate win increased interest that ballooned when Villa became the other finalists three weeks later.

Even more heavily involved in a relegation struggle than their rivals, Blues had saved themselves by winning three of their last six league matches and took that self-belief into the home leg of the final. As mentioned in the above section, they took a decisive 3-1 advantage, watched by 31,580 – only the league games with Villa (won 3-2) and Spurs had higher attendances that season. Welshman Ken Leek's opening goal was equalised by Bobby Thomson but Leek and Jimmy Bloomfield set them up nicely for the second leg. 'Brilliant goals stun timid Villa' was the headline in the *Post*. The grim return game received less favourable coverage but Blues did their job with a goalless draw in front of 37,921 to win the first major trophy of their history.

Leek's eight goals in the competition gave him 49 in 76 games since joining from Newcastle, without which relegation might have come in either season. It was an ever-present threat too in 1963/64, this time only avoided by taking three points from Villa over Easter and winning the last two matches. A humiliating FA Cup defeat at home to Port Vale did not help and manager Gil Merrick left after four seasons in which the average league position was 19th.

Joe Mallett, a coach at Nottingham Forest, was appointed, but in his first season the long-threatened relegation finally materialised, in tandem with Wolves. Blues still decided the First Division title by holding Don Revie's Leeds 3-3 in their final match, which enabled Manchester United (4-2 winners at St Andrew's a week earlier) to become champions on goal average. Stan Lynn, the old Villa full-back and penalty expert, was top scorer with ten goals – nine of them from the spot –

and the defence was pierced 96 times, including a 5-5 draw with Blackburn and a 6-1 home defeat by Chelsea.

Mallett, unlike Stan Cullis at Molineux, kept his job but early in December, with only four wins all season and crowds down to 10,000, the club announced that he would be demoted to assistant when Cullis was brought in after Christmas. Whether relieved or inspired, the team immediately won four matches in a row and ended up tenth in the table, thankful to have found a goalscorer in Geoff Vowden from Forest. The average gate of barely 14,500 was the lowest in peacetime for half a century.

Under the new management team there was an improved period of three seasons in tenth, fourth and seventh places without ever promising a return to the First Division, as well as some enjoyable cup runs and two semi-finals. In 1966/67 the Football League's first official club mascot, Beau Brummie, appeared to have every chance of walking out at Wembley when the League Cup semi-final brought a tie against Third Division leaders Queens Park Rangers; alas, the Rangers of Rodney Marsh and Les Allen romped home 4-1 at St Andrew's and 7-2 on aggregate.

In the FA Cup there were several crowds of over 50,000 and four giant-killings against Arsenal (for two seasons running), Sheffield Wednesday and Chelsea as well as draws at home to Spurs and Manchester United before heavy replay defeats. The Chelsea victory in March 1968 with a goal by Fred Pickering set up a local derby semi-final against Albion at Villa Park, in which Blues had much of the play but lost 2-0. 'Blues could surely claim that every stroke of luck was against them,' said that evening's *Sports Argus* as Albion goalkeeper John Osborne kept them at bay. And the *Post* agreed, 'Albion won because they made the most of their limited scoring opportunities and because they were protected by the luck that usually attends sides which reach Wembley.'

It was a rare blank for the sharpshooters Pickering, Vowden, Barry Bridges and Johnny Vincent in a season of 83 goals in the Second Division and 14 more in the cups. The speedy England international Bridges, signed from Chelsea, scored 29 of them but left early the next season for QPR.

In 1969/70, however, the excitement was over and so was Cullis's time. Chairman Clifford Coombs, although nominally supportive, held talks with him at the start of March amid rumours of 'dressing-room unrest' and soon after a 6-2 defeat at Millwall a fortnight later Cullis resigned, blaming pressure from supporters rather than players.

Fifteenth at the time, Blues finished three places lower. Two young forwards called Bob Latchford and Trevor Francis carried their hopes into the new decade.

* * *

Like Villa and Birmingham, **Wolverhampton Wanderers** had a bright-enough start to the 1960s before dark days crept in. Denied a championship hat-trick and with it the Double by one point in 1960 (Chapter 6), they had only a couple more good years until declining, causing the previously revered Stan Cullis to pay the price before joining Blues for a less successful finish to his glittering career. Unlike the other pair, however, they were back in the top division and ready to challenge again for trophies by the end of the decade.

From his debut as a 20-year-old at Old Trafford in September 1960, scoring twice in a 3-1 win, centre-forward Ted Farmer could have gone on to become a real star. Prolific in local football and then the club's junior teams, he ran up 16 goals in his first dozen games in the top division and finished the season with 28 in 27 matches as Cullis's emphasis on attack brought his team more than 100 goals for the fourth successive season. It was still only good enough for third place behind the Double-winning Tottenham (who won 4-0 at Molineux) and Sheffield Wednesday.

Wolves shared the Charity Shield with Burnley but as FA Cup holders went out in the third round to lowly Second Division side Huddersfield, and in the inaugural European Cup Winners' Cup, consisting of only ten teams, they lost a semi-final that was inevitably dubbed the 'Battle of Britain', to Rangers (0-2, 1-1). 'Well as Rangers played, Wolves really have only themselves to blame for their latest disappointment,' said the *Birmingham Post* correspondent, citing wasteful shooting.

Farmer missed the second leg with one of the injuries that would cut short his career after just three more truncated seasons in which he played only 30 games, scoring a further 16 goals.

After the team's slither down the table to 18th in 1961/62 he was fit enough to begin the following campaign in vintage form, scoring four in the 8-1 opening-day win against Manchester City as a dazzling start brought eight wins and three draws from the first 11 matches and a place at the head of the table. But a poor run before the snow came at Christmas meant finishing no higher than fifth with only a record 7-0 home win over West Brom to crow about.

Ray Crawford, a championship winner with Ipswich Town, had one excellent season in 1963/64, taking over the scoring mantle from Farmer and Jimmy Murray, but conceding 80 goals boded ill for the following traumatic campaign. Taking just one point from the opening seven games had Wolves rooted to the bottom of the table, but Cullis missed five of them with a debilitating virus. So it was a sensation when on the day after his return to work with a thrilling 4-3 win over West Ham, a club statement said, 'The Wolverhampton board of directors informed their manager Stanley Cullis that they wished to be released from their contract arrangements with him.' And so they were.

The story shared the front page of the *Daily Mirror* with Prime Minister Sir Alec Douglas-Home's announcement that there would be a general election in October; there was little doubt which news was the greater surprise. The *Mirror* detected the hand of the man it called 'Molineux's New Iron Man', John Ireland, appointed chairman only seven weeks earlier. The *Post* lamented the fact that 'a man generally regarded as the post-war King of managers has lost his throne', and added that the sacking, so soon after Joe Mercer and Gil Merrick left Villa and Blues respectively, was 'symptomatic of the depression in which Midland football finds itself'.

After biting his tongue for a while, a badly hurt Cullis eventually said in a ghosted *News of the World* article, 'I'm no longer angry but I'm still disgusted at my treatment by Wolverhampton Wanderers.' Thousands inside and outside the Midlands shared the sentiment.

After the next seven games in succession were lost, Andy Beattie, twice manager of Scotland and billed as 'soccer's leading rescue specialist', was hired on what appeared to be no more than a caretaker basis. A brief upturn was followed by further depression, lifted only in an FA Cup run that included victory over Villa in a second replay, but a 5-3 home defeat by Manchester United in the quarter-final, and a 7-4 loss at Tottenham the same month illustrated where the worst problem lay. Finishing above Birmingham, the only team to concede more than Wolves' 89 goals, was small consolation for a first relegation since 1923.

Goals continued to fly in at both ends down in the Second Division, flamboyant young Peter Knowles and exciting winger Dave Wagstaffe assisting centre-forward Hugh McIlmoyle, but Beattie bade a sad farewell with a 9-3 defeat at Southampton in mid-September. He was replaced by coach Ronnie Allen, a man more closely associated with Albion, who made Wolves the highest-scoring team in the division despite finishing only sixth.

Given the job permanently for the 1966/67 season, Allen justified the directors' faith by fighting Coventry all the way at the top of the table and missing out on the title itself only because of the 3-1 defeat at Highfield Road at the end of April. Once again Wolves were the top scorers, midfielder Ernie Hunt from Swindon leading the way with 20 in his first campaign; a late-season signing also worked out perfectly when Derek Dougan arrived from Leicester to join his sixth club in eight years and settle down at last. Then they set off to the USA to win a summer tournament as 'Los Angeles Wolves', beating Aberdeen 6-5 in the final with a hat-trick from Dave Burnside.

A crowd of 52,438 welcomed First Division football and Albion back to Molineux for a 3-3 draw, although former glories remained elusive for some time. There were three seasons in the bottom half, during which time Hugh Curran from Norwich superseded Dougan as top scorer, young John Richards made his debut and Knowles dramatically turned his back on football to become a Jehovah's Witness – something he later claimed never to have regretted.

In September 1968 Allen was sacked after a 6-0 home defeat by Liverpool inspired by a former Wolves prodigy, the blond-haired Alun Evans. Bill McGarry slowly rebuilt the team for the early 1970s, giving them a taste of things to come at the end of 1969/70 with four games in the Anglo-Italian Cup.

* * *

Amid all this upheaval elsewhere with all the changes of manager and status, **West Bromwich Albion**'s decade was mostly serene and often enjoyable. Comfortably mid-table in the First Division, with a high of sixth (1965/66) and a low of 16th (1969/70), they also had five successive seasons of exciting cup runs and enjoyed European competition for the first time.

At the start of the 1960s powerful centre-forward Derek Kevan was still the main goalscorer with 51 in two seasons, signing off with a hat-trick in his final match against Ipswich in March 1963. He was no doubt happy to have missed the following week's game – a 7-0 defeat away to Wolves – after joining an exodus of England internationals to London clubs; in his case Chelsea. Record-scorer Ronnie Allen had gone to Crystal Palace, Bobby Robson to Fulham and Don Howe was soon off to Arsenal.

Jimmy Hagan joined as manager from Peterborough in 1963 and made a hugely important signing in September 1964 by securing striker Jeff Astle from Notts County for a modest £25,000. The first of his 174 goals for the club came in a 5-1 win over Wolves, who were relegated that season. Astle formed such a fearsome trio with John Kaye from Scunthorpe and Lancastrian Tony 'Bomber' Brown, backed up by left-winger Clive Clark, that in 1965/66 sixth-placed Albion were the First Division's top scorers with 91 goals and won the League Cup at their first attempt.

Having scorned the competition for its first five years, they were favoured with three local derbies and consequently big gates in beating Walsall (3-1), Coventry (6-1) and Villa (3-1) before coming through a semi-final against Peterborough to play West Ham in the last of the two-legged finals. Although the Londoners won at Upton Park with a late goal by Johnny Byrne, they suffered a not uncommon defensive collapse at The Hawthorns, conceding four goals by half-time to Kaye, Brown, Clark and captain Graham Williams. 'It was the best 45 minutes of Albion football I have seen,' said the *Birmingham Post* reporter and Hagan agreed that his team had 'surpassed themselves'.

The following season they ought to have retained the trophy in the first Wembley final after demolishing Villa 6-1 in the second round and West Ham 6-2 on aggregate in the semi-final. Queens Park Rangers, an outstanding Third Division side, were not to be underestimated but seemed to freeze on the day and at the interval were trailing to two goals by Clark, their former player. In a remarkable turnaround they then scored three times, former Wolves man Mark Lazarus getting the winner.

Hagan left shortly afterwards, so Alan Ashman, having impressed with Carlisle United, was in charge for the 1968 FA Cup run. It was dogged work in a series of close games, involving replays against Colchester, Southampton and Liverpool – Bill Shankly's team being ousted 2-1 at the third attempt. Astle had scored in every round and kept up his run in the fortunate 2-0 semi-final success over Birmingham at Villa Park. Everton, three places higher in the league and 6-2 winners at The Hawthorns in March, were favourites in the final, but Astle scored the only goal in extra time – his ninth in the competition, to add to 26 in the league. Baggies fans hardly cared that the game was otherwise memorable only for BBC2 viewers, who, unlike those watching on BBC1 or ITV, were able to experience the FA Cup Final in colour for the first time.

1968 FA Cup Final: West Bromwich Albion 1 Everton 0
West Bromwich Albion: Osborne, Fraser, Williams, Brown, Talbut, Kaye (Clarke), Lovett, Collard, Astle, Hope, Clark.
Everton: West, Wright, Wilson, Kendall, Labone, Harvey, Husband, Ball, Royle, Hurst, Morrissey.

'Tempers were bad and much of the football worse,' wrote Brian Glanville in the *Sunday Times*. 'Midlands Come Back To Life' was the more positive headline in *Soccer Star*, which saw victory as a welcome boost for the region's football, whatever rival supporters might feel. 'Midland soccer, the depression area of the game for the past eight years, has at last come back to life with the success of West Bromwich Albion in winning, if not gloriously, the FA Cup. It is an honour long overdue in the area,' the magazine wrote.

When ATV introduced a Sunday afternoon football highlights programme for the start of the 1968/69 season, Albion were duly selected for the first match, at home to Sheffield Wednesday on 10 August. Industrial action meant it was never shown, and the goalless draw was in any case considerably less exciting than a 3-1 win over European Cup winners Manchester United four days later.

Influential midfielder Bobby Hope wanted to return to his native Scotland to enhance his international prospects, and for the Scots' game against Holland in Amsterdam he was prematurely listed as a Rangers player. But he actually stayed for another four years and was therefore heavily involved as the Baggies reached the FA Cup semi-final again a year later, beating Arsenal and Chelsea but surprisingly losing 1-0 to relegation-threatened Leicester with a late goal.

The year after that came a third Wembley appearance in four seasons in a League Cup run that began with a 2-1 win at Villa Park but ended in defeat by the same score against Manchester City after the ever-reliable Astle scored early on.

Winning the two cup competitions had meant entry into Europe for the first time, broadening horizons without achieving any real success. In the Fairs Cup of 1966/67 Brown scored a hat-trick in a 5-2 home win over Dutch side DOS Utrecht, but Bologna were too strong, winning 3-0, 3-1. Two years later in the Cup Winners' Cup, Bruges and Dinamo Bucharest were beaten before a home defeat by Dunfermline after a goalless draw in Scotland.

And in the 1970 Anglo-Italian Cup – a competition that tended to generate more heat than light – an away tie with Lanerossi Vicenza became so violent that English referee Kevin Howley abandoned proceedings with the score 1-1 after 75 minutes. 'I don't think you will ever get English and foreign players seeing eye to eye over how the game should be played,' he said. More than half a century on, he has yet to be proved wrong.

* * *

After eight games of the 1961/62 season **Walsall** stood proudly second in the Second Division – just behind Liverpool – a new record crowd of 25,453 having watched them beat Newcastle United to extend an unbeaten home record to 16 months. It was the high point in the club's history and the climax of three years in which, rising from sixth place in the Fourth Division, they scored a remarkable 295 goals in 138 games.

Champions of the Fourth Division in 1960, they went straight through the next level as runners-up to Bury, scoring 98 times to add to the previous season's 102. Promotion was achieved on a famous night at Shrewsbury, where thousands of Saddlers supporters swelled the attendance to a record for Gay Meadow of almost 19,000 that had still never been beaten by the time the Town left for pastures new in 2007. 'They swarmed across the pitch to shower congratulations on their heroes and it was many minutes before the players reached the dressing-room,' reported the *Post*.

Tony Richards was top scorer with a personal-best 36 in the league alone, with left-winger Colin Taylor only three behind him, but for once someone else was allowed to take the glory at Shrewsbury: Colin Askey, once a hero of Port Vale's 1954 side, headed the winner after Town equalised Taylor's goal with a disputed penalty.

From chasing Liverpool, the rest of the Second Division season was an anticlimax with a drift down to 14th place, although the side's quality was demonstrated in a 2-2 draw away to Fulham after reaching the FA Cup fourth round for only the second time since the war. Richards scored twice but in the replay the First Division side triumphed 2-0.

Unfortunately, the Saddlers became one of those clubs whose form suffered badly from the big freeze of 1962/63, when they did not play from 15 December to 2 March. Selling Richards for £9,000 to help Port Vale's promotion push, they lost six games in a row and went into a dramatic final fixture at home to Charlton Athletic needing a draw to send the Londoners down instead. On a waterlogged pitch the referee decided at half-time he would have to abandon the game, and three nights later everything went against the Saddlers in the rerun. Inside-left Graham Newton was injured early on and goalkeeper Alan Boswell fractured a cheekbone, so with substitutes still two years away they played the whole of the second half with nine fit men and right-back Grenville Palin in goal. Falling 2-0 behind, Walsall retrieved one goal through Taylor but could not quite find the equaliser and went down on goal average. 'Besides being such a vital defeat for Walsall, it was also, surely, one of the most unfortunate in the club's long history,' said the local *Observer* newspaper.

Taylor left in the summer for Newcastle and without him the Saddlers almost went straight through the Third Division, avoiding that fate by only two points. Goals from a young Allan Clarke saw them safe for another season and then up to ninth place before he left for the First Division with Fulham. Then in 1967/68 with the old Birmingham player and coach Ray Shaw having replaced Billy Moore, a strong promotion challenge fizzled out after leading the table by five points.

Otherwise, the main excitement in the latter half of the decade came from a series of cup games. In 1965/66 there was a crowd of over 41,000 at The Hawthorns to see the first Albion-Walsall derby for 65 years, which the home side won 3-1 in their first League Cup tie. Four months later came a 2-0 FA Cup win away to First Division Stoke, who they knocked out of the League Cup the following season. And in the next three seasons there were FA Cup ties with Liverpool, Tottenham and Crystal Palace from the top division, of which holding Liverpool 0-0 at Fellows Park was the pick.

Moore returned as manager in February 1969 and Taylor came back from Palace for his third and final spell but crowds were down to 5,500 for a team whose golden period was now gone.

* * *

Even football anoraks who can name Rotherham United as finalists in the first League Cup of 1960/61 might struggle with the identity of the team they beat to get there. While the Football League would doubtless have preferred Aston Villa and Burnley, founder members and both in the top half of the First Division, to contest the final, that pair were drawn together at the penultimate stage, and so were the two rank outsiders: Rotherham and – **Shrewsbury Town**.

Sitting halfway down the Third Division, Town had made the last four with by far the greatest giant-killing in their history, beating Everton 2-1 at Gay Meadow. The Merseysiders, although on a bad run, had spent lavishly to reach the top six in the First Division, hence the *Daily Herald* headline 'Shrewsbury shock the millionaires'. The great Alex Young put the visitors ahead – undeservedly said the *Herald* – before Peter Dolby from

Heanor Town, a centre-half playing at inside-right in only his third senior game, struck twice to send a crowd of over 15,000 into raptures. 'I told the boys before the match we were just as good as Everton,' said player-manager Arthur Rowley, 'and I think we proved it.'

It was hardly the sort of night anticipated when Town took three games to win their first tie in the competition, against Swindon. By the time of the semi-final, however, excitement was growing and almost 17,000 turned up for the second leg, hoping to see a 3-2 defeat at Rotherham overturned. After the local fire brigade pumped gallons of water off the pitch, Town drew level on aggregate through Malcolm Starkey but in extra time former Birmingham forward Don Weston got the decisive goal for the Second Division side.

In the league Shrewsbury had peaked by reaching third place in 1960, only a year after promotion from the Fourth Division. Rowley continued to be an inspiration and the month after the Rotherham games he broke Dixie Dean's Football League record by scoring his 380th goal, ending the season with 28 and backed up by 20 from Northern Ireland international Jim McLaughlin.

The player-manager had two more successful seasons before winding down, as Peter Broadbent was signed from Wolves and centre-forward Frank Clarke continued his progress.

When Rowley stopped playing to concentrate on management he had reached 434 league goals, still the record at the time of writing, with 152 of them for Town (plus 15 in cup games). In his final season of 1964/65 they had the first of two excellent FA Cup runs to the fifth round, beating Manchester City 3-1 before losing 2-0 away to First Division runners-up Leeds. The following season they won an exciting second replay 4-3 against Second Division Carlisle and only lost 3-2 at Chelsea, spurred on by some 10,000 travelling supporters.

In 1967, when the club tried an experiment with Saturday evening home games – quickly abandoned – they were sixth in the table, only three points from promotion, and the next year were even closer, in third place and only losing out to Bury on the final day after Clarke had moved to the top division with Queens Park Rangers. Unbeaten in FA Cup games at Gay Meadow from 1953 to 1969, Town held Arsenal 1-1 that season, but in a sign of the way football was going, the promotion challenge brought only 61 goals; when they were third in 1960, the total was 97.

In July, Rowley moved on to manage Sheffield United, where he was not a success, and former Manchester United and Northern Ireland goalkeeper Harry Gregg took over as Town finished the decade with two seasons nearer the bottom than the top.

* * *

A Shrewsbury Town coach ended up as the most successful manager of **Port Vale** in the 1960s, even though a more familiar figure returned to Vale Park early in the decade and a famous one would be at the helm for a difficult period towards the end of it.

Freddie Steele, architect of the 'Iron Curtain' defence of 1954, had resigned after a bad run three years later and been replaced by Norman Low, who lasted until the autumn of 1962 before falling out with the board. The popular Steele came back and was able to push Vale up the table, encouraging hopes of a promotion challenge by snapping up Walsall's record goalscorer Tony Richards in March. The prolific Richards ended up as leading scorer despite playing only 14 games, but even after winning eight of the last ten Vale were still four points short of second-placed Swindon.

Back in their traditional white shirts and black shorts after abandoning black and amber stripes, they revived memories of old FA Cup heroics the following season. In the third round they beat First Division Birmingham 2-1 at St Andrew's with goals by long-serving Roy Sproson and Jackie Mudie, who had signed from Stoke two months earlier. The *Birmingham Post* gave them little credit, the headline suggesting it was 'No giant-killing act slaying these meek and muddled Blues'.

The reward was a visit to Anfield, where Liverpool, rarely muddled and never meek, were on their way to winning the First Division championship. The Iron (or Steele) Curtain descended again to force a goalless draw and two days later Vale took a dramatic tie to extra time. Albert Cheesebrough, signed from Leicester, equalised a goal by Roger Hunt and it was not until the 118th minute that Peter Thompson struck a superb winner from 20 yards.

Over 42,000 saw the game, many having to be seated round the touchline after an admission gate was broken down. It was an era when fans' behaviour was coming under closer scrutiny and earlier that day British Railways had announced it would run no more football specials from Merseyside because of repeated damage. When Thompson scored, two Liverpool fans who had climbed on to the stand roof fell through it, injuring some of those below.

In the league, however, Vale were below midway, and having paid £15,000 each for Cheesebrough and Northern Ireland's Billy Bingham meant a loss of almost £50,000. Consequently there was no money for further strengthening in 1964/65 when they slumped to the bottom of the table by February, causing Steele to resign. Mudie took over as caretaker but could not avert relegation back to the Fourth Division.

In the same month as the managerial change, Sir Stanley Matthews, newly knighted, played his last Football League match for Stoke at the age of 50. He could not resist an invitation from former team-mate Mudie to join up with his boyhood favourites the following season and did so as general manager, for expenses only – an arrangement that clearly appealed to the hard-up board, especially as he spent much time travelling abroad for exhibition and charity matches.

The pair's intention was to recruit and sell on talented youngsters, largely from Scotland and the north-east, even taking on a Scottish junior team as a nursery club. For one game in January 1966 they fielded a forward line composed of five teenagers. But results in the meantime were poor and after two seasons in the bottom half Mudie resigned, leaving Matthews to run the show himself. In 1967/68, however, they were in the bottom eight again and suffered a new crisis. The club had made various illegal payments, especially to amateur and schoolboy players, and as well as being technically expelled from the Football League – though always likely to be voted back, as they were – they were hit with a £2,000 fine.

The episode left Sir Stanley disenchanted and like such fellow national heroes as Sir Bobby Charlton and Bobby

Moore he walked away with unhappy memories of football management.

The more pragmatic Gordon Lee, who had been coaching Shrewsbury, took the reins and in two years had Vale promoted. His 1969/70 team was a solid and settled one that brought back the iron curtain mentality. Four defenders plus goalkeeper Keith Ball played in every game, conceding only 33 goals, the second best in the country. They began the season with 18 games unbeaten (nine goals against) and finished it with nine unbeaten (four conceded). But for a stutter from Boxing Day until the end of January they would have been higher than fourth, five points behind the champions Chesterfield.

But dignity as well as a Third Division place had been restored.

8

Ch-Ch-Changes 1971–1992

'The club that once won at Wembley three times in five years were thumped on merit by a Southern League town famed not for football but for cider and bulls.'

The People, February 1972

'It was fitting that 35-year-old George Eastham should score the winning goal in the League Cup final and gain his and Stoke's first major honour.'

Birmingham Post, March 1972

'There's a good ball played in to Tony Morley. Oh, it must be! And it is! Peter Withe!'

ITV commentary, May 1982

'Derek Dougan was celebrating his "Molineux miracle" last night after saving bankrupt Wolves from soccer extinction by just three minutes.'

Daily Mirror, July 1982

'Hundreds were injured – many seriously – as the last day of the League soccer season erupted into a bloody nightmare at Birmingham.'

Sunday Mirror, May 1985

'Principally Coventry beat Spurs because on the day, over two hours, they were the better footballing side. They had the strength where it mattered most when it mattered most.'

Guardian, May 1987

A LOT can happen in two decades of football. Aston Villa, champions of Europe in 1982, had only ten years earlier been in the Third Division, to where Birmingham, Stoke, West Bromwich Albion and Wolves would all descend – three of them after gracing the UEFA Cup. The famous Wanderers, collapsing from first to fourth tiers in joint-record time, were on the verge of going bust and suddenly found themselves two levels below Shrewsbury Town, and on an equal footing with the former non-league giant-killers Hereford United.

Meanwhile, in the sport's grimmest decade, supporters at Heysel, Hillsborough, Bradford and Birmingham went to football matches and never returned. Fences went up and crowds went down; attendances, which stood at 41 million in 1948/49, fell below 16 and a half million. Amid the early-1980s' economic recession, a blueprint entitled 'The Fight For Survival' had several of its proposals accepted, including three points for a win, Sunday football, a paid director at each club and artificial pitches.

The repercussions of all this were profound and there was much soul-searching before, in 1992, a whole new era of blue-Sky thinking began to emerge.

The other huge change was the number of players from outside the UK now attempting to become local heroes. Birmingham took the plunge early by recruiting Argentine World Cup-winner Alberto Tarantini in the autumn of 1978. Stoke and Albion went for Dutchmen in Loek Ursem (1979) and Martin Jol (1981); Wolves, just before their swift decline, tried the easily forgotten Uruguayan Rafael Villazán (1980). Villa gave a rewarding trial to Melbourne's Tony Dorigo (1983) but had less success a year later with winger Didier Six, a 1984 European Championship winner.

* * *

At the start of the 1970s, the notion of an Australian left-back with a Frenchman in front of him would have been as, well, *foreign* to **Aston Villa** supporters as parading the European Cup through the streets of Birmingham. A core of Scots and Scousers was as exotic as it got, both tribes remaining well represented throughout the exciting odyssey from Halifax to Highbury and Rochdale to Rotterdam.

Saltergate, Chesterfield was where the club's journey back to respectability and then much more actually began. On 15 August 1970 that was the venue for Villa's first match in the third tier of English football. Several thousand visiting supporters swelled the gate to 16,760 and cheered a 3-2 win, Bruce Rioch scoring twice. Just four defeats by the end of January (albeit including humblings at Port Vale and Walsall) had them well placed for promotion but one of the great Villa Park nights turned out to have unfortunate consequences.

On 23 December in front of a joyous 58,667 a Manchester United team containing the holy trinity of Best, Charlton and Law were beaten 2-1 in the League Cup semi-final for a 3-2 aggregate success that put Villa through to Wembley. But from the week before the final until the end of March, Vic Crowe's team did not win any of their seven Third Division games and were never able to make up the lost points. In the final itself against Tottenham they fought well until succumbing in the last 12 minutes to two goals by Martin Chivers. 'Magnificent Villa Make Spurs Fight At Wembley' was the *Post*'s headline.

The lost ground in the league meant finishing no higher than fourth, a lack of goals proving crucial. Nobody reached double figures, but that was remedied the following season when four players did and the title was won by five points. Winger Ray Graydon from Bristol Rovers and centre-half Chris Nicholl proved important signings. Home form was outstanding – 20 wins out of 23 – and the average Villa Park crowd was almost 32,000. A divisional record of 48,110 watched Bournemouth beaten in February and nine days later an even bigger crowd came to see a 2-1 win over glamorous Brazilians Santos in a friendly match – though it cost chairman Doug Ellis an extra £5,000 payment for Pelé to declare himself fit.

'Villa, gaining staggering support from the fans, came bursting out of the Third Division with an authority that left observers wondering only how they had got themselves down there in the first place,' said a review of the season in the third *Rothmans Football Yearbook*.

A promising bonus was winning the FA Youth Cup for the first time (they would win it again in 1980). There might even have been a second successive promotion in 1972/73 but once more nobody managed double figures and although a commendable third, Villa had 11 points and 30 goals fewer than runners-up QPR. One poor season in 14th place then cost Crowe his job but the irredeemably dour Merseysider Ron Saunders achieved immediate success in the form of promotion back to the First Division and a League Cup triumph. Brian Little had his breakthrough season with 20 league goals, backed up by Graydon's 19, and this time a run to the League Cup Final proved an inspiration, not a distraction.

After a first-round victory over Everton the draw smoothed Villa's route to Wembley by bringing four lower-division sides as opposition. By the semi-final there was not a single First Division team left and it was one of Saunders's previous clubs, Norwich City, who lined up against them in his third successive final. Having lost the previous two with Norwich and then Manchester City, he was successful at last, thanks to Graydon following up his saved penalty ten minutes from time to score from the rebound.

The critics were not kind, 'Soccer that would have made an Isthmian League side blush,' was the *Sunday Mirror*'s verdict. Both managers demonstrated their priorities, however, by insisting they would win promotion in two months' time and duly did so. From fourth place, Villa won ten of their last 11 games, finishing as top scorers and runners-up to Tommy Docherty's Manchester United, with John Bond's Norwich third.

In the first season back in the top division they comfortably avoided relegation, made a disappointing European debut with a 5-1 aggregate defeat by Royal Antwerp in the UEFA Cup and provided a question and answer for any football trivia quiz in the 2-2 draw at Leicester: centre-half Nicholl scored all four goals.

He struck a more famous one from 35 yards a year later in the delayed second replay of the League Cup Final, before the team finished as high as fourth in the table. Top early on after putting five goals past both Ipswich and Arsenal, the real highlight was beating the champions Liverpool 5-1 on an extraordinary night at Villa Park, all the goals coming before half-time. PFA Player of the Year Andy Gray, signed from Dundee United to lead the attack, had his best season for any club, scoring 25 league goals while Little hit ten in the League Cup alone, where the semi-final and final both went to three games. His hat-trick at neutral Highbury saw off QPR to earn a final against Everton, which he settled with two goals at Old Trafford after Nicholl's blast – the second of them coming in extra time with the tie a minute away from being the first major British final decided by a penalty shoot-out.

Gray missed that game through injury, as well as a key UEFA Cup quarter-final second leg the following season against Barcelona, and the manager's insistence that he must play at other times when not fully fit became a source of friction between them. By the end of 1978/79 with Villa eighth for the second successive season but Gray having played only 15 league games, the Scot had lost all respect for Saunders and asked for a transfer. Once Wolves had received an astonishing £1.15m plus extras for midfielder Steve Daley from Manchester City, they were able to convince Villa to accept that amount plus just £25,000 extra for Gray. The total fee was £1.469m, which would stand as the British record for two years.

Villa failed to replace him and did well to finish seventh while scoring only 51 goals, but adding Peter Withe from Newcastle that summer when Coventry's Mick Ferguson proved too expensive proved the catalyst for a stunning two seasons.

With Liverpool for once out of the picture after losing 2-0 at Villa Park in January, the 1980/81 championship developed into a duel between Ipswich and Villa. Bobby Robson's team won the head-to-heads, beating them three times in the league and FA Cup, but ended up exhausted after chasing a domestic double plus the UEFA Cup (the one trophy they won); in all they played 20 games more than Saunders's team, and what seemed a crucial 2-1 victory at Villa Park in April proved to be only their second win in the last eight games. So Villa went to third-placed Arsenal on the final day needing a draw at most and, even though they lost 2-0, Ipswich were beaten at Middlesbrough to concede the title.

'Ipswich did not surrender the league championship to us, we won it on merit,' said skipper Dennis Mortimer. A four-point gap – in the last season of two points for a win – supported his argument. Remarkably, apart from good friends Gary Williams and Colin Gibson sharing the left-back position, Saunders was able to pick virtually the same team all season: the other ten players all played 35 games or more, with seven of them ever-present. Sadly, Little and full-back Mike Pejic, neither of whom had played at all because of injury, were both forced to retire; Little, taken on to the coaching staff, would return as manager (see the next chapter).

Despite this first championship since 1910, nobody was taking the former Birmingham and Nottingham Forest striker Withe too seriously when he said Villa had the ability to emulate Forest by winning the European Cup, in which English sides had triumphed for the past five seasons.

The club had picked up some European experience in the UEFA Cup as League Cup winners, enjoying a long run in 1977/78 with wins over Fenerbahçe, Górnik Zabrze and Athletic Bilbao before going out narrowly to Barcelona (2-2, 1-2). Now they were in Europe's big league for the first time and the extra commitments, together with runs to the League Cup quarter-final (losing to Albion) and FA Cup fifth round (losing to Tottenham), took its toll on a squad that Saunders had not been allowed to strengthen.

The champions were fifth from bottom but also through to the European Cup quarter-final in early February when the sensational news broke that he was quitting. The irony was that Doug Ellis, with whom most managers had a difficult relationship, had been sidelined and left the club, so it was his apparently more sympathetic replacement as chairman, Ron Bendall, who caused Saunders to walk out by refusing him another rollover contract instead of a more straightforward one of three years' duration.

'As a businessman, I don't like "rollover" contracts which go on forever,' Bendall said. 'With football in its present recession, we have to know what our liabilities are.' Saunders took this as meaning that 'the club have less confidence in me' and later hinted at other frustrations: 'I'm paid to manage, not to be an office boy who has to ask about everything he does.'

His assistant and former Portsmouth team-mate Tony Barton, a very different character, took over as caretaker and, before the club had decided whether to bring in someone from outside, results picked up. Wins over Birmingham (who jubilantly installed Saunders as their new manager) and Coventry were followed by a 2-0 aggregate success against Dinamo Kiev to bring Barton a contract and a semi-final with Anderlecht. Winger Tony Morley's goal won the home leg and in Brussels a fortnight later his team, 'bubbling with re-found confidence', held out for a goalless draw amid serious crowd trouble.

Newly confident or not after hauling themselves up to finish 11th in the First Division, few gave them much of a chance in the Rotterdam final against the Bayern Munich of Paul Breitner, Uli Hoeneß and Karl-Heinz Rummenigge. Having to replace goalkeeper Jimmy Rimmer with the inexperienced Nigel Spink after only eight minutes appeared to diminish those chances further and they were on the back foot for most of the game. 'Villa scored at a time when the tide of the game was not just running against them – it was threatening to drown them,' wrote Frank McGhee in the *Daily Mirror*.

As they built a rare attack in the 67th minute, commentator Brian Moore's summing up for ITV viewers was, 'Villa hanging on at 0-0.' Every Villan knows the rest, 'Shaw, Williams, prepared to adventure down the left. There's a good ball played in to Tony Morley. Oh, it must be! And it is! Peter Withe!' Withe had bobbled the ball in off a post to earn a place in Aston Villa's Hall of Fame with one mishit shot.

Barton received many plaudits, but the following day's *Evening Mail* just as correctly remembered the man who put the side together: 'Just for a moment a thought for former manager Ron Saunders. Whatever the current feeling about him at Villa Park, it would be churlish to deny that he created this team.'

1982 European Cup Final: Aston Villa 1 Bayern Munich 0
Aston Villa: Rimmer (Spink), Swain, Williams, Evans, McNaught, Mortimer, Bremner, Shaw, Withe, Cowans, Morley.
Bayern Munich: Müller, Dremmler, Horsmann, Weiner, Augenthaler, Kraus (Niedermayer), Dürnberger, Breitner, Hoeneß, Mathy (Güttler), Rummenigge.

The following busy season – without a single new player – Barton's team beat Barcelona to win the European Super Cup

(0-1, 3-0), lost 2-0 in the World Club Championship in Tokyo to Peñarol of Uruguay and went out of the European Cup in the quarter-final to Juventus (1-2, 1-3). Significantly, Ellis returned as the club's first paid director, claiming as he had on his arrival in 1968 that the financial position was dire.

Sixth place in the First Division earned one more European adventure in the 1983/84 UEFA Cup. It ended with a home defeat by Spartak Moscow, which together with a fall to tenth place – in a season when Gordon Cowans and Gary Shaw were seriously injured – meant Barton's contract was not renewed. Less than ten years later he was dead, aged only 56.

Within three more seasons under Graham Turner from Shrewsbury Town (several bigger names turned the job down) and then the disappointing Billy McNeill, Villa were unthinkably relegated, their decline from European champions to the Second Division having come in five years – even quicker than Manchester United a decade earlier. A couple of League Cup semi-finals, welcome as they would have been a few years previously, were small beer now after the continental champagne.

It is a common view that a winning team was broken up too quickly, but the fact is that of the 12 players who effectively won the title in 1981, seven were still in the side that started the 1984/85 season, finishing tenth for the second successive year. The problem was the quality of replacements for those few who left; French winger Six, a successor to Morley, being only one of the signings that did not work out.

After Cowans and Paul Rideout were sold cheaply to Bari in Serie A, Andy Gray had returned in the summer of 1985, having won the FA Cup, First Division championship and European Cup Winners' Cup with Everton. Knee problems handicapped him, however, to the extent that in 54 league games he scored only five goals and after relegation joined his third West Midlands club, West Brom.

Back in the Second Division, Graham Taylor, who had done great work at Watford, revived the club after a slow start (including a 2-0 defeat by Birmingham in his first home game) and Villa finished runners-up to Millwall in a tight finish. Two years later they were second in the top division with Paul McGrath among the three central defenders. David Platt's goals from midfield meant that the lack of a free-scoring striker was not as costly as it might have been.

That achievement earned Taylor the dubious honour of becoming England manager in succession to Bobby Robson and was followed by an unsuccessful year in the bottom four with a UEFA Cup defeat by Inter Milan under the former Czechoslovakia manager Dr Jozef Vengloš – a rabbit produced from a hat by Ellis as the first of many foreign managers in English football's top tier. Platt departed to Bari for £5m as Ron Atkinson arrived from Sheffield Wednesday to usher Villa into the new Premier League.

* * *

By becoming champions of England and then Europe without excessive expenditure on players, and by dropping out of the First Division for only one season, Villa were able to ride out the 1980s economic storms – just. Even in their case, a payments scandal over construction of the new Witton End stand in the late 1970s could have had greater repercussions, and crowds more than halved from 1980 to barely 15,000 in 1986.

In the same period average attendances for **Wolverhampton Wanderers** collapsed from 21,500 to a pathetic 4,000. No team has ever sunk from the top division of English football to the bottom one faster. That was the club's fate between May 1984 and May 1986. Along the way humiliations included one Molineux 'crowd' numbering 2,205; cup defeats by Walsall and Chorley; a sale to unsuitable new owners with minutes to spare before liquidation; and later a second winding-up order.

There was little hint of such horrors in the previous decade, which included two Wembley wins and several seasons in Europe. Even when relegated after one bad season in 1976, Wolves came straight back up.

An experienced squad put together by Bill McGarry finished as high as fourth in 1970/71, an attacking team in a dull era with Bobby Gould, Hugh Curran and Derek Dougan all in double figures and popular young midfielder Kenny Hibbitt starting the first of over 550 games. There was even a trophy at the end of it, when the Texaco Cup, a British Isles competition, was won by beating Hearts in a two-legged final.

Fourth place also meant a UEFA Cup spot for the following year and a dozen games from September to May in which the only one lost was the first leg of the all-English final at home to Tottenham, who won 2-1. At White Hart Lane Dave Wagstaffe's goal could not prevent a 3-2 aggregate defeat. The highlight along the way was knocking out Juventus, but the season's biggest crowd of 53,379 turned up in between the two Spurs games for a match of no importance to mid-table Wolves. Visiting Leeds, FA Cup winners two days earlier, needed a point to become champions, but on a night of wild rumour and controversial penalty decisions, they were beaten 2-1 by goals from Derek Dougan and Frank Munro which handed the title to Brian Clough's Derby County.

Fifth place and two semi-finals made 1972/73 another fine season as John Richards established himself at centre-forward with 36 goals in all competitions. After over 50,000 had watched Coventry being beaten 2-0 in the FA Cup quarter-final, Leeds took partial revenge by the only goal at Maine Road, and Spurs repeated their UEFA trick in the League Cup by winning 2-1 at Molineux and drawing at home. Wolves won the short-lived FA Cup third-place play-off match against Arsenal which had been introduced in the early 1970s.

The following season seven Richards goals were instrumental in winning the League Cup, though he then missed the rest of the campaign.

His individual effort knocked out champions Liverpool at Molineux in the fifth round and he scored all three in the 3-2 semi-final aggregate success over Norwich. At Wembley, Alan Sunderland, in his first full season, made goals for Hibbitt and Richards on either side of Colin Bell's equaliser, and reserve goalkeeper Gary Pierce was named man of the match for his defiance of City's all-star forward line. 'We kidded everyone that Phil [Parkes] would be fit to play, simply to take the pressure off Gary but he never had a chance,' manager McGarry said. 'And what a game he had.'

1974 League Cup Final: Wolves 2 Manchester City 1
Wolves: Pierce, Palmer, Parkin, Bailey, Munro, McAlle, Sunderland, Hibbitt, Richards, Dougan, Wagstaffe (Powell).

Manchester City: MacRae, Pardoe, Donachie, Doyle, Booth, Towers, Summerbee, Bell, Lee, Law, Marsh.

Dougan, by now chairman of the PFA, retired with 123 Wolves goals to his name and the burden weighed too heavily on Richards in an unexpectedly bad 1975/76 campaign that ended in relegation. On the final night of the season either Birmingham or Wolves were destined to go down but, while the Blues managed a draw at Sheffield United, Molineux saw Liverpool recover from Steve Kindon's goal to score three times in the last quarter of an hour and become champions.

McGarry made way for his assistant Sammy Chung, who was able to inspire a Second Division championship win at the first attempt to celebrate the club's centenary. Five different players, led by Hibbitt, reached double figures in a total of 84 goals. While Clough's Nottingham Forest went up with them to win the First Division and then the European Cup, Wolves sat in the bottom eight, then lost 11 of the first 14 games in 1978/79 to cost Chung his job.

John Barnwell secured safety and took them to the FA Cup semi-final and defeat by Arsenal. The following September, with Emlyn Hughes already signed from Liverpool, the manager was able to use the exorbitant fee received for Steve Daley to recruit Andy Gray, whose four goals in his first three games brought victories over Everton, Manchester United and Arsenal. Hero status was confirmed six months later when his goal won the 1980 League Cup Final after a mix-up involving Peter Shilton in the Nottingham Forest goal.

1980 Football League Cup Final: Wolves 1 Nottingham Forest 0
Wolves: Bradshaw, Palmer, Parkin, Daniel, Berry, Hughes, Carr, Hibbitt, Gray, Richards, Eves.
Nottingham Forest: Shilton, Anderson, Gray, McGovern, Needham, Burns, O'Neill, Bowyer, Birtles, Francis, Robertson.

It seemed a reasonable time to be expanding, with the Molineux Street stand and 70 houses demolished to make way for a futuristic curved edifice, the John Ireland Stand, executive boxes and all. But apart from a run to the 1981 FA Cup semi-final, ended in a replay against bogey team Spurs, little went right from that moment.

Relegation, avoided by only two points, came to pass a year later, Barnwell having resigned after a run of nine successive defeats; crowds were down to 12,000, atmosphere at the stadium had died and in June debts of £2.6m were announced, brought on largely by the new stand and its interest payments. Doug Ellis, out of favour at Villa, briefly became chairman, controversially calling in the official receiver, and Walsall's Ken Wheldon led a rival consortium with Sir Jack Hayward, but it was Derek Dougan who in the words of the *Daily Mirror* 'was celebrating his "Molineux miracle" last night after saving bankrupt Wolves from soccer extinction by just three minutes'.

A new company called Wolverhampton Wanderers FC (1972) Ltd was formed, but the money men turned out to be Saudi brothers Mahmud and Mohammad Bhatti, whose main interest lay in developing the valuable site by adding a superstore. Once the local council rejected their plans and a surprisingly quick return to the First Division was followed by immediate relegation, they lost interest.

In May 1984 a crowd of 7,405 saw the last top-tier game at Molineux for nearly 20 years. Graham Hawkins had come and gone as manager and in Tommy Docherty's one season in charge, 1984/85, a reasonable autumn was followed by 19 games without a win and a second successive relegation, Dougan quitting in frustration as chief executive.

On the same day as the last game, a 3-0 defeat at Blackburn, the Bradford City fire cost the lives of 56 supporters and led to new safety measures that meant closing both the old main stand on Waterloo Road and the North Bank. The 1985/86 season was another ghastly one, starting with seven defeats in eight matches, of which the one at home to Bristol Rovers was watched by 3,241 people. By mid-March, against Bury, that had dropped to an even more embarrassing 2,205 – the lowest crowd since 1906.

McGarry had returned for two months as manager but decided he could not stick around to be associated with 'killing off one of the finest clubs in the world'. As the third successive relegation followed – something previously achieved only by

This Ticket is not available after 3.15 p.m.

Kick off at 3.30 p.m.

CRYSTAL PALACE.

Football Association Challenge Cup.

FINAL TIE.

30TH APRIL, 1895.

RING.

No 531

HALF-A-CROWN.

THIS TICKET DOES NOT ADMIT TO THE PALACE

Three times in nine seasons Aston Villa met local rivals West Bromwich Albion in the FA Cup Final, winning the first and third – this one in 1895. (John Lerwill)

Little Teddy Bear about to stick it to the mighty Gunners on the greatest day in Walsall's history, Saturday, 14 January 1933. (Getty)

The great Harry Hibbs of Birmingham City and England helping to save the Blues from relegation in 1935 during a 2-2 draw at Chelsea. (Alamy)

Port Vale's 'Iron Curtain' defence of 1953/54 defies local man Stanley Matthews as visiting Blackpool are knocked out 2-0 in the FA Cup fifth round. (Getty)

England's Masters win in the mud

Hail, Wolves 'Champions of the world' now

By DAVID WYNNE-MORGAN

SALUTE the wonderful Wolves this morning for giving Britain her greatest football victory since the war. Last night

The quote from Wolves manager Stan Cullis after beating Honvéd in December 1954 that led to the European Cup being instigated.

Two masters of management: Stan Cullis and Jimmy Hill at Highfield Road in 1964. (Alamy)

The first of two pitch invasions greets non-League Hereford United's equaliser by Ronnie Radford (11) in their famous 1972 FA Cup victory over First Division Newcastle. (Getty)

In safe hands: Gordon Banks and Peter Dobing show off the Football League Cup in the Potteries after beating Chelsea in the 1972 final to earn Stoke's first major trophy. (Getty)

Birmingham director Jasper Carrott at the club's training ground in 1976 with, among others, Howard Kendall, Trevor Francis, Peter Withe and Kenny Burns. (Getty)

Peter Withe (centre) writes himself into Villa's Hall of Fame with one mishit shot to win the 1982 European Cup. (Getty)

While the Bradford fire was raging on one of the worst days in English football history, 11 May 1985, Leeds fans rioted at St Andrew's, where one supporter was killed as a wall collapsed. (Alamy)

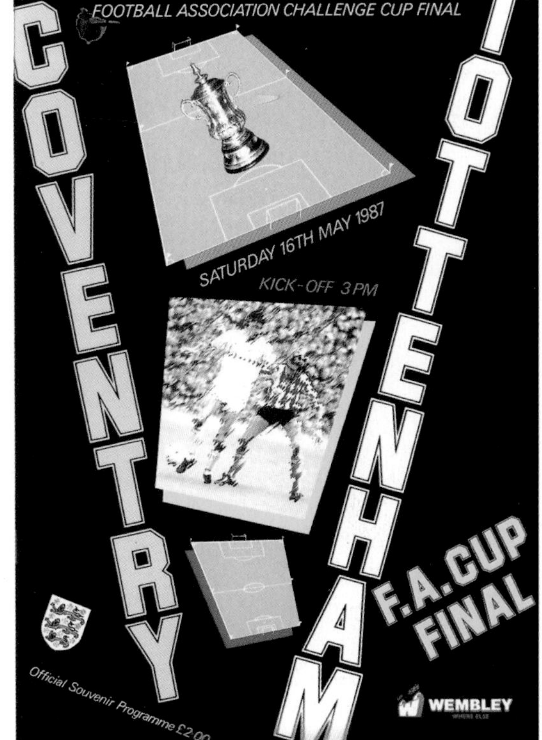

'Play up Sky Blues': and they did, to win the thrilling 1987 final against Spurs.

PAGE 60 SUNDAY MIRROR, November 6, 1994

BIG RON By The Doc

'You'll get sack for Christmas!'

BIG Ron Atkinson is heading for the sack at the hands of his Aston Villa chairman 'Deadly' Doug Ellis.

The once-proud club – which only two seasons ago was challenging Manchester United for Premiership supremacy – has become a "rest home for elderly gentlemen."

And last night former Villa boss Tommy Docherty – speaking on the [illegible] anniversary of his own sacking at the hands of Ellis – declared: "Atkinson could be gone by Christmas."

Big Ron will this afternoon take his side into action against Manchester United – another club managed by both him and the Doc – but the outspoken Scot marks Villa's victory chances at "less than zero."

Flash

He makes no bones about his own dislike for the man ... describing him as 'flash' and 'a guy who doesn't stick around at clubs long enough to be found out.'

Doc roared: "He's got an old team on his hands which is going absolutely nowhere. If they fail to progress in the Coca Cola Cup and are kicked out of the FA Cup early I am sure he'll be gone.

"Doug is not the most patient of men. He will be looking at the balance sheet, wondering about the money that's been spent on players and lost as a result of going out of Europe.

"If the bottom line doesn't look too clever, then I think Ron will be in trouble.

"I remember the night before Doug sacked me – he told me he was right behind me. I wish he'd been in front."

Ageing

The Doc is critical of Big Ron's signings and believes he is paying a heavy price for investing in ageing, limited term players.

He was astonished at the signing of John Fashanu in particular, describing it as an "extraordinarily bad piece of business."

Doc went on: "Don't ask me why Ron bought him. At £[illegible] it was ridiculous. It would have been ridiculous at £[illegible]."

[illegible]-year-old Fash joined a squad of players described by Docherty as "Ron's short-term certs."

He said: "He buys guys who have done it but are probably just past their peak. My view is that he doesn't like to gamble in the transfer market on youthful potential.

"Just look at the first team squad. Eight of them are in their thirties: Nigel Spink, Paul [illegible]

MR NOWHERE MAN: Ron Atkinson and his creaking Villa crew are heading for oblivion, taunts Tommy Docherty

One of 'Deadly' Doug Ellis's Aston Villa victims, Tommy Docherty, correctly predicts the fate of Ron Atkinson – who was sacked four days after this Sunday Mirror article from 6 November 1994.

Luke Rodgers and goalscorer Nigel Jemson celebrate Shrewsbury's 2-1 FA Cup victory over Everton at Gay Meadow in 2003. (Getty)

Kevin Campbell gives manager Bryan Robson a champagne shower as Albion achieve the great escape of 2005 – avoiding relegation after being bottom of the Premier League at Christmas. (Getty)

Manchester United's Phil Bardsley clears a shot off the line as Nigel Clough's non-League Burton Albion hold them 0-0 in a 2006 FA Cup tie before losing the replay at Old Trafford. (Getty)

Bristol City four years earlier – and Molineux became a one-sided ground with closure of the South Bank, supporters endured another fraught summer in receivership.

The saviours turned out to be Wolverhampton Council, which had turned down the Bhattis' proposal but now bought the stadium and adjoining land while a Birmingham property developer paid off the debts once Asda received planning permission to build a store behind the North Bank. As is the way of these things, negotiations dragged on until barely a week before the new season, when 6,001 turned out to see a home defeat by Cambridge United.

From that unpromising start but with the Bhattis gone, optimism grew as Graham Turner from Villa replaced the popular caretaker Brian Little to begin a long stint at the club after seven different managers in five years. In a stroke of genius he paid £70,000 to Albion for midfielder Andy Thompson and powerful young striker Steve Bull, whose 15 goals in 30 games alongside Andy Mutch propelled Wolves from 17th place in January to the play-offs. There they beat Colchester but were shocked in the two-leg final by unfancied Aldershot, who won 3-0 on aggregate.

After an unruly start at Scarborough, where their supporters were involved in serious crowd trouble and were banned for six away games, the 1987/88 season became an overdue triumph. Bull's 52 goals, plus 23 from Mutch, brought the Fourth Division championship and the lower divisions' Sherpa Van Trophy, in which almost 81,000 watched the 2-0 Wembley final victory over Burnley.

'Football, the people's sport, has once again revived the pride of a town,' said the leading article in the *Sandwell Evening Mail*. 'The gold and black of Wolverhampton shines anew ... Wolves and Aston Villa, the West Midlands' two most charismatic clubs, are on the climb upwards. The coincidence that the former's manager, Graham Turner, was sacked by the latter cannot be overlooked for his is as heart-warming a story as that of his club.'

Wolves were indeed on the way back and the following season stormed to the Third Division title with even more points (92) and goals (96), Bull scoring 37 of them and adding 13 in cup competitions to earn an England cap against Scotland. Mutch again backed him up splendidly with 21 league goals and played for England B.

While some supporters were no doubt dreaming of returning to the First Division as quickly as they had left it, consolidating at the level below was a more realistic target and was achieved with a run of solid mid-table finishes. Bull played in the 1990 World Cup and his remarkable run continued with hauls of 27, 27 and 23 goals to make him the highest scorer in the club's history.

* * *

West Bromwich Albion were lording it two divisions above Wolves and in the top six in November 1986 when manager Ron Saunders (now on his third West Midlands club) allowed Bull to move to their greatest rivals. Three years later the clubs were competing at the same level and Bull was scoring winning goals against Albion at Molineux and The Hawthorns on his way to Italia 90. Saunders by then was long gone, one of nine different managers in 16 years – three of whom bravely came back for more. Yet not long beforehand there had been something of a golden era at The Hawthorns under two of them, Johnny Giles and Ron Atkinson.

The first of the nine, and longest serving, was former Baggies full-back Don Howe, one of those fine coaches who never quite cut it as a manager. But it was unfortunate for him that his return to the club to take over from Alan Ashman in 1971 coincided with the dramatic decline of Jeff Astle and Tony Brown as one of the country's most potent striking partnerships. From 1965/66 to 1970/71 that pair's joint goals total in First Division games alone was 35, 30, 37, 38, 35 and 41. The last of those, significantly, was the first in which Brown was the major contributor. Astle's injuries reduced his effectiveness and goalscoring to eight in 42 games over the next three seasons as Albion followed two years in the division's lower reaches with relegation in 1972/73.

They finished rock bottom with only 38 goals in total and were sent on their way by defeats against a gleeful trio in Wolves, Stoke and Birmingham. Astle made his last half-dozen appearances in the Second Division, including one victory at Villa Park that kept them in the promotion race, but winning only one of the 11 games after that meant finishing no higher than eighth.

He departed for South Africa while player-manager Giles arrived from Leeds to succeed Howe and inspire recovery. In an exciting finish to the 1975/76 season, thousands of Baggies supporters followed the team to Oldham, where appropriately it was Brown, soon to become the club's record scorer, who grabbed the only goal to seal promotion. Winning the FA Youth Cup for the first time and beating Wolves of all people in both legs of the final was an enjoyable bonus.

Giles oversaw an excellent season in seventh place back in the First Division from his midfield berth, often alongside a young if injury-prone Bryan Robson and then gifted winger Laurie Cunningham. It was a huge disappointment when he walked out because of not being given sufficient control over transfers, but Ronnie Allen, briefly, and then Ron Atkinson from January 1978 brought about a further improvement to sixth place. There could well have been an FA Cup Final too but after ending newly promoted Nottingham Forest's hopes of a stunning Double with a 2-0 FA Cup win, Albion fell to lowly Ipswich 3-1 in the semi-final.

The players had to make do instead with a groundbreaking summer tour to China, followed by a series of shorter trips in the UEFA Cup, a good run to the quarter-final ending in narrow defeat by Red Star Belgrade (0-1, 1-1). Allen had recommended signing Cyrille Regis from Hayes for £5,000, who became a real force in an outstanding 1978/79 season. The Baggies would have been runners-up had they not lost to Forest, the other contenders, by a last-minute goal at The Hawthorns in the final game. Left-back Derek Statham, Regis and Cunningham were all named in the PFA team of the season and were among the same 11 Albion players who appeared more than 30 times each and featured together on a memorable December day when Manchester United were spanked 5-3 on their own pitch, a month before the Baggies went top of the table.

'Three Black Aces' was the *Sunday Mirror* headline in a reference to Regis, Cunningham and full-back Brendon Batson, a trio who Atkinson, in a stunt that has not worn well, dubbed 'The Three Degrees'. 'As good a game as I've ever seen,' the manager called the Old Trafford performance.

Two and a half years on he was working there himself after another good season in fourth place, but he upset Albion by taking key midfielders Robson and Remi Moses, both of whom had begged to join him. Cunningham had already gone to Real Madrid and Brown finally bowed out in October 1981 with 218 league goals in 574 games (both club records). That same month goalkeeper Tony Godden ended a remarkable run of 228 consecutive appearances, and despite 1982 semi-finals in the two domestic cup competitions, lost to QPR and Tottenham, the team was on the slide. Allen, Ron Wylie, the returning Giles, his brother-in-law Nobby Stiles and Saunders in quick succession were all unable to arrest it.

Goalscorers Regis and Garry Thompson were further unpopular departures and the season after they left, Albion hit the bottom of the barrel with only four wins out of 42 games, finishing 1985/86 a full 18 points from safety. It was little consolation that two of the wins were over Birmingham, who went down with them.

Like Wolves, who dropped to the Fourth Division the same season, Albion were now in serious decline, not helped when Saunders – a former centre-forward who might have been expected to recognise a good one – sold Bull to the old enemy for a song.

He believed the player's first touch was not good enough, although the obvious rejoinder was that regardless, his second touch tended to end up in the back of the net.

For three seasons out of four the Baggies sat marooned in the Second Division's bottom eight, and in the other one blew a chance of promotion after Atkinson's second spell abruptly ended with a move to Atlético Madrid. He had arrived back in September 1987 and found 'the place was in disarray and close to being skint'.

Brian Talbot's tenure as player-manager finished with the humiliation of a 4-2 FA Cup defeat at home to non-league Woking in January 1991 and four months later Albion were relegated to the Third Division under Bobby Gould, who spoke of 'the worst feeling I've ever had in the game'. Many supporters shared it.

* * *

Birmingham became fellow strugglers alongside Albion without having enjoyed quite so much success earlier, despite the emergence of a club legend in Trevor Francis.

Not quite a genuine local hero, he was born a Devonian in April 1954 and was spotted by a Blues scout when scoring a hat-trick for Plymouth Schools in Bordesley Green, just a couple of miles from St Andrew's. Although 'frail' on his own admission, he was sharp enough to make history as the Blues' youngest player when coming on as substitute away to Cardiff in the Second Division on 5 September 1970, aged only 16 years and 139 days. In the starting XI a week later, he scored on his home debut against Oxford in a 1-1 draw and was on his way. 'Francis at last set the game alight with a goal that thoroughly vindicated manager Goodwin's gamble in including him,' reported the *Sunday Mirror.*

After four more games it was back to the reserves until the second half of the season, when it was hardly coincidence that his regular selection marked an upturn in the team's humdrum fortunes. From the start of February, Francis, still a 16-year-old apprentice, scored in eight successive matches, the highlight being the day that 25,600 saw him hit four goals past Bolton Wanderers to earn the tabloid tag 'Superboy'. *The People*'s player ratings awarded him the rare accolade of ten out of ten and Bolton's manager Nat Lofthouse – no mean goalscorer himself – said, 'What a future this kid must have.' Three home games later the crowd was nearly 50,000 to see a sixth successive win and only then did Blues fall away, ending any promotion talk and finishing ninth.

Twelve months on, however, they made it with an adventurous team featuring Bob Latchford (23 goals), Bob Hatton (15) and Francis (13) in attack, supported by Gordon Taylor on the left wing. Reaching the FA Cup semi-final (a 3-0 defeat by Leeds) had no adverse effect on an unbeaten run of 18 Second Division games in a dramatic finish: thousands of Millwall supporters turned up at Orient hoping to see their promotion rivals Blues beaten but on a wild night Latchford's goal won the prize in front of a capacity crowd swollen by an even larger number of Birmingham followers. They even won the FA Cup third-place match against Stoke, the first tie in that competition ever to be decided on penalties.

A terrific run at the end of the first season back in the First Division pushed them up to tenth place, with the fourth-best crowds in the country averaging 36,663 – nearly 10,000 more than Second Division Villa. When they drew 2-2 with West Brom in August, Latchford was delighted to put Blues' second goal past his younger brother Peter, Albion's keeper. Then the third of the brothers, Dave, played in goal for Blues for the rest of the season.

At Christmas they had been 21st, and the following three years finished 19th, 17th and 19th, one point, four points and three points clear of relegation respectively. Bob Latchford was sold to Everton in February 1974 and the following season Francis suffered a bad injury at Sheffield United in October, returning just in time for the huge disappointment of another FA Cup semi-final defeat. Unlike the Leeds tie, Blues were the favourites against Second Division Fulham, but after a 1-1 draw they lost the Maine Road replay in extra time, earning Bobby Moore and Alan Mullery a last hurrah at Wembley against West Ham.

Manager Freddie Goodwin left early the following season and under his assistant Willie Bell, Francis's goals kept the team up: 17, 21 and 25 in successive seasons. The latter campaign featured a six-month interlude from September 1977 to March with Sir Alf Ramsey in charge. A board member since January 1976, he won four of his first five games, including a popular one at Villa Park – one of Blues' record five straight wins over the old enemy – but in February a dispute over Francis's future caused his resignation. He had fined the England international for a newspaper article about needing a bigger club and wanted him sold to raise some money. The board, having agreed, infuriated the manager by changing their mind, so after a 'disgraceful' 4-0 defeat at Coventry on 4 March, Ramsey walked away from his last job in English football.

Jim Smith took over but after finishing in the top half for the first time in five seasons, Blues went down with QPR and Chelsea after Francis finally moved to Nottingham Forest in February 1979. He had stayed loyal for ten years, scoring 133 goals, but having played only nine league games in an injury-plagued season he took his leave of a team that had won two games out of 25. Becoming Britain's first £1m footballer, he won the European Cup with his header for Brian Clough's team in the final against Malmö three months later.

Buying in some experience with the Francis money, Smith took Blues straight back up on goal difference from Chelsea thanks to a 3-3 draw with Notts County in the final game and a very tight 38-goal rearguard. Colin Todd joined Joe Gallagher in central defence, Archie Gemmill was in midfield and Frank Worthington livened up the attack and the dressing room.

They stayed up for three seasons without scoring many goals, Smith being sacked in February 1982, which caused professional comedian Jasper Carrott to resign as a director. Smith's successor was none other than Ron Saunders, who had just walked out on Villa. Long coveted by Blues chairman Clifford Coombes, he was able to double his wages and claim, 'I would still have been at Villa Park if I had been given the same security and freedom of management I have been given by Birmingham.' The players were not immediately roused, losing at home to Villa before he officially took over, but better results against Stoke, West Brom, Wolves and Coventry kept them up by two points, new signing Mick Harford scoring nine goals in a dozen games.

In Saunders's first visit back to Villa Park at Christmas 1982, Blues produced their joint-biggest win of the season, 3-0. They lost the return in April when in trouble at the bottom but won five and drew one of the last six to stay up with more crucial goals from Harford.

The following season, however, it was back down for another year, scoring only 39 goals and with an average gates as low as 14,000. Again they went straight back up, runners-up to Jim Smith's Oxford United, but celebrations on the final Saturday were spoilt for the biggest crowd of the season at 25,000 when a 12ft-high boundary wall collapsed under pressure from Leeds fans, killing a 15-year-old from Northampton who was attending his first professional match.

'Hundreds were injured – many seriously – as the last day of the League soccer season erupted into a bloody nightmare at Birmingham,' said the *Sunday Mirror* under the headline 'It's A Riot'. It was the same day as the Bradford fire and the two events were bracketed together for the subsequent government inquiry, which blamed the St Andrew's trouble on 'spectators bent from the outset on violence'. Recommendations included an identity-card scheme for all fans, closed-circuit television for all First and Second Division grounds and an alcohol ban. Birmingham were later fined £5,000 by the FA.

With the Heysel tragedy having occurred later the same month, the 1985/86 season began under a cloud dark enough to make St Andrew's a dismal place. Even while winning four of their first five home games, Blues could not attract a crowd as high as even 12,000 except for the visit of Villa. Worse, that winning form proved deceptive. From the end of September, Saunders's team lost 15 league games out of 17, drawing the other two, and in January he left for West Brom following a home defeat in the FA Cup by Altrincham – one of the rare occasions a non-league team has ever won away to First Division opposition.

The Coombs family (Keith had replaced his father Clifford as chairman) had had enough and in December sold out to Ken Wheldon, the former Walsall chairman, whose plan for the two clubs to share St Andrew's as well as a training ground was thwarted by the Football League. John Bond was unsurprisingly not able to prevent relegation, with only 30 goals scored – a historical low. Rare bonanzas of a 3-0 win at Villa Park and 4-4 draw at Coventry meant they stayed ahead of Albion at the bottom.

These were hard times and Wheldon felt obliged to embark on a period of austerity that badly affected results. The club was almost £3m in debt and losing £10,000 a week. The penultimate First Division gate against Southampton was as low as 5,833 and the rollercoaster, instead of swooping up again, dipped towards the Third Division. For two successive seasons, under Bond and then former defender Garry Pendrey, Blues survived by two points. In the next one, 1988/89, they lost seven of the first eight games – one of them by 5-0 at Walsall – and in April, with another demotion inevitable, Wheldon sold out to the Kumar brothers, based in Manchester with no discernible football background. Dave Mackay took over as manager and with crowds dipping below 5,000 it was little consolation to take Walsall and Shrewsbury down to the third tier with them, as Wolves and Port Vale went in the other direction.

This was not to be one of the more glorious chapters in Mackay's football history, which may be why he devoted precisely one page out of 250 to Birmingham in his autobiography. From the promise of seventh place in 1990 and 12 matches without defeat to start the next season, they fell to 15th in January, when he resigned two days after being given a vote of confidence.

One of the reasons was illustrated when the next man in, Lou Macari, was told there was no money for a hotel and so slept in the club offices, a supporter having provided a sofa bed. The bubbly Macari decided to concentrate on the Leyland DAF Cup, and his team progressed all the way to Wembley, where some 45,000 Bluenoses saw big John Gayle score two of the best goals of his career to beat Tranmere. Hugely disappointed with the contracts offered to him and those players out of contract, however, Macari left barely four months after joining and moved to Stoke.

Fortunately the board came up with another winner in former Leeds and England full-back Terry Cooper, before bowing to the financial problems that left the club in administration for five months after Cooper's team won promotion as Third Division runners-up; they should have been champions but lost the last two matches.

So although in the summer of 1992 there would be no Olympics in Birmingham, which had applied six years earlier to stage the Games – with Blues possibly using a proposed new Olympic Stadium at the NEC thereafter – the club had second-tier football to look forward to again, as well as the ups and downs of the Sullivan era to come.

* * *

Brian Joicey's winning goal away to Wolves in April 1970 earned **Coventry City** an unprecedented sixth place in the First Division and with it a Fairs Cup spot the following season, in which a gentle introduction was followed by a sharp reality check. In the club's first European game John O'Rourke's hat-trick brought a 6-1 romp away to Bulgarians Trakia Plovdiv, who were then beaten 2-0 at Highfield Road.

The excitement of being drawn against Bayern Munich, just establishing themselves as one of West Germany's top clubs, was dampened on a wet Bavarian night that kept the crowd below

13,000 and led to young goalkeeper Eric McManus, deputising for the injured Bill Glazier, being beaten four times in the first 20 minutes. The final damage was 6-1, a measure of pride being restored by a 2-1 home win in the second leg with barely half the all-ticket limit of 48,000 in attendance.

In the league, the best moment of a dull campaign was the 'donkey kick' goal scored in a 3-1 win at home to Everton: little Scot Willie Carr put the ball between his feet and flipped it up behind him for fellow midfielder Ernie Hunt to volley into the net. This party trick – which had been tried in a pre-season friendly at Blackpool and failed miserably – won *Match of the Day's* Goal of the Season award but was then banned.

It was an achievement (mainly down to Glazier and his defenders) to finish tenth despite scoring only 37 goals, a deficiency that was not really remedied for some years. In the meantime there were a succession of relegation fights, as well as red-faced FA Cup defeats by Rochdale and Hull that led to Noel Cantwell making way in February 1972 for a progressive alliance of Gordon Milne and general manager Joe Mercer.

By the time Jimmy Hill returned as unpaid managing director in 1975, (while continuing as presenter of *Match of the Day*), however, he found that 'gates were down, results were unexciting and the diminishing crowd was losing confidence'.

In the second season of this new arrangement the struggle to avoid relegation was tighter than ever, and ended with the bottom ten teams separated by just five points. On the final midweek night Tottenham and Stoke were already doomed and two of the three clubs who could still join them, Coventry and Bristol City, were meeting at Highfield Road while Sunderland were at mid-table Everton. So many wanted to see the Sky Blues' game that the referee agreed to delay the start, which meant that well before the end the crowd knew Sunderland had lost and would go down as long as Coventry and City stayed level at 2-2. Just to make sure they got the message, Hill insisted the Sunderland score should be given out to the crowd, whereupon the tempo slowed even more in a non-aggression pact that lasted until both teams were able to celebrate at the final whistle. He was subsequently reprimanded by the Football League.

Supporters had been upset by outgoing transfers, above all the loss of former apprentice Dennis Mortimer to Aston Villa, but Milne made some good buys and in particular ginger-haired Glaswegian Ian Wallace, who became the goalscorer lacking for so long. Having landed a match-winning hat-trick at home to Stoke in the 1977 escape, he went on to score 21 and 15 goals in the next two seasons, which led to finishes of seventh and tenth, even after a 7-1 hammering at The Hawthorns in October 1979. That game was not the best advert for a brown change strip once voted the worst kit of all time, but City fans soon had more than shirt colours to worry about.

The early 1980s was a grim period of further struggles to preserve First Division status, which in six successive seasons was achieved by margins of three points, eight, one, two, one and two, hence the joke that if the *Titanic* had been painted sky blue it would never have gone down.

After Milne was made general manager, Dave Sexton, Bobby Gould and Don Mackay all found themselves handicapped by the club's financial position. The novelty of First Division football, introduced to an average crowd of 35,000 in 1967/68, had since long worn off and by 1982/83 the figure was 10,552. Fine new training headquarters and an accompanying leisure centre at Ryton had to be financed by selling Wallace to Nottingham Forest for a seven-figure sum, and losing the 1981 League Cup semi-final to Second Division West Ham (3-2, 0-2) meant another lost payday.

Hill had become chairman in 1980, still full of ideas. They included trying to change the club's name to Coventry Talbot, then controversially incorporating the car company's logo into the shirt design at a time when shirt sponsorship was not allowed in televised matches. In an attempt to combat hooliganism he made the typically far-sighted but also unpopular decision to convert Highfield Road into the first all-seater stadium in England; sitting in the rain with no roof cut attendances further and visiting Leeds fans used the seats as weapons anyway.

A 5-5 draw at Southampton in May 1982, Mark Hateley equalising in the last minute to complete his hat-trick was rare excitement, and after the following season Hill left, undermined, he felt, by his fellow directors. The team finished 19th for two years running and in 1985 only stayed up by winning the three final games, against Stoke, Luton and Everton. Mackay resigned in April the following year with relegation threatening yet again, whereupon George Curtis and John Sillett began their famous partnership by winning two of the last three matches to ensure safety.

Having retired from playing after his three years at Aston Villa, Curtis had worked for the Sky Blues' commercial department and then become executive director, while Sillett had been employed on and off as a coach depending who the manager was. Signing only Keith Houchen from Scunthorpe and David Phillips from Norwich, then promoting young Steve Sedgley, the genial pair had their charges in the top half of the table for almost all of the 1986/87 season and increased attendances from barely 11,000 in the first home game against Arsenal to double that for a thrilling 4-3 win over Tottenham at Christmas.

Nobody knew at that point how large Spurs would loom in Coventry history a few months later. Two weeks after the Londoners were beaten at Highfield Road, the FA Cup run began with a comfortable 3-0 win over Third Division strugglers Bolton. The draw sent City to Old Trafford for the fourth round, where Alex Ferguson was only two months into his new job as Manchester United's manager; his hopes of an early trophy were ended by Houchen scoring the only goal on a frozen pitch.

City were already revelling in newfound confidence summed up in Birmingham's *Evening Mail*: 'More by luck than design, Coventry have found a managerial partnership that through its no-nonsense, down-to-earth approach has created one of West Midlands football's rarest sights – a club flourishing once more.'

Six successive wins from mid-February included further FA Cup triumphs at Stoke (1-0) and Sheffield Wednesday (3-1) to set up a semi-final back at Hillsborough against Second Division promotion contenders Leeds. An exciting tie went to extra time, in which Dave Bennett was given a tap-in to win it 3-2.

Having finished third to City's tenth, Tottenham were unsurprisingly made favourites in the final, not least because their leading scorer Clive Allen had 48 goals to his name – three of them in two games against the Sky Blues. At Wembley he added a 49th within two minutes, and after Bennett's swift equaliser a dramatic first half ended with Brian Kilcline nudging Glenn Hoddle's free kick into his own net. Just after the hour, Houchen brought City level again with a diving header, and in extra time a cross by Lloyd McGrath, whose main role was to subdue Hoddle, brought the second own goal of a memorable final, deflected in by the unfortunate Gary Mabbutt.

'Principally Coventry beat Spurs because on the day, over two hours, they were the better footballing side,' wrote David Lacey in *The Guardian*. 'They had the strength where it mattered most when it mattered most. Steve Ogrizovic made two uncharacteristic errors and one of these cost Coventry a goal but in the end his was the expertise that stopped Clive Allen snatching the Cup back for Tottenham.' Sillett rightly claimed of one of the best post-war finals, 'It was a classic, with both sides trying to go forward and attack. They both showed the best of English football, but our boys were superb.'

The BBC's Jimmy Hill, casting neutrality aside, led the players in a chorus of the Sky Blue anthem, and next day in Coventry a crowd well over ten times the average gate of 16,000 turned out to show their appreciation.

1987 FA Cup Final: Coventry City 3 Tottenham Hotspur 2 (after extra time)
Coventry City: Ogrizovic, Phillips, Downs, McGrath, Kilcline (Rodger), Peake, Bennett, Gynn, Regis, Houchen, Pickering.
Tottenham Hotspur: Clemence, Hughton (Claesen), Thomas, Hodge, Gough, Mabbutt, C. Allen, P. Allen, Waddle, Hoddle, Ardiles (Stevens).

Being FA Cup holders after 20 consecutive seasons in the First Division was worthy of new respect and with Sillett promoted to team manager, the club produced three further solid seasons in tenth, seventh and 12th places. There was nevertheless an FA Cup sensation of a different sort in January 1989 when City were dumped out of the competition 2-1 by non-league Sutton United.

A year later came a narrow League Cup semi-final defeat to Forest (1-2, 0-0) but even with record-signings David Speedie and Kevin Gallacher on board the lack of goals was worrying. After losing the final game of 1989/90 6-1 at home to Liverpool, the next campaign began badly and in November Sillett said he would not be signing a new contract. The club immediately sacked him and just as quickly appointed as player-manager Terry Butcher, who had been about to move from Rangers to Leeds.

In the event he played just half a dozen games and lasted a mere 14 months, being sacked in January 1992. Only the fact that Luton lost on the last day of that season brought another great escape and allowed City, beaten at Villa Park, to gain a place in the brave new world of the Premier League.

* * *

For three consecutive seasons in the 1970s the highest-placed West Midlands club was **Stoke City** – a hat-trick they had never achieved before and would not repeat until 2013–16 (see Appendix I). Twice in that period Tony Waddington's mixture of mainly local lads and old heads competed in Europe, as well as narrowly losing two FA Cup semi-finals and winning a first major trophy at last, the 1972 League Cup. Yet later they were not immune to the downward syndrome that blighted the region, sharing time in the third tier of English football with Birmingham and West Bromwich Albion as Wolves finally moved in the other direction.

For a club that had never reached the FA Cup Final, the two successive semi-final defeats by Arsenal were hard to take. Stoke were never closer than at Hillsborough on 27 March 1971 when they led 2-1 with a minute to play. Gordon Banks claimed he was then fouled before conceding a corner from which John Mahoney handled Frank McLintock's flicked header. Peter Storey calmly put away the penalty to leave Waddington fuming, 'There were 55,000 people here and they must all have seen Gordon shoved in the back.' *The People* reported, 'Stoke should have made their Wembley place secure long before. They went in at half-time two goals up. They had outplayed Arsenal.'

The psychological advantage was now with the London side, who dominated the replay at Villa Park four days later in winning 2-0 and went on to do the Double. It was very little consolation to the Potters to win the third-place match against Everton – the second of five ever played – staged in front of a tiny crowd at Selhurst Park.

A second successive moderate league campaign a year later became insignificant amid two exciting cup runs. First came the Football League Cup, which turned into a marathon of 12 games. Three of them were in the fourth round against the runaway First Division leaders Manchester United, who were overcome after Stoke won the toss to stage the second replay at home, where they came through 2-1 with John Ritchie's goal. The three games were watched by 130,000 people and there were also packed houses for the fifth-round tie at Bristol Rovers (4-2) and then four semi-final matches against West Ham.

The Londoners seemed to have the advantage after winning their away leg 2-1, Geoff Hurst putting a penalty past his England friend Banks. But at Upton Park, Ritchie brought the aggregate score level and with three minutes of extra time remaining Banks pulled off a save from another Hurst penalty that the goalkeeper rated better than his famous one from Pelé in the 1970 World Cup.

It was a more important one too, keeping Stoke in the competition for a third game – goalless – at Hillsborough and then a momentous fourth meeting in an Old Trafford mudbath. On 26 January, seven weeks after the tie had begun, Stoke won 3-2 with goals by Mike Bernard, Peter Dobing and Terry Conroy, two of them going past Bobby Moore, who was deputising in goal for the concussed Bobby Ferguson.

At Wembley, Chelsea's glamour boys and European Cup Winners' Cup holders were expected to repeat their league victory at the Victoria Ground earlier in the season. Peter Osgood equalised Conroy's header, but veteran George Eastham tapped in the winner from two yards as Banks defied Chelsea throughout.

So, *The People* reported, the final was the story of 'The Golden Oldies'. 'Gordon Banks lived up to his reputation as the world's greatest goalkeeper,' said the *Daily Mirror*. And for the *Birmingham Post*, 'It was fitting that 35-year-old George Eastham should score the winning goal in the League Cup final and gain his and Stoke's first major honour. Eastham returned from South Africa encouraged by the campaign for restrictions on tackling from behind and now he will delay his departure to help Stoke in their assault on the FA Cup.'

1972 League Cup Final: Stoke City 2 Chelsea 1
Stoke City: Banks, Marsh, Pejic, Bernard, Smith, Bloor, Conroy, Greenhoff (Mahoney), Ritchie, Dobing, Eastham.
Chelsea: Bonetti, Mulligan (Baldwin), Harris, Hollins, Dempsey, Webb, Cooke, Garland, Osgood, Hudson, Houseman.

With a Wembley win and even a hit record to their name ('We'll Be With You' reached number 34), that assault on the other domestic cup competition continued by knocking out Manchester United after drawing at Old Trafford. In another drawn semi-final against Arsenal they had some luck this time as Bob Wilson injured a knee, Peter Simpson scored an own-goal equaliser and then striker John Radford had to take over between the posts. The replay was closer than the previous one, Jimmy Greenhoff and Charlie George exchanging penalties before Radford scored what most observers felt was a deserved winner, 'Rightly punishing Stoke for their defensive attitude to the whole tie,' said the *Post*.

Not often could Waddington's Stoke be called negative, with little midfielders Eastham and Dobing complemented by the attacking power of Greenhoff, Geoff Hurst and Ritchie, the latter scoring 91 goals in five seasons before breaking his leg at Ipswich and being forced to retire with a club record of 176 in his two spells. When Banks (having suffered an eye injury in a car crash), Eastham and Dobing also retired, maverick midfielder Alan Hudson was recruited from Chelsea for £240,000 and the club paid £325,000 for Leicester's Peter Shilton, a world record for a goalkeeper.

The blend worked well. Finishing fifth in 1973/74, the Potters were the first team to beat Leeds all season, at the end of February, which came a month after staging the First Division's first Sunday game, against Chelsea. The following season they were in with a shout of winning the title itself. Beginning with a 3-0 demolition of champions Leeds in Brian Clough's demoralising first league match, the Potters topped the table in November and again at the end of February. Even after a cruel run of injuries they lay third with three games to play but failed to score in any of them, losing to Sheffield United and drawing with Newcastle and Burnley. In fifth place again, they were just four points short of champions Derby, having won only four of the last 13 games.

Competing in the UEFA Cup could not be counted as an excuse, however: just as two years earlier against Kaiserslautern, City went out in the first round, this time to Ajax.

As the transfer fees paid for Hudson and Shilton illustrated, Stoke seemed to be in better financial shape than many of their Midlands rivals, crowds having picked up to over 27,000. But they had made a loss of almost £450,000 and from the time of a freak accident in January 1976 matters deteriorated on and off the pitch. The roof was blown off the Butler Street stand in a violent storm, a First Division game against Middlesbrough had to be played at Vale Park and when the bill for a new roof came in at £250,000 the stars had to be sold.

Manchester United, Arsenal and Everton swooped down on players like Greenhoff, Hudson and left-back Mike Pejic, and suddenly Waddington had a fight on his hands with a badly weakened squad. From ninth place in November they plummeted after that trio's departure and in March Waddington gave up after 17 years as manager.

Even then they were outside the bottom eight but under caretaker Eastham only one match was won out of the unlucky last 13, and in the tight finish that saved Coventry, the Potters went down with Sunderland and Tottenham. They had scored just 28 goals.

The following season, with Shilton next out of the door, was most notable for a shocking FA Cup defeat at home to non-league Blyth Spartans and the subsequent arrival of Alan Durban as manager from Shrewsbury Town. Lifting City from 18th place to seventh, with local boy Garth Crooks as leading scorer, he continued the upward climb in 1978/79. Top of the table early on, the Potters faltered in March but finished strongly and just pipped Sunderland to the final promotion place when Paul Richardson scored the only goal with a couple of minutes to spare at Notts County.

Youngsters Adrian Heath and Lee Chapman were introduced during a First Division campaign that achieved its main objective with survival by a five-point margin, which led to Crooks, top scorer again, moving on to a successful spell with Spurs. Fortunately, the taller, wiry Chapman was ready to replace him and his 15 goals helped the team finish in the top half of the table in 1980/81. The football, however, was often attritional, Durban upsetting the London press after a dull defeat at Highbury by snorting, 'If you want entertainment, go and watch a bunch of clowns.' With attendances dropping to a new post-war low, it was not the most tactful comment, especially as Stoke's gates were falling by a quarter to 15,500.

Durban then left for Sunderland, and his replacement Richie Barker, who had been John Barnwell's coach at Wolves, avoided relegation in his first season by two points (finishing level with Durban's Sunderland), and was comfortable in his second after signing future England winger Mark Chamberlain from Port Vale. But he was sacked in December 1983 amid another relegation struggle. From 21st place, Barker's assistant, former Potter Bill Asprey, staved off the worst on the last day with a 4-0 win over bottom club Wolves, Glaswegian Paul Maguire from Shrewsbury Town scoring all four goals.

Even with finances in a poor state again, nobody could have predicted how catastrophic the next season would prove. Maguire surprisingly left for the United States and in his absence the two highest scorers from open play were defenders Steve Bould and Paul Dyson – with three each. To relate the season's statistics seems almost cruel: only three wins and 24 goals; 31 defeats and 91 goals conceded; bottom from the first week of November onwards; an utterly dispirited team finishing with 12 losses from the last 13 games. Asprey, who must have found his coaching jobs in Syria and Iraq a piece of cake in comparison, departed in April, leaving the caretaker Tony Lacey to lose the last eight matches. One of those games, against Norwich, attracted a crowd of 4,597.

Former England captain Mick Mills was the brave man who took over. In four seasons his best finish was eighth, but he was sacked in November 1989 with one win (over West Brom) from the first 16 outings. His recently appointed coach Alan Ball could do little better and by the end of the season City were 13 points from safety and destined for the Third Division.

Local businessman Peter Coates became majority shareholder and chairman, appointing Lou Macari, who had just walked out on Birmingham, to succeed Ball in the summer of 1991 and overseeing the first revival. In Macari's first season Stoke had the disappointment of a play-off semi-final defeat by Stockport (0-1, 1-1) but took revenge on them three days later at Wembley, winning the Autoglass Trophy in front of more than 48,000 with Mark Stein's goal.

Losing in the FA Cup to Telford United was less impressive and summed up how poorly the club had performed in the two main domestic cups since those heady days of the early 1970s.

* * *

Alan Durban (Stoke), Richie Barker (Wolves and Stoke) and Graham Turner (Aston Villa and Wolves) all earned jobs at bigger West Midlands clubs by making an important contribution to the most successful period in the history of **Shrewsbury Town**.

From 1974–78 Durban lifted the club out of the Fourth Division and consolidated in the Third before moving on to the Potteries, whereupon Barker, his eventual successor there, and then Turner took the Shrews one stage further to a record high of eighth place in the Second Division as well as two FA Cup quarter-finals.

After three mid-table seasons, during one of which converted centre-half Alf Wood scored 35 league goals and was sold to Millwall, a drop down to the fourth tier had occurred in the miserable Three-Day Week season of 1973/74; one midweek crowd against Charlton was just 1,232. Welsh international midfielder Durban joined from Derby early on, getting a goal on his debut and finishing as leading scorer with a modest nine after becoming player-manager. Continuing in that arduous role, he led them straight back as runners-up to Mansfield Town, having recruited Ray Haywood from Stourbridge to score 21 of the 80 league goals, which included a hat-trick in the eventful 7-4 win over Doncaster.

After two solid seasons in the Third Division's top ten, Durban left for Stoke in February 1978, Barker declining to accompany him but leaving nine months later to join John Barnwell at Wolves. Turner at that point was a stalwart defender whose £30,000 fee from Chester in January 1973 made him the club's record signing; they could afford him because Manchester United paid three times as much for Shrewsbury's centre-half 'Big' Jim Holton.

Taking over from Barker with the team well placed in third position, Turner kept them in an exciting four-team promotion race that climaxed with home wins over Rotherham (3-1) and Exeter (4-1) to secure the title itself and preserve an unbeaten record at Gay Meadow. The final match was watched by 14,441. 'Shrewsbury carved out their own little piece of soccer history by winning Second Division status for the first time since they became a League club almost 30 years ago,' wrote the *Birmingham Post*.

The team's strength was also shown in their club-best FA Cup run the same season, knocking out Mansfield, Doncaster, Cambridge United, Malcolm Allison's First Division Manchester City (2-0) and Aldershot for a lucrative local derby quarter-final against Wolves. At Molineux a penalty by Ian Atkins earned them a draw in front of almost 41,000 but three days later Wolves won 3-1 with 15,279 at Gay Meadow.

So on 18 August 1979 Town played their first match in the Second Division, losing 2-0 at Swansea but recovering from a slow start to finish a comfortable 13th. Doing the double over both Chelsea and West Ham was a high spot and as well as the Londoners, visitors like Birmingham, Leicester, Newcastle and Sunderland drew good crowds to Shropshire, enabling the club to make their first six-figure signing in Aldershot forward John Dungworth.

More remarkably, they stayed in the second tier for ten years, finishing in a new high of eighth place during 1983/84 and 1984/85. The former season included a famous 5-1 win over Leeds after being 1-0 down, Paul Petts scoring a hat-trick in the last ten minutes. In 1982 they reached another FA Cup quarter-final, beating First Division runners-up and UEFA Cup holders Ipswich 2-1 before going out at Leicester. The Welsh Cup was a further source of success, with nine semi-finals in 11 years and trophy wins in 1977, 79, 84 and 85; unfortunately as an English club they were not allowed entry to the Cup Winners' Cup, so Gay Meadow was denied European football.

In the summer of 1984 Turner was given a chance in the First Division with Villa and was succeeded for three years by former forward Chic Bates, initially as another money-saving player-manager. He enjoyed a good first season with 20 goals from striker Gary Stevens, which included a double over Wolves and a sixth Welsh Cup success. But Town soon began to find themselves struggling against relegation and after finishing 19th, 18th and 18th they went down in 1989 with Birmingham and Walsall.

Bates had left to follow Lou Macari around as his coach and Ian McNeill was unsuccessful as the next manager. Gates dipped and players like Bernard McNally (to West Brom for a record £385,000) and John McGinlay, after scoring 22 goals in 1989/90, had to be sold. Others could be persuaded that Shrewsbury was a pleasant place to wind down a career; in December 1990, one of them, European Cup winner Gary Shaw, scored a hat-trick in four and a half minutes at Bradford City.

That was a comparatively rare highlight. Asa Hartford – yet another player-manager – was dismissed shortly afterwards and after three seasons in the Third Division the Town were relegated under John Bond in 1992, dropping back to the bottom rung where they had begun two eventful decades earlier.

* * *

In a region of so many professional clubs, large and small, it is perhaps surprising that there have not been even more cases down the years of mergers and groundsharing. The most dramatic proposal was probably for Stoke City and Port Vale to amalgamate in the 1920s (Chapter 4). In 2019 Coventry City ended up at St Andrew's, and some 30 years earlier that might have been the fate of **Walsall** – had they not moved to Molineux first.

The key figure was Ken Wheldon, a local man with a metal merchant's business, who first came to the notice of Saddlers supporters just before Christmas 1972. With crowds down to 5,000 or fewer in the Third Division there was continuing talk of financial woe, and chairman Ken Robinson was under pressure from fans. Instead of stumping up more money, he resigned, making way for Wheldon, who was described in the *Birmingham Post* as a 'wealthy racehorse owner', and who told readers, 'There are many clubs in the Football League who are in a worse plight than us.'

He also predicted that the team, top of the Third Division table two months earlier, had 'a good chance of winning promotion'. As they had already slipped to tenth following a change of manager, it might have been wiser to hold fire on that one: they dropped as far as 20th and finished 17th, two points off relegation.

Billy Moore had walked away from his second period as manager following a disagreement with assistant John Smith, who replaced him but left in turn at the end of the season. In an illustration of Wheldon's ruthlessness and the club's financial problems, Ronnie Allen, hired in July 1973, and his assistant David Burnside were then sacked as an economy measure five days before Christmas. With the team struggling again, the last home gate had been only just over 3,000 and Wheldon had now experienced a year in the life of a lowly Third Division football club. 'The economic crisis is hitting clubs and it will be survival of the fittest,' he said.

For five years they managed to survive at that level, as well as earning fame and finance from the FA Cup run of 1974/75. After a goalless draw at Old Trafford, Manchester United, the runaway Second Division leaders, were toppled 3-2 in the replay with two goals by Alan Buckley, and First Division Newcastle were beaten 1-0 in front of almost 20,000. Only Birmingham, also in the First Division, halted the run, by 2-1.

The quicksilver Buckley, only 5ft 5in, was in his prime with 120 goals in five seasons, and in 1977/78 the Saddlers finished sixth, only three points behind the promoted trio, as well as knocking First Division Leicester out of the FA Cup. But after accepting £175,000 for Buckley from Birmingham in October 1978 they went down to the Fourth Division. Happily for the Saddlers, Birmingham were relegated too and sold him back for the same sum that summer to become player-manager and lead Walsall to the runners-up spot behind Huddersfield – pipped to the title by losing at home on the final day. For once he was not top scorer, youngster Don Penn beating him with 25 league goals.

There were narrow escapes in the next two seasons. In 1980/81, knowing that the losers in their last game away to

Sheffield United would go down, the Saddlers won it with a penalty by Penn. A year later they were made to sweat a few extra days after completing their programme, until rivals Swindon lost their last match and went down.

This insecurity – and one home crowd of below 2,500 – persuaded Wheldon to seek drastic solutions. As Wolves sank further into the financial mire in the summer of 1982, he became very interested in a proposal from their board to groundshare at Molineux. Derek Dougan, not involved at the time (though it later transpired he had ideas of his own), wrote in a newspaper column, 'It makes no practical sense, none at all. Walsall is eight miles from Molineux. The towns do not identify with their Black Country neighbour, so how could Walsall supporters feel at home at Molineux.'

While those supporters formed the Save Walsall Action Group, Wheldon joined forces with Sir Jack Hayward in a consortium opposing that of Doug Ellis to take control of Wolves. If successful, he would presumably have urged the groundshare on Walsall; instead, as mentioned in the Wolves section of this chapter, it was none other than Dougan who rode to the Wanderers' rescue.

A seed had, however, been sown and grew after the disasters at Bradford and Brussels in 1985 led to increasing concern about the safety of football grounds. The first victims were Charlton Athletic, forced to leave The Valley and share Selhurst Park with unloved rivals Crystal Palace. Walsall avoided that fate, but Fellows Park, like most lower-division grounds, needed extensive, expensive work, as was shown in February the previous year when a serious incident marred a great achievement in reaching the League Cup semi-final.

Top of the Third Division before falling away and missing promotion, Buckley's team had knocked out Arsenal at Highbury with Ally Brown's late goal and drawn the first leg of their semi-final at Liverpool 2-2. Almost 20,000 packed in to see a 2-0 defeat in the second leg, when a wall collapsed, injuring 20 people.

In November 1985, Wheldon, tired of waiting for Walsall to move up in the world, did so himself by taking over Birmingham, who would be a First Division club for a few more months, although their financial position was worse than that of the

Saddlers. Links between the two clubs immediately became much closer, as the *Evening Mail* reported in March 1986: 'Their futures appear more and more intertwined by the cost-cutting influence of St Andrew's chairman Ken Wheldon. Off the field the clubs will share the Elmdon training facilities next season and are already serviced by dual accountants and groundstaff. All this has fuelled speculation that groundsharing and even amalgamation are part of Wheldon's grand design to rescue the ailing St Andrew's giant from extinction.'

After a campaign led by furious supporters, the Football League killed that plan but such was the precarious state of football in the mid-1980s that such a suggestion was not unique. Three years earlier, Oxford United owner Robert Maxwell had proposed merging with Reading to produce 'Thames Valley Royals'. In London, Wimbledon's owner Ron Noades was always a keen turf warrior, with his eye on Crystal Palace; eventually buying them and sharing a ground but failing to amalgamate. Then Queens Park Rangers wanted to merge with Fulham.

The latter deal, seen off by furious supporters with Jimmy Hill becoming Fulham chairman, became linked with events in the West Midlands when Terry Ramsden bought Walsall. A flamboyant Londoner who made millions of pounds in Japanese bonds, Ramsden held shares in Marler Estates, the controversial property developers who at one time owned both Stamford Bridge and Craven Cottage with ambitions to build on one or the other.

With no obvious connection to Walsall or even the Midlands, he took over officially on 1 August 1986 and immediately sacked club legend Buckley, bringing in the little-known Scot Tommy Coakley. A season finishing in eighth place was made memorable by an FA Cup run in which victory away to First Division Charlton brought an away tie with none other than Birmingham. Nicky Cross scored the only goal to earn a fifth-round tie in which the Saddlers lost to another First Division side, Watford, only in a second replay after drawing 1-1 and 4-4.

Unfortunately the economic crash of 1987 eventually ruined both Ramsden's empire and any hopes of a new era for Walsall following promotion to the Second Division in 1987/88.

Irish international David Kelly's 20 goals helped them finish third in the Third Division and he scored seven more in five play-off games that took them past Notts County and Bristol City, the final requiring a third match that Walsall won 4-0 with a Kelly hat-trick. West Ham immediately signed him for £600,000, and after beating Birmingham 5-0 early on, a weakened team was unable to cope at the higher level. They finished bottom with only five wins all season, having suffered one dreadful run of 15 successive defeats that climaxed with a rampant Chelsea winning 7-0 at Fellows Park. Coakley made way for John Barnwell, who could not prevent a second successive relegation, once again after finishing bottom of the pile.

What is remarkable is that amid all this uncertainty and failure the club was able to press ahead with a far-sighted move away from Fellows Park – home since 1896 – to only the second new ground built by a Football League club since the 1950s (Scunthorpe's Glanford Park being the first).

The £3m Bescot Stadium, barely half a mile away and even closer to the M6, was opened for business by Sir Stanley Matthews in August 1990 before a friendly against Aston Villa, watched by almost 10,000 spectators. A week later Torquay United drew 2-2 there in the first league match. Stuart Rimmer remained a trusty goalscorer but from ninth at Christmas the team finished 16th, then 15th in 1992 – the year Terry Ramsden was declared bankrupt.

* * *

Another illustration of the dramatic changes two decades can bring occurred in the Potteries. **Port Vale** began the 1970s in the Fourth Division while Stoke City were well established in the First; 20 years later they were lording it at a higher level than their more famous neighbours, for only the second time in history.

At the end of the 1969/70 season, Vale had won promotion to the Third Division, where they suffered an early 7-3 defeat at Shrewsbury despite Bobby Gough scoring a hat-trick, but then drew more than 11,000 to Vale Park to see struggling giants Aston Villa beaten 2-0. The following year a similar-sized crowd for Villa's visit saw a dramatic 4-4 draw and in both those seasons Vale finished safe from relegation, and even had an international striker on the books: Belfast-born Sammy Morgan was capped by Northern Ireland, scoring against Spain on his debut.

In the summer of 1973 he moved to Villa after Vale finished sixth in a strange campaign. They went top early on shortly after losing 7-0 at Rotherham (who were relegated) and despite conceding more goals than any team, except three who went down, were in contention for one of the two promotion spots until two 5-0 defeats in the last four games.

Gordon Lee, making an impression in his first managerial job, was old school, a believer in hard work and discipline, although some opposing managers believed his team were too physical. In January 1973 Ron Greenwood accused them of 'diabolical intimidation' after his West Ham side came through an FA Cup tie 1-0, and two months later Blackburn's Ken Furphy called them 'brutal'. It did not seem to worry the Blackburn directors, as when Furphy left for Sheffield United later that year they turned to Lee to succeed him. Having regularly criticised the small crowds at Vale Park, he was keen to move on and within a few years was challenging at the top of the First Division with Everton.

To replace him Vale chose a man who was already a club legend – and ran the risk of tarnishing that reputation in an unforgiving role. Roy Sproson played almost 850 games for the club in a 22-year period, bowing out in April 1972 in front of a crowd of just 2,743. That gave some indication of what he was up against when moving up from coach to manager early in 1974, as did taking his team to Rochdale soon afterwards where the gate was barely 1,000. Sinking fast from ninth position, they finished only one place from relegation, albeit with seven points to spare.

In Sproson's first full season, however, they were sixth, four points behind the promoted trio and only out of contention in the last couple of games. Brian Horton's 13 goals from midfield attracted attention and in the centenary season of 1975/76 – marked by a friendly against Stoke – he went to Brighton for £30,000. Sproson oversaw the best FA Cup run since 1962, culminating in a fifth-round defeat at Villa Park with almost 47,000 present, but he could not change the image: Burnley (one of the FA Cup victims) and Rotherham called his players 'kickers' and 'thugs' respectively.

League results were nevertheless not good enough and in October 1977, club legend or not, he was sacked after defeat at Shrewsbury left Vale 23rd in the table. 'We offered him a job in charge of the club's youth policy but he has declined,' said chairman Arthur McPherson. Bitterly upset, Sproson never returned to Vale Park, where a statue paid for by fans was erected in 2012, 15 years after his death. He was honoured too in a local beer, Burslem's Legend, which carried his picture.

Six months after the sacking, nephew Phil, the son of post-war Vale player Jess Sproson, played the first of his 500 games as a substitute at Peterborough. New manager Bobby Smith from Bury could not bring about much improvement, however, and without a win in the final ten matches the Valiants went down to the Fourth Division, gates having dropped well below 4,000.

In a period of managerial flux, Smith soon left for Swindon, Dennis Butler was sacked, Alan Bloor resigned and even Gordon Banks, on the coaching staff for a year, was forced out. Under John McGrath, who brought in John Rudge as his assistant, the club sank in 1979/80 to the lowest point in their history, avoiding a re-election application only by winning the last two games. Far from rallying round, supporters drifted away and the last of those matches was watched by 2,338.

Another poor season, including a shameful 3-0 FA Cup defeat by Enfield, did nothing to encourage them back, and in May against York City the crowd of 1,924 was the lowest on record. Best players regularly had to be sold and in August 1982 future England winger Mark Chamberlain and goalkeeper Mark Harrison went to Stoke, followed shortly afterwards by Chamberlain's older brother Neville. The three deals raised some £210,000. Yet the 1980s still brought promotion three times. In 1982/83 with a young Robbie Earle appearing in midfield, 20 goals from Bob Newton led to third place and a return to the Third Division, only to come straight back down, McGrath being sacked soon after a dreadful day at Burnley when Vale went in at half-time trailing 6-0.

Thus began the John Rudge era, the best in the club's history. Forced to sell Mark Bright cheaply to Leicester, the seventh manager in as many years did well to find Andy Jones as a replacement, from Rhyl. The bustling Welsh striker was second-top scorer to Earle in the 1985/86 promotion campaign, then scored 29 league goals the season after, including five at home to Newport and a hat-trick in the 6-0 win at Fulham.

That meant losing him to First Division Charlton, and with Vale drifting down the table in the winter of 1987/88 there were rumblings about Rudge's job ahead of a third-round FA Cup tie against non-league Macclesfield. It took a late goal by teenager Kevin Finney to win it and earn the reward of a home tie with Tottenham Hotspur.

A month into the reign of new manager Terry Venables, Spurs had not yet settled and the sight of the sodden Vale Park pitch did nothing to ease any apprehension. 'Spurs seemingly didn't fancy it from the moment they arrived for their first glimpse of the stadium,' chortled the *Evening Sentinel* after a famous 2-1 home win enjoyed by millions on *Match of the Day*. 'With their quagmire pitch levelling the skill factor, the Third Division strugglers slugged it out as star-studded Spurs went to pot in the Potteries,' reported the *Sunday Mirror*.

Ray Walker, the former Villa midfielder, drove in the first goal from 25 yards and Phil Sproson was presented with a tap-in for the second. Neil Ruddock, preferred to World Cup winner Ossie Ardiles because of the heavy pitch, gave Tottenham hope of forcing an undeserved replay but Vale held out. An even bigger crowd than the 20,000 for that game turned out for the next round to see another First Division side, Watford, leave with a goalless draw before winning the replay 2-0.

Darren Beckford from Manchester City now took over the principal striking role, assisted to such good effect the following season by the experienced Ron Futcher and Earle that the trio scored more than 50 goals. Third behind Wolves and Sheffield United, Vale went into the play-offs where Beckford's hat-trick got them past Preston, and an Earle goal in each leg of the final beat Bristol Rovers to secure promotion.

Back in the Second Division for the first time since 1957, they lived comfortably for two seasons among some big fish. West Brom were beaten in the first home game, top-flight Derby knocked out of the FA Cup (before a 6-0 hiding at Villa Park) and, best of all, hostilities were revived with Stoke. Although both derbies were drawn, it was a shocking season for the Potters, who finished bottom, 13 places and 24 points behind Vale.

Another 39 league goals from Beckford in those two seasons – 'A brilliant striker but a nightmare to manage,' Rudge said – made him too hot to keep when Norwich offered £925,000. The same summer Earle also stepped up to the top division, Wimbledon paying £775,000, and although the club spent the latter fee on replacements including Martin Foyle for a record £375,000 from Oxford, there was a price to pay for the near £1m profit. From 11th place at Christmas 1991, Rudge's team went four months without a win, hit the bottom and stayed there, finishing five points from safety.

'Vale have a chance of retaining the support they have attracted over the last three seasons – providing they set their stall out and adopt a positive attitude,' the *Sentinel* reported. And so it would prove.

* * *

The history of football in Herefordshire is confusing, not least because the most prominent clubs around the end of the 19th century all tended to use the name of the county town, adding appendages like Town, City, Thistle or nothing at all. For more on those teams, see the following Non-League chapter.

Fortunately, the backstory of the club which finally brought the Football League to the county, as late as 1972, is clearer. **Hereford United** were formed in 1924 by a merger of St Martin's and the Royal Ordnance Army Corps team at Rotherwas, a munitions factory built in a south-eastern suburb during the First World War. They played from the start at Edgar Street, shared with Hereford City, who, like the equally prominent Hereford Thistle, were not interested in an amalgamation.

While the latter pair fell into decline, the new club soon progressed. Accepted straightaway into the Birmingham Combination (the junior version of the powerful Birmingham League), United played a first game on 30 August against Atherstone Town, losing 3-2 after leading at the interval. Only a week later they faced a difficult FA Cup debut and went down 7-2 away to Kidderminster Harriers of the Birmingham League.

They finished 11th of 18 teams, and at the end of that first season shared the Herefordshire Cup after drawing the final against Hereford City.

The *Birmingham Gazette* was sufficiently impressed to write at the start of the following season, 'The prospects are very bright and a new grandstand is to be opened by the Mayor of Hereford this afternoon.'

The optimism was justified for within the next three seasons United were fourth and later third, prompting a move with champions Walsall Reserves to the stronger Birmingham League. There they finished 11th of 18, as in the first Combination season, but scored an impressive 86 goals and began a long rivalry with Shrewsbury Town, who would eventually beat them into the Football League by 22 years.

In 1932/33 United reached the first round proper of the FA Cup, the competition in which they would make a national reputation 40 years on. They went out 2-1 away to Accrington Stanley. Normally to be found in the top half of the table, they were able to hold their own against numerous other Football League reserve teams who joined the competition, including those of Wrexham, Cardiff City and Bristol Rovers. During the Second World War they moved to the Southern League, greater travel notwithstanding, and in the first post-war season of 1945/46 were only pipped to the title on a points-per-game basis by Chelmsford City.

In an inconsistent period the club once went from 19th in 1950 to runners-up the following season, which gave them first dreams of the Football League. Although Shrewsbury and Gillingham were admitted when the two Third Divisions were expanded in 1950, the voting in normal years was hopelessly split by having so many teams applying. Thus in 1951, Hereford were one of no fewer than 12 non-league applicants, and did not receive a single vote. In 1953 they were given one vote, but did not try again for six years, this time as the Southern League North-Western champions; the competition having been regionalised that season, they won their section from Kettering, but lost a play-off 2-1 to the South-East champions Bedford.

In the meantime they had built a reputation as FA Cup fighters, even appearing on television while winning a first-round replay against amateurs Leyton in 1952 and then the following year beating Football League opposition for the first time, 2-0 at Exeter after a 1-1 draw; floodlights had been installed that year, much earlier than many clubs higher up the scale.

Aldershot were beaten in 1956 but the most spectacular victory was the following season, a 6-1 demolition of Queens Park Rangers in December 1957. It brought First Division opposition to Edgar Street in the form of Sheffield Wednesday, who won 3-0 in front of a record crowd of 18,114 that would never be beaten. 'Hereford put up a grand display and if things had run more kindly for them in a glorious opening spell of 20 minutes they could have built up a lead,' reported the *Birmingham Post*. Receipts of £2,900 were a welcome consolation.

The club achieved a coup in July 1966 by signing the great John Charles, hero of Leeds United, Juventus and Wales, when he left Cardiff City. Only 34, he scored 37 goals in his first season and played for five years, latterly as player-manager. He left in September 1971 to concentrate on business interests in Cardiff, praising Hereford as 'the most go-ahead club in non-league football today' but having no idea of the dramatic events that would follow under another player-manager, the former Nottingham Forest, Arsenal and Sheffield United man Colin Addison.

The beginnings were humble: a goalless draw in the FA Cup first round away to fellow Southern League side King's Lynn. United scraped through the replay 1-0, then drew at home to Fourth Division Northampton in the second round and used the incentive of a tie away to Newcastle United to come through at the third attempt, winning 2-1 on neutral ground at The Hawthorns.

And so to St James' Park on 24 January 1972 for a third-round tie that the Geordies, sitting comfortably in the middle of the First Division, were naturally expected to win. The game had been postponed by nine days but 2,500 United supporters still made the long Monday night trip and mobbed the jubilant players after a thrilling 2-2 draw.

All the goals came in the first 25 minutes, Brian Owen putting the visitors ahead after barely 15 seconds and Addison later equalising after two quick Newcastle goals. 'This is Hereford's finest hour,' said club chairman Frank Miles. But a finer one was to come.

Frustratingly, the replay had to be postponed four times because of a waterlogged or frozen Edgar Street pitch, finally taking place on 5 February, the date of the scheduled fourth round, as West Ham waited to see which of the teams they would be visiting. With capacity lowered slightly since the ground record was set 14 years earlier, the *Post* reported that there were fans 'clinging from the tree-tops and others precariously perched in the floodlighting towers'. They saw Hereford fight well once more but when Malcolm Macdonald, who had scored a controversial penalty in the first game, headed Newcastle in front with only seven minutes remaining, young *Match of the Day* commentator John Motson instinctively shouted, 'That's it!'

It wasn't. Ronnie Radford prompted a first pitch invasion by driving in gloriously from almost 35 yards, and then in extra time Dudley Tyler, United's best player, fed substitute Ricky George to bring the excited hordes streaming back on again. It was the first time for 23 years – since Yeovil knocked out Sunderland – that a non-league team had beaten a First Division side. *The People* had former Sunderland hero Len Shackleton reporting on the sensation. 'The club that once won at Wembley three times in five years were thumped on merit by a Southern League town famed not for football but for cider and bulls,' he wrote.

Only four days later the ground was packed again for West Ham's visit, with the pitch still more conducive to giant-killing than silky skills. The notoriously flaky Londoners held out for a goalless draw and won the replay 3-1 with a Geoff Hurst hat-trick.

Hereford had attracted such interest that despite playing on a Monday afternoon, the Upton Park crowd of 42,271 was only a few hundred short of the stadium record. More importantly, their reputation had been established nationwide, and despite only finishing as runners-up to Chelmsford in the Southern League that season, they clearly had a strong case for joining the Football League, which was no longer quite such a closed shop; Cambridge United had been elected two years earlier in place of Bradford Park Avenue.

It still proved a close-run thing. Northampton, Crewe and Stockport were all comfortably re-elected but Barrow and

Hereford received 26 votes each. That meant a second ballot, in which the desire for some new blood proved decisive by 29-20. Herefordshire finally had a Football League club.

In the close season Tyler joined West Ham for £15,000 and without him United lost their opening Fourth Division game 1-0 at Colchester on 12 August, but a week later they beat Reading 3-0 in front of 8,839 at Edgar Street, Londoner Ken Wallace scoring the first goal. Winning none of the other opening ten games, and standing 21st in the table, Addison's team learnt lessons with remarkable speed, shot up to second place in March and finished runners-up to Southport. The average attendance of almost 9,000 was the best by far in the division.

After two seasons of consolidation, a triumphant 1975/76 campaign brought further promotion, as Third Division champions. John Sillett had succeeded Addison as manager and Dixie McNeil, signed from Lincoln, was the country's leading scorer with 34 of the team's 86 goals, giving him 66 in two seasons. He was well supplied by Tyler, back from West Ham, and former England winger Terry Paine, who overtook the Football League record of 764 appearances; he finished in 1977 with 824.

These heady days ended all too soon. In September 1976 United were sixth in the Second Division but won only one more game before March and ended up bottom despite another 16 goals from McNeil. Early the next season he moved to Wrexham, who won the Third Division while United sank straight through it, relegated for the second successive season while scoring only 34 goals.

In the early 1980s they struck serious difficulties all too common to the region's clubs. In 1980, 1981 and 1983 they were forced to apply for re-election, having an uncomfortably narrow escape on the first occasion when receiving only three votes more than leading applicants Altrincham. Chairman Peter Hill wrote a positive letter to every club entitled to vote but later admitted, 'If I'd revealed our true financial position there's no doubt we would have been voted out.'

Like many lower-division clubs, United had regularly balanced the books by selling a player or two, but there were few Dixie McNeils. The promising Kevin Sheedy went very cheaply to Liverpool in 1978, and receiving £100,000 from Derby for midfielder Steve Emery in 1979 remained the record for a full ten years.

In 1982 the club accepted a £450 fine in order to save £2,000 annually by withdrawing from the Football Combination but that summer they almost went under with debts of £400,000. Supporters launched a Save Our Soccer campaign but saw a dreadful 1982/83 season – the one with six goalkeepers, including 40-year-old John Jackson – in which the team was bottom of the Fourth Division virtually from start to finish. In March 1983 the gate against Stockport was 1,294.

The worst, however, was over. In 1985, with John Newman as manager and Emery back, they were only one place off promotion and held Arsenal 1-1 in the FA Cup before going down 7-2 at Highbury. Double European Cup winner Ian Bowyer took over in 1987 but, apart from becoming the last English club to win the Welsh Cup in 1990, as well as running Manchester United close in the FA Cup (0-1), life was lived almost exclusively in the bottom half of the Fourth Division.

9

Non-League

'The Malvernians had all the best of the play, their combination being far in advance of their rivals.'

The Referee, March 1902

'Enjoying their finest hour since the club was formed 56 years ago, Worcester City beat Liverpool at Worcester yesterday to pass into the fourth round of the FA Challenge Cup competition.'

Birmingham Post, January 1959

'Doctors at Solihull Hospital yesterday lost their 22-hour battle to save the life of Anthony Allden, aged 23, Highgate United's centre-half, who was struck by lightning on Saturday.'

Birmingham Post, February 1967

'Stan Storton's Telford troopers left jam-packed Goodison Park with boos ringing in their ears.'

Sunday Mirror, February 1985

THE FA Amateur Cup, competed for between 1893 and 1974, brought surprisingly little success to the two areas that produced the first 12 professional Football League clubs in the world: Lancashire and the Midlands. Those who won it more than once, led by Bishop Auckland with ten successes, were exclusively from the north-east and south-east of England.

Even the 1902 winners **Old Malvernians**, former pupils of Malvern College, played mainly in Norwood, south London, where they defeated Ipswich Town 10-0 in the quarter-final before winning the semi-final against Ilford 6-4 and the final at Headingley 5-1 against the mighty Bishops. 'The Malvernians had all the best of the play, their combination being far in advance of their rivals,' said *The Referee*.

The star player was R.E. 'Tip' Foster, Malvern-born and the only man to captain England at both football and cricket (he scored a world record 287 on his Test debut in Sydney). The Old Boys followed up their triumph by winning the London Senior Cup the following year, but still play an occasional home match in Malvern.

Evesham Town in 1923 were otherwise the only Midlands team ever to reach the FA Amateur Cup Final, where they lost 2-1 to London Caledonians at Crystal Palace after extra time.

Perhaps the region, like the north-west, took its sport too seriously to have much time for amateurs. For sure, a good crop of semi-professional teams in the area had long been making their mark.

Shrewsbury Town (Chapter 6) finally fought their way into the Football League in 1950 and would later be joined by Hereford United (Chapter 8), Kidderminster Harriers and Burton Albion (both Chapter 10).

By the time of the FA Trophy (1969/70) and a national Alliance Premier League (1979/80), the area was well represented – much more so than the north-west. Local teams played in the first three FA Trophy Finals, winning two of them. And there were six West Midlands clubs in the inaugural Alliance competition: AP Leamington, Nuneaton Borough, Redditch United, Stafford Rangers, Telford United and Worcester City.

* * *

Founded in 1872 as the Parish Church Institute and soon becoming Wellington Town, **Telford United** were allowed, like Shrewsbury and several other English clubs, to cross the border for the Welsh Cup, returning with it in their hands in 1902, 1906 and 1940.

Four times champions of the Birmingham and District League in the 1930s before switching to become Cheshire County League winners immediately after the war, they made their name nationally only after changing it; adopting the name of Telford in 1969 once the new town was established there. Losing the first FA Trophy Final 2-0 to Macclesfield Town with 28,000 present at Wembley, they went back the following year to beat Hillingdon Borough 3-2 after trailing 2-0 at half-time.

Ambitious enough to apply regularly for Football League membership, they only attracted one or two votes until the 1980s, even under two World Cup-winning managers. Geoff Hurst was still playing during his spell from 1976–79 but Gordon Banks was less successful in the inaugural Alliance season of 1979/80, finishing 13th and claiming it 'broke my heart' to be sacked the following November.

A series of fine FA Cup runs thereafter attracted greater attention. The best of them was in 1984/85, beating four Football League clubs – Lincoln, Preston, Bradford City and Darlington – before losing 3-0 in the fifth round at Everton, where according to the *Sunday Mirror*, 'Stan Storton's Telford troopers left jam-packed Goodison Park with boos ringing in their ears' on account of an over-vigorous approach. Two years later they knocked out Burnley and were narrowly beaten 2-1 by Leeds after moving the home tie to The Hawthorns.

Further FA Trophy wins came in 1983 and 1989 (as well as losing a replayed final in 1988). The highest finish in the Alliance was third place in 1982; as the only non-league team put forward for election to the Fourth Division they received 13 votes – still far too few to achieve it. Frequently in the top six, they slipped in the early 1990s and in 1997/98 enjoyed a lucky reprieve from relegation before reviving somewhat.

A further FA Cup flourish came in 2003/04 with victories over Brentford and then Crewe, who were tenth in the Championship at the time. But after finishing 12th in the Conference that season, fans were shocked to learn that owner Andy Shaw's business had collapsed and the club would have to fold. Nearly 3,500 saw the final game at home to Farnborough and another 2,000 on top of that had been at the FA Cup fourth-round defeat by eventual finalists Millwall. A phoenix club, **AFC Telford United**, soon materialised under Brendan McNally, still playing at the New Bucks Head stadium, and within four years had fought their way back via the Evo-Stik League (and one home crowd of 5,710) into the National League North division, where they were runners-up but play-off losers.

Losing the play-off final the following year, they finally made it back to the top level of non-league football in 2011, beating Nuneaton and then Guiseley with Andy Sinton as manager. Relegated in 2013, winning the National League North title a year later and then going back down again in 2015, they have remained in the northern section; the fans grateful at least still to have a senior football club representing the town.

* * *

Stafford Rangers, long-time rivals to Wellington/Telford, date back to 1876 and have been playing at Marston Road since 1896, settling in the Birmingham and District League from the start of the 20th century.

They were particularly strong from 1926–31, in the top three every year and champions in 1927. Disbanding and re-forming at the beginning and end of the Second World War, Rangers survived financial problems in the 1950s and like Telford began to flourish with the advent of the FA Trophy and the Alliance. In 1971/72 they achieved a treble as Northern Premier League champions, FA Trophy winners (3-0 v Barnet) and Staffordshire Cup winners, all on the back of goals by the prolific Ray Williams, a schoolteacher who then joined Port Vale.

After losing the 1976 Trophy final 3-2 to Scarborough, a second win followed three years later, 2-0 against Kettering with a record crowd for the competition of 32,000. In the FA Cup they reached the competition proper in 1972/73 for the first time since 1885 and had their best run in 1974/75. Stockport, Halifax and Rotherham were all beaten, the latter in front of Marston

Road's record crowd of 8,536. The fourth-round tie at home to Peterborough was moved to Stoke's Victoria Ground, where a remarkable 31,160 saw the visitors win 2-1.

The club were founder members of the Alliance in 1979 but have never finished high enough in the fifth tier to come close to a Football League place. In 1993, with Dennis Booth as manager, they were sixth, having two years earlier sold a young Stan Collymore to Crystal Palace, where he made half a dozen appearances as the London club finished third in the top division. In 2011 Rangers were relegated from National League North and nine years later had sunk to the bottom of the Northern Premier League.

* * *

Until Hereford United knocked Newcastle United out of the FA Cup in 1972 (Chapter 8), the best result ever achieved by a West Midlands non-league club was arguably on 15 January 1959 when **Worcester City** took on Liverpool in the third round and won 2-1. Liverpool were a Second Division side but a formidable one, forever just missing out on promotion, and at the time of the tie they had won six successive league games.

Led by Roy Paul, the former Manchester City and Wales half-back, Southern League Worcester had shocked Fourth Division Millwall 5-2 in the second round and were disappointed when a frozen pitch caused the Liverpool game to be put off until the following Thursday afternoon – the St George's Lane ground, next to the canal, had no floodlights at that time.

The pitch was still hard and City adapted to it much better than their visitors, who were without the legend that was Scottish forward Billy Liddell but included England's Alan A'Court at outside-left, with future international Jimmy Melia inside him. City's own left-winger, Tommy Skuse, opened the scoring after only ten minutes and Liverpool centre-half Dick White conceded an own goal before Geoff Twentyman replied with a disputed penalty.

'Enjoying their finest hour since the club was formed 56 years ago, Worcester City beat Liverpool at Worcester yesterday to pass into the fourth round of the FA Challenge Cup competition,' reported the *Birmingham Post*. An impressed *Liverpool Echo* correspondent wrote, 'The longer the match went, the more obvious it became that Worcester's ideas of how to play were the right ones.'

A home tie with Sheffield United, another strong Second Division side (they finished third), was Worcester's reward and a ground record 17,042 turned out to see the visitors win 2-0. Liverpool also missed out on promotion once again and before the end of the year had appointed a certain Bill Shankly as their new manager.

The club had been formed in 1903, when Worcester Rovers took over the fixtures of local outfit Berwick Rangers in the Birmingham League and changed their name to City. Often near the bottom early on, they became champions four times, scoring 150 goals once in the early 1930s and beating Bilston United 19-1. Progressing to the Southern League, they won the Premier Division in 1979 to earn a place in the new national Alliance Premier and did best of all the Midlands clubs by finishing third.

Relegated in 1985, they have never been back and after the 2012/13 season left St George's Lane, which was sold for housing, causing a long exile from the city. They shared at Kidderminster Harriers until 2016, then with Bromsgrove before a return to Worcester for 2020/21. One notable achievement in exile was another FA Cup giant-killing with a 2-1 win away to Coventry City in 2014. In the second round, defeat against Scunthorpe came only after a 1-1 draw and a record penalty shoot-out margin for the competition proper of 14-13.

Like Stafford Rangers, they provided a striker for the top tier of English football in Roger Davies, bought by Derby County in 1971; and in 1987 defender Andy Awford made history as the youngest player to appear in the FA Cup at under 15 and three months, subsequently going on to play for and manage Portsmouth.

* * *

Founded in 1889 but liquidated twice, **Nuneaton Borough** are now on their third incarnation, another club proud to have kept their town's flag flying in the face of frequent financial difficulty without ever having been in sight of the Football League.

Nuneaton St Nicholas was formed by Bible class students at a local school, becoming Nuneaton Town five years later and soon playing league football. In 1931 they won the Birmingham Senior Cup for the first time but six years later had to form a new club after being wound up.

In 1956 they moved from the Birmingham League to the Southern League and enjoyed three spells in the Alliance (which later became the Conference, and now the National League), the most recent ending in 2015. David Pleat made his management debut with the club in the 1970s and was doing great work at Luton Town when Borough finished runners-up in both 1984 (only a point behind Maidstone) and 1985. In each of those seasons Paul Culpin was by far the league's top scorer with 41 goals and then 36. He totalled 131 in 150 games before joining Coventry City, returning via four other clubs in 1992 to score another 72 in 102 appearances.

An FA Cup tie with Rotherham in January 1967 attracted Manor Road's biggest crowd of 22,114 and Stoke City were giant-killing victims in 2000/2001 after a goalless draw at the Victoria Ground.

In January 2006 Borough held Middlesbrough, UEFA Cup finalists at the end of that season, to a 1-1 draw in the third round, but a year later, selling the ground and moving to Liberty Way failed to raise sufficient revenue to erase serious debts. A new club was effectively formed, being demoted two divisions and reverting to the old name of Town, which became Borough again in 2018.

* * *

Qualifying for the Alliance Premier competition in 1979 after only a few years in the Southern League, **Redditch United** found themselves out of their depth. They not only finished bottom, scoring just 26 goals, but in the following two seasons were bottom but one and then bottom of the Southern League Midland Division – from which, fortunately, there was no relegation. The rise in fortunes had come a little too fast.

Formed in 1891 as Redditch Town, they followed the tried and trusted route through the Birmingham leagues, though rather more slowly than the likes of Nuneaton, Stafford and Worcester. In 1960 they were still playing in Division Two of the Birmingham League against Worcester's reserves and Coventry City 'A' when it was revamped and restricted to first teams only.

Becoming Redditch United in 1971, they celebrated with a first appearance in the FA Cup proper, holding Peterborough 1-1 in front of a record crowd of 4,500 before a heavy defeat in the replay. It took almost 20 years to reach that stage again and the most notable feature of the 1990s was once playing nine games in nine days because of a fixture backlog.

Briefly reaching Conference North in 2004, the Reds went down again in 2011 after winning only two games out of 40 and have remained in the Southern League since, while concentrating on greater involvement in the local community. Installing an artificial 3G pitch in 2016 allowed over 900 people in 50 different teams to play at the Valley stadium each week.

* * *

Completing the local contingent in the original Alliance competition were the club known at the time as **AP Leamington**, who adopted that name when local firm Lockheed changed their name to the grander-sounding Automotive Products in 1973.

As the Lockheed works team from 1933, nicknamed the Brakes, they began to make significant progress in the 1950s and 60s, winning the Birmingham Senior Cup three times, then the Birmingham, West Midlands and Midlands Leagues between 1961 and 65. The 1970s were spent in the Southern League after another step up, entertaining Southend United and Torquay United in the FA Cup – although a 1979 tie away to Tranmere Rovers proved a bridge too far with a 9-0 defeat.

In the Alliance they finished above Stafford and Redditch but nobody else, managing only two more seasons before relegation in 1982. Unable to return despite winning the Southern League because the ground was not up to scratch, they suffered badly from the loss of AP's sponsorship, dropping the name, dropping down the divisions and dropping out of football altogether for 12 years from 1988–2000 after crowds fell to just a few hundred.

It took a group of dedicated supporters to revive the club, getting them back as far as National League North, but with sensible plans for the future to go the same way as Redditch at a new venue with an artificial pitch.

* * *

Forty years on from the start of a national non-league division, **Solihull Moors** were the only local representatives – but the new kids on the block, formed by a merger of two old rivals in 2007, came close to becoming the area's newest Football League club.

Deep in the south of the region by the M42, **Solihull Borough** had only existed from 1953, initially as Lincoln FC, but **Moor Green** to the north-west were much longer established, having been formed early in the 20th century as winter recreation for a local cricket club.

They achieved little success until just before the Second World War, then established themselves in the 1970s in the Midland Combination, reaching the FA Cup first round and joining the Southern League in 1983. From the Premier Division they reached the Conference North but the ground in Hall Green, long coveted by developers, suffered two arson attacks in 2005 that would eventually lead to the merger.

Having hosted Borough as their tenants for ten years from 1989–99, they reversed roles and shared their rivals' new Damson Park stadium, deciding to join forces with them for the 2007/08 season. The FA generously allowed the new club to keep Moor Green's place in the Conference North, which meant Borough had effectively been promoted two steps up from the bottom half of the Southern League Midlands Division.

Finishing no higher than the bottom six in four of the first five seasons, and stunned by the death of long-serving manager Bob Faulkner in February 2011, the Moors finally began to find a berth in the top half from 2012/13 and three years later won National League North by nine points. At the higher level, managers like Marcus Bignot and Mark Yates were lured away by Football League clubs, but in a first season under Tim Flowers, the former Blackburn goalkeeper, the Moors were runners-up and only three points behind champions Leyton Orient before losing to AFC Fylde in the play-offs.

* * *

As well as Telford United, Stafford Rangers and Kidderminster Harriers, one other West Midlands team has lifted the FA Trophy. In 2004 **Hednesford Town**, by beating Canvey Island 3-2, became one of those winners who were denied a Wembley triumph and had to settle for Villa Park because the national stadium was being rebuilt.

Hednesford, 'The Pitmen', had little on their honours board for many decades after being formed in 1880. But the Trophy success followed a Southern League title in 1995, and third place in the Conference the following season at the new £1.3m Keys Park stadium, when local legend Joe O'Connor scored 23 of his 220 goals for the club. In 1996/97 he bagged the winner in an FA Cup tie at Blackpool and then got two more in the 3-2 defeat away to Middlesbrough of the Premier League, watched by over 27,500.

The Pitmen were back in the Southern League when reaching the Trophy Final, returning to Conference North in 2005 for one year and again in 2013 after four successive play-off seasons. More recently they have competed in the Northern Premier League.

* * *

The FA Cup has often been the best way of bringing a small club to the attention of a wider audience. Several of those mentioned above have benefited from famous performances; in the case of others like **Alvechurch** it was through setting a record, wanted or otherwise. 'The Church', for instance, attempting to reach the first round for the first time in 1971/72, made history by playing no fewer than five drawn games against Oxford City before beating them 1-0 at Villa Park. With four lots of extra time, the tie lasted for 11 hours, something never to be even approached again since the abolition of second replays; and after all that effort an exhausted set of players lost the delayed first round game away to Fourth Division side Aldershot 4-2. Formed in 1929, Alvechurch reached the 1966 FA Amateur Cup semi-final at Stamford Bridge, a year after a record crowd of 13,500 watched a quarter-final defeat at home to Enfield. They were wound up in 1993 but started up again the following year.

Brierley Hill Alliance made the record books in September 1955 when visiting Kidderminster Harriers for the first FA Cup tie to be played under floodlights. Six years later they reached the first round proper for the only time in their 94-year history, which ran from 1887–1981. They won the Birmingham and District League in 1951 and 1952, and four Birmingham Senior Cups.

Coventry Sporting, founded as the works team of the Coventry Tile Company in the 1930s, had their day in the national limelight in November 1975 when drawn at home to the Fourth Division leaders Tranmere Rovers. Switching the tie to Highfield Road, they won 2-0, and played there again in the second round, losing 4-0 against Peterborough in front of 8,556. After reaching the Southern League in 1983 they were dissolved in 1989.

An FA Amateur Cup tragedy brought **Highgate United** widespread sympathetic attention. 'Doctors at Solihull Hospital yesterday lost their 22-hour battle to save the life of Anthony Allden, aged 23, Highgate United's centre-half, who was struck by lightning on Saturday,' reported the *Birmingham Post* in February 1967.

The occasion was a quarter-final at home to Enfield. One reporter described involuntarily closing his eyes after a deafening clap of thunder and opening them to find that 'there seemed to be bodies everywhere on the ground'. Half a dozen players were affected but all except Allden survived. When the abandoned match was replayed at Villa Park the Midlands football community rallied round to support his young widow, and a crowd of 31,000 turned out to see Enfield's 6-0 victory.

Highgate, formed in 1948 before moving south-east to Solihull, now have a Tony Allden Room at their Coppice ground. They went on to enjoy their best period in the 1970s, including three successive Midland Combination titles.

* * *

Since amateurism and with it the Amateur Cup were abolished in 1974, there have been three West Midlands winners of its successor, the FA Vase.

Tamworth, (founded 1933) triumphed in 1989 when beating Sudbury Town in a replayed final at Peterborough, and from there went on to greater things. Winning the Southern League Premier Division in 2003 (when also Trophy runners-up) and Conference North six years later earned the Lambs two spells in the top non-league competition. They lasted for nine seasons in total on gates of around 1,000, making most of their money from an FA Cup tie at Everton in 2012, which was honourably lost 2-0 in front of almost 30,000.

Rugby Town, formed in 1955 as New Bilton Juniors, won the 1983 final at Wembley when known as **VS Rugby**, and subsequently drew FA Cup ties with Northampton, Leyton Orient and Bristol Rovers. The team they beat at Wembley, **Halesowen Town**, then became one of only three clubs to win the Vase in successive seasons, defeating Fleetwood in 1985 and Southall a year later. Established as long ago as 1873, they have played at the same ground since 1876.

* * *

Many other clubs have been an important part of their community for up to 140 years, while coming together in the various Birmingham, Staffordshire, Shropshire or Worcestershire leagues and cups.

The resilient **Atherstone Town** (formed 1887), who style themselves as a 'Community Football Club', reached the FA Amateur Cup semi-finals as long ago as 1908 and 1909. Soon after Jeff Astle finished his playing career there in the late 1970s, they survived a financial setback in 1979, resuming as Atherstone United, then folded again in 2003/04 and simply started up once more with the old Town epithet.

Bromsgrove Rovers (1885) were at their best in the 1990s under former West Brom midfielder Bobby Hope. He took them from the Southern League Midland Division to finish 1992/93 as runners-up in the Conference to Martin O'Neill's Wycombe Wanderers. After a notable FA Cup win over Northampton and an unlucky defeat by Viv Anderson's Barnsley, the club went into decline and following administration in 2010 the fans' consortium trying to save the club ended up starting a new one, **Bromsgrove Sporting**, at the same Victoria ground.

Dudley Town are another club dating all the way back to the 1880s who have proved tough to kill off. Folding twice in between the wars, they were unfortunate in having to leave their ground just after reaching the Southern League Premier Division for the first time in 1985 and closed down briefly in 1997. Rejoining the West Midlands League with landlords **Gornal Athletic**, they have led a nomadic existence ever since but have managed to keep going.

Evesham United replaced former Amateur Cup finalists Evesham Town after the Second World War, reaching the Southern League Premier Division in 2005 with the former Coventry City defender David Busst as manager, and again in 2008 during a six-year spell groundsharing with Worcester.

Leek Town failed to add to the list of local FA Trophy winners when losing the 1990 final 3-0 to Barrow, but they joined Hednesford in the Conference in 1997/98 as Northern Premier League champions, lasting there for just two seasons. From their formation in 1946 until then, the Blues spent many seasons in Lancashire or Cheshire leagues. A much older club, **Leek FC**, represented the town in the 19th century, once reaching the last 16 of the FA Cup.

Rushall Olympic, based to the north of Walsall, played league football in the 1890s but disbanded before the Second World War, starting up again in 1951. They settled at a new ground in 1977 and found themselves shuttled between the Southern League and Northern Premier League.

Stourbridge, originally Stourbridge Standard (from 1876), and still known as The Glassboys after the town's traditional main industry, were Worcestershire Senior Cup winners early on and champions of the Birmingham League in the 1920s. The 1970s saw them in the Southern League, when strikers Chic Bates and Ray Haywood scored 50 goals apiece to help win the Division One North title, beat Swansea and Wrexham in the Welsh Cup and earn the pair a move to Shrewsbury Town. It took 133 years to reach the FA Cup first round, when a home tie with Walsall brought a 1-0 defeat. And in 2016/17 they made the third round, losing narrowly at Wycombe after knocking out Northampton with 2,520 present.

Stratford Town first reached the Southern League in 2013, 72 years after being founded as Stratford Rangers and five years after moving into a new ground at Tiddington. They made it to the competition's Premier League in 2015.

Sutton Coldfield Town are another 19th-century club whose best achievements have been far more recent. They reached the FA Cup first round in 1981 (losing to Billy Bremner's Doncaster Rovers) and 1993 (losing at Bolton Wanderers), got to the Southern League Premier for one season in 1983, and won the Birmingham Senior Cup for the only time in 2011.

10

Sky High
1993–2010

'The battle for Birmingham City was today won by Karren Brady, undoubtedly the best looking managing director in the history of British football. The Daily Sport executive immediately announced there would be money for new players to help Blues avoid relegation.'

Evening Mail, March 1993

'Doug Ellis has delivered many a shock and many a sacking in his 70 years but the dismissal of Ron Atkinson was a combination of both that exploded like a Molotov cocktail on the consciousness of Villa fans.'

Evening Mail, November 1994

'Stoke City can expect major support from fans if they decide to quit the Victoria Ground in favour of a new home. Seventy per cent of fans who took part in the Sentinel's phone poll voted in favour.'

Evening Sentinel, November 1994

'It doesn't matter who they support, most football fans in the West Midlands are unanimous in their choice of the region's team-of-the-year – Walsall.'

Evening Mail, May 1999

'The repercussions are likely to be widespread and [Coventry] chairman Bryan Richardson has warned relegation will cost the club £15million in lost revenue.'

Daily Telegraph, May 2001

'They billed it as the great escape, and in Premiership history there has been none greater. West Bromwich Albion propelled themselves to a final position of fourth from bottom with a combination of victory over Portsmouth and a goal at The Valley by a man named Fortune.'

The Independent, May 2005

THE FIRST dozen Football League members in 1888/89 may have been evenly split between the Midlands and the north-west, but by the time of the FA Premier League 104 years later, geographical balance had changed markedly.

Of the 22 clubs who kicked off what satellite television company BSkyB dubbed 'a whole new ball game' in August 1992, only Aston Villa, Coventry City and Nottingham Forest represented the Midlands; the so-called 'Big Five' clubs who had lobbied hardest for change (only one of whom finished in the top five places, incidentally) were exclusively from Lancashire and London: Manchester United, Liverpool, Everton, Arsenal and Tottenham.

That group had led the campaign throughout the 1980s for a greater share of television revenue to go to the bigger clubs like themselves, and having achieved that once regular live football was introduced in 1983, they turned to restructuring the Football League with a smaller First Division. Over the course of two seasons from 1987–89 the top tier was reduced from 22 clubs to 20 but, when a majority voted to increase it back for 1991/92, the Big Five found a new ally in the Football Association. Picking up on England's success and popularity in the 1990 World Cup, the FA produced 'The Blueprint For The Future Of Football', proposing among many other things a breakaway Football Association Premier League, which by 1996 would be reduced to 18 clubs.

It never was and the 'FA' prefix was quietly dropped within a few years as the governing body lost any control it had ever had. But arrangements were agreed with surprising speed, including a stunning television deal said to be worth £304m over five years (though that figure was not achieved) with which BSkyB pipped a furious ITV.

* * *

For 16 of the 18 seasons covered in this chapter, **Aston Villa** were the highest-placed West Midlands club in the Premier League, losing out only to Coventry City in 1995 and Birmingham City in 2003. But could they compete with the best in the land?

Initially it seemed so. Despite being 40-1 outsiders for the inaugural title in 1992/93 (ten teams had shorter odds), Ron Atkinson's side shook off a slow start once he finally persuaded Doug Ellis – 'the only chairman in the English game I knew I could never comfortably work alongside' – to pay Liverpool a national record £2.3m for striker Dean Saunders.

The Welshman proved the catalyst with six goals in three games; a heavy Boxing Day defeat at Coventry was a rare setback, and from mid-February Villa were top of the table for six weeks. They held closest rivals Manchester United at Old Trafford, but Saunders ran out of goals, fellow striker Dalian Atkinson was injured and Villa were left over-reliant on a defence that finally cracked with three games left. They lost 3-0 at Blackburn, then slipped 1-0 at home to relegation candidates Oldham to give United their first title for 26 years. Alex Ferguson's team won their last seven games, Villa lost their last three and were ten points behind in the end in second place with Saunders having scored two goals in 15 matches.

League runners-up in 1990 and now 1993, with their average gate below only Liverpool and United, Villa should have been in an ideal position to kick on as the Premier League began to offer some serious money – finishing second in that first season of the new league alone earned the club £778,155. Atkinson was allowed to spend £3.3m on Andy Townsend, Gordon Cowans and the Portsmouth striker Guy Whittingham, but, although winning the League Cup to deny United a domestic Treble was a personal pleasure against the club who had sacked him in 1986, sliding from second place in the autumn to finish tenth did not bode well.

This time Ellis refused to invest, taking more in transfer income during the summer than he spent. Just as at Old Trafford almost exactly eight years earlier, Atkinson found himself dismissed, in November 1994, with Villa in 19th. They had taken one point from nine games in a season when four teams were going down.

Supporters and pressmen were largely sympathetic. 'Doug Ellis has delivered many a shock and many a sacking in his 70 years but the dismissal of Ron Atkinson was a combination of both that exploded like a Molotov cocktail on the consciousness of Villa fans,' said the *Evening Mail*. Bearing in mind that he would pitch up next at Highfield Road, it did at least give Big Ron a good after-dinner joke: 'What's the best way to get to Coventry? Lose six on the bounce at Villa.'

Brian Little, once a Holte End hero, was the replacement following an acrimonious departure from Leicester City, taking assistants Allan Evans and John Gregory with him. After the club's record Premier League win, 7-1 at home to Wimbledon, he kept Villa up on the final day and in a fine 1995/96 season a much-changed team won the League Cup against Leeds, reached the FA Cup semi-final (0-3 v Liverpool) and finished fourth in the table.

The following season, after reluctantly letting Paul McGrath move on, they were fifth but early in 1998 a weary Little resigned, having failed to get the best out of his £7m signing Stan Collymore – who would later be diagnosed with clinical depression. One of the players Little had most trouble with was Serbian midfielder Saša Ćurčić from Bolton, who once booked himself into a London clinic for cosmetic surgery on his nose, ruling himself out of contention for several weeks. It was another import, defender Fernando Nélson, who woke the manager at 3am to complain that the broken gate at his house was banging and keeping him awake (he got a two-word response).

Despite an unwelcome FA Cup fifth-round derby defeat at home to Coventry, Villa had reached the quarter-final of the UEFA Cup, in which Atlético Madrid squeaked home on an away goal after losing 2-1 at Villa Park shortly after Little left. That was the latest in a series of appearances in the competition and the furthest the club had progressed in half a dozen attempts since 1978. Deportivo la Coruna, Trabzonspor and Helsingborgs had all knocked them out in tight contests and a year after Atlético did the same, Celta Vigo repeated the trick.

Those latter ties were under John Gregory, who returned to take charge after two years as manager of Wycombe. His first full season, 1998/99, was his best, Villa leading the league from September until Boxing Day despite having sold Dwight Yorke to Manchester United after the opening game. But ten matches without a win meant they fell away to finish sixth, still the lowest position of any team top of the Premier League at Christmas.

The following season it was sixth again, with two good cup runs. In the League Cup a weakened United were emphatically beaten 3-0 but Leicester's Matt Elliott scored the only goal of the two-legged semi-final. In the FA Cup there was an equally tight semi-final – a goalless draw at Wembley against wasteful Bolton, which Villa won 4-1 on penalties after Mark Delaney was sent off. Chelsea, one place above them in the league, won the final with a goal by Roberto Di Matteo following a mistake by goalkeeper David James.

'We didn't do enough in the final third, that's been the story of our season,' said Gregory, another Villa manager who found his relationship with the chairman strained. Having won one of the finals of the Inter Toto Cup to earn a UEFA Cup place, then raised hopes by topping the Premier League table for a week in the autumn, he resigned in January 2002, complaining of lack of transfer funding after being refused permission to buy Leicester's Muzzy Izzet.

Graham Taylor, back at the club as a non-executive director and now manager again, had learnt how to handle Ellis early on: 'We had a massive row at my first board meeting. So I stopped going.' The 2002/03 season turned out to be a bad one to manage Villa, however, as Birmingham returned to the top flight, completing the double over their neighbours and finishing three places above them in 13th. With only one away win all season, it was fortunate that Villa Park saw 11 home victories as relegation was avoided by three points.

Exit Taylor, enter David O'Leary, having taken Leeds United to a Champions League semi-final amid the sort of financial extravagance and subsequent implosion that Ellis would never have allowed. There should have been a halfway house between the two approaches for clubs of that size; but at the end of O'Leary's third season after finishing sixth, tenth and 16th, with only one League Cup semi-final as a bonus (lost 5-4 on aggregate to Bolton), a group of Villa players issued a statement to the press complaining about cutbacks, which said in part, 'The chairman should be behind the club and not working against what we're trying to achieve. There've been a series of cutbacks and we feel we have to mention this because they are now starting to affect us.'

O'Leary resigned shortly afterwards and new manager Martin O'Neill, fresh from five successful years at Celtic, soon found himself working for a new Villa chairman. At the age of 82 Ellis did as supporters had been urging for some years and finally relinquished control in the autumn of 2006, to the American billionaire Randy Lerner, an Anglophile who had given millions of pounds to the National Portrait Gallery and his former Cambridge University college.

As owner of the Cleveland Browns American football team, Lerner was reckoned to know something about running a major sports organisation and he endeared himself to Villa fans by not only backing the manager but by gestures like restoring the Holte pub behind the ground at a cost of £4m.

Three times in as many years O'Neill broke or equalled the club's transfer record, signing Ashley Young from Watford for £9.6m in January 2007, James Milner from Newcastle in August 2008 and Middlesbrough's Stewart Downing the following July, both for £12m. Tenth in his first season, Villa were sixth three times in a row, every time hitting what appeared to be a glass ceiling and finding the big hitters just too powerful on and off the pitch.

It did mean three seasons of European football, the first of which in 2008/09 comprised 12 games from mid-July in the Inter Toto Cup to late February and a UEFA Cup defeat by CSKA Moscow when O'Neill, prioritising the Premier League, fielded a virtual reserve team; the next two campaigns were far briefer, losing a play-off round of the Europa League, each time to Rapid Vienna. Further domestic disappointment came in the 2010 League Cup Final and FA Cup semi-final, losing 2-1 to Manchester United in the former (after a bizarre 6-4 win over Blackburn in the semi-final second leg) and 3-0 to Chelsea in the senior competition. In August that year, just five days before the first Premier League games, O'Neill became the latest Villa manager to walk away, his timing questionable but his frustration understandable.

* * *

It was typical of **Coventry City** not only to qualify for inclusion in the Premier League by the skin of their teeth but to hang in there with such tenacity until finally surrendering in 2001 after 34 unbroken years in the top flight – at which point only Arsenal, Everton and Liverpool had been there for longer. From then on, however, there was no realistic chance of returning and more than once it was a struggle to avoid disappearing into the lower divisions. It was indicative of the club's struggles that in two decades 13 different managers came and went, of whom only Gordon Strachan (1996–2001) lasted for more than two years.

The Sky Blues only made the Premier League in the first place because, as recounted in Chapter 8, Luton Town lost their final game of the preceding season at Notts County; otherwise Villa supporters would have been rejoicing at sending City down by beating them (as, ironically, they did nine years later).

Bobby Gould, having finished at Albion, was back for a second spell as manager, which would last for only 15 months this time. Until a disappointing last dozen games, that first season of the new era in 1992/93 was a resounding success with Gould's signing Mick 'Sumo' Quinn – 'the best natural finisher I ever worked with' he said – scoring 17 goals in 26 games. City sat proudly on top of the table after three games, and were fourth as late as February, the highlights being successive home wins over Liverpool (5-1) and Villa (3-0).

Slumping to finish 15th with ten home defeats was therefore disappointing and meant that average home crowds were still below 15,000. Financial constraints increased when Peter Robins made way as chairman for Bryan Richardson, brother of the former England batsman Peter, and in October 1993 after one attendance of 9,837 was followed by a 5-1 defeat at QPR, Gould resigned in the toilets.

His assistant Phil Neal took over and kept the team in a comfortable 11th place, only one behind Villa, but when they dropped from tenth in mid-season to 20th the following February he was sacked and replaced by Ron Atkinson. Now on his third West Midlands club, Atkinson found more boardroom trouble in a period he described as 'full of intrigue, relegation campaigning and backroom manoeuvrings'.

The arrangement was that he would do two full seasons, then hand over to a player-coach he had picked and groomed. After considering names like Ray Wilkins and Chris Waddle, he went for Strachan, who he had wanted to buy while at Sheffield Wednesday, only for the little Scot to choose Leeds instead and win a championship medal there.

Coventry, for all their struggles, had important players in the Zimbabwean Peter Ndlovu, who scored a hat-trick to win a crucial game at Anfield, and Dion Dublin, who would be top scorer four seasons in a row (once sharing the Premier League's Golden Boot). Strachan added his own midfield expertise just in time to help the team to safety by five points but the next two campaigns were stressful until the very last whistle.

Early in 1995/96 the Sky Blues went 14 games without a win and they only survived on the final day because Manchester City played for a draw at home to Liverpool, believing they were safe.

Amid another dreadful run the following autumn – one win in the first 16 games – Atkinson, to his annoyance, was moved upstairs six months ahead of schedule without any clearly defined role and Strachan took over. The latest great escape came with a 2-1 win on the last day at Tottenham, and only then because Middlesbrough, who had suffered a three-point deduction, and Sunderland both failed to win.

'We haven't let down 30 years of players and managers who have kept their club in the top division,' Strachan said. 'The players are so excited at just staying up.'

That was nevertheless an attitude he was determined to change and for three years City were unusually comfortable, finishing 11th, 15th and 14th. There were even three decent FA Cup runs, to the quarter-final in 1998 (losing on penalties to Sheffield United after winning at both Liverpool and Villa for the first time), then the fifth round twice, beaten by Everton and Charlton.

With Dublin sold to Villa for almost £6m, the board spent that amount on Robbie Keane from Wolves. But after one season they accepted more than twice as much from Internazionale for him and also sold the influential Gary McAllister to Liverpool. In the relegation zone by December, Strachan's charges were finally doomed at just about the worst possible venue – a gloating Villa Park, where they had been 2-0 up at half-time but lost 3-2.

'The repercussions are likely to be widespread and chairman Bryan Richardson has warned relegation will cost the club £15million,' reported the *Daily Telegraph*.

The manager resolved to stay for the second-tier campaign but found supporters turning against him after a third defeat in the first five games, and he was sacked with the team in 18th place. He had been in charge for two months short of five years – an impressive stint by modern standards. The stability of those years now gave way to a period of eight managers in the next decade, none of them coming close to a return to the Premier League, as well as a new stadium that would prove a distinctly mixed blessing.

Talk of moving from Highfield Road, home since 1899 but with its capacity reduced to below 24,000 and little room to expand, first began after almost 100 years there. Ambitious chairman Richardson announced plans for what was called Arena 2000, 'the national arena in the heart of England' with a 40,000 capacity at Holbrooks, three miles to the north.

Highfield Road was sold in 1999 for £4m – the cost of a moderate Premier League striker – and leased back, which simply added to the club's running costs. Plans were slowly scaled down and Ricoh replaced Jaguar as the proposed sponsor for the new stadium, but crucially the club did not own it.

In the first season there, 2005/06, the Sky Blues improved on a poor first half to finish in the top eight for the first time in five seasons in what was now named the Championship, and average gates were up by a third. A crowd of 23,000 came to the opening game, a 3-0 win over QPR, and almost 27,000 saw Wolves beaten to start the new year.

Former City defender Micky Adams was by then the manager, after Roland Nilsson, McAllister, Eric Black and the unpopular Peter Reid had come and gone in the space of four years. The optimism of that season soon diminished, however, and early in 2007 Adams was sacked too with the team 17th, where Iain Dowie kept them at the season's end.

'Operation Premiership' was launched but the one real highlight during its planned three-year period proved to be in the League Cup, when two goals by Maltese forward Michael Mifsud knocked Manchester United out at Old Trafford with 74,000 present. After an unlucky defeat by West Ham in the next round, league form fell away, Dowie was replaced by Chris Coleman and relegation to the third tier was only avoided by a single point. It was an underwhelming way to celebrate the club's 125th anniversary.

Overshadowing all this, however, was the change of ownership in December 2007, when, with minutes to spare before going into administration, the former Manchester City player Ray Ranson and the SISU group took control. SISU, a London-based hedge fund that had earlier tried to buy Southampton, would eventually become a dirty word for City supporters. Seventeenth and 19th places in the first full seasons of the new regime hardly suggested a golden age and in May 2010 Coleman departed after losing six and drawing four of his last ten games. But worse was to follow in the new decade.

* * *

The quartet of West Midlands clubs who had sunk to a historic low in the mid-1980s and early-1990s – Birmingham, Stoke, West Brom and Wolves – missed out on the Premier League riches early on but all revived sufficiently to get there in the first decade of the new century. With the exception of the Potters, there would still be an awful lot of to-ing and fro-ing for their supporters to enjoy and endure, above all by **West Bromwich Albion**.

As the breakaway league began, the Baggies were down in the third tier – known then as the Second Division – where Ossie Ardiles led them through an exciting promotion chase with not only Stoke but Port Vale too. 'His attitude was just that however many the opposition score, we'll score more,' said skipper Darren Bradley of the manager's philosophy. Most of the time they did, and in mid-October they were top, but losing all four derbies with the Potteries pair meant finishing behind both of them and going into the play-offs. There they thrilled a 26,000 crowd at The Hawthorns by overturning a 2-1 first-leg defeat against Swansea and at Wembley overcame Vale 3-0 with over 53,000 present. Including an 8-0 FA Cup win over Aylesbury, it was a season of more than 100 goals, 34 of them scored by centre-forward Bob Taylor.

The higher division in 1993/94, with Ardiles having taken over at Tottenham, was a struggle. Having scored more goals than Birmingham – 18 of them to Taylor – was all that kept them up in the first season and although invariably below Wolves, they became a mid-table side, even when local favourite Lee Hughes was the country's top scorer with 31 in 1998/99.

A lot was going on in the boardroom, meanwhile, as the club became a public company. Old warrior John Wile was appointed as CEO, chairman Tony Hale left to be replaced by Paul Thompson, and in March 2000 manager Brian Little, continuing his round of the region's clubs, was sacked after only seven months following a 3-0 home defeat by Blues. Gary Megson, following Little from Stoke, oversaw narrow survival that season as Taylor's five goals in the last six games after returning from Bolton sent Walsall down instead.

Celebrating 100 years at The Hawthorns in September 2000, the club enjoyed two good seasons by reaching the play-offs before a rock-steady defence, conceding only 29 times, carried them to second place in 2001/02 ahead of Wolves, who missed out in third despite scoring 15 goals more than the Baggies, and Birmingham, who won the play-offs.

Once in the Premier League, however, Albion became the archetypal yo-yo club. Hughes, sold to Coventry for £5m and bought back for half the price, didn't score in 23 league games as they went down in 19th place. He fared better back in the Championship, where Albion stayed in the top two from October 2003 onwards to go straight back up, but just before the new season began Hughes was sent to prison for six years (serving four) for causing death by dangerous driving.

Despite signing ten new players, it looked again as though the Premier League would prove too much. Megson, who found life difficult under yet another new chairman in Jeremy Peace, left after winning one of the opening 11 games and when that run was extended to one in 23 under former hero Bryan Robson, supporters were resigned to another demotion.

At that point Kevin Campbell from Everton joined Hughes's replacement, record-signing Robert Earnshaw, in attack. After a draw at Villa Park the Baggies clawed their way up to 17th place, but going into the final day's home game with Portsmouth they were bottom again. On that famous afternoon, however, everything went in their favour: Geoff Horsfield and Kieran Richardson scored in the second half to earn three points that carried them above Norwich and Southampton, who both lost, as well as Crystal Palace, who conceded a late equaliser to local rivals Charlton. It would go down as 'The Great Escape', the only time in the first 21 seasons of the Premier League that a team bottom at Christmas survived. Albion were the lowest scorers and had only six wins and 34 points – two years earlier West Ham had been relegated with 42.

'The turning point,' said *The Independent*, 'was a last-gasp own-goal equaliser at Manchester City, a game in which Albion mustered neither a shot nor a header on target. Since New Year's Day, they have collected 24 points, the final three arriving yesterday on an afternoon when the nerves, as well as the history books, were shredded at The Hawthorns.'

They were not going to get away with that sort of record again, although the next season, 2005/06, the pattern was reversed; hovering just above the relegation places for eight months, they failed to win any of the last 13 games and finished with even fewer goals and points than the previous year, going down with Birmingham and Sunderland.

Robson clung on for eight games of the following season, and under his successor Tony Mowbray, there should have been yet another promotion. In Kevin Phillips and Senegal's Diomansy Kamara, Albion found two badly needed goalscorers, who routed Coventry 5-0, Barnsley 7-0 and scored all four goals to beat Wolves in the play-off semi-finals. Only in the final did the goals dry up, Derby County's Stephen Pearson scoring the crucial one in front of almost 75,000 in the first final at the rebuilt Wembley.

Derby's fate in the Premier League – record lows of one win and 11 points in 38 games – emphasised what Baggies fans knew all too well about the difference between the two levels. So it was hardly a shock when in the next three seasons they went up twice more, coming back in between times.

As well as reaching the 2008 FA Cup semi-final (lost 1-0 to Portsmouth), Mowbray marched them up to the top of the hill with 88 goals and marched them down again, bottom of the table from November onwards. He left for Celtic, Roberto Di Matteo then proving briefly successful in another promotion campaign in 2009/10 with 89 goals spread around the squad.

For seven seasons out of nine the Baggies had been either promoted or relegated, losing a play-off final and surviving by one point in the others. Supporters could hardly complain that life was dull.

* * *

It was not surprising that **Birmingham City**, also trudging up hill and down dale with great frequency, should repeatedly have bumped into Albion, becoming entangled in several promotion and relegation fights with them along the way. So it was appropriate that the pair both ascended to the promised land of the Premier League in 2002, then descended together four years later before swapping places in 2008 and 2009.

All this occurred under a new regime. In March 1993 Londoner David Sullivan, proprietor of the racy *Sport* newspapers, bought out the Kumars, whose business failure had caused Blues to be in administration for five months as the threat of relegation back to the third tier after only one season increased.

'This will be the dawn of a new era for Birmingham City,' said Sullivan's appointee Karren Brady, a 23-year-old described by the *Evening Mail* as 'undoubtedly the best looking managing director in the history of British football'. 'We are serious, have money and are going to take the club places,' she promised; whereupon in one month seven new players were signed and four games were won.

Despite an extraordinary 6-4 home defeat by Swindon, a jubilant 22,000-strong crowd was able to celebrate survival on the final day by beating Charlton 1-0.

'Taking the club places' proved to be an unfortunate phrase a year later when those places included the likes of Shrewsbury, Stockport, Crewe and Chester – after relegation to the Third Division. Manager Terry Cooper left in December following an unexpectedly poor run and for a long time his successor Barry Fry's only good result was a 2-0 Christmas win over relegation rivals West Brom in front of 28,000. It was the only success in three months and a final flourish of seven games without defeat came just too late, Albion finishing above them on goal difference to stay up.

The irrepressible Fry characteristically promised they would 'bounce straight back as champions' and was able to live up to the boast. Flying forward Ricky Otto became the club's record signing at £800,000 and the much-travelled Steve Claridge hit 20 of the 84 league goals. It took penalties to knock them out of the FA Cup at Liverpool after Otto equalised Jamie Redknapp's goal and in the lower divisions' Auto Windscreens Shield, Paul Tait's golden goal beat Carlisle in the Wembley final with nearly 77,000 present.

That fine double and then a mid-table finish plus a League Cup semi-final (lost 1-2, 0-3 to Leeds, missing out on a Wembley final against Villa) and an Anglo-Italian Cup quarter-final did not spare Fry the sack at the end of the 1995/96 season, in which he had famously used 46 players in league games alone.

A key factor was that Trevor Francis was available to make a return to his spiritual home, which he did that summer, lasting five and a half frustrating years of near misses at reaching the Premier League.

He inherited a huge squad, no youth system, 'pretty abysmal facilities' and a striker, Paul Peschisolido, who was married to the managing director, which Francis did not consider good for the dressing room. Selling him to West Brom only four months after the player's return to St Andrew's from Stoke upset Karren Brady at the start of a difficult relationship, but Francis had supporters on his side, even before making Manchester United's captain Steve Bruce his first signing and adding several other Premier League players as a show of intent.

After a first season in tenth place, the near misses began in 1997/98 when Blues would have been in the play-offs but for a new Football League rule that goals scored and not goal difference decided between teams level on points. So having easily the best defensive record in the division counted for nothing; nor did winning 7-0 away to Stoke in January.

Once they did start to reach the play-offs – for three seasons running – there was only the heartache of semi-final defeats by Watford on penalties (1999), Barnsley (2000) and Preston on penalties (2001). The dreaded spot-kicks even denied them a League Cup triumph that year, after Liverpool had been held 1-1 in the final at Cardiff.

Crowds, having dropped to 6,000 at the end of the 1980s, were regularly up to 20,000 and more, but after what were now being seen as failures, the 2000/01 season always looked a crucial one. From winning four of the first five games, Blues slipped to 14th at the end of September, and after a 3-1 success at Barnsley Francis was sacked.

'Once the chemistry goes there is no going back and that's really what has happened here,' said co-owner David Gold. 'We have all worn each other out. I think in the best interests of Birmingham City and Trevor Francis we have done what we think is best.'

To his credit, Francis admitted, 'I got enough opportunities to win promotion.' He ended up at Crystal Palace, swapping places with Steve Bruce, who built on the good work and was able to achieve success at the end of that season. Although only 12th in mid-November, Blues finished strongly with ten unbeaten games, came through a play-off semi-final at last, on a wild night at Millwall, and even won a penalty shoot-out in the final against Norwich after a 1-1 draw.

Accompanying Albion into the Premier League for the 2002/03 campaign, they survived where the Baggies failed, even though nobody scored more than six league goals. Bruce's team delighted in taking four points from them and, even better, doing the double over Villa by 3-0 and 2-0 to finish three places above them in 13th. It was the first time they had looked down on their nearest neighbours in the same division since 1970.

In three seasons from 2002 Blues' triumphant record against Villa was four wins and two draws from six games. Premier League money enabled the acquisition of record signings such as David Dunn at £5.5m and Emile Heskey for £5.9m, but in 2005/06 neither of them could inspire a recovery from one victory in the first dozen games (3-2 at The Hawthorns) and relegation followed.

Bruce was kept on and took them straight back from the Championship, finishing runners-up to Sunderland with a younger, cheaper squad. But the Sullivan-Gold regime, faced with trying to establish the club in the Premier League again, announced they were prepared to sell up. 'I think the public have had enough of us,' Sullivan said, which was probably correct. The one thing that might have encouraged them to stay was a proposed new 'City of Birmingham Stadium' in nearby Saltley, but when Warwickshire County Cricket Club dropped out and the idea of a super-casino failed to materialise, they could not make the finances add up.

In the summer of 2007 Carson Yeung's Hong Kong company GIH began its protracted takeover. By the time the process was complete two years later, Blues had changed divisions for the fourth successive season, vying with Albion as the country's yo-yo club. Bruce took advantage of the uncertainty to leave for Wigan Athletic and in 2008 it was relegation again by a single point after Scotland manager Alex McLeish replaced him; then back up at the first attempt once more, Kevin Phillips, signed from Albion, leading the scorers. In 2009/10 they relied more on solid defence as a settled side enjoyed the club's best season in the top division since 1959 by finishing ninth. For 12 successive matches from November to February – a Premier League record – the starting XI was unchanged: Hart, Carr, Ridgewell, Ferguson, Dann, Johnson, Larsson, Bowyer, Jerome, Benítez, McFadden.

* * *

Less erratic than some of their West Midlands rivals, **Wolves** established themselves as a reliable top-half Championship side with just one blip, and although initially surviving for only one season after reaching the Premier League in 2003 under Dave Jones they regrouped and got back there five years later with Mick McCarthy in charge. Meanwhile, Molineux had become a proper stadium once more, thanks to Sir Jack Hayward's patronage, three new stands lifting capacity to 28,525 in 1993/94.

The ground was almost full for West Brom's visit that season after the old rivals were reunited following Albion's promotion, and although the visitors won 2-1 to complete a league double Wolves finished above them six times in seven years. In the second of those, 1994/95, with Graham Taylor returning to club management from the England job and Steve Bull still going strong, they reached the play-offs, only to lose narrowly to Bolton (2-1, 0-2). Dropping to 18th place the following November cost Taylor his job but that proved to be the only poor season and Mark McGhee, in his first full campaign, had them finishing third, but losing the play-off semi-final again, this time to Crystal Palace (1-3, 2-1).

In 1998 Wolves reached the FA Cup semi-final by winning a sixth-round tie at Leeds, and were only beaten 1-0 by Arsenal's Double-winning side. Distracted in the league, they dropped from sixth in February to ninth, and November again proved the cruellest month for a manager – McGhee was made the fall Guy on Bonfire Night.

The sharp little Dubliner Robbie Keane was now the main goalscorer, injuries having hampered Bull for two years. Bull made four substitute appearances at the end of the 1998/99 season and reluctantly decided in the summer to retire, with a magnificent record of 306 goals in 561 games over the course of 13 seasons at Molineux. He became an MBE later that year, had a stand named after him at the ground in 2003 and after a brief spell assisting former Wolves manager Graham Turner at Hereford United tried management himself, without success, at Stafford Rangers in 2008.

Another goalscoring legend, John Richards, had become managing director in 1997 for a frustrating period of near misses. Having missed out on the play-offs by one place in Bull's farewell season, Wolves did so again the following year after Keane was sold to Coventry for £6m. Half of that fee was spent on Ade Akinbiyi from Bristol City, who scored 16 goals and was sold to Leicester for a healthy profit. Manager Colin Lee went the way of Taylor and McGhee before the following Christmas after a home defeat by Birmingham left his goal-shy team 16th.

The arrival of Dave Jones as manager in January 2001 led to two successive seasons back in the play-offs, and the long-desired promotion. He found a goalscorer in Dean Sturridge (21 in 29 games) but a last-minute Norwich goal in the first leg of the 2002 semi-final proved decisive in taking them through 3-1, 0-1. Twelve months later, with joint-record-signing Kenny Miller from Rangers now among the goals, Wolves saw off Reading in the semi-final (2-1, 1-0) and romped to a surprisingly easy win over Sheffield United by 3-0 in the Cardiff final, all the goals coming in the first half.

Joy at replacing relegated Albion lasted only as long as the first month of the next season. Back in the top tier for the first time in 19 years, Wolves lost their opening games 5-1 and 4-0, went seven without a win and were bottom, where they stayed; Albion, in contrast, won five of their first six and remained in the First Division's top two almost all season to change places with their neighbours again.

It was all too predictable that Jones would depart in Molineux's sacking month of November; less so that another former England manager, Glenn Hoddle, would take what was clearly seen as an attractive job at a big club. His team were unbeaten in the Championship from 4 January onwards, finishing ninth, but Hoddle suddenly left after missing the play-offs by a familiar one place in 2006. He was unhappy with the new age of austerity at the club, relegation parachute payments having ended and Sir Jack Hayward having decided he had spent enough of his money and was looking to sell up.

Mick McCarthy, yet another former international manager after his time with the Republic of Ireland, did well in the circumstances to make the play-offs in 2007, albeit for a bitter defeat there by West Brom, who won both legs of the semi-final. Merseysider Steve Morgan, the founder of property builders Redrow, bought the club before the 2007/08 season, another one in which the play-offs were missed by one place. But a year later striker Sylvan Ebanks-Blake confirmed his promise with 25 goals in a total of 80 and Wolves became champions by seven points from Birmingham. In doing so they changed places with relegated Albion for the third time in seven years and this time stayed up in 15th place, as the Premier League's lowest scorers. Despite having warned supporters that his initials did not stand for 'Merlin the Magician', McCarthy had pulled off quite a trick.

* * *

Of the local quartet who put many dark days behind them to reach the Premier League, **Stoke City** took longest but – coincidentally or not – then established themselves the most securely. It still took one further setback before they did so, dropping down to the third tier again for three more years in 1998 following a dismal first season at a smart new home.

Building on 1992's fourth place and the Autoglass Trophy success at Wembley, Lou Macari led his side to the Second Division (third tier) title a year later. He threw himself into the job that season with greater enthusiasm than ever after the relief of being found not guilty of tax offences in a court case in the summer dating back to his Swindon Town days three years earlier; the Swindon chairman, Brian Hillier, went to prison.

Macari found Stoke 'a fun place to work' and after a slow start the 1992/93 season was enjoyable all round as the Potters topped the table with 93 points, going unbeaten from 5 September to 27 February in a run of 25 league games and doing the double over promotion rivals West Brom and Port Vale. Losing to Vale in an FA Cup first-round replay was the only blot. 'This is an important achievement for Stoke City, who have never been regarded as a club who win championships,' the manager said (after 1933, 1963 and 1993, a 30-year cycle meant the next one was due in 2023).

Two months into a new season, however – after further enhancing his reputation with a first-leg victory over Manchester United in the League Cup – Macari could not resist an invitation to take over from Liam Brady at Celtic, another of his old clubs and the one he had supported as a boy. Mark Stein, the diminutive striker who scored 30 goals in all competitions in that championship-winning season, then moved on to Chelsea and without him new manager Joe Jordan did well to finish tenth at the higher level.

Meanwhile his predecessor had endured a torrid time with Celtic's new owner Fergus McCann, who sacked him after less than eight months, which meant he was available when Jordan made a poor start to the 1994/95 campaign and was dismissed. Steadying the ship, Macari lifted them to 11th, with Paul Peschisolido as top scorer, and the following season City had a sniff of the Premier League on the back of Mike Sheron's goals in seven successive games – a club record – before losing the play-off semi-final to Leicester (0-0, 0-1).

Chairman Peter Coates, having survived a supporters' campaign to oust him, had given up on a £5m plan to modernise the Victoria Ground and so 1996/97 was to be the last season at a home the club had known since March 1878 – the longest occupation of one ground by any Football League club. Coincidentally, the final league game there turned out to be against their first Football League opponents in 1888, old rivals West Brom. City won it 2-1, watched by 22,500, which was the biggest gate of a disappointing season that ended in 12th place. It became the last goodbye too for Macari who, unlike 70 per cent of fans in an *Evening Sentinel* poll, had never wanted them to leave the atmospheric ground; he also felt money was being diverted away from team building to fund the Britannia Stadium.

The little Scot resigned and looked on sadly as a local resident while the first season at the new home went pear-shaped. Auguries were not good when a delayed first home game was lost 2-1 to Swindon, and after the shocking 7-0 home defeat by Birmingham in January chairman Coates and then manager Chic Bates both stepped down.

Chris Kamara, recently sacked by Bradford City, was appointed and did not even last until the end of the season. Alan Durban, previously in charge from 1978–81, took over but could not stem the tide and the Potters went down alongside Manchester City, whose 5-2 win at the Britannia on the final day brought an inglorious end to that first season in residence.

It took three more managers and four seasons to return, although all of them were spent in the top eight. Brian Little resigned after a year, disappointed at finishing eighth following a good start; Gary Megson lasted only a few months before new Icelandic owners bought the club and installed one of their countrymen, Gudjon Thordarson, as the club's first foreign manager. Peter Thorne from Swindon Town was leading scorer three seasons out of the four, racking up 30 in all during 1999/2000, including the winner at Wembley against Bristol City when the Potters won the Auto Windscreens Shield watched by more than 75,000.

Home crowds, however, dropped below 11,500 until picking up through three successive play-off campaigns. In 2000 City lost to Gillingham 3-2, 0-3; the next year Walsall beat them 0-0, 4-2; and in 2002 they overcame Cardiff 1-2, 2-0 after trailing in the last minute of the second leg, and went back to the Welsh capital to beat Brentford 2-0 in the final.

Thordarson was controversially sacked within a week of that triumph, a club statement describing his relationship with the board as 'untenable', but his successor Steve Cotterill stayed for less than three months into the new season before moving to Sunderland as assistant manager. George Burley was lined up but pulled out, and Tony Pulis stepped in at the start of November to eventually bring about the club's most successful era since the 1970s.

It had a nervous beginning when they were only saved from relegation back to the third tier on the last day of the season, and there was an interruption when he was sacked by the Icelanders after two seasons in mid-table, returning after a year at Plymouth when Peter Coates regained control of the club.

After missing out on the play-offs by two points in 2007, Pulis led a triumphant promotion campaign as runners-up to Albion. Coates's backing enabled him to break the club's transfer record in the January window by signing Ryan Shawcross and Leon Cort for £1.5m each, while the powerful top scorer Ricardo Fuller and Rory Delap with his long-throw missiles typified the no-nonsense style of play. Striker Dave Kitson was a considerably less successful signing at £5.5m but from losing six of the first nine Premier League games, the Potters defied expectations in finishing 12th and then 11th.

In those two seasons, the home team conceded only 36 goals in 38 games. Full houses roared them on, the wind howled round and Pulis kept the grass so long to handicap close-passing sides that Sir Alex Ferguson once joked he saw rabbits hiding in it. For all of Lou Macari's earlier scepticism, the Britannia had become an inhospitable place for visiting sides.

* * *

Having enjoyed two seasons at the start of the 1990s in a higher division than Stoke, **Port Vale** rejoined their neighbours in the third tier after relegation in 1992 and were one match away from winning promotion alongside them. The following season the Valiants did indeed go up and went on to enjoy probably the best decade in their history.

John Rudge was just over halfway through his 15-year spell – easily the longest stint of any Vale manager – and he continued to prove an inspiring leader, taking every setback in his stride. Forced to sell Darren Beckford and Robbie Earle for a total of £1.7m, he plucked midfielder Ian Taylor out of non-league football at Moor Green to become leading goalscorer in the exciting 1992/93 season. Sitting in an automatic promotion place behind Stoke throughout the spring, the Valiants lost out by a point to Bolton's storming late run and then went down 3-0 in the play-off final against West Brom, who they had beaten home and away in the league. Defender Peter Swan was sent off in the second half with the score at 0-0, an incident 'unquestionably the turning point of a game Vale had under control' according to the *Sentinel*.

Having waited 117 years for a Wembley visit, the club had found two arriving in the space of eight days; on 22 May they won the Autoglass Trophy there by 2-1 against Stockport. The season's other highlights were knocking Stoke out of both the FA Cup (3-1 following a goalless draw at the Victoria Ground) and the Autoglass (1-0 away).

Taylor was backed up in midfield by Robin van der Laan, the club's first major European import, and with striker Martin Foyle justifying a record £375,000 fee in his second season of 1993/94, it was Vale who finished strongest by winning eight of the last nine games to take the runners-up spot behind Reading and return to the second tier. 'A year ago we were on the floor after losing in the play-off final,' said tearful chairman Bill Bell after the decisive win at Brighton. 'Now look what we have achieved.'

Foyle hit 16 goals at the higher level as Vale took four points off Stoke, comfortably avoided the four relegation places and reaped a financial bonus from two close games against Manchester United in the League Cup; Paul Scholes scored twice on his first-team debut at Vale Park, but local MP Joan Walley asked questions at Parliament about why United were allowed to field so many young reserves after home fans had bought tickets.

The 1995/96 campaign was rescued from serious relegation worries after a double over Stoke and two fine cup runs. In the FA Cup, Crystal Palace and holders Everton were beaten (the latter 2-1 after a 2-2 draw at Goodison) and Leeds were held at Elland Road before scraping through the second game. Rudge's team even reached the Anglo-Italian Cup Final at Wembley after beating West Brom, but then lost 5-2 to Genoa. With renewed confidence they won six games in a row to finish 12th and from another slow start in 1996/97 were on course for their highest finish in history before ending up eighth in the second tier – still the best since 1934. It would have been seventh but for allowing QPR a 4-4 draw after leading 4-0 at half-time.

That was four places above the Potters, who went down a year later as Vale stayed up by winning their last game 4-0 at Huddersfield. In January 1999, however, an era came to a sad end when Rudge, the country's second-longest serving manager behind Dario Gradi at Crewe, was sacked after 15 years and almost 850 matches, with the team in trouble again following one win in 14 games. He declined a director of football role and under Brian Horton Vale survived on the same number of points as relegated Bury. It was a temporary reprieve and a year later they went down with Walsall, 13 points from the safe spot occupied by Albion.

The dramatic decade was over and the new one brought difficult times off the field. Although the FA Cup had again provided much-needed finance with ties in successive years against Premier League Blackburn (0-1), Arsenal (0-0 away and 1-1, lost on penalties), Liverpool (0-3) and Leeds (0-2), bids like the £2m Wimbledon offered for midfielder and would-be rock star Gareth Ainsworth were impossible to resist even if it meant weakening the team.

Victory over Brentford in the LDV Vans Trophy Final (having beaten Stoke again on the way) did not significantly swell the coffers and by December 2002, with the FA Cup now offering only the humiliation of a home defeat by Canvey Island in front of 3,566, the club was in administration. A supporters' trust took over and Horton, having done sterling work, finally gave up in February 2004 under threat of further budget cuts.

He left the team in a good position and under Foyle they only missed the play-offs on goal difference, but otherwise his three and a half years were notable only for some more cup adventures. In 2005/06 they won three FA Cup rounds and held out away to Villa for 70 minutes before succumbing 3-1. The following season there was a new League Cup best by reaching the fourth round with home wins against Preston, QPR and Norwich (all from a higher division) before a trip to Tottenham, also honourably lost 3-1.

Londoner Leon Constantine, who gave Vale the lead at White Hart Lane, scored 38 goals over the course of those two seasons, earning a move to Leeds. In a dismal 2007/08 season without him they slipped into relegation danger early on, sacked Foyle, crashed out of the FA Cup to tiny Staffordshire club Chasetown and went down after winning fewer games than any other team and suffering the division's smallest attendance of 2,869.

Down among the financial mayhem of the fourth tier, where four clubs had double-figure points deductions, the main objective was just to stay in the Football League, which was achieved despite only two teams scoring fewer goals.

Under the down-to-earth Micky Adams, however, there was hope of an uplift for the next decade with an improved effort in 2009/10, which included 23 goals from Marc Richards and League Cup wins over the two Sheffield clubs, both Championship sides.

* * *

Like Port Vale, **Walsall** made it to one level below the new Premier League, but only for two brief spells and never with a sniff of reaching the big time. Four promotions and three relegations meant it was not an uninteresting period, however, as ten different managers coped with the changing fortunes.

Kenny Hibbitt and Ray Graydon stayed longest, both making a reasonable fist of four years in their first managerial posts. Hibbitt's team reached the fourth-tier play-offs in 1993 with 23 goals from another former Wolves man, Wayne Clarke, but suffered a heavy 9-3 aggregate defeat by Crewe in the two-leg semi-final. Two years later there was no mistake as runners-up to Carlisle, Chris Nicholl having replaced Hibbitt, and Bermudan Kyle Lightbourne enjoying the first of three prolific seasons that brought him 58 goals and a move to Coventry in the Premier League.

Graydon took over in 1998 and immediately led the Saddlers to a further promotion alongside the big spenders of Fulham and Manchester City after being widely tipped as relegation fodder. 'It doesn't matter who they support, most football fans in the West Midlands are unanimous in their choice of the region's team-of-the-year – Walsall,' wrote the *Evening Mail*. Not surprisingly, perhaps, they struggled in the second tier and, despite beating West Brom twice and Wolves at Molineux, went down just three points below Albion.

But it was straight back 12 months later after play-off success against Stoke (0-0, 4-2) and Reading, who were beaten 3-2 in the Cardiff final after leading in extra time. The main goalscorer was now Portuguese import Jorge Leitão, who also got the winner away to Premier League Charlton to equal a club record in reaching the FA Cup fifth round in 2002 – something achieved again the following year.

The latest spell in the higher echelons lasted three nervous seasons, costing Graydon and then Colin Lee their jobs and leading to the headline-grabbing appointment as player-manager of Paul Merson. Looking safe a month from the end of the 2003/04 season, the Saddlers lost five in a row without scoring and went down despite beating Rotherham on the last day in front of a record Bescot crowd of 11,049.

Two years later they dropped into the fourth tier, winning two games out of the last 21 and using 46 players, but Richard Money led them straight back as champions, Trinidadian goalkeeper Clayton Ince keeping 21 clean sheets. Talking of money, it was a sign of the club's thin resources that the £175,000 paid to get Alan Buckley back from Birmingham in 1979 was still Walsall's record transfer outlay by 2010 – and would be for six more years.

Even the record fee from David Kelly's move to West Ham remained for 20 years until 2008, when about £1m was received from Coventry for centre-half Scott Dann. Coffers thus replenished, the Saddlers finished the decade with a rare period of stability – three mid-table finishes in the third tier, as a hard-drinking young Brummie tearaway called Troy Deeney led the scorers.

* * *

As a Second Division club from 1979–89 in the most sustained period of success in their history, it was a horrible shock for **Shrewsbury Town** to drop out of the Football League altogether in 2003 – not least because that was the season of a famous FA Cup win over Everton. Fortunately they returned immediately and within three years were installed in a smart new stadium.

John Bond's unsuccessful attempt to win promotion from the fourth tier in 1992/93 led to his departure but his assistant Fred Davies led Town back as champions a year later, conceding fewer goals than anyone outside the Premier League. From losing the first three games, including a 6-1 drubbing at Preston, it was quite a feat. So was drawing away to Kenny Dalglish's Blackburn Rovers in the League Cup and only losing the replay 4-3 in extra time against full-strength opposition.

By 1997 it was back down again despite the boost of a first Wembley appearance when losing the previous year's Auto Windscreens Shield Final 2-1 to Rotherham in front of 35,000.

There was a serious warning under new manager Kevin Ratcliffe in 2000 when Town only avoided relegation to the Conference by winning 2-1 at Exeter on the final Saturday, and after two mid-table seasons the worst happened in 2002/03.

Making national headlines by knocking Everton out of the FA Cup with two goals by Nigel Jemson was followed by a 4-0 defeat at home to Chelsea in the next round and a collapse in league form. It was the first season that two teams were automatically cast out of the Football League, and winning only two of the 23 games after Christmas made certain long before the end that Town would be one of them. Unsurprisingly they finished rock bottom, losing the last eight in a row and ending up eight points from safety. Their fate was sealed by losing the penultimate one, at home to fellow-strugglers Carlisle, in front of the biggest crowd of the season, 7,236.

'Given the funereal atmosphere on the final whistle it was apt that a hat-trick from Brian Wake should relegate Shropshire's only league club,' wrote *The Guardian* reporter. 'It ended in calls for Kevin Ratcliffe's head; today there is only emptiness on the banks of the Severn.'

If the Conference season was not entirely convincing, third place – 17 points behind runners-up Hereford – took the

Blues into the play-offs, where Scottish goalkeeper Scott Howie regained his place from a 17-year-old Joe Hart and made crucial saves to win the semi-final and final on penalties. Derbies against champions Chester, Hereford and Telford helped Shrewsbury record the league's best average attendance of just over 4,000.

Northern Ireland international Jimmy Quinn, having replaced Ratcliffe after relegation, played more than a dozen games at the age of 44 in the promotion season but stood down in a difficult start back in the Football League.

Londoner Gary Peters, who had narrowly failed to prevent Exeter going out of the Football League along with Town, joined in November immediately after an FA Cup defeat by Histon, steering them away from trouble and then into mid-table in 2006, when Manchester City paid £600,000 for goalkeeper Hart. The following season was the final one at Gay Meadow after 97 years and could have brought a glorious finale. The last match there, on 14 May 2007, was a play-off semi-final against MK Dons, but despite winning through to Wembley after the away leg, and taking an early lead there against Bristol Rovers, Peters's side were beaten 3-1.

So the last football had been retrieved by the Davies family coracles from the River Severn and Gay Meadow was turned into flats. Life at what was popularly known as the New Meadow, a 10,000 all-seater on the southern outskirts of town costing £11m, brought a 20 per cent increase in crowds despite a poor second half of the season, Peters departing in March.

With £170,000 record-signing Grant Holt the division's joint-top scorer, Paul Simpson took Town to another play-off final in 2009 where they lost 1-0 to Gillingham, and in the summer of 2010 the popular Graham Turner came back 26 years after his departure, having managed Villa, Wolves and Hereford in the meantime, to lead another revival.

* * *

Turner's 15-year stint at **Hereford United** from 1995–2010, ending up as manager, chairman and owner, was more than could reasonably have been asked of any man.

United's romantic ascent to the Football League in 1972 and then the Second Division four years later had soon run into hard reality. By the summer of 1995, when Turner became manager, they had finished in the bottom half of the lowest division for nine seasons in a row and attendances of little more than 2,000 were lower than during the club's financial crisis of the early 1980s (Chapter 8). Despite holding Tottenham 1-1 in the FA Cup in January 1996 and taking welcome receipts from the White Hart Lane replay (lost 5-1), a tenth successive placing in the lower reaches seemed likely late in March, when the crowd at home to Lincoln was 1,631. But on the back of a club-record six successive wins in April, a sixth place finish was achieved before a play-off semi-final defeat by Darlington, striker Steve White totalling 29 league goals – second highest in the country behind Blackburn's Alan Shearer.

White was inevitably soon sold, as was midfielder Richard Wilkins, and the 1996/97 season proved calamitous right at the finish. Brighton were in such dire straits for most of the season – 13 points adrift at one stage – that they seemed certain to occupy the bottom spot which would mean dropping into the Conference. In a dramatic revival under Steve Gritt, however, they pulled just above Hereford with one match to play – at Edgar Street. The Sussex club needed only a draw, but United had to win, and in front of an 8,532 crowd took the lead with an own goal. Just after the hour, however, Robbie Reinelt equalised for the visitors, who hung on to save themselves and condemn Hereford to non-league football after quarter of a century.

Beating Brighton 2-1 in the FA Cup six months later was little consolation as the club's very existence was hanging in the balance again. The Conference proved more of a struggle than anticipated and after finishing only sixth, 20 points behind champions Halifax, chairman Peter Hill resigned and Turner bravely took on the majority shareholding to keep the club afloat.

Being unable to buy new players and having to sell any who would command a decent fee restricted possibilities of a return to the Football League and in the next four seasons United were only once even in the top ten. A brave FA Cup performance in 1999/2000 against Premier League Leicester City (0-0, 1-2 after extra time) was a rare high spot.

In 2002, after finishing 17th with an average crowd of barely 1,500, Turner completely revamped the squad with impressive results: sixth place was only one outside the newly introduced play-offs, which United then reached for three seasons running. The first, which included a 9-0 away win at Dagenham & Redbridge, ended with ten men and a defeat on penalties by Aldershot in the semi-final. Next time, despite finishing runners-up again, came a defeat by Stevenage Borough, but finally in 2006 they made it. Morecambe were beaten 1-1, 3-2 and in the final at Leicester, Ryan Green's goal in extra time beat Halifax 3-2.

'As manager, chairman and majority shareholder, Turner is entitled to take all the plaudits that will follow promotion,' said *The Guardian*. 'I've dedicated 11 years of my life to Hereford United, so that's the personal expense but it's been worth it,' he told reporters. 'After nine years it has put right what went wrong on that day against Brighton.'

Comfortable in 16th place back in the Fourth Division and now making a profit, they even won promotion a year later after knocking Leeds out of the FA Cup at Elland Road, but Turner's group of free transfers and loanees struggled at the higher level and finished bottom. After one season back in the bottom tier and a familiar berth in the lower half, he was more than entitled to a change of scene at last up the road at Shrewsbury. Without him, however, further woe awaited.

* * *

For five of the seasons that Hereford languished in the Conference, the region gained a replacement Football League side – Worcestershire's only ever representatives – in the shape of **Kidderminster Harriers**. Five years but no more, with a highest position of tenth, which was poor reward for a club striving to reach that level since 1886.

As the name implies, the club's origins were in other sports, notably athletics and rugby, only switching from an oval ball to a round one for the 1886/87 season.

Two of the town's clubs dominated the first season of the Birmingham and District League in 1889/90, unbeaten Kidderminster Olympic beating Harriers to the title by 12 points, whereupon the pair merged, moved for one season to the stronger Midland League but quickly returned, intending to compete as separate sides again. Olympic, however, folded, leaving Harriers to fly the flag from then on.

They remained in the Birmingham League without conspicuous success until suddenly improving in the 1930s, winning the title as unbeaten champions in 1938 and finishing top of two different sections played the following year. War interrupted a move to the Southern League but from 1948/49 they were regulars there and in that season set the ground record of 9,155 at Aggborough – home since 1887 – for a 3-0 FA Cup defeat by neighbours Hereford. The cup, although not a source of any great success at that point, did turn the Harriers into history-makers in September 1955 when they entertained Brierley Hill Alliance in the competition's first floodlit match.

Dropping back down for financial reasons to the Birmingham League in 1960, two years before it became the West Midlands League, proved a good move and they were regularly a top-six club, winning the title in 1965 and then successively from 1969–71. The hat-trick prompted a return to the Southern League and promotion in 1983 to the Alliance Premier.

AP Leamington's Graham Allner was appointed manager and under him greater success in cup competitions enhanced the club's reputation, their original red and white halved shirts, which returned in 1986, becoming widely recognised after a series of well-publicised exploits.

With Kim Casey rattling in the goals they were runners-up in the Welsh Cup in 1985/86 after knocking out Shrewsbury, and the following year won the FA Trophy by beating Burton 2-1 at The Hawthorns after a goalless draw at Wembley. And in the FA Cup they began to achieve some distinction at last, most notably in 1993/94. Chesham United, Kettering and Woking were beaten before a first third-round tie in the club's history took them to St Andrew's, where they shocked Birmingham 2-1 with goals by Neil Cartwright and Jon Purdie, plus a heroic goalkeeping performance from Kevin Rose.

In the fourth round Preston fell 1-0 to bring West Ham to Aggborough in the last 16. A crowd of 8,000 saw the Premier League side scrape through 1-0 with Lee Chapman's goal. 'Despite the defeat, this was a day for Graham Allner's side to be proud, and maybe a signal that the best is yet to come,' said the *Evening Mail*. 'Harriers showed on and off the field that they would not be out of place in Division Three.'

They duly went on to win the Conference but as feared were denied promotion because the Football League did not accept that a new main stand would be ready to replace the existing wooden one before the new season. So Northampton Town were reprieved and it took Kiddy six more years to achieve their goal.

Runners-up to Macclesfield in 1997, when Smethwick boy Lee Hughes scored 30 goals before joining West Brom for £380,000, they failed for the next two seasons, and Allner left after 15 years and more than 900 games. The big name to replace him was Jan Mølby, backed by chairman Lionel Newton and turning Harriers into champions by nine points in his first season, with former Liverpool team-mate Mike Marsh one of the key players.

Asked if his team were good enough for the Football League, the great Dane replied, 'We'll have a lot of fun finding out.' After an opening-day 2-0 victory against Torquay in front of 5,122 and winning two of the next three, finishing 16th with an average of just under 3,500 was solid enough and for two seasons they improved on it in tenth and 11th places.

Mølby, who had left briefly for Hull, returned for the 2003/04 season but a drop to 16th despite coming within a minute of knocking Premier League Wolves out of the FA Cup foreshadowed the disaster to come. Lacking a goalscorer, they struggled from the start and Mølby resigned in October after defeat at Chester left them bottom. They stayed in the bottom two relegation places from then on and 23rd place would have been 24th but for Cambridge United suffering a ten-point deduction. The last home game in the Football League on 30 April 2005 drew little more than 2,000 fans, who saw a 4-1 defeat by Grimsby; a week later Kiddy bade farewell with a third successive three-goal defeat, this time at Northampton.

The average home gate for the season of 2,785 was almost exactly the same as when they joined five years earlier and had only topped 3,000 in the first year; it had been impossible to attract significant new support. The 2002 collapse of ITV Digital, owing £172m in TV rights to Football League clubs, did not help either, although it affected all 72 members. Since joining, Harriers had hardly been profligate, never again paying as much as the £80,000 they spent on record-signing Andy Ducros from Nuneaton in the summer of 2000.

Three survivors from the final Third Division game set off in the Conference with a 2-1 win over Woking but changes on the field and in the boardroom meant adjusting was difficult. Only once in the first five seasons back did the Harriers finish in the top six and what little joy there was came from the FA Trophy. In 2007 they made the final, losing 3-2 to Stevenage at the rebuilt Wembley in front of 53,262 after holding a 2-0 lead at half-time, and two years later they reached the semi-final.

But the best days were gone and a hard slog was under way.

* * *

Having lost Kidderminster in 2005, the region gained a replacement four years later who would surpass the Harriers' achievements.

As recounted in the first three chapters, the brewery town of Burton had a chequered football history, fielding two different teams in the Football League Second Division – Swifts and Wanderers – who then joined forces as Burton United before losing Football League status in 1907. Amalgamating with Burton All Saints three years later and changing their name yet again to **Burton Town** in 1924, they played in the Birmingham Combination and Birmingham League between the wars, winning the championship of the latter once (1928) before moving up to the Midland League. One season of wartime football, however, back in the Birmingham competition, proved to be the last for a senior team in the town for exactly ten years.

Then on 6 July 1950 the *Derby Daily Telegraph* reported, 'Almost 700 "fans" decided at a public meeting at Burton Town Hall last night to establish **Burton Albion** Football Club, which will compete next season in the Birmingham League.' The ground, it was announced, was to be in Wellington Street and one player had already been signed – local boy Norman Smith, a 25-year-old inside-forward who had once played for Accrington Stanley and Oldham. A later recruit, winger Bertie Mee, would attract wider attention 20 years on as manager of Arsenal's Double-winning side.

Don McPhail, who had played on the wing for Burton Town, was appointed manager and saw them through the first season. The enduring post-war enthusiasm for any form of entertainment was shown on 19 August when the new club drew more than 5,000 people to see a first Birmingham League game against Gloucester City's reserves. From finishing only two points off the bottom that first season, Albion, in their black and amber stripes, quickly established themselves, finishing runners-up to Wolves 'A' in 1954 as well as winning the Birmingham Senior Cup. Two years later they came through seven rounds of the FA Cup, knocking out Halifax Town to reach the third round proper, and earning some national publicity with an away tie against Charlton Athletic, fifth in the First Division, who beat them 7-0. A year later the damage was worse with an 8-0 defeat at Bournemouth in the first round.

In 1958, leaving Wellington Street for Eton Park, they progressed to the Southern League, struggling early on but winning the Southern League Cup in 1964 under Peter Taylor, who was taking his first steps in management before rejoining former team-mate Brian Clough at Hartlepools the following year. Taylor had made it to the Football League but that notion was still a distant dream for Albion (who had applied in 1955 and 1958 without receiving a single vote).

Apart from an unbeaten run of 31 Southern League games from March 1971 to February 1972, the 1970s were unexceptional, but from the mid-1980s they began to make a mark with Neil Warnock in charge. An unlucky defeat in the 1987 FA Trophy Final against Kidderminster (see previous section) confirmed the progress they had made while coming to the notice of a wider audience with the controversial FA Cup tie of 1985 against Gary Lineker's Leicester City. Warnock's Brewers, having moved the home game to Derby's Baseball Ground, lost 6-1 (with a Lineker hat-trick) after their goalkeeper Paul Evans was hit by a wooden missile, and persuaded the FA to order a replay behind closed doors at Coventry, where the First Division side won only 1-0.

When English football was revolutionised by the Premier League, Burton were a mid-table Southern League team. In 1997 they won both the Southern League Cup and Birmingham Senior Cup and in October 1998 entered a new era with the appointment of Manchester City's 32-year-old Nigel Clough as player-manager.

He proved an inspired choice and after switching to the Northern Premier League, the Brewers became champions in 2002, losing only twice and scoring 106 goals to reach the Conference for the first time. After three years in the lower half of the table they began to progress each season and in 2005/06 held Manchester United to a goalless draw in the FA Cup, banking some £600,000 after losing the replay 5-0 at Old Trafford.

'Nigel Clough and his players will relish those sporadic moments when their neat triangular football bridged the gulf between the two clubs. And their supporters, old and new, will always remember the time they questioned whether the mighty Manchester United were Tamworth in disguise,' reported *The Guardian*.

United were visiting the new Pirelli Stadium for the second time in three months, having officially inaugurated the new ground in November 2005. Ninth place that season became sixth, fifth (35 league goals in two seasons from centre-forward Daryl Clare) and then, in 2008/09, first.

Continuing a long run without defeat even after Clough left for Derby County in January had them on course to romp home before almost throwing automatic promotion away with five defeats in the last six games as Cambridge United drew ever closer. On the final day Albion were beaten 2-1 at Torquay, but Cambridge, with a better goal difference, could only draw and finished two points behind. 'I've had a few sleepless nights but we've done it over 46 matches, through effort and hard work, with a lot of skill thrown in,' said temporary manager Roy McFarland.

So Burton had a Football League club again for the first time in 102 years. Imaginative chairman Ben Robinson continued his policy of blooding untried managers by appointing Paul Peschisolido, who after an opening 3-1 defeat at Shrewsbury on 8 August 2009, steered the Brewers to 13th place. Two of the season's smaller crowds saw the most eventful games: a 6-1 win over Aldershot in December, when Greg Pearson scored the club's first Football League hat-trick, and an extraordinary 6-5 home defeat by Cheltenham. The average gate was 3,191 and for all Robinson's backing, Albion could hardly be accused of buying success: Russell Penn at just £25,000 from Kidderminster was the most expensive player recruited.

11

Endings 2011–2021

'This was Birmingham's first major trophy since 1963 and one that has seen them qualify for next season's Europa League, a detail McLeish said he had not realised.'

The Guardian, February 2011

'Stoke, 39 years on from winning their one significant honour, were nothing like the team who had demolished Bolton 5-0 in the semi-final.'

Independent on Sunday, May 2011

'The new Hereford Football Club, founded by supporters after their beloved, historic Hereford United crumpled into liquidation last year, has been reborn with a pre-season friendly against FC United of Manchester, attended by a remarkable, emotional crowd of 4,000.'

Guardian, July 2015

'Wolverhampton Wanderers have been cleared by the Football League over their close relationship with "super-agent" Jorge Mendes.'

Daily Telegraph, April 2018

'In the second half the Baggies looked more likely to win it with their physically intense style that fed off one of the most electric atmospheres at The Hawthorns in recent years. But in the 80th minute, Albion lost their captain and leader Chris Brunt to a red card, swinging the tie in Villa's favour.'

Express & Star, May 2019

'Supporters of Coventry City Football Club are now facing, for a second time, the prospect of enforced groundshare and the decision to attend matches or not – a situation and decision that no football fan should have to ever face.'
Club statement, June 2019

IT WAS a decade in which the Premier League's half-dozen biggest (i.e., richest) clubs established a stranglehold. Leicester City may have caused a sensation with their 5,000-1 title win in 2016 but in the three following seasons the same six teams topped the table, well ahead of the rest – something that had never happened in 130 years. Emboldened by their dominance, they even proposed awarding themselves a larger share of television money and greater voting rights, then shamelessly applied to join a midweek European Super League offering them permanent membership.

The West Midlands was not represented among this new elite. Aston Villa, who in the previous decade had finished sixth for three years running, now dropped out of the Premier League altogether for three seasons, in one of which (2018/19) Wolves were the only local representatives.

One thing the big four in the second city and the Black Country did have in common was ownership – every one of them at that stage being under Chinese control. From the same country, catastrophically, came the outbreak of coronavirus that the World Health Organization declared to be a public health emergency at the end of January 2020, when the first cases were reported in the United Kingdom. But it was not until mid-March, with the death toll in Britain having risen to 55, that the country went into the first of the lockdowns that would have such serious implications for football at all levels.

On Monday, 9 March Villa lost 4-0 at Leicester in the last Premier League game played for more than three months, during which discussion raged about whether or when the season should be ended. Villa, 19th at the time with ten matches still to play, were left contemplating enforced relegation and Wolves, who were sixth, wondered about their European prospects; Albion fretted over whether they would be promoted from the Championship, Blues whether they would drop back into the third tier; Coventry, sitting on top of League One, worried that their efforts would simply be wiped out, and many other lower-division clubs were concerned about simply surviving the financial hit.

In the event, the top two tiers decided to play on behind closed doors from mid-June, but the lower divisions, so dependent on gate receipts, cut their losses and ended a first incomplete season since 1939 on a points-per-game basis. Port Vale's chief executive summed up their financial predicament, estimating that restarting would have cost £100,000 per month just to take players and staff off the government furlough scheme (which paid 80 per cent of wages up to £2,500 a month) and that regular testing would eat up another £125,000 to £140,000. And the following season, it turned out, was worse.

* * *

When the 'Big Six' from Manchester, Merseyside and London established their dominance from 2017 onwards, **Aston Villa** were nowhere to be seen, having just been relegated to the Championship. At the start of the decade they had finished in sixth place for a third year running under Martin O'Neill. Yet all that was about to end.

Anyone wondering why the manager walked out five days before the opening game of the 2010/11 season need only check a list of Premier League clubs' transfer activity that summer: on the day he left, Villa had not spent a penny on new players. Worse, after James Milner scored in the 3-0 victory over West Ham in the first match, he was sold to Manchester City for £26m.

Nobody was expecting owner Randy Lerner to keep up with newly mega-rich City (who spent almost £130m on half a dozen new players) and he could claim to have given O'Neill plenty of spending money for the previous two seasons, resulting in wages at an unhealthy 88 per cent of turnover and losses of almost £40m. That was the price of a regular sixth place in the table. But seeing local rivals Birmingham, Stoke, West Bromwich and Wolves each spend between £10m and £15m net on new recruits did not encourage much belief that Villa could even maintain their status, let alone improve it under a new manager who did not take over until late-September.

That man turned out to be Gérard Houllier, who had not worked in England since leaving Liverpool six years earlier. By the new year he was being booed, Villa had gone out of the League Cup to Birmingham and were 18th in the table with significant injuries, forcing Lerner to authorise the purchase of Darren Bent for a club-record £18m from Sunderland. The striker's nine goals in 16 matches enabled them to finish as high as ninth, but in March Houllier was taken to hospital with a recurrence of heart problems, missing the remaining games, and at the start of June he left the club.

The identity of his successor caused a sensation, Alex McLeish becoming the first manager to switch directly from St Andrew's to Villa Park (although Ron Saunders had gone the other way in 1982). Having underestimated the depth of local feeling, Lerner did not help his new appointee by using the summer transfer window to reduce new losses of £54m, selling England wingers Stewart Downing and Ashley Young to Liverpool and Manchester United respectively.

Without them McLeish endured a poor second half of the 2011/2012 season to finish 16th, only two points above relegation and with the second-lowest goals total. He found himself facing first a Holte End banner that read 'It's not where you came from, it's where you are taking us' and then the sack, just one day after the final game at Norwich.

Norwich's Paul Lambert took on the challenge of restoring Villa as the region's top club – Albion and Stoke both having finished above them. He could have eased the pressure by winning a trophy in his first year but Bradford City, tenth in League Two, somehow knocked his team out 4-3 in the League Cup semi-final before losing 5-0 to Swansea at Wembley. Lerner allowed Lambert two low-scoring seasons in 15th place but in February 2015 felt obliged to make another change with the team in the relegation zone amid a dreadful run of one goal in eight games.

Tim Sherwood dragged them to safety with a new low of just 31 goals, and more surprisingly to the FA Cup Final by beating

Leicester, West Brom and in the semi-final Liverpool. Wembley opponents Arsenal, who had won the two league meetings by an aggregate of 8-0, settled for 4-0 in a one-sided final. 'Though Aston Villa will always be filled with regret for playing with so little wit and cohesion, they should also realise they came up against an Arsène Wenger side displaying all the qualities of his greatest moments', said *The Observer*.

Outclassed as Villa were on the day, few could have imagined the following 2015/16 campaign turning into the very worst in the club's history. There were perhaps two bright moments: winning the opening game at Bournemouth and knocking Blues out of the League Cup in September. The following month, however, Sherwood was gone after eight defeats in nine games; Frenchman Rémi Garde, an acolyte of Wenger, was then given five months in charge until April, by which time relegation was assured. A total of 17 points, three wins all season and 27 goals scored, plus 11 successive league defeats and 19 games without a win were all new lows from 142 years of Aston Villa history.

'No fight, no pride, no effort, no hope' read one supporter's banner; 'Rotterdam to Rotherham' said another – though 'Bayern to Burton' would have done just as well.

Lerner, having initially put the club up for sale in 2014, got out at last in June 2016. 'I have come to know well that fates are fickle in the business of English football. And I feel that I have pushed mine well past the limit,' he said, adding that he was 'hoping for a stronger future performance appropriate to our size and heritage'.

It would take a while. Chinese businessman and former Harvard student Tony Xia bought the club for £76m, and appointed Roberto Di Matteo, five years after the Italian had left Albion, and then won the FA Cup and Champions League at Chelsea. He lasted for just 12 Championship games, winning only one of them. Steve Bruce, another former Birmingham man, signed John Terry on a free transfer as his captain for a first full season and reached the 2018 play-off final, only to lose 1-0 to Fulham.

Promotion at that point might not have been the blessing it seemed, for Xia was having trouble getting money out of China, and when a £4m tax bill arrived to add to existing debts reported to be £50m there was some doubt whether Villa could pay it. 'The club faced being wiped out,' according to new chief executive Christian Purslow.

Xia sold his majority stake to the Egyptian-based group NSWE, who proved equally demanding owners: at the start of the 2018/19 campaign, Bruce won the first two games but only one of the next nine and was sacked.

On 10 October boyhood fan Dean Smith was brought in from Brentford, with Terry as assistant head coach, but next day the club was in mourning for Sir Doug Ellis, who died aged 94. 'Ellis had an infamously frosty relationship with Villa fans but their fortunes have taken a turn for the worse since his departure,' said the *Daily Mail.* The upturn was about to start.

Fifteenth when Smith took over, Villa finished fifth with ten straight wins in the run-in and 25 goals from Chelsea loanee Tammy Abraham. They did the double over Blues but took only one point from Albion, their semi-final play-off opponents for another two fiercely contested games that ended all square, before Villa won the penalty shoot-out 4-3 with Jed Steer saving two. 'In the second half the Baggies looked more likely to win it with their physically intense style that fed off one of the most electric atmospheres at The Hawthorns in recent years,' reported the *Express & Star.* 'But in the 80th minute, Albion lost their captain and leader Chris Brunt to a red card, swinging the tie in Villa's favour.'

At Wembley they beat Derby County 2-1 with goals by Anwar El Ghazi and Scottish international John McGinn. 'Aston Villa are headed back to the Premier League. Had you told that to any fans in claret and blue in December they'd have laughed you back onto the train at New Street station,' said *The Independent*.

2019 Championship play-off final: Aston Villa 2 Derby County 1

Aston Villa: Steer, Elmohamady, Tuanzebe, Mings (Hause), Taylor, McGinn, Hourihane, Grealish, Adomah (Green), Abraham, El Ghazi.

Derby County: Roos, Bogle, Keogh, Tomori, Cole, Mount, Huddlestone (Marriott), Johnson, Wilson, Lawrence (Jozefzoon), Bennett (Waghorn).

The previous season, Premier League newcomers Fulham managed to spend £100m and still get relegated; Villa backed Smith with the record signing of Wesley Moraes at £22m from Club Brugge as part of no less than £130m of investment. It proved just enough to avoid Fulham's fate, although it was a close-run thing. Deep inside the relegation zone when football paused for 100 days and still there with four games to play, they survived by drawing 1-1 on the last day at West Ham with a goal by gifted local boy and future England cap Jack Grealish. Relegated Bournemouth, who beat them twice, were only a point behind, with a better goal difference.

For the following more successful season, Ollie Watkins from Smith's former club Brentford became the club's most expensive signing at £28m and then a hero with his hat-trick in the extraordinary 7-2 demolition of reigning champions Liverpool. That was part of another £75m of expenditure on new players, which produced a fine start of four straight wins – for the first time in the top division since 1930 – amid some wild media talk, quickly forgotten, about emulating Leicester's 2016 triumph. But 11th place was solid enough and a first FA Youth Cup success since 2002 was encouraging.

* * *

After returning to the Premier League for three seasons from 2009–12, **Wolves** were in danger of bringing on back the bad times amid two successive relegations, but Kenny Jackett proved successful in steering them quickly up from the third tier, and new foreign owners and coaching staff ushered in the closest thing to glory days for some 40 years.

Mick McCarthy battled doggedly to keep them at the highest level and in 2011 survived by one point at Birmingham's expense, helped by Steven Fletcher's late scoring burst and crucial wins over Villa and Albion.

The 2011/12 campaign soon became a struggle, however, and a humiliating 5-1 home defeat by Albion in February proved too much for supporters and owners to take. McCarthy was dismissed, and conceding five goals twice more in quick succession under his assistant Terry Connor meant there was little doubt about the team's fate. They finished rock bottom, 12 points from safety and without a win in three months.

Norwegian Ståle Solbakken, who had played briefly for Wimbledon and won the Danish title eight times as FC Copenhagen's coach, was appointed the club's first foreign manager, owner Steve Morgan insisting it was 'not a gamble'. He fared miserably after a bright start and was sacked in January 2013 following an FA Cup defeat away to National League club Luton Town. Under Dean Saunders, beating Birmingham at the start of April left six teams below Wolves, but losing five of the last six matches proved fatal for the manager and the club, who suffered a second successive demotion.

Jackett, cast out by Millwall after six seasons, proved a better appointment and took them straight up on the back of a club record nine straight wins in the new year, finishing with 89 goals spread around the squad and a record 103 points. With crowds back up to over 20,000 an impressive seventh place in the Championship followed, before two seasons of treading water in the lower half as Morgan sold to a Chinese investment group. Jackett was quickly dismissed, but his successors Walter Zenga and Paul Lambert were no more successful and it took a third foreign manager to bring further progress.

Nuno Espírito Santo, once a goalkeeper and formerly in charge at Valencia and Porto, arrived in the summer of 2017 as part of the Portuguese revolution inspired by his relationship with super-agent Jorge Mendes. Failure would have been expensive, as Nuno brought in his own staff plus seven Portuguese players, of whom Rúben Neves at £15.8m cost almost £10m more than any other signing in the club's history. The result was a £57m loss for the year – but supporters loved it as his team romped to the Championship title with 99 points, playing exciting football and missing the century only by drawing and losing the final two games. Over 30,000 saw a 2-0 home win over Villa; Diogo Jota, later to join Liverpool, topped the scorers and Rúben Neves was voted the club's player of the season.

Less impressed were Championship rivals like Villa, Derby and Leeds, who complained in vain to the EFL about Mendes's relationship with the club. 'Wolverhampton Wanderers have been cleared by the Football League over their close relationship with "super-agent" Jorge Mendes,' the *Daily Telegraph* reported in April that year. 'The EFL has concluded that Wolves have not broken any regulations despite their link-up with Mendes, insisting he does not hold any official role at the Championship title winners.'

Back in the Premier League as the West Midlands' only representatives, the spending continued with six new Portuguese signings, including the nation's most capped goalkeeper Rui Patrício, and Wolves exceeded expectations by finishing seventh. It was the highest placing since the days of John Richards and Andy Gray in 1980. There should have been an FA Cup Final too after knocking out Liverpool and Manchester United, then leading Watford 2-0 in the semi-final with 12 minutes to play – only to lose in extra time.

Just as impressive was another seventh place the following year, which would have been a top-six berth but for losing the final game at Chelsea. A return to European competition after almost 40 years brought a long run in the Europa League before losing a quarter-final to Seville when Mexican Raúl Jiménez, the new record £30m signing from Benfica and yet another Mendes client, missed a penalty.

Eyebrows were raised at the even higher fee paid for the latest Portuguese arrival in September 2020; teenager Fábio Silva had played only a dozen senior games for Porto but cost an eye-watering £35m. There was no faulting the club's ambition – it was the sixth time the new owners had broken the transfer record in four years – and the dark days of the mid-1980s seemed light years away.

'Wolves are not short of resources and have a serious powerbroker as their friend. It is only a matter of time before they are knocking on the door of the Champions League spots,' predicted *The Independent*. But after a serious head injury to striker Jiménez led to a disappointing finish in 13th place, ten points behind Villa, supporters were stunned by the departure of Nuno and his entourage. 'We had very special moments together that will forever stay in our memories,' he said.

* * *

As well as handsome backing from their new owners, Wolves were once more savouring the financial delights of the Premier League. Neighbouring **West Bromwich Albion** had been in a position to boast all about that when they stayed for eight lucrative seasons from 2010–2018, the club's longest spell in the top tier since the infinitely less lucrative days of 1976–86.

Without matching Wolves' spending, Albion were regularly able to sign players for £10m or more. The difference between the two leagues was illustrated, however, by relegation in 2018; income dropped from £125m to £70m, the latter figure bolstered only by the controversially high parachute payments that many wanted to stop as part of football's overdue reset following coronavirus.

Of those eight Premier League seasons, the first three were spent in the top dozen places, though not entirely without fear of relegation. In the first season of 2010/11, which began with a 6-0 drubbing at Chelsea, the Baggies lost five games in a row over Christmas and New Year, beginning with defeat at Villa Park (where they failed to win a league game from May 1979 until October 2011). After a seventh loss in ten at Manchester City early in February they were 17th and Roberto Di Matteo was fired. Roy Hodgson took over a month after ending his bruising spell with Liverpool, where he was never a good fit, and steered the Baggies to a creditable 11th, losing only two of the remaining games (albeit one was away to Wolves).

The unpredictable Peter Odemwingie finished top scorer with 15 after a late burst and did so again the following season with ten, three of which came in the famous 5-1 romp at Molineux that cost Mick McCarthy his job and pushed the old enemy closer to relegation. Hodgson's long career was on the up again and a top-ten finish earned him nothing less than the England job.

Tenth was the Baggies' best since 1981 and they rose two more places in 2012/13 under Hodgson's replacement, Steve Clarke, having been third at the end of November. The powerful Romelu Lukaku, on loan from Chelsea, got 17 league goals. Odemwingie ended up with only five, the last of them earning a late draw at Villa Park in January, after which he demanded a transfer and tried to force a move by driving himself to Queens Park Rangers on deadline day, but ended up turning round and going home to be disciplined by the club. He did not start another match and was moved on to Cardiff City in the summer.

Missing Lukaku's goals more than the Nigerian's, Albion dropped to 17th, only three points from relegation after a mid-season slump that led to Clarke being replaced by the unsuccessful Spaniard Pepe Mel. Young striker Saido Berahino, later to join Stoke for £12m, topped the list of scorers with almost as many goals in two League Cup matches (four) as in the league (five).

Tony Pulis, another grizzled Premier League veteran, brought about a return to mid-table without exciting the fans, as, in the summer of 2016, Albion followed Wolves into Chinese ownership. Pulis departed 15 months later after being allowed to spend £43m for little return. Successor Alan Pardew had a dreadful time, with one league win in 18 games (plus, bizarrely, an FA Cup triumph at Liverpool) and the popular Darren Moore could not prevent relegation in his caretaker role despite a brave attempt. The goals total was a miserable 31.

Rewarded with the full-time job, Moore and two assistants were sacked next March with the team having taken one point from three Championship games but still sitting in fourth place. 'We have to place the club's best interests at the forefront of our thinking and we must do everything we can to try to deliver the promotion we have targeted,' a club statement said.

They stayed in the same position with 87 goals, 23 of them from loanee Dwight Gayle and 22 from Jay Rodriguez. Losing on the final day meant a play-off semi-final with Villa, against whom they had taken four points in the league, three of them in the away game in February. Returning there three months later for the first leg, Albion took the lead through Gayle then conceded twice in the last quarter of an hour. Craig Dawson levelled matters on aggregate at The Hawthorns and although Chris Brunt was sent off his team would have gone through if the EFL had an away goals rule. Instead they played out extra time with ten men and lost 4-3 on penalties.

The hurt was eased, though not forgotten, as the Baggies went up automatically the following season with a fresh, younger squad. Slaven Bilić had been appointed as manager, the club citing his 'presence, experience and management qualities'.

These proved sufficient to earn promotion behind Leeds United, and above Brentford in dramatic circumstances. On a fluctuating final day Albion could only draw with QPR, but Brentford, needing a win at home to struggling Barnsley to secure the second automatic spot, were caught out chasing a winning goal and lost 2-1.

Back in the Premier League, Bilić was disappointed at the club's transfer business, and conceding 11 times in the first three games suggested a struggle would be forthcoming. The manager departed before Christmas to be replaced by former coach Sam Allardyce from Dudley, who as a player had trained or had trials at Albion, Wolves and Villa. A welcome win at Molineux was the only one in his first 13 games and despite an astonishing 5-2 victory at Chelsea the Baggies stayed 19th, where they had been before the change, and went down once more.

* * *

In an eventful decade **Stoke City** reached the FA Cup Final for the first time, Tony Pulis moved on after seven years and Premier League status was lost following two seasons as the top side in the whole of the Midlands – another historic first for the club.

The 2010/11 cup run came amid fluctuating league fortunes, positions varying from 19th early on to eighth with only two games left, but finally 13th. From the unimpressive start of a third-round draw at home to Cardiff, Wolves were beaten at Molineux, as were Brighton and West Ham at the Britannia. In the Wembley semi-final Owen Coyle's Bolton, four places above the Potters in the Premier League, were drubbed 5-0, three of the goals coming before half-time; it was the most decisive win at that stage of the competition since Wolves beat Grimsby by the same score in 1939.

In a disappointing final, goalkeeper Thomas Sørensen kept the newly enriched Manchester City at bay until the 74th minute, when Yaya Touré scored the only goal. 'Stoke, 39 years on from winning their one significant honour, were nothing like the team who had demolished Bolton 5-0 in the semi-final,' said the *Independent on Sunday*.

2011 FA Cup Final: Manchester City 1 Stoke City 0
Manchester City: Hart, Richards, Kompany, Lescott, Kolarov, De Jong, Touré, Barry (Johnson), Silva (Vieira), Tevez (Zabaleta), Balotelli..
Stoke City: Sorensen, Wilkinson, Shawcross, Huth, Wilson, Pennant, Whelan (Pugh), Delap (Carew), Etherington (Whitehead), Jones, Walters.

While City became champions the following season, Stoke scored fewer goals than any other Premier League team despite having paid a record £10m to Tottenham for Peter Crouch. He managed ten of their 36 in the league, and a reasonably tight defence ensured they dropped no lower than one place to 14th. Again there was more fun to be had from other competitions, with a run to the FA Cup quarter-final, lost narrowly at Anfield, plus 12 European games – the first for 36 years – ending with defeat by Valencia (0-1, 0-1) after coming through the group stage of the Europa League.

In the Premier League, the Potters were treading water and after another 13th place in 2013 Pulis decided to move on. 'We had seven very good years with Tony Pulis,' said owner Peter Coates. Once again they were only a couple of points away from the top half of the table, but the football had become too attritional for many supporters, as was reflected in a further drop in goals scored to just 34 – better than bottom club QPR but nobody else.

Under Mark Hughes, an extra dozen goals per season brought three successive finishes in ninth place, the first of which in 2013/14 made them the highest -placed team in all the Midlands for the first time. It was all done by way of modest spending too, including one notable investment: the volatile Austrian forward Marko Arnautović cost £2m from Werder Bremen and was eventually sold to West Ham for ten times as much. He did not immediately increase the firepower but like Senegal's Mame Biram Diouf did at least reach double figures in one campaign.

The second season of the three ninth-placed finishes ended with a 6-1 win over Liverpool, who almost unthinkably trailed 5-0 at the interval. Their embarrassed manager, Brendan Rodgers, returned to the Potteries to win the first game of the new season 1-0 but lasted for only seven more matches before being replaced by Jürgen Klopp. Stoke felt emboldened to spend £18m on midfielder Giannelli Imbula from Porto, who proved not worth it, and with a League Cup semi-final lost to Liverpool on penalties and another ninth place, Hughes had peaked. Having dropped four positions in 2016/17, he departed the following January after an FA Cup defeat at Coventry and with relegation a strong possibility. Despite the creative promptings of little Xherdan Shaqiri, new man Paul Lambert, continuing his round of the West Midlands, won only one game in 15 before the drop was confirmed, West Brom being the only team beneath them.

Unlike the Albion, however, there would be no quick return from the Championship, just three seasons in the lower half under first Gary Rowett from Derby, then Nathan Jones, who left them bottom in November, and finally Michael O'Neill, also continuing for a while as manager of Northern Ireland, whose side were 21st with four games to play but beat Blues 2-0 and finished 15th and then 14th.

* * *

Three months before Stoke became FA Cup runners-up, **Birmingham City** had their own day in the Wembley sun. It brought greater success but came amid a bizarre 2010/11 campaign that saw them win the League Cup, reach the FA Cup quarter-final, suffer relegation, lose their manager to Villa and find the club's owner, Carson Yeung, arrested for money laundering.

Only four clubs had spent more money in the summer transfer window, with goalkeeper Ben Foster and the 6ft 8in Valencia striker Nikola Žigić costing £6m each, while Alex Hleb on loan from Barcelona was supposed to provide extra craft in midfield. But Žigić scored just once before February, by which time it was clear that only the cups would provide much to remember the season by. Knocking Villa out of the League Cup quarter-final amid serious crowd trouble at St Andrew's was just about the only highlight before Christmas but in the new year two double successes kept minds off Premier League problems.

A near-capacity crowd roared Blues to Wembley after trailing West Ham 3-1 on aggregate at half-time in the semi-final and three days later they beat Coventry 3-2 in the FA Cup fourth round. The next month, successive matches brought a fifth-round 3-0 win over Sheffield Wednesday and, most remarkably of all, Arsenal. Arsène Wenger's side had just beaten Barcelona in the Champions League, but were shocked 2-1 in the League Cup Final when Obafemi Martins took advantage of a hideous defensive mix-up in the last minute.

'This was Birmingham's first major trophy since 1963 and one that has seen them qualify for next season's Europa League, a detail McLeish said he had not realised,' *The Guardian* pointed out. The manager told reporters, 'It is all the sweeter because nobody gave us a prayer. I am so delighted for everyone, especially the long-suffering Blues fans. It was a Titanic performance. It's Carson Yeung's birthday and he must think it's easy being an owner.'

2011 League Cup Final: Birmingham City 2 Arsenal 1
Birmingham City: Foster, Carr, Ridgewell, Bowyer, Jiránek, Johnson, Larsson, Ferguson, Žigić (Jerome), Gardner (Beausejour), Fahey (Martins).
Arsenal: Szczęsny, Sagna, Clichy, Song, Djourou, Koscielny, Rosický, Wilshere, Van Persie (Bendtner), Arshavin (Chamakh), Nasri.

In fact, Yeung's financial problems were making his life anything but easy, and the comedown was swift both on and off the pitch. A home defeat by Albion put McLeish's men in the relegation zone and Bolton immediately knocked them out of the FA Cup at St Andrew's. Then a steadier run pushed them up to 15th, with half a dozen matches left and the manager claiming that one win would see them safe. It still would have done on the final day at Tottenham, going into which West Ham were already down but Wigan, Blackpool and Birmingham all had 39 points, Wolves and Blackburn (who were playing each other) 40.

Blackpool predictably lost at Old Trafford but Wigan won at Stoke and the Blues, needing all three points to overtake Wolves, were beaten 2-1 at Tottenham by a last-minute goal. The goals tally summed up a strange season: 27 scored in 11 cup games but only 37 – easily the lowest of any team – in 38 league matches.

McLeish was kept on, but was told he would need to win promotion the next season. Villa, sensing an opportunity after being turned down by Wigan Athletic's Roberto Martínez, immediately made a play for him and succeeded, infuriating the Blues, who demanded and received compensation. At the end of June, Yeung was arrested and charged with five counts of money laundering. He was eventually jailed in 2014 for six years, a month after finally severing connections with the club.

By that time Birmingham had failed in their only realistic attempt at returning to the Premier League, losing the 2012 play-off semi-final against Blackpool 0-1, 2-2 after being three goals down on aggregate at one point. Chris Hughton was the manager that season, during which they narrowly failed to reach the knockout stage of the Europa League, but with the club under a transfer embargo and ownership up in the air he soon departed for the more stable atmosphere of Norwich City.

For the rest of the decade they were never in the top eight, and under seven different managers often flirted with relegation. The closest shave came in 2014, just after Yeung's conviction in a Hong Kong court; following five successive defeats, Blues were going down until the 93rd minute of the final game at Bolton, when Paul Caddis scored an equalising goal to saved them.

A few months later, after Lee Clark was sacked, came the embarrassment of a record 8-0 home defeat to Bournemouth, after which Gary Rowett steered the side from 23rd place to mid-table. The takeover by Trillion Trophy Asia, a Hong Kong investment company, in October 2016 (a month after the original gypsy curse on the stadium was supposedly lifted by a local priest) led to Rowett making way for a short-lived trophy manager Gianfranco Zola, and two years later to the name Trillion Trophy being added to the stadium name after 112 years as plain St Andrew's. Whatever extra revenue accrued, two 19th places, one 20th and one 18th all within a few points of going down, under eight managers in five years, were desperately poor reward for 20,000 loyal Bluenoses.

* * *

Coventry City's stadium problems amounted to far more than a mere change of name, so much so that in the period under review they played at three different home grounds – including St Andrew's. It was all the more credit to the boys of 2020 that they should return the club to the Championship, eight years after dropping into the third tier for the first time since 1964.

In those halcyon mid-60s days of Jimmy Hill, the birth of the Sky Blues and 51,000 at Highfield Road, supporters might have imagined the lower divisions had been left behind forever. But in August 2013 'Jimmy's Hill' was the name given to the slope overlooking Sixfields Stadium, Northampton where diehard followers protested on matchdays against the hated owners SISU, who had condemned City to play home games there, 33 long miles from home.

The move to the Ricoh Arena in 2005 (see previous chapter) led to only one good season, finishing eighth in the Championship with average attendances up by a third to 21,302, from which point crowds regularly dropped as every subsequent campaign was spent in the bottom eight. By May 2012 gates of 15,000 were lower than at Highfield Road and relegation for Andy Thorn's side was confirmed after they had spent every week since November in the bottom three. 'Under a financial choke hold inflicted by owners SISU, Coventry have dropped into the third tier of English football for the first time in 48 years, condemned by a defeat against Doncaster on home turf,' reported *The Guardian*.

SISU's four and a half years had become a relentlessly downward spiral, which now threatened to take the club off a cliff. As the team failed to challenge at the lower level in 2012/13 despite David McGoldrick's 18 goals (the best return since Dion Dublin in 1998), crowds understandably fell further to below 11,000 and in March 2013 City went into administration over unpaid rent. An inevitable ten-point deduction proved one of the least costly – effectively demoting Steven Pressley's team from 13th to 15th – the real damage being done that summer when the stadium managers Arena Coventry Ltd (ACL) refused to re-negotiate the rent, which the club claimed they could no longer afford as a League One side.

The solution to the impasse was apparently to be another brand-new stadium 'designed and delivered in three years' and in the meantime City would groundshare. After an unsuccessful campaign by local politicians and supporters and the *Coventry Telegraph*, the question became 'with whom?' Walsall were one of the three clubs involved in talks, but fans were shocked when it was announced that the venue was to be faraway Northampton.

By the start of the new season the club were still in administration, so the Football League imposed another ten-point deduction, their chairman Greg Clarke making the football authorities' displeasure known: 'Once again, it is a source of immense frustration to everyone involved that the two parties in this dispute have failed to reach any agreement. The Board is dismayed at the level of intransigence being shown.'

A majority of equally dismayed supporters decided to boycott 'home' matches, although those up on Jimmy's Hill with their anti-SISU banners for the opening game against Bristol City had a partial view of a thrilling 5-4 win. The crowd of 2,348, which was not going to solve any financial problems, fell for Carlisle's visit in February to a record low of 1,603. And the second successive points deduction was more damaging than the previous season's, leaving the Sky Blues 18th instead of ninth, only three places from relegation.

It was a situation that could clearly not continue and agreement was finally reached with ACL for a return to the Ricoh. Delayed for two further games at the start of 2014/15, it was celebrated on 5 September by a joyous crowd of 27,306 – more than ten times the previous gate – for a 1-0 win over Gillingham achieved with Frank Nouble's goal. 'It hasn't felt like our team, it wasn't Coventry City,' a Sky Blue Trust member said of the year's exile. 'It's really a victory for fan power and common sense.'

Life was still far from smooth. Pressley left before the end of a season that ended no higher than 17th place with eight home defeats in League One and another in the FA Cup by non-league Worcester City. The down-to-earth Tony Mowbray then had them top of the table until falling away to eighth in his one full season before the bittersweet campaign of 2016/17 brought a Wembley win – and another relegation. After Mowbray resigned to spend more time with his family, Russell Slade managed just one win in his 13 league games and the season finished in 23rd place with only 37 goals scored. Before that, however, came a glorious day at Wembley when almost 75,000 watched a 2-1 victory over Oxford United in the EFL Trophy Final.

Off the field, meanwhile, Wasps rugby club had become the surprising new owners of the Ricoh from late in 2014, paying less than £5.5m. Coventry rugby club, 140 years old, were among those far from pleased and City even contemplated moving in with them at the Butts Park Arena, now shared instead with non-league Coventry United – who were founded in 2013 as a reaction to the Sky Blues' move to Northampton.

SISU were equally upset, claiming that the value of the stadium had been grossly undervalued and legal appeals rumbled on as far as the European Commission. In 2017/18, their first season down in League Two, City revived under Mark Robins (returning for a second spell in the tenth managerial change in ten years of SISU ownership) and made the play-offs, where they defeated Notts County 5-2 on aggregate in the semi-final – drawing over 17,000 for the home leg – and then beat Exeter 3-1 at Wembley with more than 50,000 present. The official man of the match was the Sky Blues' Scottish striker Marc McNulty, who scored 28 in all competitions before moving on to Reading.

Without him they managed a commendable eighth place in League One before SISU's continuing dispute with Wasps led to the shock of a second groundshare from 2019, this time at St Andrew's. 'The Ricoh Arena is the stadium built to be the football club's home, and our fans should be able to watch their team play in the city that we are proud to represent,' said a club statement.

The first season in Birmingham proved a far happier one than at Northampton, however, and Robins's team were five points clear of the field and deservedly declared League One champions after lower-division clubs voted to halt the campaign and decide the final tables on a points-per-game basis as a result of the coronavirus pandemic. There were two further very welcome developments: a partnership with the University of Warwick, who would provide land for a new stadium, and the announcement of a return to the Ricoh for 2021/22 during Coventry's year as UK City of Culture.

* * *

Burton Albion's first season in the Football League, 2009/10, had been a perfectly acceptable one in finishing 13th, but far from building on it they slipped the other way for two years. Going into the last month of the second campaign they were in danger of returning to the National League before half a dozen unbeaten games carried them to the safety of 19th place. The third season was more promising, spending Christmas in the top five with Billy Kee, Calvin Zola and Justin Richards scoring well, but a dreadful run from then on of 12 defeats and four draws got Paul Peschisolido the sack. Coach Gary Rowett kept them out of trouble in 17th place and then laid the seeds for three successive seasons in the top six and a promotion that he missed, having moved on to Birmingham.

The Blues had recognised his work in leading Burton – still without any expensive signings – to successive play-offs. Finishing fourth in 2013, Albion lost the semi-final 5-4 to Bradford City after leading 3-1 at half-time in the away leg, and the following year they beat Southend but were beaten 1-0 in the Wembley final by Fleetwood Town. After Rowett was lured away in October 2014 with the Brewers having knocked Premier League QPR out of the League Cup and sitting third in the table, Jimmy Floyd Hasselbaink lifted them higher, going top in February and staying there for the rest of the season. Promotion was confirmed at Morecambe with two games to spare and the title was secured on the final day with another win at Cambridge.

Success on gates of 3,000 at a club whose record signing cost £25,000 continued to attract admiring glances and with Albion racing to the top of League One in December 2015, Hasselbaink, like Rowett before him, was lured away, in his case to QPR. To supporters' delight, chairman Ben Robinson was immediately able to persuade Nigel Clough to return after almost seven years away at Derby and Sheffield United. Keeping them top until a late stutter, he secured promotion as runners-up by winning the final game at Doncaster to stay one point ahead of Walsall.

Rarely heavy scorers – 57 that season was the same total as relegated Colchester – the Brewers not surprisingly found the going hard in the second tier. They did spend some real money at last by paying Milton Keynes £500,000 for defender Kyle McFadzean, and in beating Clough's old teams Derby and Nottingham Forest, plus Birmingham twice, they scraped to safety by a point with a record average gate of 5,228.

In the summer, however, Australian international midfielder Jackson Irvine went to Hull City for £2m, and another £500,000 signing, Northern Ireland striker Liam Boyce from Ross County, badly injured a knee in a pre-season friendly. He could not play until an away game at Villa Park in February, when losing 3-2 despite his first goal confirmed them in bottom place; three late wins in a brave revival could not prevent relegation.

Ninth place just below Coventry in 2018/19 was followed by the difficult first coronavirus-impacted season of 2019/20. Albion were a comfortable 12th but the last home gate was only 2,034. In May, Clough, his assistant Gary Crosby (who later returned) and chief scout Simon Clough, Nigel's brother, all stood down to help finances. Jake Buxton was appointed manager, before Hasselbaink returned in January 2021 to lead a revival from the bottom of the table to safety.

* * *

Like Burton with Nigel Clough, **Shrewsbury** welcomed back an old favourite who had enjoyed adventures with more prosperous employers elsewhere and on his return was also able to get them promoted once more but not to keep them up. His successors, however, fared better and the club should have reached the Championship in 2018.

Graham Turner came back in June 2010 after 26 years away and brought about an immediate upturn. Top of League Two early on and in the play-off places for most of the season, Town finished fourth, only a point from automatic promotion, but could not recover from conceding two first-half goals at Torquay in the play-off semi-final. The following season they made no mistake even while scoring fewer goals, finishing strongly and maintaining an unbeaten record at the New Meadow. There was welcome extra finance too from the cup defeats at Tottenham and Arsenal.

In the higher division with a revamped squad, however, they lasted for only two seasons. In the first came an impressive double over Coventry but only seven goals each from the leading scorers, and in 2013/14 a new record crowd of 9,510 against champions-elect Wolves (plus a goalless draw at Molineux) were rare highlights. Turner resigned in January with the team 19th and they won only three of the remaining 19 games, finishing a full eight points from safety in 23rd place.

Micky Mellon got them straight back as runners-up to Burton. James Collins returned from two years at Swindon and Hibernian to top the scorers again, and Chelsea's visit for the League Cup after Town had knocked out Leicester and Norwich brought the New Meadow's first five-figure crowd of 10,210. Keeping them in League One by one place, Mellon left early in 2016/17 after a poor start and they survived by two points under Paul Hurst with an improved second half of the season.

On the back of that recovery came an unexpectedly exciting 2017/18 that should have brought a return to the second tier. Fans able to enjoy safe standing with 550 'rail seats' – the first in England – saw their team top of the table after starting with 15 unbeaten games. Towards the end of March Hurst's men were still at the summit but then allowed the Lancashire pair Wigan and Blackburn to overhaul them. In the play-offs they beat Charlton home and away but at Wembley fell 2-1 to Rotherham in extra time after Alex Rodman's equaliser. It was the club's second visit of the season to the national stadium, where they had earlier lost the Checkatrade Trophy Final 1-0 to Lincoln.

Hurst left to manage Ipswich, which led to two seasons in the bottom half of the table. Holding Premier League champions-elect Liverpool 2-2 in a thrilling FA Cup tie before narrow defeat at Anfield was a highlight but in the league a big chance to return to the 1980s heights had gone.

The 2020/21 season, like the previous one, was spent in the bottom half of the League One table, further troubled by having workaholic manager Steve Cotterill in hospital twice suffering from coronavirus.

* * *

Shrewsbury's Paul Hurst, like Nigel Clough and Graham Turner, was one of many managers whose success with the region's smaller clubs earned them a route to supposedly greater things. The grass was by no means always greener: Hurst lasted just two months into the new season at Ipswich and Sheffield-born Micky Adams, leaving **Port Vale** for Bramall Lane in December 2010, did not fare much better. He was sacked after failing to save the Blades from relegation and gratefully returned to the Potteries for the 2011/12 campaign, telling the *Sentinel*, 'I always said Sheffield United would be the only club to tempt me away from Vale, and ultimately I let my heart rule my head.'

At times in a difficult decade at Vale Park, owners, chairmen and chief executives seemed to come and go as fast as managers. Despite unsubstantiated talk of £5m investment from an American outfit called Blue Sky International, Adams soon discovered the club to be in a familiar position of financial difficulty and in March they went into administration. Without the inevitable ten-point deduction they would have been close to a play-off place, but having lost leading scorer Marc Richards to Chesterfield it was a pleasant surprise that the 2012/13 season went so well. The key turned out to be the transformation of local man and Vale fan Tom Pope, the lanky striker who after ten goals in 58 league games since joining from Rotherham hit four in a 6-2 win against his old club and added two further hat-tricks to finish the season with 31 as Vale, easily League Two's highest scorers, took the third automatic promotion place – just ahead of Burton, whose hopes they had dented with a 7-1 victory.

As Wolves romped to the League One title the next season, drawing a 12,000 crowd to Vale Park, Adams's team finished a respectable ninth but he resigned after five successive defeats the following September.

The club's first foreign manager, Portuguese former Leeds and Sheffield United player Bruno Ribeiro, was appointed in 2016 but had an unhappy time after bringing in a dozen foreign players and resigned at Christmas with the team 17th. Relegation soon began to look a possibility, which became reality after failing to score more than one goal from the final seven games.

A dreadful start to the new season led to the sack for Michael Brown with Vale bottom of League Two. Seventeen goals from club captain Pope, who had returned after two seasons at Bury, brought salvation, albeit only one point ahead of Barnet, who dropped out of the Football League with Chesterfield.

A second successive season in the bottom five was then followed by narrowly missing out on the play-offs in the truncated 2019/20 campaign under John Askey's management after husband and wife Kevin and Carol Shanahan took on the task of keeping the club afloat in troubled times following the exit of widely disliked owner Norman Smurthwaite.

* * *

History suggests **Walsall** are a club who belong in the third tier of English football, which is where they settled from 2007 to 2019 before dropping back for one of their occasional spells in the lowest division. That has rarely been good enough to satisfy the owners, however, which is why the number of managers in the post-war period soared towards 40 – since the Second World War, that is, not the First.

Stable in mid-table as a League One side from 2007–10, they faded after leading scorer Troy Deeney left for Watford and were in the bottom six for the next two seasons, surviving by a point in 2011 after having been ten behind.

That season's saviour, Dean Smith, had taken over from Chris Hutchings for one of the club's longer stretches in the manager's chair, lasting for almost five years. Under him the Saddlers finished in the top half of the table in 2013, with Northern Ireland's Will Grigg catching fire to hit 19 goals; they inflicted Wolves' first defeat of the following season in a rare league meeting and as one of only four league teams never to have played at Wembley they went at last for the 2015 Johnstone's Paint Trophy Final, more than 72,000 watching the 2-0 defeat by Bristol City.

Smith's team were well in the promotion hunt in November 2015 when he shocked supporters by leaving for Championship side Brentford. 'He has been fantastic for Walsall Football Club and, in turn, we have been fantastic for him,' said a disappointed chairman, Jeff Bonser.

Sean O'Driscoll had them top at Christmas but was suddenly sacked in March after his side took three points from six games.

Bonser could claim it was the right decision when they revived to win eight of the remaining dozen matches, losing out to Burton by only a point for automatic promotion. A 5-0 win at Port Vale in the last game sent them into the play-offs in good heart and good form but sixth-placed Barnsley, whose 3-1 win at the Bescot had cost O'Driscoll his job, repeated the dose after winning their home leg 3-0.

Smith helped his old club's financial position by paying a record £1.5m for England under-19 full-back Rico Henry in August 2016 but a steady decline over three seasons then culminated in the drop in 2019, falling from 11th place at Christmas to 22nd. The final game was a relegation decider at Shrewsbury, where the Saddlers had famously won promotion to the Second Division in 1961. At the New Meadow rather than the old ground, there was also a near-capacity crowd, who saw a goalless draw that saved the Town but cost Walsall dear.

So they were back in the lowest tier for the two Covid seasons, happy to finish the first in 12th place after sitting 22nd at one time, before dropping to the bottom six in 2020/21.

* * *

Having dropped out of the Football League from 1997 to 2006, **Hereford United** returned for only six more seasons. Two years after that, in 2014, they were wound up when debts became too heavy to bear, but in the modern manner a phoenix club quickly emerged from the ashes and with familiar colours, nickname and motto flew through three divisions in successive seasons to end up just two steps from the EFL again, and in two Wembley finals.

Where the average gate at Edgar Street way back in the club's first Football League season of 1972/73 had been almost 9,000, barely a third of that number were ever tempted back for the second spell, which was at the heart of the problem. As chairman and manager, Graham Turner ran the tightest of ships – reportedly paying a fee for only three players in ten years – and as late as 2008, while winning promotion for a one-year spell in the third tier and enjoying a good FA Cup run (Chapter 10), he was able to report a £400,000 profit. But there was little good news once he left a year later to return to rivals Shrewsbury.

In 2010/11 the Bulls were under pressure from a poor start – which led to one home crowd of 1,444 against Stevenage – plus a three-point deduction for fielding a player not registered in time the previous day. Turning a 3-0 half-time deficit away to Northampton into a 4-3 win in October could not keep them off the bottom of the table but from Boxing Day they revived and survived, finishing three points clear.

The following season's revival came just too late. Going into the final month they were bottom again, having sacked manager Jamie Pitman. Winning the last two games almost saved them, but relegation rivals Barnet, with a worse goal difference, won 2-1 on the final day away to Burton, who missed a penalty that would have kept Hereford up.

'The road back to the Football League will not be paved with gold,' reported *The Observer*. 'David Keyte, the owner, has made it clear that losing the £400,000 of annual funding the Football League provides will hit the club hard. But it will not finish it off.'

Two and a half years later, however, it did just that. The first season back in the National League had gone well enough on the field, just missing the play-offs, although one crowd of below 700 against Dartford was ominous. A year later, winning the last two games again seemed to have prevented another relegation but six weeks later United were expelled for non-payment of bills to staff and other clubs totalling £148,000.

Walsall supporters who remembered Londoner Terry Ramsden arriving in his helicopter 30 years earlier (Chapter 8) must have had a wry smile at the potential saviours who journeyed up from the capital to Herefordshire. Tony Agombar was a London property developer who took control for a matter of weeks, claimed that debts were £1.3m, not the £300,000 he had been told and then failed the Football Association's 'officers and directors test' because he had a criminal conviction. His associate Andy Lonsdale, the former owner of Feltham FC, was equally unpopular with United fans, many of whom boycotted the club for the 2014/15 season.

Having been accepted into the Southern Premier League, where they had made their name 40-odd years earlier, the Bulls were threatened with eviction by their council landlords and had not completed half a season when on 19 December 2014

Lonsdale – 'stuck in traffic' – failed to arrive in time for a High Court hearing that wound up the club after 90 years.

The final match had been against Dunstable on 13 December, a 1-1 draw leaving the Bulls in 14th place. Interested parties, including the club's Supporters' Trust, had concluded by this time that the best way forward was to fold and start again, which was why local MP Jesse Norman portrayed the High Court outcome as a victory, clearing the way for 'something very significant and good and long-term and new in football for Herefordshire'.

Only three days later a new club, named plain **Hereford**, was born, securing a five-year lease on the Edgar Street ground early in the new year and appointing as manager Peter Beadle, who had been in charge of United when they left the Football League.

It was a triumphant resurrection from the start, as *The Guardian* reported in July: 'The new Hereford Football Club, founded by supporters after their beloved, historic Hereford United crumpled into liquidation last year, has been reborn with a pre-season friendly against FC United of Manchester, attended by a remarkable, emotional crowd of 4,000.'

Accepted into the Midland League Premier Division, part of the football pyramid's ninth tier, they attracted an equally large crowd for the first league game against the Nottingham club Dunkirk on 8 August 2015, which was won 4-1, and went on to win the league with 108 points while scoring 138 goals. The season even finished with a trip to Wembley for the FA Vase Final, where they lost to Morpeth.

The following two seasons were equally successful, winning the Southern League South and West in 2017 by fully 18 points after losing only one game; then in 2017/18 the new Bulls won five games to reach the second round proper of the FA Cup and won the Southern Premier League while scoring more than 100 goals for the third successive season.

Sacking Beadle early the next season when they were 12th in National League North seemed ungracious if not ungrateful. Harsh reality soon kicked in with finishes of 17th and 16th over the next two seasons but in 2021 they kept going while the league ended prematurely for a second successive year, having a day out at Wembley for the FA Trophy Final. It was lost 3-1 to AFC Hornchurch after leading with 15 minutes to play, but the

Bulls were back in business, which was what mattered most in Herefordshire.

* * *

If the second Covid season of 2020/21 was a disappointing one for so many of the local teams, it was a time to be grateful for small mercies, which in many cases meant mere financial survival. Playing-wise, outside the Premier League, Stoke were always comfortable in the Championship, while Coventry and Birmingham, Burton and Shrewsbury, Port Vale and Walsall all avoided demotion from their respective divisions and, more importantly, were still – like the new Hereford – alive to fight another day.

Further north, historic clubs like Bury (formed in 1885 and twice FA Cup winners) and Macclesfield Town (1874) were on the rocks even before the potentially ruinous season began. Too late for them was the £250m bail out in loans and grants to EFL clubs from the Premier League. Loans, grants and furlough payments or not, it was a tribute to fans paying for either season tickets they never used or matches on television and laptops, as well as supportive owners and sponsors, that struggling communities throughout the West Midlands region could continue to be represented by so many football clubs bearing their name.

Well over 100 years on, the principal local rivalries still existed and were even being extended, as Villa and Blues found themselves in a (successful) relegation fight in the Women's Super League. Not even the visionary William McGregor had thought of that one.

Appendix I

Top West Midlands club each season by league position
(Football League First Division from 1888/89; Premier League from 1992/93)

1888/89 Aston Villa (2nd)
1889/90 Wolves (4th)
1890/91 Wolves (4th)
1891/92 Aston Villa (4th)
1892/93 Aston Villa (4th)
1893/94 **Aston Villa (1st)**
1894/95 Aston Villa (3rd)
1895/96 **Aston Villa (1st)**
1896/97 **Aston Villa (1st)**
1897/98 Wolves (3rd)
1898/99 **Aston Villa (1st)**
1899/00 **Aston Villa (1st)**
1900/01 Wolves (13th)
1901/02 Aston Villa (8th)
1902/03 Aston Villa (2nd)
1903/04 Aston Villa (5th)
1904/05 Aston Villa (4th)
1905/06 Birmingham (7th)
1906/07 Aston Villa (5th)
1907/08 Aston Villa (2nd)
1908/09 Aston Villa (7th)
1909/10 **Aston Villa (1st)**
1910/11 Aston Villa (2nd)
1911/12 Aston Villa (6th)

1912/13 Aston Villa (2nd)
1913/14 Aston Villa (2nd)
1914/15 West Bromwich (10th)

1919/20 **West Bromwich (1st)**
1920/21 Aston Villa (10th)
1921/22 Aston Villa (5th)
1922/23 Aston Villa (6th)
1923/24 Aston Villa (6th)
1924/25 West Bromwich (2nd)
1925/26 Aston Villa (6th)
1926/27 Aston Villa (10th)
1927/28 Aston Villa (8th)
1928/29 Aston Villa (3rd)
1929/30 Aston Villa (4th)
1930/31 Aston Villa (2nd)
1931/32 Aston Villa (5th)
1932/33 Aston Villa (2nd)
1933/34 West Bromwich (7th)
1934/35 West Bromwich (9th)
1935/36 Stoke City (4th)
1936/37 Wolves (5th)
1937/38 Wolves (2nd)
1938/39 Wolves (2nd)

1946/47 Wolves (3rd)
1947/48 Wolves (5th)
1948/49 Wolves (6th)
1949/50 Wolves (2nd)
1950/51 Stoke City (13th)
1951/52 Aston Villa (6th)
1952/53 Wolves (3rd)
1953/54 **Wolves (1st)**
1954/55 Wolves (2nd)
1955/56 Wolves (3rd)
1956/57 Wolves (6th)
1957/58 **Wolves (1st)**
1958/59 **Wolves (1st)**

1959/60 Wolves (2nd)
1960/61 Wolves (3rd)
1961/62 Aston Villa (7th)
1962/63 Wolves (5th)
1963/64 West Bromwich (10th)
1964/65 Stoke City (11th)
1965/66 West Bromwich (6th)
1966/67 Stoke City (12th)
1967/68 West Bromwich (8th)
1968/69 West Bromwich (10th)
1969/70 Coventry City (6th)
1970/71 Wolves (4th)
1971/72 Wolves (9th)
1972/73 Wolves (5th)
1973/74 Stoke City (5th)
1974/75 Stoke City (5th)
1975/76 Stoke City (12th)
1976/77 Aston Villa (4th)
1977/78 West Bromwich (6th)
1978/79 West Bromwich (3rd)
1979/80 Wolves (6th)
1980/81 **Aston Villa (1st)**
1981/82 Aston Villa (11th)
1982/83 Aston Villa (6th)
1983/84 Aston Villa (10th)
1984/85 Aston Villa (10th)
1985/86 Aston Villa (16th)
1986/87 Coventry City (10th)
1987/88 Coventry City (10th)
1988/89 Coventry City (7th)
1989/90 Aston Villa (2nd)
1990/91 Coventry City (16th)
1991/92 Aston Villa (7th)
1992/93 Aston Villa (2nd)
1993/94 Aston Villa (10th)
1994/95 Coventry City (16th)
1995/96 Aston Villa (4th)
1996/97 Aston Villa (5th)

1997/98 Aston Villa (7th)
1998/99 Aston Villa (6th)
1999/00 Aston Villa (6th)
2000/01 Aston Villa (8th)
2001/02 Aston Villa (8th)
2002/03 Birmingham City (13th)
2003/04 Aston Villa (6th)
2004/05 Aston Villa (10th)
2005/06 Aston Villa (16th)
2006/07 Aston Villa (11th)
2007/08 Aston Villa (6th)
2008/09 Aston Villa (6th)
2009/10 Aston Villa (6th)
2010/11 Aston Villa (9th)
2011/12 West Bromwich (10th)
2012/13 West Bromwich (8th)
2013/14 Stoke City (9th)
2014/15 Stoke City (9th)
2015/16 Stoke City (9th)
2016/17 West Bromwich (10th)
2017/18 Stoke City (19th)
2018/19 Wolves (7th)
2019/20 Wolves (7th)
2020/21 Aston Villa (11th)

Total: Aston Villa 62, Wolves 27, West Bromwich 14, Stoke City 11, Coventry City 6, Birmingham City 2.

League champions: Aston Villa 7, Wolves 3, West Bromwich 1.

Appendix II

Lowest West Midlands club each season by league position
*Denotes left Football League, permanently or temporarily

Football League:
1888/89 Stoke (12th)
1889/90 Stoke (12th)*
1890/91 West Bromwich (12th)
1891/92 Stoke (13th)

Second Division:
1892/93 Walsall Town Swifts (12th)
1893/94 Walsall Town Swifts (10th)
1894/95 Burslem Port Vale (15th)
Walsall Town Swifts (14th) not re-elected*
1895/96 Burslem Port Vale (14th)*
1896/97 Burton Wanderers (15th)*
1897/98 Burton Swifts (13th)
1898/99 Burton Swifts (13th)
1899/00 Burton Swifts (15th)
1900/01 Burton Swifts (18th)
Walsall (16th) not re-elected*
1901/02 Burslem Port Vale (12th)
1902/03 Burton United (13th)
1903/04 Burton United (14th)
1904/05 Burton United (17th)
1905/06 Burton United (19th)
1906/07 Burton United (20th)
Burslem Port Vale (16th) resigned*

1907/08 Stoke (10th) resigned*
1908/09 Birmingham (11th)
1909/10 Birmingham (18th)
1910/11 Birmingham (14th)
1911/12 Birmingham (12th)
1912/13 Wolves (10th)
1913/14 Birmingham (14th)
1914/15 Birmingham (6th)

1919/20 Coventry City (21st)
1920/21 Coventry City (20th)

Third Division North or South:
1921/22 Walsall (8th)
1922/23 Walsall (3rd)
1923/24 Walsall (17th)
1924/25 Walsall (19th)
1925/26 Walsall (21st)
1926/27 Coventry City (15th)
1927/28 Coventry City (20th)
1928/29 Walsall (14th)
1929/30 Walsall (17th)
1930/31 Walsall (17th)
1931/32 Walsall (16th)
1932/33 Coventry City (6th)
1933/34 Walsall (4th)
1934/35 Walsall (14th)
1935/36 Walsall (10th)
1936/37 Walsall (17th)
1937/38 Walsall (21st)
1938/39 Walsall (21st)

1946/47 Port Vale (10th)
1947/48 Port Vale (8th)
1948/49 Walsall (14th)
1949/50 Walsall (19th)
1950/51 Shrewsbury Town (20th)
1951/52 Walsall (24th)

1952/53 Walsall (24th)
1953/54 Walsall (24th)
1954/55 Walsall (23rd)
1955/56 Walsall (20th)
1956/57 Coventry City (16th)
1957/58 Walsall (20th)

Fourth Division:
1958/59 Walsall (6th)
1959/60 Walsall (1st)

Third Division:
1960/61 Coventry City (15th)
1961/62 Shrewsbury Town (19th)
1962/63 Shrewsbury Town (15th)
1963/64 Walsall (19th)
1964/65 Port Vale (22nd)

Fourth Division:
1965/66 Port Vale (19th)
1966/67 Port Vale (13th)
1967/68 Port Vale (18th)
1968/69 Port Vale (13th)
1969/70 Port Vale (4th)

Third Division:
1970/71 Walsall (20th)
1971/72 Port Vale (15th)

Fourth Division:
1972/73 Hereford United (2nd)

Third Division:
1973/74 Shrewsbury Town (22nd)

Fourth Division:
1974/75 Shrewsbury Town (2nd)

Third Division:
1975/76 Port Vale (12th)
1976/77 Port Vale (19th)
1977/78 Hereford United (23rd)

Fourth Division or equivalent:
1978/79 Port Vale (16th)
1979/80 Hereford United (21st)
1980/81 Hereford United (22nd)
1981/82 Hereford United (10th)
1982/83 Hereford United (24th)
1983/84 Hereford United (11th)
1984/85 Port Vale (12th)
1985/86 Hereford United (10th)
1986/87 Hereford United (16th)
1987/88 Hereford United (19th)
1988/89 Hereford United (15th)
1989/90 Hereford United (17th)
1990/91 Hereford United (17th)
1991/92 Hereford United (17th)
1992/93 Hereford United (17th)
1993/94 Hereford United (20th)
1994/95 Hereford United (16th)
1995/96 Hereford United (6th)
1996/97 Hereford United (24th)*
1997/98 Shrewsbury Town (13th)
1998/99 Shrewsbury Town (15th)
1999/00 Shrewsbury Town (22nd)
2000/01 Kidderminster Harriers (16th)
2001/02 Kidderminster Harriers (10th)
2002/03 Shrewsbury Town (24th)*
2003/04 Kidderminster Harriers (16th)
2004/05 Kidderminster Harriers (23rd)*
2005/06 Shrewsbury Town (10th)
2006/07 Hereford United (16th)
2007/08 Shrewsbury Town (18th)
2008/09 Port Vale (18th)
2009/10 Hereford United (16th)

2010/11 Hereford United (21st)
2011/12 Hereford United (23rd)*
2012/13 Burton Albion (4th)
2013/14 Burton Albion (6th)
2014/15 Shrewsbury Town (2nd)

League One:
2015/16 Shrewsbury Town (20th)
2016/17 Coventry City (23rd)

League Two:
2017/18 Port Vale (20th)
2018/19 Port Vale (20th)
2019/20 Walsall (12th)
2020/21 Walsall (19th)

Total: Walsall 31, Hereford 23, Port Vale 19, Shrewsbury 13, Coventry 8, Birmingham 6, Burton United 5, Burton Swifts 4, Kidderminster 4, Stoke 4, Burton Albion 2, Burton Wanderers 1,West Bromwich 1, Wolves 1.

Select bibliography

Atkinson, Ron, *Big Ron* (Andre Deutsch, 1998)
Blanchflower, Danny, *The Double And Before* (Nicholas Kaye, 1961)
Bradbury, Mike, *Lost Teams of the Midlands* (XLibris, 2013)
Butler, Bryon, *The Football League 1888–1988 – The Official Illustrated History* (Queen Anne Press, 1998)
Buxton, Peter, *Stoke City FC Centenary Handbook* (Pyramid Press, 1963)
Carr, Steve, *The History of the Birmingham Senior Cup 1876 to 1905* (Grorty Dick, 2000)
Collett, Mike, *The Complete Record Of The FA Cup* (Sports Books, 2003)
Cullis, Stan, *All For The Wolves* (Rupert Hart-Davis, 1960)
Curry, Graham and Dunning, Eric, *Association Football* (Routledge, 2015)
Dean, Rod and others, *Coventry City, A Complete Record* (Breedon Books, 1991)
Docherty, Tommy, *My Story* (Headline, 2006)
Francis, Trevor, *One In A Million* (Pitch Publishing, 2019)
Giles, John, *A Football Man* (Hodder & Stoughton, 2010)
Goodyear, David and Matthews, Tony, *Aston Villa, A Complete Record* (Breedon Books, 1998)
Gould, Bobby, *24 Carat Gould* (Thomas Publications, 2010)
Gray, Andy, *Shades of Gray* (Queen Anne Press, 1986)
Green, Geoffrey, *Soccer in the Fifties* (Ian Allan, 1974)
Harris, Nick, *England, Their England* (Pitch Publishing, 2003)
Henderson, John, *The Wizard: The Life of Stanley Matthews* (Yellow Jersey Press, 2013)

Hill, Jimmy, *My Autobiography* (Hodder & Stoughton, 1998)
Holden, Jim, *Stan Cullis, the Iron Man* (Breedon Books, 2000)
Hugman, Barry, *Football Players Records 1946–84* (Rothmans, 1984)
Inglis, Simon, *League Football and the Men Who Made It* (Willow Books, 1988)
Inglis, Simon, *Soccer In The Dock* (Collins Willow, 1985)
Inglis, Simon, *The Football Grounds of Great Britain* (Collins Willow, 1987)
Jawad, Hyder, *Strange Magic: Birmingham City v Aston Villa* (Birmingham Post, 2005)
Jones, Mike, *Breathe On 'Em Salop* (Yore, 1995)
Kent, Jeff, *The Story of Port Vale* (Witan Books, 1990)
Little, Brian, *A Little Is Enough* (Goodyear, 2018)
Lupson, Peter and Lerwill, John, *The Inspirational William McGregor* (A & JL Solutions, 2011)
Macari, Lou, *Football, My Life* (Transworld, 2008)
Matthews, Stanley, *The Way It Was* (Headline, 2000)
Matthews, Tony, *Birmingham City, A Complete Record* (Breedon Books, 1989)
Matthews, Tony, *The Saddlers* (Breedon Books, 1991)
Matthews, Tony with Mackenzie, Colin, *West Bromwich Albion, A Complete Record* (Breedon Books, 1987)
Matthews, Tony with Smith, Les, *Wolverhampton Wanderers, A Complete Record* (Breedon Books, 1994)
Metcalf, Mark, *The Origins of the Football League, The First Season 1888/89* (Amberley, 2013)
Morris, Peter, *Aston Villa* (Naldrett Press, 1960)
Motson, John and Rowlinson, John, *The European Cup, 1955–80* (Queen Anne Press, 1980)
Moynihan, Leo, *Gordon Strachan* (Virgin Books, 2005)
Page, Rex, *Burton Albion, The Complete History* (Burton Mail, 2010)
Radford, Brian, *Through Open Doors* (Harrap, 1984)
Robinson, Michael, *English Football League and FA Premier League Tables 1888–2019* (Soccer Books, 2019)
Robinson, Michael, *Non-League Football Tables of the West Midlands 1889–2019* (Soccer Books, 2019)

Rollin, Jack, *Soccer At War 1939–45* (Headline, 2005)
Samuels, John, *Where Did It All Go Wrong?* (Brewin Books, 2019)
Sydenham, Richard, *Ticket to the Moon* (deCoubertin, 2018)
Tabner, Brian, *Through the Turnstiles* (Yore,1992)
Tyler, Martin, *Cup Final Extra!* (Hamlyn, 1981)
Wright, Billy, *Captain of England* (Stanley Paul, 1950)
Young, Percy, *Centenary Wolves* (Wolverhampton Wanderers FC, 1976)

Rothmans Football Yearbook, 1970–2002
Sky Sports Football Yearbook, 2003–2018
Football Yearbook, 2019–2021

Selected websites
blackcountryhistory.org
britishnewspaperarchive.co.uk
enfa.co.uk
englandfootballonline.com
fchd.info
footballsite.co.uk
historicalkits.co.uk
lerwilllife.org.uk
nonleaguematters.co.uk
rsssf.com
soccerbase.co.uk
thebeautifulhistory.wordpress.com
thefootballarchives.com
thefootballhistoryboys.com
wikipedia.org
youtube.com
Official club websites

Main index to clubs

(note to editor: page details to come)